The Cavalier
King Charles Spaniel
Handbook

BY

LINDA WHITWAM

Copyright © 2018 Linda Whitwam

ISBN: 978-1731551061

Copyright

Acknowledgements

My sincere thanks to the dedicated Cavalier King Charles Spaniel breeders, owners and canine experts who have generously contributed their time and expertise to this book. Their knowledge and love of their dogs shines through; without them, this book would not have been possible.

Specialist Contributors:

DENNIS AND TINA HOMES

JINA EZELL

Contributors:

Special thanks to: Dennis and Tina Homes, Jina Ezell, Philippa Biddle, Sandra Coles, Kathy Hargest, Julie Durham, Philip Lunt, Nicola Byam-Cook, Laura and Mustafa Rakla, and Dr Sara Skiwski

(Full details of breeders appear at the back of the book)

TABLE OF CONTENTS

1. Meet the Cavalier

This handsome, affectionate little dog with its wonderful gentle temperament, intelligence, great love of humans and desire to please his owners is simply unique. And when listing the attributes of all the different breeds, it's hard – if not impossible - to think of one with a sweeter nature, or a dog that is more child-friendly.

The word *Companion* sums up the Cavalier in a single word. This little Love Machine has boundless affection for his or her owners and loves nothing more than snuggling up with them - preferably after a good walk. The Cavalier is at one with the world; happy with everything and everybody. As one of our contributing breeders said: "They haven't got a bad bone in their body."

Photo of Ch Leogem Rhapsody courtesy of Dennis and Tina Homes.

Properly socialised, they are completely non-aggressive with other dogs and infinitely patient with children – sitting accommodatingly as they are dressed up as Santa Claus or Superman – it's more often the dog that needs protecting from the kids, rather than the other way round.

Sporting Toy with a Royal Connection

Historically, the Cavalier is a strange anomaly of Toy breed and sporting dog. Its origins lie with the field Spaniel, a hardy dog bred to flush and retrieve game for the guns. The Cavalier is the only Spaniel to be classed in the Toy Group, the others are all in the Gundog (UK) or Sporting (USA) Group. As with all dogs of sporting origins, Cavaliers love a challenge, both physical and mental, especially games and retrieving.

However, the modern Cavalier does not have the "drive" of a sporting Spaniel; he or she is far more laid back. Hundreds of years ago, Spaniels were bred down to create a smaller, gentler dog for lords and ladies. Queen Elizabeth I (1533-1603) had a "spaniel gentle" as a comforter. This type of dog was probably a forerunner to the Cavalier and was popular with aristocratic ladies as a plaything and bed warmer! It is said that Mary, Queen of Scots' little Spaniel was found hidden in her petticoats after she was beheaded.

Just over half of all of today's Cavaliers are the rich chestnut and white Blenheims, developed by the first Duke of Marlborough (1650-1722) who lived at Blenheim Palace. It is thought Charles II had Blenheims and black and tans. The tricolour (the second most popular colour today) was originally called the Prince Charles, and the ruby was the last colour to be developed.

In some Blenheims there is a highly-prized chestnut mark in the middle of the forehead called the *Blenheim Spot* or *Duchess Thumb Print*. Legend has it that while Sarah Churchill, Duchess of Marlborough, was awaiting news of her husband's safe return from the Battle of Blenheim, she anxiously kept pressing her thumb on the head of an expecting female. The story goes that this resulted in five puppies bearing the "lucky mark" after news arrived that the battle had been won.

The Modern Cavalier

Today's dog has anything but *a Cavalier attitude* to life. Not at all domineering, stand-offish or egotistic, the Cavalier is sweet and gentle, friendly, incredibly loyal and easy to train – provided you put a bit of time in at the beginning. It's not often the word "kind" is used to describe a breed - but it sums up this one.

The Cavalier's athletic side is complemented with a kind and generous temperament with a streak of sensitivity. Many owners say that their Cavaliers are compassionate and can pick up on the emotions within their household. They are also tactile and love to be petted - for as many hours as you are prepared to give them; you'll tire of it before they do!"

They will jump on your lap if you sit down or follow you from room to room like a little shadow; they love physical contact and want to be close. This desire to be close extends to other dogs too; if you have more than one, you will find that they like to sleep in piles!

They are generally excellent with other dogs and seem to have an affinity with other Cavaliers. Often happy to share their house with a cat, as long as they have been introduced at an early age, but once outdoors, some take great delight in chasing small birds, squirrels and other people's cats.

Once socialised, Cavaliers are not generally noisy dogs. Some may bark when a person comes to the door; however, they are not known as excessive barkers. But if you're looking for a guard dog, then look elsewhere. If a truckload of robbers arrived to make off with the family silver, the Cavalier's main priorities would be to make friends with, and get petted by, them all.

Not only is the Cavalier a companion second to none for young and old alike, but the breed, with its soft, silky coat and trademark long ears, is also graceful and attractive. The sight of a fully-groomed Cavalier gliding around the ring at a conformation show is a beautiful sight to behold. Although the Cavalier King Charles Spaniel Alansmere Aquarius won Best in Show at Crufts in 1973, the breed has yet to repeat this success at America's Westminster Kennel Club Dog Show.

The breed's playful nature and sporting background mean that they can be trained in several different disciplines, including Agility, Obedience, Rally and Canine Freestyle (Dancing with Dogs). And their sensitive nature, combined with their love of humans, makes them well-suited to therapy work with disabled people, children and the elderly.

They do not respond well to harsh voices or rough treatment, which stresses them. Neither do they like being left alone for very long; they can even become depressed if they are badly treated.

Downsides to Cavaliers?

Does the Cavalier have any downsides and, with all of these amazing attributes, how come some end up in rescue centres? Well, sometimes people enter into dog ownership without considering all of the consequences, and although Cavaliers have all of the qualities listed, these dogs are demanding of you and your time. Here are some other things to consider:

- Cavaliers are most definitely *Velcro dogs*. They like to stick to you and don't like being left alone for long. This means they are not a suitable choice for people who are regularly out of the house for hours on end. They can become depressed or miserable with their own company

- Cavaliers are high maintenance and expensive when it comes to their long, silky coat. They require regular grooming – anything from daily to two or three times a week - to keep them clean and matt-free

- Their floppy ears are prone to infections, so owners need to make time to pluck hair out of the inside of the ears – or pay a groomer to do it

- Like other Toy breeds, Cavaliers are prone to dental issues, so regular teeth cleaning is another necessary maintenance job

- Several health issues can affect the breed, and it is particularly prone to inherited heart disease. Choose your puppy carefully and ask to see the parents' health certificates before committing. Once you have your dog, take out canine health insurance

- A Cavalier from fully-health tested parents will cost four figures.

- Cavaliers shed hair and can get wet and muddy when running free or swimming, so this is not a breed for the very house-proud

- Some Cavaliers can be stubborn, requiring more time and patience to train and socialise

- Toy breeds have a reputation for being slow to housetrain. Some Cavaliers pick it up very quickly, but others take longer – vigilance on the part of the owner speeds up the process

- The Cavalier is an escape artist extraordinaire - and has NO road sense whatsoever. You will need to have a secure fence and plug every little gap

- Although the Cavalier was bred as a companion, he still needs regular walks – up to an hour or more a day. If you can't devote the time, consider a smaller breed or one without a sporting ancestry

What the Experts Say

Despite all of this, ask anyone who has owned a Cavalier and they will say that there is something very special about this breed. Several breeders have been involved in the writing of this book, all of them are Kennel Club Assured Breeders in the UK and AKC Breeders in the USA. Between them, they have countless years of experience with Cavaliers. Here are some of their thoughts: Philippa

Biddle, of Hearthfriend Cavaliers, Norfolk: "I have bred Blenheims, tricolours and black and tans for 18 years. I first got a Cavalier as I just wanted an easy-to- live-with family pet.

"Once I got one, I completely fell in love with the breed. I've had dogs all my life, but never met one like a Cavalier. They have enough sporting instinct and fun in them to go for long walks and do other activities and games, but at the same time they are very quiet and placid in the house. They will tolerate less exercise if you are ill or busy.

"They are very affectionate, willing, easy to train, friendly and totally non-aggressive with other dogs, even if growled at by one. They are also very emotionally tuned in. They are marvellous with children; very affectionate and tolerant.

"My daughter has three-year-old twins and had the Cavalier before they were born. The Cavalier will protect them when with the buggy by placing herself in front of their buggy or jumping up and sitting on the toddler!"

Photo of these Hearthfriend Cavaliers courtesy of Philippa

"I have eight. If I lie down on a sun lounger, garden swing seat or sofa for a nap, every single one will try to lie on top of me! This is typical. They all snuggle in and find a space and you end up with a living Cavalier fur blanket — it's very cosy!

"When visitors arrive, they are amazed that every Cavalier I have wants to greet them personally and close up - and usually wants to sit on them too. However many dog beds I have out, they always try to squeeze into just one or two. They are very tactile and like to sleep in a heap."

Tina and Dennis Homes have been breeders for nearly 40 years and bred the UK's Top Cavalier in 2017: "In the 18th and 19th century, Cavaliers were used in hunting for retrieving small game such as woodcock, but at the same time were also used as "comforter" Spaniels. They love to cuddle and be cuddled.

"It's those large dark eyes with a hint of soulfulness that gives these dogs their lovely soft expression. Apart from their soulful expression, they have the kindest disposition for everyone they meet. We recommend Cavaliers to families with children; their gentle demeanour makes for every child's friend. They are natural pleasers and are happy when you are. They are also amusing - we have had several dogs that regularly look at the television screen and if they see a four-legged animal (horse, dog, cat, etc). appear on the screen, they immediately run to the back of the TV in an effort to find it!"

Kathy Hargest, of Kathysgirls Cavaliers, Gloucestershire: "I have been breeding all four colours of Cavalier for 14 years. I met one on a bus one day and was hooked! They are the most loving and loyal dog; not a mean bone in their body. They are lapdogs, hunters, companions, funny and cheeky, and can be stubborn. Each colour has its own characteristics.

"Cavaliers are like chocolates; one is never enough."

Julie Durham, of Donrobby Cavaliers, Berkshire: "I bought my first Cavalier in 1982, I bred her in 1985 and have been in love with the breed ever since. This is a wonderful breed; kind and loving - especially for families as they are so keen to please. Having said that, I would never sell a puppy or adult dog to a family with young children under school age, simply because children like to explore various orifices and I could not place one of my fur babies in that situation.

"Cavaliers are loyal, kind, and keen to please. My advice is: Don't expect too much from your Cavalier intelligence-wise and you will not be disappointed. But never ever will you be disappointed by their kind, loving, loyal disposition. They were good enough for kings and queens for a very good reason."

Sandra Coles, of Twyforde Cavalier King Charles Spaniels, Devon: "I have been breeding and showing Cavalier King Charles Spaniels since 1974. We had our first puppy from a local breeder that I had known for a long time and she encouraged me to show and breed. Not long after we acquired our second Cavalier and we were really hooked.

"They are such a loving and endearing breed. They love to be with you wherever you go, like little shadows. Regardless of how many, they will follow you anywhere. You dig in the garden, they come along behind and dig. I have only ever bred Blenheims and tricolours and each one has had its own personality: Tali, who is very naughty but loves everyone; Homer, who doesn't like getting his feet dirty and is always immaculate, despite being a boy. On the whole, they are very clean little dogs and I am always amazed at how well they clean themselves."

Sandra added: "Cavaliers can be very amusing. Janie, a little tricolour girl that I hand-reared, just loves to fish for pebbles on the beach. Her head goes right under the water and you can see the bubbles rising – it's is only certain pebbles that she is interested in. Her owners have sent me several videos!

"Our vegetable garden is separate from the dog's garden. In the spring, if I have very little growing, the dogs love to go in and rummage their new territory. That particular year I had let it overgrow. I was in the top garden when one of my dogs, Gemma, came towards me with something that looked like a sock in her mouth. She dropped it at my feet and it was a baby rabbit. She proceeded to do this again and we ended up with three baby rabbits, all alive and well! Bless her. They were all sent to a local wildlife rescue centre."

Philip Lunt, of Oaktreepark Cavaliers, Staffordshire: "I have bred Cavaliers for 24 years, my current colours are tricolour and Blenheim, but I have also had black and tan. The nature of the breed was the most appealing thing for me; Cavaliers are a loyal, friendly outgoing dog that is non-aggressive.

"Due to their nature, they get on well with children; if a child is not sure around dogs then a Cavalier

can be well suited for them. If anything surprises new owners, it is the breed's friendliness, affection and loyalty and the fact that they always want to be close to human contact.

"Dr Stanley Coren ranks Cavaliers 73rd out of 138 dogs in his *Intelligence of Dogs* List, but I think they should be higher up the list as they are very obedient and are known to be good working/assistance dogs."

Jina Ezell, of Kalama Cavaliers, Washington State, USA is a member of the gold standard American Kennel Club (AKC) Bred With H.E.A.R.T. Program. Breeders have to fulfil certain requirements in the following areas: Health, Education, Accountability, Responsibility and Tradition.

Photo courtesy of Jina.

She says: "The Cavalier is like the best Golden Retriever combined with the best Persian Cat. They are absolutely fun-loving, yet will lay on or by me all day long and let me pet their silky coat for hours on end."

"They are portable and want to go, go, go with me anytime, anywhere! When I am sad or tired, they are the first to give me a look, attention and their own sweetness to brighten my day. They are super easy-going and love people and animals of all sizes and varieties. They do not demand much and are trainable.

"Mine are typical lapdogs: I will be working inside or outside and the moment I sit down (anywhere), they will all pile up on me. I have my "Morning Coffee Chair" and, thankfully, it's wide enough and has arms, so that when I pull the feet out, I have room enough for all five to pile on. In my experience, the females love you, but the males, well, they are completely in love with you!

"The energy of Cavalier puppies always surprises the new owners, as well as how many naps they take until they are about four months old. Cavalier puppies have two speeds: ON and OFF!"

Owner Nicola Byam-Cook of Hampshire: "Ruby is our first Cavalier and I would definitely get another. She gets on very well with all dogs; we regularly walk with friends and there are six or seven dogs and she is sociable and kind. They can go on a five-mile walk, but if they don't get walked every day, don't go crazy. A Cavalier is a great dog for those with busy lives and fab with kids.

"We have children and poor Ruby tolerates being picked up, dressed in bonnets and hairbands. They get in her bed and cuddle her and she is part of their games - she has never snapped and is very patient with them. The children often lead her on walks, but she prefers to be off the lead running round. Ruby always sits under my feet wherever I am and is very loyal and will move to where I am in the room, day or night. She is part lapdog, part hunter; she loves to sit on our laps, but loves chasing birds and going shooting - and has even caught a baby rabbit!"

The Cavalier has worldwide appeal. Laura and Mustafa Rakla have two Cavaliers and live in Dubai. Laura says: "We were initially attracted to their long ears and coat; so adorable.

"Alfred and Bertie *(pictured)* like human interactions and respond well to talking and petting - they seem to listen and react well to your emotions. They are very gentle. We have found them quite easy to train and they are obedient.

"Ours are still young dogs; we haven't had many instances of them chewing furniture, but have lost four pairs of flip-flops! They are more lapdogs than

hunters and enjoy a lot of attention; very happy to be docile and sleep or rest, but Bertie does have more inclination to chase cats and birds. They have been surprisingly energetic and jumped to catch birds in mid-air. We have never had any problems with other dogs.

"They have not had that many interactions with children but generally, they may be a little intimidated at first, but then respond well. They let small children pet them and play with them without being aggressive."

"We have found both our Cavaliers to be intelligent from a training and problem-solving perspective. We gave them some structured training as pups, which they responded well to. They seem to be able to problem-solve quite well when faced with similar scenarios multiple times. Now also they use signals to show when they need the bathroom, by putting a paw on your leg."

We also asked breeders and owners to sum up their Cavaliers in a few words. This is what they said:

- Gay, friendly, relaxed, tactile, willing
- Gentle, inquisitive, fearless and friendly
- Passionate, compassionate, snuggle-bunny
- Loyal, kind, best friend
- Great companions, friendly temperament and fearless
- Kind, easy, family dog, easy to train
- Affectionate, adorable, amusing and amiable
- Active, well balanced with a gentle expression
- They leave paw prints on your heart
- Gentle, friendly, companionable, tactile
- Devoted, kind, patient
- Hairy bundle of love

Read on to find the right puppy and, if you already have yours, learn how to take good care of the newest member of the family for the rest of his or her life, and how to build a unique bond that will become one of the most important things in your life - and certainly theirs.

2. History of the Cavalier

Instinct plays a big part in the way dogs perceive, and then react to, the world around them. Learning about the history of the Cavalier not only gives owners a fascinating glimpse of how their breed has developed over the centuries, but also an insight into the unique traits bred into the Cavalier, which goes some way to explaining why their dogs look and behave as they do today.

Spaniel Origins

The clue is in the name! The ancestors of the Cavalier King Charles Spaniel were different types of Spaniel, which is one of the oldest breeds in history. Today's Cavalier retains some of the appearance and traits of the breed.

The Spaniel's origins date back over a thousand years and the breed has been recorded for posterity in literature, law and art. It is generally thought that the name 'Spaniel' derives from the word Spain, or Hispania as it used to be called.

Between 910 and 948 Wales was ruled by King Hywel Dda (Hywel the Good), who drew up a new legal code. The Spaniel was at that time already present in Wales, brought, some say, by the Spanish clan of Ebhor or Ivor many centuries before. In his Book of Laws (pictured), mammals were divided in three kinds: Birds, Beasts and Hounds, and the Hounds had three subdivisions:

➢ Hounds for the Scent
➢ Greyhounds
➢ Spaniels

The Greyhound and Spaniel were the favourite hunting dogs for many generations. King Hywel Dda also laid down in his Book of Laws that *"The Spaniel of the King is a pound of value."* We have to remember that in the year AD 948, a pound could buy several wives, slaves, horses, oxen, turkeys and geese! So the Spaniel was certainly a dog of both high reputation and value at that time.

During the Crusades of 1095 to 1291, noblemen were often accompanied by huntsmen and their dogs, which interbred with dogs in the Arabian countries, and the noblemen brought these crossbreeds back to their own country. These dogs became very popular with the Royals because of their excellent hunting abilities and were also regarded as status symbols; their owners had, after all, fought for their religion.

Between the 10th and 15th centuries, these crossbreeds produced offspring with excellent hunting qualities. They spread out over the continent and developed in different ways, according to the country where they lived and the work they were asked to do. In France they became Épagneuls (French for Spaniel), in Germany Wachtelhunde, in the Netherlands they were the Spioen and in Great Britain the Spaniel.

Much of the Spaniel's history can be found in literature. Mention of a Spaniel is made in Geoffrey Chaucer's (1343-1400) *Canterbury Tales*. The Tales are about a group of pilgrims travelling together who pass the time by each telling a story, the themes of which are courtly love, treason, avarice and adultery. *The Wife of Bath's Tale* is about a woman who had been married five times (very unusual in those days) and who was looking for Husband Number Six. The storyteller compared her with a Spaniel: "She coveteth every man that she may se: for as a spaynel she wol on hym lepe".

A contemporary of Chaucer, Gaston III, Count of Foix, owned an estate in south west France. Between 1350 and 1390 he was the leader of a band of adventurers who travelled from the Pyrenees to Scandinavia. Between his travels he stayed on his estate, Orthez, where he dedicated himself to his three passions: weapons, love and hunting. In 1387, at over 50 years of age and finding himself too old for warfare and love, he decided to devote himself solely to the hunt.

Between 1387 and 1391 he wrote a book on hunting, *Livre de Chasse*, which was translated into English by Edmund de Langley as *The Book of Hunting*. It contained beautiful images (pictured) and was one of the first books on hunting.

De Foix, who also used the name Gaston Phébus, referred to the Spaniel: "Another kind of hound there is that be called hounds for the hawk and Spaniels, for their kind cometh from Spain, notwithstanding that there are many in other countries. A good Spaniel should not be too rough, but his tail should be rough."

In 1486 the first list of domesticated dogs appeared in 'The Book of St. Albans'. The book was probably meant as teaching material for the pupils of the school in the Hertfordshire town. Dame Juliana Berners (pictured), said to be Prioress of the nearby St. Mary of Sopwell Convent, is considered to be the author.

In the chapter on hunting, she writes: "Thyse ben the names of houndes, fyrste there is a Grehoun, a Bastard, a Mengrell, a Mastiff, a Lemor, a Spanyel, Raches, Kenettys, Teroures, Butchers' Houndes, Myddyng dogges, Tryndel-taylles, and Prikherid currys, and smalle ladyes' poppees that bere away the flees." The last part refers to small lapdogs to fend off the fleas of their mistress!

During the hunt, the *Spanyels* were used to flush the game so that a bird of prey, usually a hawk, could catch the game. During Henri VIII's reign (1509-1547), large parties were held at the court with great feasts and the demand for game was inexhaustible. Partridge, quail, pheasant, rabbit and hare were caught with the snare, but demand surpassed supply. Huntsmen began to look for other means to catch the game and they discovered the use of the net.

A dog flushed the game from its cover, sat down and the huntsman threw a net over the game and the dog. The dogs they used with the net were called 'setting' or 'sitting Spaniels' and are the ancestors of our modern Setters. The dogs that were used to flush the game were called 'springing Spaniels'; this does not mean that the dogs had to spring, but rather that it was their job to make the game spring from its cover. The Cocker Spaniel was originally called the Cocking Spaniel as it was used to flush woodcock out of the undergrowth.

In 1570, there is a mention of a Toy spaniel in literature. Dr John Keye (or Kaye) published *Canibus Britannicus* in Latin under his pseudonym, Dr Caius. Later it was translated into English as *Treatise of English Dogges*. Dr Caius described four kinds of dogs: the Venatici for the hunt of big game, the Aucupatorii for the hunt of small game, the Delicati such as Toy Spaniel or Comforter, and the Rustici such as the Pastoralis (herding dog) and the Villaticus (mastiff). (The group of Aucupatorii he subdivided into Hispaniolus or Spainel, Setter and Aquaticus or Water Spaniel).

Development of the Toy Spaniel

Spaniels continued to hunt game, as they do today. But some of them were bred down to create a smaller, more docile dog with less "drive" which was to become a ladies' comforter popular with the aristocracy. They were known as Toy Spaniels and it is from these that the modern Cavalier is descended.

There have been several theories put forward as to the origin of the small Toy Spaniel. One is that smaller types of European Spaniels were crossed with oriental dogs, such as Pugs or Asian Spaniels. Breeding wasn't regulated until the last quarter of the 1800s, when the Kennel Clubs were formed and dogs were registered by breed. There was a lot of cross breeding and experimentation among dog fanciers, as well as indiscriminate mating from dogs that ran free, which is why it is difficult to pin point the exact origins of any breed.

However, most experts seem to agree that the ancestor of the Toy Spaniel originally came from the Far East. It's most likely that these dogs were first brought to Europe from China by Italian traders, perhaps as early as the 12th and 13th centuries. Many of the earliest paintings of Toy Spaniels were by Italian artists and they showed small red and white Spaniels similar to Blenheim Cavaliers.

Painting, 1635-6, by Antoon van Dyck: 'The Three Eldest Children of Charles I'.

Throughout Europe, a number of different Toy Spaniels evolved from these Far Eastern dogs. The Italian Spaniel was a pale red and white, similar to a small Blenheim. In France there was a small black Spaniel, the Gredin, with tan flashes around the eyes - probably where the black and tan genes came from. These tan flashes were also known as "fire marks" and folk legend has it that these flashes are the eyes of their sixth sense which enables them to see ghosts and spirits!

It is thought the Gredin may have influenced the Cocker Spaniel, and also the Pyrame, a curly-coated black and tan favoured by Charles II. These dogs had fused toes - a feature often found in the King Charles Spaniels of today.

Spanish Truffle dogs were also brought to Britain in the 1600s and kept by members of the nobility. Most were black and were described as small water dogs with very curly coats, possibly the ancestor of the Miniature Poodle. It is also a possibility that the bloodlines of these dogs were crossed with the Toy Spaniels of the time. In Holland a small Spaniel evolved that was both black and white and solid black. This became known as the Dutch Spaniel or Holland Spaniel. Although all these are now both extinct, their genes are no doubt in the Cavalier and King Charles Spaniels of today.

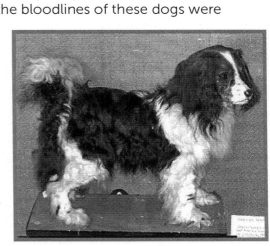

Some black and white Holland Spaniels were used as water dogs, and over the years evolved into a breed known as the Toy Trawler Spaniel, a breed that is believed to have died out in the 1920s. In the National History Museum in Tring there is a Trawler Spaniel (pictured) among the large display of stuffed dogs. Despite its curly coat and long muzzle, it is somewhat similar to a tricolour Cavalier. Small Toy Spaniels became popular all over Europe from the 1500s. They were mainly favoured by the aristocracy and wealthy merchants, and many were probably given as gifts to the ladies of prominent households. There are many old paintings of European royal families, notably the French and English, that also depict small Toy Spaniels.

A famous painting by William Allan shows Mary Queen of Scots arrive at Leith (in 1587) with a small tricolour. It is known that she brought her small spaniels to Scotland from France. There has been a reference to a small Toy Spaniel hidden in the clothing of Mary Queen of Scots when she was executed and the small dog being covered in blood. The narrative of her execution states:

". . . . one of the executioners, pulling off her garters, espied her little dogg which was crept under her clothes which could not be gotten forth but by force, yet afterwards would not depart from the dead corpse, but came and lay between her head and her shoulders, which being inbued with her bloode, was caryed away and washed, as all things ells were that had any bloode was either burned or clean washed."

In Dr. Caius's writings, he stated that the Toy type of Spaniel could be used to soothe stomach sickness! The Spaniel should be worn as a plaster by the sick and weak because the warmth of the body could transfer to dog, hence the patient became well (and the dog more often than not would die). His remedy for curing a patient of gout was that a two-day-old Spaniel should be *"boiled up in nettles, terpentyn, oyle of balm and other secret drugs to anoint where the grief was."*

He mentioned the "Comforter Spaniels" that were kept by the ladies of the court and claimed that they used to sit under their skirts against their legs. This would both keep their feet warm and also attract fleas and other insects from the bodies of the ladies.

Charles I (1600-1649) kept small Spaniels and his daughter, Princess Henrietta (pictured), was totally devoted to her dogs. Her brother, Charles II was the monarch famed for his love of these Spaniels. He had lots of them and it was through him that the breed got its name. When Henrietta married Philippe d'Orleans and became the Duchess of Orleans, she took her Spaniels to France, where she also kept black and tan Pyrames. Toy Spaniels were already very popular with the French aristocracy. The family of Louise XIV, the Sun King (1638-1715), owned several - as can be seen in some old masters.

The day after Charles II returned to England in May 1660 after his exile, Samuel Pepys wrote in his diary, "The King was rowed ashore in the admiral's barge, while I followed in a smaller boat with Mr Mansell, one of the footmen, and a dog that the King loved".

Pepys also wrote on another occasion that the King (pictured) paid far more attention to his dogs than to business at a Privy Council meeting. It is well documented that the King allowed his dogs to go everywhere with him, much to the displeasure of many of his courtiers. Lord Rochester wrote:

In all affairs of Church and State

He very zealous is and able

Devout at prayers and sits up late

At the Cabal or Council Table

His very dog at Council Board

Sits grave and wise as any Lord.

Charles II was married to Catherine of Braganza, who was given oriental Chin dogs from Portuguese missionaries. Whether any of her dogs mated with Charles's Spaniels is not known, but in a palace full of dogs it is indeed a possibility and the Chin genes could have easily crept into Charles's Spaniel line. As there was no legitimate heir from their marriage, when Charles II died he was succeeded by his brother James II. James also kept small Toy Spaniels and legend has it that during a storm at sea when orders were given to abandon ship he was alleged to have said, *"Save the dogs!!. . . and the Duke of Monmouth".*

When William of Orange succeeded James II to the throne of England in 1689 he kept Pugs, the national dog of Holland. Short-faced dogs soon then started to become popular among the ladies of the nobility. During the Victorian era, short-faced Toy dogs, such as Japanese Chins and Pugs, became extremely popular and some cross-breeding went on to give the Toy Spaniel a much shorter face. *Pictured is a modern Japanese Chin.*

Toy Spaniels were mainly favoured by the aristocracy, wealthy merchants and the landed gentry. Shortly after the death of Charles II, Huguenots began settling in England. They were Protestant refugees from France escaping religious persecution. Many settled around Spitalfields in East London and worked as silk weavers. Some of also brought their Toy Spaniels, so for the first time these small Spaniels were being kept as pets by working class people in England.

The British Royal family have loved their dogs over the centuries, and Queen Victoria was no exception. Her large tricolour Toy Spaniel, Dash (pictured with her), was especially dear to her heart. He was given to her as a present in 1833 when she was a teenager, and the dog and princess soon became inseparable. She sometimes dressed him in a scarlet jacket and blue trousers, and at Christmas gave him three India rubber balls and two bits of gingerbread decorated with holly and candles.

Victoria had him painted at least a half a dozen times (pictured).When Dash died in 1840, three years after she became Queen, she buried him herself at Adelaide Cottage in the grounds of Windsor Castle, and had inscribed on his tombstone: *"His attachment was without selfishness; His playfulness without malice; His fidelity without deceit; Reader if you would live beloved; and die regretted, profit by the example of Dash."*

When Victoria first met Prince Albert of Saxe-Coburg in 1836, Victoria was taken with the tall, blue-eyed Albert, but it was his behaviour toward Dash that sealed her opinion of him. Victoria recorded in her diary how Albert 'played with and fussed over' Dash. Thus, with Dash's seal of canine approval, Albert's fate was set. Soon after, the Queen proposed and rest -as they say - is history!

The Blenheim Connection

General John Churchill (1650-1722) was a great soldier, keen dog breeder and huntsman, and in his day, the most popular gundogs were Cocking Spaniels and Springing Spaniels. But the Duke much preferred to hunt with small chestnut and white Spaniels that were descended from the Toy Spaniels favoured by the nobility.

He developed a line that were not just lapdogs, but also hardy, small retrieving Spaniels that could work well in the field, being mainly used to retrieve woodcock. The story goes that while his wife, Sarah, was awaiting news of the General's safe return from the Battle of Blenheim, she was holding a small pregnant bitch for comfort and kept anxiously pressing the dog's head with her thumb. When the litter arrived, all the pups had lozenge marks on their heads - and this is where the famous Blenheim spot (pictured, previous page) comes from!

What we do know is that upon his victorious return, Queen Anne granted Churchill the title (1st) Duke of Marlborough and gave him a massive estate in Oxfordshire, together with a grand house she had built for him; Blenheim Palace. The late Diana, Princess of Wales, was a direct descendant of the first Duke.' *A Marlborough Spaniel', by Charles Towne, early 1800s.*

The various Dukes of Marlborough kept these small chestnut and white Spaniels on the estate for more than two centuries; the dogs becoming firmly associated with the Marlborough family and the Blenheim estate. The more robust ones were worked in the field, while the smaller ones became *"lady's carpet spaniels"*.

They became known as both Marlborough Spaniels and Blenheim Spaniels - although in some quarters they were still called Italian Spaniels. In 1820 the Sportsman Review described them as *"very small or carpet spaniels, have exquisite noses and will hunt truly and pleasantly."*

This photo, taken at Blenheim Palace in 1898, shows the dogs owned by the 9th Duke of Marlborough, together with their handlers. Smaller and lighter and with a shorter muzzle than the Marlborough Spaniel of a few decades earlier, these dogs look far more akin to today's Cavalier Kind Charles Spaniel.

Fast forward to 1921 when the 9th Earl of Marlborough married Gladys Deacon, a somewhat eccentric American who decided to resume the breeding of the Marlborough Spaniels.

She believed that the rearing of puppies should be done in a near-to-nature way and ripped up an ancient palace floor to allow the bitches to whelp below the floorboards! On another occasion she imported some chocolate imitation dog poo(p) from a Paris joke shop and left them in strategic places on the stairs. When distinguished guests arrived, she would pop the poo(p) into her mouth! Unsurprisingly, the marriage did not last and, sadly, the Duke destroyed all the dogs to spite Gladys.

In 1926, before the divorce, the Duchess had sold the dog Blenheim Palace Poppet to Mrs Jennings of the Plantations Kennel. The dam and sire were Blenheim Palace Trixey and Blenheim Palace Billy. Poppet was mated to Timon of Ttiweh and produced Timonetta of Ttiweh, who became an influential bitch behind present-day Cavaliers. In another mating to Mark of Ttiweh, she produced Plantation Pixie, another key dog behind many pedigrees.

So, despite the tragic end of the Marlborough Toy Spaniels at Blenheim, they were instrumental in laying the foundations for the modern Cavalier King Charles Spaniel.

The Blenheim Spaniel connection with the Marlborough dynasty was briefly rekindled in the mid-1950s when Lady Ivor Spencer-Churchill, wife of the brother of the 10th Duke, bred the first Cavalier to be shown in Canada. This was Deanhill Panda, a Blenheim dog owned by Mrs C. Cunningham. Deanhill Cavaliers were also exported to several other countries.

In August 2010, the UK's Cavalier King Charles Spaniel Club held a celebratory Cavalier Extravaganza weekend in the grounds of Blenheim Palace, the ancestral home of the breed. Hundreds of people attended from some 22 different countries, including many from the USA and even some enthusiastic owners from Australia. As well as a huge dog show, various other events took place: dogs in fancy dress, display team, obedience, junior handling, along with a barn dance and cabaret in the evening.

....

Birth of The Cavalier KCS as a Separate Breed

The first official dog show took place on June 28th and 29th, 1859, in Newcastle-upon-Tyne, when 60 Pointers and Setters were entered; no other breeds. The dogs were entered under the name of their owner, such as 'Mr. Murrel's Spot' and 'Mr Brown's Venus'. In 1870 it was decided that regulations were necessary and this resulted in the formation of The Kennel Club in1873. Since most dogs were named simply Spot, Bob, Jet and Vic, it soon became necessary to create some order among all these dogs, so one of first tasks of The Kennel Club was to introduce a Stud Book.

Victorian gentlemen of pleasure became very interested in dog shows; the new railways made travelling throughout the country to visit shows possible. At the same time, working class fanciers began experimenting with breeding smaller dogs that lived in the house, and began to hold their own shows, initially in London's East End taverns in London. At the UK Kennel Club is a famous painting , 'An Early Canine Meeting', which shows a meeting of gentlemen and their dogs at Jemmy (or Jimmy) Shaw's Queen's Head Tavern in 1855. Among the breeds depicted in the painting are Bulldogs, Bull Terriers, Black and Tan Terriers and Toy Spaniels. Ladies tended to hold their shows in somewhat more genteel surroundings.

At this time, there were still two similar types of Toy Spaniel in England. William Youatt outlines some of the differences in his 1848 book, 'The Dog':

The Blenheim Spaniel

"For its beauty and occasional gaiety, it is often an inhabitant of the drawing room than the field; but it occasionally breaks out, and shows what nature designed for it. Some of the carpeted pets acquit themselves boldly in the covert. There they ought oftener to be; for they have not much individuality of attachment to recommend them, and like other spoiled animals, both quadruped and biped, misbehave. The breed has degenerated of late (1848) and is not always to be had pure, even in the neighbourhood of Blenheim. This spaniel may be distinguished by the length and silkiness of the coat, the deep fringe about the ear, the arch and deep feathering of the tail, the full and moist eye and the blackness of the palate."

The King Charles Spaniel

"The ears deeply fringed and sweeping the ground, the rounder form of the forehead, the larger and moister eye, the longer and silken coat and the clearness of the tan, and white and black colour sufficiently distinguish this variety. His beauty and diminutive size have consigned him to the drawing room or parlour. Charles the First had a breed of Spaniel, very small, with the hair black and curly. The spaniel of the Second Charles was of the black and tan breed. The King Charles's breed of the present day is materially altered for the worse. The muzzle is almost as short, and the forehead as ugly and prominent as the vermiest bulldog. The eye is increased to double its former size and has an expression of stupidity with which the character of the dog too accurately corresponds. Still there is the long ear and the silky coat and the beautiful colour of the hair and for these the dealers do not scruple to ask 20, 30 or even 50 guineas."

In 1885 a number of keen enthusiasts got together with the aim of forming a Toy Spaniel Club. A standard was drawn up for each of the colours: the King Charles (black and tan), the Blenheim (red and white), the Prince Charles (tricolour), and Ruby (red). Until then, these colours had all been judged separately, but at a meeting in 1902 at Crystal Palace, they decided that, as all four colours could be produced in one litter, they must all be of the same family and should therefore be classed as colour variants of the same breed.

To keep the link with King Charles, the club decided to call the breed The King Charles Spaniel. The Kennel Club overruled this decision and said that they should retain the existing name of The English Toy Spaniel. However, some club members appealed to the king, His Majesty Edward VII, and he sided with them, agreeing that they should retain the historical link with Charles II. The Kennel Club had to comply with the royal wish.

Édouard Manet's 'A King Charles Spaniel' (ca. 1866)

The birth of the Cavalier was in some part due to an American lover of Toy Spaniels, Mr Roswell Eldridge who came to England and was very disappointed not to find any Blenheim Spaniels with long noses and sporting natures like he'd seen in classical paintings. He offering prizes at Crufts from 1926 to 1930 for *'Blenheim spaniels of the old type'* and the word *'Cavalier'* was chosen to distinguish this type from the flatter-faced type, which was known as The King Charles. It was not a popular move, as breeders had worked hard for years to do away with the long nose. Just a few enthusiasts carried on the breeding experiment; foremost amongst them was Mrs Hewitt Pitt, who founded the TTewih (Hewitt backwards) line of Cavaliers.

In 1928 a club was founded, and the title "Cavalier King Charles Spaniel" was chosen. At the first meeting, held the second day of Crufts 1928, the Breed Standard was drawn up; it was practically identical to today's Breed Standard. The "live pattern" on the table was Miss Mostyn Walker's dog Ann's Son, and members brought reproductions of paintings from the 16th, 17th and 18th centuries. Thus the Cavalier King Charles spaniel was born.

It wasn't, however, until 1945 that the breed was recognised by the Kennel Club, and a full half century later that the American Kennel Club gave full recognition to the Cavalier King Charles Spaniel.

....

Numerous references were used in the research of this history. The main source was:

"The Cavalier King Charles Spaniel: The Origin and Founding of the Breed"

Excerpts reproduced here by kind permission of the authors, Tina and Dennis Homes. The book is available from The Cavalier King Charles Spaniel Club and is widely regarded as the most detailed and accurate history of the breed – www.thecavalierclub.co.uk/pay/cavshop.html

Other sources:
- "All About Dogs," 1901, Charles Henry Lane
- "Dogs of All Nations," 1915, W.E. Mason
- "The Book Of Dogs – An Intimate Study Of Mankind's Best Friend," 1919, National Geographic Society
- The Kennel Club www.thekennelclub.org.uk/services/public/breed/display.aspx?id=6149
- Wikipedia https://en.wikipedia.org/wiki/Cavalier_King_Charles_Spaniel
- Chest of Books www.chestofbooks.com
- The Cocker Spaniel Handbook www.amazon.com/Cocker-Spaniel-Handbook-Essential-Prospective/dp/1523798203

3. Breed Standard

The **breed standard** is what makes a Great Dane a Great Dane and a Chihuahua a Chihuahua. It is a blueprint not only for the appearance of each breed, but also for character and temperament, how the dog moves and what colours are acceptable. In other words, it ensures that a Cavalier King Charles Spaniel looks and acts like a Cavalier King Charles Spaniel.

The breed standard is laid down by the breed societies. In the UK it's the Kennel Club, and in the USA it's the AKC (American Kennel Club) that keeps the register of pedigree (purebred) dogs. Dogs entered in conformation shows run under Kennel Club and AKC rules are judged against this ideal list of attributes. Breeders approved by the Kennel Clubs - called 'Assured Breeders' in the UK - agree to produce puppies in line with the Breed Standard and maintain certain welfare conditions.

Good breeders select only the best dogs for reproduction, based on factors such as the health, looks, temperament and character of the parents and their ancestors. They do not simply take any available male and female and allow them to randomly breed. The same is true of AKC Breeders of Merit and Breeders with H.E.A.R.T. in the USA: "AKC Breeders are dedicated to breeding beautiful purebred dogs whose appearance, temperament, and ability are true to their breed."

An excellent place to source a reputable breeder is the relevant breed club in your country. In the UK the national club is The Cavalier King Charles Spaniel Club: www.thecavalierclub.co.uk There's also a number of regional clubs and you can find a full list with contact details by typing *"Kennel Club Cavalier Clubs"* into Google.

In the USA, the Cavalier King Charles Spaniel Club's website can be found at: www.ckcsc.org At the top right of the home page, there are the words *Regional Clubs,* click on this to find your nearest one.

The UK Kennel Club and AKC also have lists of breeders, and if you have not yet got a puppy, they are a good place to start looking for one near you. In the UK, look for an *Assured Breeder* and in the AKC 'Find a Puppy' or 'Marketplace' section, try and stick to *Breeders of Merit* or *Breeders with H.E.A.R.T.* as the AKC does not carry out any checks on the others.

Tip *The fact that a puppy is registered with the Kennel Club or AKC does NOT mean that his or her parents have been screened for hereditary diseases, or that you have any guarantee of a healthy pup. A Kennel Club or AKC pedigree certificate simply means that the puppy's family tree can be traced back several generations. Always ask to see health certificates.*

Responsible breeders aim to reduce or eradicate genetic illnesses by screening their dogs and not breeding from the ones that carry faulty genes. In the case of Cavaliers, the major health tests cover eye and heart diseases and Syringomyelia, a serious disorder which affects the spine and brain. After World War II, there were only six Cavaliers left in the world and all of today's Cavalier King Charles Spaniels are their descendants. Unfortunately, as well as passing on good genes, they also passed on some bad ones, so it is extremely important that you check the health of your future Cavalier's parents. Hereditary diseases are common among unscreened dogs.

Today, the Cavalier gene pool is much larger. The COI (Coefficient of Inbreeding) measures how big the gene pool is for each breed. The UK Kennel Club average COI for Cavvies is 5.5%, which is quite good. To put this in perspective, 12.5% would be the genetic equivalent of a dog produced from a grandfather to granddaughter mating, and 25% would equate to the genetic equivalent of a dog produced from a father and daughter.

UFAW (Universities Federation for Animal Welfare) says: "Essentially, COI measures the common ancestors of dam and sire, and indicates the probability of how genetically similar they are. There are consequences to being genetically similar, some good, some bad. The fact that dogs within individual breeds are so genetically similar is what makes them that breed." Which is why when you breed a Cavalier to a Cavalier, the resulting pups look like Cavaliers.

It goes on to explain why a high COI can be a problem: "Inbreeding will help cement 'good' traits but there's a danger of it also cementing bad ones. In particular, it can cause the rapid build-up of disease genes in a population. Even if a breed of dog is lucky enough to be free of serious genetic disorders, inbreeding is likely to affect our dogs in more subtle, but no less serious, ways."

 Prospective UK owners can check the COI of a prospective puppy by typing in the name of the dam and sire (mother and father) using the Kennel Club's **Mate Select** programme at www.thekennelclub.org.uk/services/public/mateselect - the lower the number, the wider the gene pool. The US equivalent of Mate Select is the K9 programme at www.k9data.com

If you are serious about getting a Cavalier King Charles Spaniel, then study the Breed Standard before visiting any puppies, so you know what a well-bred example should look like.

....

Kennel Club Breed Standard (UK)

General Appearance: Active, graceful and well balanced, with gentle expression.

Characteristics: Sporting, affectionate, absolutely fearless.

Temperament: Gay, friendly, non-aggressive; no tendency to nervousness.

Head and Skull: Skull almost flat between ears. Stop shallow. Length from base of stop to tip of nose about 3.8 cm (1½ in). Nostrils black and well developed without flesh marks, muzzle well tapered. Lips well developed but not pendulous. Face well filled below eyes. Any tendency to snipiness undesirable.

Eyes: Large, dark, round but not prominent; spaced well apart.

Ears: Long, set high, with plenty of feather.

Mouth: Jaws strong, with a perfect, regular and complete scissor bite, i.e. upper teeth closely overlapping lower teeth and set square to the jaws.

Neck: Moderate length, slightly arched.

Forequarters: Chest moderate, shoulders well laid back; straight legs moderately boned.

Body: Short-coupled with good spring of rib. Level back.

Hindquarters: Legs with moderate bone; well turned stifle – no tendency to cow-hocks or sickle-hocks.

Feet: Compact, cushioned and well feathered.

Tail: Length of tail in balance with body, well set on, carried happily but never much above the level of the back. Docking previously optional when no more than one-third was to be removed.

Gait: Free-moving and elegant in action, plenty of drive from behind. Forelegs and hind legs move parallel when viewed from in front and behind.

Coat: Long, silky, free from curl. Slight wave permissible. Plenty of feathering. Totally free from trimming.

Colours: Recognised colours are:-

- **Black and Tan**: Raven black with tan markings above the eyes, on cheeks, inside ears, on chest and legs and underside of tail. Tan should be bright. White marks undesirable.

- **Ruby**: Whole coloured rich red. White markings undesirable.

- **Blenheim**: Rich chestnut markings well broken up, on pearly white ground. Markings evenly divided on head, leaving room between ears for much valued lozenge mark or spot (a unique characteristic of the breed).

- **Tricolour**: Black and white well spaced, broken up, with tan markings over eyes, cheeks, inside ears, inside legs, and on underside of tail.

- *Any other colour or combination of colours highly undesirable.*

Weight and Size: Weight – 5.4–8.2 kg (12–18 lb). A small, well balanced dog well within these weights desirable.

Faults: Any departure from the foregoing points should be considered a fault and the seriousness with which the fault should be regarded should be in exact proportion to its degree and its effect upon the health and welfare of the dog.

Note: Male animals should have two apparently normal testicles fully descended into the scrotum.

Last Updated – February 2012

American Kennel Club Breed Standard

General Appearance: The Cavalier King Charles Spaniel is an active, graceful, well-balanced toy spaniel, very gay and free in action; fearless and sporting in character, yet at the same time gentle and affectionate.

It is this typical gay temperament, combined with true elegance and royal appearance which are of paramount importance in the breed. Natural appearance with no trimming, sculpting or artificial alteration is essential to breed type.

Size, Proportion, Substance:

Size - Height 12 to 13 inches at the withers; weight proportionate to height, between 13 and 18 pounds. A small, well balanced dog within these weights is desirable, but these are ideal heights and weights and slight variations are permissible.

Proportion - The body approaches squareness, yet if measured from point of shoulder to point of buttock, is slightly longer than the height at the withers. The height from the withers to the elbow is approximately equal to the height from the elbow to the ground.

Substance - Bone moderate in proportion to size. Weedy and coarse specimens are to be equally penalized.

Head: Proportionate to size of dog, appearing neither too large nor too small for the body.

Expression - The sweet, gentle, melting expression is an important breed characteristic.

Eyes - Large, round, but not prominent and set well apart; color a warm, very dark brown; giving a lustrous, limpid look. Rims dark. There should be cushioning under the eyes which contributes to the soft expression. **Faults** - small, almond-shaped, prominent, or light eyes; white surrounding ring.

Ears - Set high, but not close, on top of the head. Leather long with plenty of feathering and wide enough so that when the dog is alert, the ears fan slightly forward to frame the face.

Skull - Slightly rounded, but without dome or peak; it should appear flat because of the high placement of the ears. Stop is moderate, neither filled nor deep.

Muzzle - Full muzzle slightly tapered. Length from base of stop to tip of nose about 1½ inches. Face well filled below eyes. Any tendency towards snipiness undesirable. Nose pigment uniformly black without flesh marks and nostrils well developed. Lips well developed but not pendulous giving a clean finish. Faults - Sharp or pointed muzzles.

Bite - A perfect, regular and complete scissors bite is preferred, i.e. the upper teeth closely overlapping the lower teeth and set square into the jaws. **Faults** - undershot bite, weak or crooked teeth, crooked jaws.

Neck, Topline, Body:

Neck - Fairly long, without throatiness, well enough muscled to form a slight arch at the crest. Set smoothly into nicely sloping shoulders to give an elegant look.

Topline - Level both when moving and standing.

Body - Short-coupled with ribs well sprung but not barrelled. Chest moderately deep, extending to elbows allowing ample heart room. Slightly less body at the flank than at the last rib, but with no tucked-up appearance.

Tail - Well set on, carried happily but never much above the level of the back, and in constant characteristic motion when the dog is in action. Docking is optional. If docked, no more than one third to be removed.

Forequarters: Shoulders well laid back. Forelegs straight and well under the dog with elbows close to the sides. Pasterns strong and feet compact with well-cushioned pads. Dewclaws may be removed.

Hindquarters: The hindquarters construction should come down from a good broad pelvis, moderately muscled; stifles well turned and hocks well let down. The hindlegs when viewed from the rear should parallel each other from hock to heel. Faults - Cow or sickle hocks.

Coat: Of moderate length, silky, free from curl. Slight wave permissible. Feathering on ears, chest, legs and tail should be long, and the feathering on the feet is a feature of the breed. No trimming of the dog is permitted. Specimens where the coat has been altered by trimming, clipping, or by artificial means shall be so severely penalized as to be effectively eliminated from competition. Hair growing between the pads on the underside of the feet may be trimmed.

Color:

- *Blenheim* - Rich chestnut markings well broken up on a clear, pearly white ground. The ears must be chestnut and the color evenly spaced on the head and surrounding both eyes, with a white blaze between the eyes and ears, in the center of which may be the lozenge or "Blenheim spot." The lozenge is a unique and desirable, though not essential, characteristic of the Blenheim.

- *Tricolor* - Jet black markings well broken up on a clear, pearly white ground. The ears must be black and the color evenly spaced on the head and surrounding both eyes, with a white blaze between the eyes. Rich tan markings over the eyes, on cheeks, inside ears and on underside of tail.

- *Ruby* - Whole-colored rich red.

- *Black and Tan* - Jet black with rich, bright tan markings over eyes, on cheeks, inside ears, on chest, legs, and on underside of tail.

Faults - Heavy ticking on Blenheims or Tricolors, white marks on Rubies or Black and Tans.

Gait: Free moving and elegant in action, with good reach in front and sound, driving rear action. When viewed from the side, the movement exhibits a good length of stride, and viewed from front and rear it is straight and true, resulting from straight-boned fronts and properly made and muscled hindquarters.

Temperament: Gay, friendly, non-aggressive with no tendency towards nervousness or shyness. Bad temper, shyness, and meanness are not to be tolerated and are to be severely penalized as to effectively remove the specimen from competition.

Approved Date: January 10, 1995. Effective Date: April 30, 1995

Glossary:

Hock - tarsal joint of the hind leg corresponding to the human ankle, but bending in the opposite direction (looks like a low backwards knee on the back leg). *Cow Hocks* bend inwards (knock knees) and *Sickle Hocks* bend outwards (bow legged)

Muzzle – Upper and lower jaws

Occiput - bony bump seen at the top rear of the skull on some breeds

Parti colors – different colors, one of which is usually white

Pastern – the area below the wrist or hock but above the foot

Snipiness - a weak, pointed muzzle lacking in substance in a dog's underjaw, or fill beneath the eyes

Stifle – technically the knee, but higher than the hock and closer to the body

Stop - area between a dog's eyes, below the skull

Withers - the ridge between the shoulder blades

4. Finding Your Cavalier Puppy

Once you have decided that the Cavalier King Charles Spaniel is the dog for you, the best way to select a puppy is with your head - and not with your heart. With their Teddy bear looks, button noses, soft, wavy coats and affectionate personalities, there are few more appealing things on this Earth than Cavalier puppies. If you go to view a litter, they are sure to melt your heart and it is extremely difficult – if not downright impossible - to walk away without choosing one. So, it's essential to do your research before you visit any litters.

Unfortunately, The Cavalier is a breed recognised as having some serious health issues. So you want to make sure that you avoid buying a puppy with inherited diseases. If you haven't yet chosen your pup yet and take only one sentence from this entire book, it is this:

Find a responsible breeder with health-tested parents (of the puppy, not the breeder!) and one who knows Cavaliers inside out.

After all, apart from getting married or having a baby, getting a puppy is one of the most important, demanding, expensive and life-enriching decisions you will ever make.

Just like babies, Cavalier puppies will love you unconditionally - but there is a price to pay. In return for their loyalty and devotion, you have to fulfil your part of the bargain.

In the beginning, you have to be prepared to devote much of your day to your new puppy. You have to feed her several times a day and housetrain virtually every hour, you have to give her your attention and start to gently introduce the rules of the house as well as take care of her health and welfare. You also have to be prepared to part with hard cash for regular healthcare and pet insurance.

If you are not prepared, or unable, to devote the time and money to a new arrival, if you have a very young family, a stressful life or are out at work all day, then now might not be the right time to consider getting a puppy. Cavaliers are gentle, loving dogs that thrive on being close to their owners.

If left alone too long, these beautiful dogs can become unhappy, bored and even destructive. This is a natural reaction and is not the dog's fault; she is simply responding to the environment, which is failing to meet her needs. Pick a healthy pup and he or she should live for more than a decade if you're lucky - so getting a Cavalier is definitely a long-term commitment. Before taking the plunge, ask yourself some questions:

Have I Got Enough Time?

In the first days after leaving her mother and littermates, your puppy will feel very lonely and probably even a little afraid. You and your family have to spend time with your new arrival to make him feel safe and sound. Ideally, for the first few days you will be around all of the time to help him settle and to start bonding with him.

If you work, book a couple of weeks off (this may not be possible for some of our American readers who get shorter vacations than their European counterparts), but don't just get a puppy and leave him all alone in the house a couple of days later. Housetraining (potty training) starts the moment your pup arrives home.

Then, after the first few days and once he's feeling more settled, start to introduce short sessions of a couple of minutes of behaviour training to teach your new pup the rules of the house. Cavalier puppies want to please you and, while they are often gentle souls, all puppies are lively. This energy can become boisterous and mischievous if not channelled - so start training early to discourage puppy biting and jumping up.

Some Cavaliers are sensitive and may be affected by all kinds of things: loud noises, shouting, arguments, unhappiness, other animals or new situations, to name but a few things. Begin the socialisation process by taking him out of the home to see buses, noisy traffic, other animals, kids, etc. - but make sure you CARRY HIM until the vaccinations have taken effect. It's important to start the socialisation process as soon as possible, as the more positive experiences he is introduced to at this early stage, the better, and many good breeders will already have started the process.

Once he has had the all-clear following vaccinations, get into the habit of taking him out of the house and garden or yard for a short walk every day — more as he gets older. New surroundings stimulate interest and help to stop puppies becoming bored and developing unwanted behaviour issues. He also needs to get used to different noises.

The Cavalier has a beautiful silky coat, which is more high maintenance than many breeds with shorter hair. Make time right from the beginning to get your pup used to being handled, gently brushed, ears checked, and having his teeth touched and then cleaned.

We recommend that you have your pup checked out by a vet within a couple of days of arriving home. You'll also need to factor in time to visit the vet's surgery for annual check-ups as well as vaccinations, although most of these now last several years — check with your vet.

How Long Can I Leave My Puppy?

This is a question we get asked all of the time and one that causes much debate among new and prospective owners. All dogs are pack animals; their natural state is to be with others. So being alone is not normal for them - although many have to get used to it. The Cavalier has not been bred to be a guard dog; he or she most definitely wants to be around you and/or other dogs.

Another issue is the toilet; Cavalier puppies have tiny bladders. Forget the emotional side of it, how would you like to be left for eight hours without being able to visit the bathroom? So how many hours can you leave a dog alone?

Well, a useful guide comes from the canine rescue organisations. In the UK, they will not allow anybody to adopt if they are intending to leave the dog alone for more than four or five hours a day.

Dogs left at home alone a lot get bored and, in the case of Cavaliers, i.e. a breed that thrives on companionship, they can become depressed and even destructive. Of course, it depends on the character and temperament of your dog, but a lonely Cavalier may display signs of unhappiness by barking, chewing, digging, urinating, soiling, bad behaviour, or just being plain sad and disengaged.

In terms of housetraining, a general rule of thumb is that a puppy can last without going to the toilet for **one hour or so for every month of age.** So, provided your puppy has learned the basics, a three-month-old puppy should be able to last for three hours or a little longer without needing the toilet. Of course, it doesn't work like this – until housetraining kicks in, young puppies just pee at will!

A puppy or fully-grown dog must NEVER be left shut in a crate all day. It is OK to leave a dog in a crate if he or she is happy there, but all our breeders said the same: the door should never be closed for more than a few hours during the day. A crate is a place where a dog should feel safe, not a prison. Ask yourself why you want a dog - is it for selfish reasons or can you really offer a good home to a Cavalier for 10 or more years?

Family and Children

Cavaliers are great with children; they are gentle, patient, tolerant and love being with people. Of course, that comes with the usual caveat – you have to socialise your Cavalier AND the kids! Your children will, of course, be delighted about your new arrival. But remember that Cavalier puppies are very small and delicate with tiny bones, so you should never leave babies/toddlers and dogs alone together – no matter how well they get along.

Small kids lack co-ordination and may inadvertently poke a puppy in the eye, tread on him or pull a joint out of place, causing serious injury. Some breeders have said they would not place a Cavalier puppy in a family with very young children for this reason.

Often puppies regard children as playmates - just like a child regards a puppy as a playmate - young pups are playful and can be boisterous. They may chase, jump and nip a small child – although it is more often the other way round. Cavaliers are so gentle, it is often them that need protecting from the children.

Lively behaviour is not aggression; it is normal play for puppies. See **Chapter 11. Training** on how to deal with puppy biting.

Train your pup to be gentle with your children and your children to be gentle with your puppy.

Dennis Homes says: "We remind parents not to allow young children to pick up a very young puppy, as he or she could easily jump out of the child's arms. It is far preferable for a young child to sit on the floor and play with the puppy. When holding a young puppy, people should ensure that they have both hands over the puppy and NOT with the pup's front legs tucked over the owner's hands."

Your dog's early experiences with children should all be positive; if not, a dog may become nervous or mistrustful - and what you want around children is most definitely a relaxed dog that does not feel threatened by a child's presence.

Discourage the kids from constantly picking up your gorgeous new puppy. They should learn respect for the dog, which is a living creature with his or her own needs, not a plaything. Cavaliers are extremely loyal once humans and animals have found their way into their affections. Take

things steady in the beginning, and your Cavalier will form a deep, lifelong bond with your children. He or she may even become protective and watch over them.

Make sure puppy gets enough time to sleep – **which is most of the time in the beginning** - so don't let children (or adults!) constantly pester him. Sleep is very important to puppies, just as it is for babies. Also, allow your Cavalier to eat at his or her own pace uninterrupted; letting youngsters play with the dog while eating is a no-no as it may promote gulping of food or food aggression.

One reason that some dogs end up in rescue centres is that owners are unable to cope with the demands of small children AND a dog. On the other hand, it is also a fantastic opportunity for you to educate your little darlings (both human and canine) on how to get along with each other and set the pattern for wonderful lasting friendships.

Sandra Coles has bred Twyforde Cavalier King Charles Spaniels in Devon since 1974 and said: "Their temperament is second to none and I always had to rescue the dogs from the children! Both my boys were brought up with Cavaliers and would join them in the garden with their toys and paddling pool; my eldest is particularly fond of the breed. Cavaliers' tails never stop wagging and they just want to please, they are very loyal. Being very good with children and older people, they are often used as PAT (Pets as Therapy) dogs."

Single People

Many single adults own dogs, but if you live alone, getting a puppy will require a lot of dedication on your part. There will be nobody to share the responsibility, so taking on a dog requires a huge commitment and a lot of your time if the dog is to have a decent life.

If you are out of the house all day as well, it is not really fair to get a puppy, or even an adult dog. However, if you work from home or are at home for much of the day and can spend considerable time with the pup, then a Cavalier will undoubtedly become your best friend.

Older People

If you are older or have elderly relatives living with you, Cavaliers can be great company, as they are very adaptable as far as exercise goes. They are a very affectionate breed and love to snuggle up. Puppies generally require a lot of energy and patience from any owner; if you are older and/or less mobile, an adult Cavalier may be a better option.

Dogs can, however, be great for fit, older people. In his mid-80s my father still walked his dog for an hour to 90 minutes every day - a morning and an afternoon walk and then a short one last thing at night – even in the rain or snow. He grumbled occasionally, but it was good for him and it was good for the dog, and helped to keep them both fit and socialised! They got fresh air, exercise and the chance to communicate with other dogs and their humans. His dog recently passed away, but my father, now 88, still walks with a friend's dog every day.

Dogs are also great company indoors – you're never alone when you've got a dog. Many older people get a canine companion after losing a loved one (a husband, wife or previous much-loved dog). A pet gives them something to care for and love, as well as a constant companion.

However, owning a dog is not cheap, so it's important to be able to afford annual pet insurance, veterinary fees, a quality pet food, etc. The RSPCA in the UK has estimated that owning a dog costs an average of around £1,300 (around $1,700) a year!

Other Pets

However friendly your puppy is, if you already have other pets in your household, they may not be too happy at the new arrival. Cavaliers generally get on well with other animals, but it might not be a good idea to leave your hamster or pet rabbit running loose; many young puppies have play and/or prey instincts – although if introduced slowly, they may become best friends!

Some Cavaliers do have quite a strong hunt instinct outdoors, when they love to chase cats, birds and other small creatures - but once back indoors they often get along perfectly happily with other small animals sharing their home.

Cavaliers usually do well with other dogs – especially Cavaliers - and cats, provided they have been introduced under the right conditions. In the beginning, spend time to introduce them to each other gradually and supervise the sessions. Cavalier puppies are naturally curious and playful and they will sniff and investigate other pets. They may even chase them in the beginning. Depending on how lively your pup is, you may have to separate them to start off with, or put a playful Cavalier into a pen or crate initially to allow a cat to investigate without being mauled by a hyperactive pup who thinks the cat is a great playmate.

This will also prevent your puppy from being injured. If the two animals are free and the cat lashes out, your pup's eyes could get scratched. A timid Cavalier might need protection from a bold cat - or vice versa. A bold cat and a gentle Cavalier will probably settle down together quickest!

If things seem to be going well with no aggression, then let them loose together after one or two supervised sessions. Take the process slowly; if your cat is stressed and frightened he may decide to leave. Our feline friends are notorious for abandoning home because the board and lodgings are better down the road.

iheartdogs asked 101 owners if their Cavaliers got along with cats - 37% said "Yes, very well", 29% said "Gets along OK", and 35% said "Does not get along well." The main factors appeared to be that some dogs need longer to accept a cat, and it's important to give both the dog and the cat time to get used to each other.

Here are a few comments from Cavalier owners: "Give the cat its space, most likely the Cavalier will stay clear until the cat is ready to come closer. Rubbing your cat or dog scent in common areas of the house can help adjust." "Introduce slowly, more for the safety of your dog than your cat." "Mine barks at the neighbour's cats." "Patience from the cat... introduce slowly for the cat's sake. Our two cats are old and see the dogs daily, but don't care for them - but the dogs love them." "If Pluto sees a cat in the garden he goes mental. But when we are my sister's house, he doesn't bother with her cat." "Zara was two when I got the two eight-week-old kittens. She mothered them and two years on they all love each other."

Gender

You have to decide whether you want a male or a female puppy. In terms of gender, much depends on the temperament of the individual dog - the differences WITHIN the sexes are greater than the differences BETWEEN the sexes.

One difference, however, is that females have heat cycles and, unless you have her spayed, you will have to restrict your normal exercise routine when she comes into heat (every six months or so) to stop unwanted attention from other dogs. Another is that some Cavaliers can be territorial and it is not unusual for them, particularly males, to regularly 'mark' their territory by urinating.

At one time, vets routinely recommended neutering or spaying from an early age, but with new evidence emerging that sex hormones also play a role in health, neutering is no longer such a straightforward subject - with some breeders now recommending that owners leave their dogs entire (unneutered), or at least wait until they are two years old before neutering. If you think you may leave your dog entire, then think carefully about which gender would be most suitable.

If you already have dogs or are thinking of getting more than one, you do, however, have to consider gender. You cannot expect an unneutered male to live with an unspayed female without problems. Similarly, two uncastrated males may not always get along; there may simply be too much testosterone and competition.

If an existing dog is neutered (male) or spayed (female) and you plan to have your dog neutered or spayed, then gender should not be an issue. Some breeders will specify that your Cavalier pup has to be spayed or neutered after a certain timeframe. This is not because they want to make more money; it is to protect Cavaliers from indiscriminate breeding.

Unlike most other breeds, there is not a big difference between the size of fully-grown male and female Cavaliers. Your main points of reference in terms of size, physical appearance and temperament are the puppy's parents; see what they are like and discuss with your breeder which puppy would best suit you.

More than One Dog

Well-socialised Cavaliers normally have no problem sharing their home with other dogs. Supervised sessions from an early age help everyone to get along and for the other dogs to accept your new pup. If you can, introduce them for the first time outdoors on neutral ground, rather than in the house or in an area that one dog regards as his own. You don't want the established dog to feel he has to protect his territory, nor the puppy to feel he is in an enclosed space and can't get away.

All that said, reasons for the Cavalier's popularity include their lack of aggression, gentle temperament and ability to get on with children and other dogs. They also seem to have an affinity with other Cavaliers - several of our breeders literally have piles of Cavaliers! As Gloucestershire breeder Kathy Hargest says: "They have not a mean bone in their body." *Photo courtesy of Kathy.*

If you are thinking about getting more than one pup, consider waiting until your first Cavalier is a few months old or adult before getting a second, so have the housetraining out of the way and your older dog can help train the youngster.

Coping with training and housetraining one puppy is hard enough, without having to do it with two. On the other hand, some owners prefer to get the messy part over and done with in one go and get two together — but this will require a lot of your time for the first few weeks and months.

Owning two dogs can be twice as nice - it's also double the food and vet's bills. There are a number of factors to consider. This is what one UK rescue organisation has to say: "Think about why you are considering another dog. If, for example, you have a dog that suffers from separation anxiety, then rather than solving the problem, your second dog may learn from your first and you then have two dogs with the problem instead of one. The same applies if you have an unruly adolescent; cure the problem first and only introduce a second dog when your first is balanced."

"A second dog will mean double vet's fees, insurance and food. You may also need a larger car, and holidays will be more problematic. Sit down with a calculator and work out the expected expense – you may be surprised. Two dogs will need training, both separately and together. If the dogs do not receive enough individual attention, they may form a strong bond with each other at the expense of their bond with you.

"If you are tempted to buy two puppies from the same litter – DON'T! Your chances of creating a good bond with the puppies are very low and behaviour problems with siblings are very common. If you have a very active dog, would a quieter one be best to balance his high energy or would you enjoy the challenge of keeping two high energy dogs? You will also need to think of any problems that may occur from keeping dogs of different sizes and ages.

"If you decide to purchase a puppy, you will need to think very carefully about the amount of time and energy that will be involved in caring for two dogs with very different needs. A young puppy will need to have his exercise restricted until he has finished growing and will also need individual time for training.

"If you decide to keep a dog and bitch together, then you will obviously need to address the neutering issue."

Which Colour?

There are four colours of Cavalier King Charles Spaniels:

- ❧ *Blenheim* - tan/chestnut and white
- ❧ *Tricolour* - black and white with tan markings on eyebrows, cheeks, underside of tail, inside ears and legs
- ❧ *Black and Tan* - black with tan markings on eyebrows, cheeks, chest, underside of tail, inside ears and legs
- ❧ *Ruby* – rich red all over. Some have white markings, but these are frowned upon in the show ring

If someone is trying to sell you a dog of any other colour, it isn't a Cavalier!

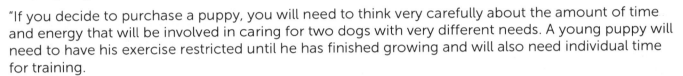

More than half of all Cavaliers worldwide (51%) are Blenheim, 22% are Tricolour, 13.4% are Black and Tan and the remaining 13.5% are the newest colour; Ruby.

This is according to the UK Cavalier Club's 2013 Health Census, involving more than 5,500 Cavaliers. It makes fascinating reading on behaviour, health and colour. The full report can be found at: www.thecavalierclub.co.uk/health/survey_13/reports/uk_census_analysis_2013_iss3.pdf

According to owners who participated in the survey, there is no great difference between the four colours with regards to:

- ❧ Weight
- ❧ Eating habits
- ❧ Friendliness
- ❧ Sociability
- ❧ Obedience
- ❧ Aggression

In other words, these are mainly down firstly to the breeder and secondly to you, the owner. Black and tans were, however, considered to be slightly noisier than the other three colours by their owners.

Puppy Stages

It is important to understand how a puppy develops into a fully-grown dog. This knowledge will help you to be a good owner. **The first few months and weeks of a puppy's life will have an effect on his or behaviour and character for life.** This Puppy Schedule will help you to understand the early stages:

Birth to seven weeks	A puppy needs sleep, food and warmth. He needs his mother for security and discipline and littermates for learning and socialisation. The puppy learns to function within a pack and learns the pack order of dominance. He begins to become aware of his environment. During this period, puppies should be left with their mother.
Eight to 12 weeks	A puppy should NOT leave his mother before eight weeks - modern thinking says that nine weeks is better. At this age the brain is fully developed and **he now needs socialising with the outside world.** He needs to change from being part of a canine pack to being part of a human pack. This period is a fear period for the puppy, avoid causing her fright and pain.
13 to 16 weeks	Training and formal obedience should begin. **This is a critical period for socialising with other humans, places and situations.** This period will pass easily if you remember that this is a puppy's change to adolescence. Be firm and fair. His flight instinct may be prominent. Avoid being too strict or too soft with her during this time and praise his good behaviour.
Four to eight months	Another fear period for a puppy is between seven to eight months of age. It passes quickly, but be cautious of fright or pain which may leave the puppy traumatised. The puppy reaches sexual maturity and dominant traits are established. Your Cavalier should now understand the following commands: 'sit', 'down', 'come' and 'stay'.

These photos show the progress of Tina and Denis Homes's female Cavalier, Leogem Rhapsody, aged (left to right): eight weeks, seven months and two years.

Plan Ahead

The age at which a puppy leaves a breeder varies, but NO puppies should leave the litter before they are eight weeks old. It is important that they have enough time to physically develop and learn the rules of the pack from their mothers and litter mates.

A puppy that leaves the litter too early often suffers with issues, such as nervousness or problems interacting with other dogs, throughout life. Toy breeds, like the Cavalier, tend to mature later than larger breeds and for this reason, many breeders like to hold on to the puppies for a little longer. If you have bought from a good breeder, expect your puppy to be aged eight to 12 weeks when he comes home.

Much depends on how much socialising the breeder is doing. If the pup is waiting in a crate until the new owners arrive, he or she is not learning very much. On the other hand, a young puppy will be learning a great deal after the age of eight weeks if the breeder has a socialisation programme. This is yet another question to ask!

Breeders who allow their pups to leave home before eight weeks are probably more interested in a quick buck than a long-term puppy placement. In the USA, many states specify that a puppy may not be sold before eight (or sometimes seven) weeks of age. And if you want a well-bred Cavalier, it certainly pays to plan ahead as most good breeders have waiting lists.

Choosing the right breeder is one of the most important decisions you will make. Like humans, your puppy will be a product of his or her parents and will inherit many of their characteristics. His temperament and how healthy your puppy will be now and throughout his life will depend on the genes of his parents. (Character is what develops as a result of how you treat your dog). Responsible breeders health test their dogs, they check the health records and temperament of the parents and only breed from suitable stock.

Here are some steps to take to find a good breeder:

1. Plan ahead – start a few months before your planned arrival. Good pups are usually spoken for as soon as or even before they are born.

2. Contact a breed club – see **Useful Contacts** at the end of this book – email the secretary and ask to be put in touch with members who are planning a litter.

3. In the USA you can also look on AKC Marketplace for future litters. Ideally look for a breeder who is a member of a club, the Bred With H.E.A.R.T. programme or one of the few AKC Breeders of Merit. https://marketplace.akc.org/puppies/cavalier-king-charles-spaniel

4. In the UK, find a Kennel Club **Assured Breeder** with the KC's online Find a Puppy Service at: www.thekennelclub.org.uk/services/public/findapuppy NOTE: this is no guarantee of health testing, you still need to ask. Champdogs is another place to look. Breeders now have to state if they health test their dogs, choose one that does and ask to see certificates: www.champdogs.co.uk/breeds/cavalier-king-charles-spaniel/breeders

5. Email the breeders and find out about future litters and potential dates, and ask for a list of health tests carried out on the dam and sire.

6. When the breeders contact you, you will have to give some more details about yourself.

7. If everything moves ahead, ask for the names of the dam and sire (parents), and check the COI – coefficient of Inbreeding – see **Useful Contacts** for details. The UK Kennel Club breed average for the Cavalier is 5.5% - very near this figure or less is good, it means the parents are not too closely related.

Prices vary a great deal for Cavalier puppies, with ancestry, colour and region all having a part to play. For a fully health-tested pet puppy from a breed club member, Kennel Club Assured Breeder or AKC breeder, expect to pay anything from £900 to £1,500 or more in the UK and around $1,500 to $3,000 in the USA, depending on various factors including where you live. If a Cavalier pup is being sold for much less, you have to ask why. Dogs with show or competition potential cost more.

A healthy Cavalier will be your irreplaceable companion for the next decade or more, so why buy an unseen puppy, or one from a pet shop or general advertisement? Would you buy an old wreck of a car or a house with structural problems just because it was cheap? The answer is probably no, because you know you would be storing up stress and expense in the future.

If a healthy Cavalier is important to you, wait until you can afford one. Good breeders do not sell their dogs on general purpose websites, in pet shops or car parks or somebody else's house. Many reputable Cavalier breeders do not have to advertise, such is the demand for their puppies. Many have their own websites; you must learn to spot the good ones from the bad ones, so do your research.

We strongly recommend visiting the breeder personally at least once and follow our **Top 12 Tips for Selecting a Good Breeder** to help you make the right decision. Buying a poorly-bred puppy may save you a few hundred pounds or dollars in the short term, but could cost you thousands in extra veterinary bills in the long run - not to mention the terrible heartache of having a sickly dog. Rescue groups know only too well the dangers of buying a poorly-bred dog; years of problems can arise, usually health-related, but there can also be temperament issues, or bad behaviour due to lack of socialisation.

....

Where NOT to buy a Cavalier Puppy

There are no cast iron guarantees that your puppy will be 100% healthy and have a good temperament, but choosing a Cavalier breeder who is registered with the Kennel Club in your country or who belongs to a Cavalier club increases these chances enormously. There are several Cavalier clubs in the UK and USA and most have strict entry guidelines and Code of Ethics; see back of book for details.

If, for whatever reason, you're not able to buy a puppy from a breeder with a proven track record, how do you avoid buying one from a 'backstreet breeder' or puppy mill (puppy farm)? These are people who just breed puppies for profit and sell them to the first person who turns up with the cash. Unhappily, this can end in heartbreak for a family months or years later when their puppy develops problems due to poor breeding.

Price is a good guide. A cheap puppy usually means that corners have been cut somewhere along the line. If a pup is advertised at a price that seems too good to be true; then it is. You can bet your last dollar that the dam and sire are not superb examples of their breed, that they haven't been fully health screened, and that the puppies are not being fed premium quality food or even kept in the house with the family where the breeder is starting to socialise and housetrain them.

Here's some advice on what to avoid:

Unscrupulous breeders have sprung up to cash in on the high price of purebred dogs. While new owners might think they have bagged 'a bargain,' this more often than not turns out to be false economy and an emotionally disastrous decision when the puppy develops health problems due to poor breeding, or behavioural problems due to poor temperament or lack of socialisation.

Buying from a puppy mill or someone breeding for profit means that you are condemning other dogs to a life of misery. If nobody bought these cheap puppies, there would be no puppy mills.

The UK's Kennel Club has issued a warning of a puppy welfare crisis, with some truly sickening statistics. As many as one in four puppies bought in the UK may come from puppy farms - and the situation is no better in North America. The KC Press release stated: "As the popularity of online pups continues to soar:

* **Almost one in five pups bought (unseen) on websites or social media die within six months**

* One in three buy online, in pet stores and via newspaper adverts - outlets often used by puppy farmers — this is an increase from one in five in the previous year

* The problem is likely to grow as the younger generation favour mail order pups, and breeders of fashionable breeds flout responsible steps."

The Kennel Club said: "We are sleepwalking into a dog welfare and consumer crisis as new research shows that more and more people are buying their pups online or through pet shops, outlets often used by cruel puppy farmers, and are paying the price with their pups requiring long-term veterinary treatment or dying before six months old. The increasing popularity of online pups is a particular concern. Of those who source their puppies online, half are going on to buy 'mail order pups' directly over the internet." The KC research found that:

* One third of people who bought their puppy online, over social media or in pet shops failed to experience 'overall good health'

* Almost one in five puppies bought via social media or the internet die before six months old

* Some 12% of puppies bought online or on social media end up with serious health problems that require expensive on-going veterinary treatment from a young age

Caroline Kisko, Kennel Club Secretary, said: "More and more people are buying puppies from sources such as the internet, which are often used by puppy farmers. Whilst there is nothing wrong with initially finding a puppy online, it is essential to then see the breeder and ensure that they are doing all of the right things. This research clearly shows that too many people are failing to do this, and the consequences can be seen in the shocking number of puppies that are becoming sick or dying. We have an extremely serious consumer protection and puppy welfare crisis on our hands."

The research revealed that the problem was likely to get worse as mail order pups bought over the internet are the second most common way for the younger generation of 18 to 24-year-olds to buy a puppy (31%) Marc Abraham, TV vet and founder of Pup Aid, said: "Sadly, if the "buy it now" culture persists, then this horrific situation will only get worse. There is nothing wrong with sourcing a puppy online, but people need to be aware of what they should then expect from the breeder.

"For example, you should not buy a car without getting its service history and seeing it at its registered address, so you certainly shouldn't buy a puppy without the correct paperwork and health certificates and without seeing where it was bred. However, too many people are opting to buy directly from third parties such as the internet, pet shops, or from puppy dealers, where you cannot possibly know how or where the puppy was raised.

"Not only are people buying sickly puppies, but many people are being scammed into paying money for puppies that don't exist, as the research showed that 7% of those who buy online were scammed in this way." The Kennel Club has launched an online video and has a Find A Puppy app to show the dos and don'ts of buying a puppy. View the video at www.thekennelclub.org.uk/paw

Caveat Emptor – Buyer Beware

Here are some signs that a puppy may have arrived via a puppy mill, a puppy broker (somebody who makes money from buying and selling puppies) or even an importer. Our strong advice is that if you suspect that this is the case, walk away. You can't buy a Rolls Royce or a Lamborghini for a couple of thousand pounds or dollars - you'd immediately suspect that the 'bargain' on offer wasn't the real thing. No matter how lovely it looked, you'd be right - and the same applies to Cavaliers. Here are some signs to look out for:

- Websites – buying a puppy from a website does not necessarily mean that the puppy will turn out to have problems. But avoid websites where there are no pictures of the home, environment and owners. If they are only showing close-up photos of cute puppies, click the **X** button

- Don't buy a website puppy with a shopping cart symbol next to his picture

- Don't commit to a website puppy unless you have seen it and the mother face-to-face. If this is not possible, at the very least you must speak (on the phone) with the breeder and ask questions; don't deal with an intermediary

- At the breeder's, you hear: *"You can't see the parent dogs because......"* ALWAYS ask to see the parents and, as a minimum, see the mother and how she looks and behaves

- If the breeder says that the dam and sire are Kennel Club or AKC registered, insist on seeing the registration papers

- Ignore photographs of so-called 'champion' ancestors (unless you are buying from an approved breeder), in all likelihood these are fiction

- The puppies look small for their stated age. A committed Cavalier breeder will not let her puppies leave before they are eight weeks or older

- The person you are buying the puppy from did not breed the dog themselves

- The place you meet the puppy seller is a car park, somebody else's house or place other than the puppies' home

- The seller tells you that the puppy comes from top, caring breeders from your or another country. Not true. There are reputable, caring breeders all over the world, but not one of them sells their puppies through brokers

❧ Price – if you are offered a very cheap Cavalier, he or she almost certainly comes from dubious stock. Careful breeding, taking good care of mother and puppies and health screening all add up to one big bill for breeders. Anyone selling their puppies at a knock-down price has certainly cut corners

❧ Ask to see photos of the puppy from birth to present day. If the seller has none, there is a reason – walk away

❧ If you get a rescue Cavalier, make sure it is from a recognised rescue group – see **Chapter 16. Cavalier Rescue** for details - and not a 'puppy flipper' who may be posing as a do-gooder, but is in fact getting dogs (including stolen ones) from unscrupulous sources

In fact, the whole brokering business is just another version of the puppy mill and should be avoided at all costs. Bear in mind that for every cute Cavalier puppy you see from a puppy mill or broker, other puppies have died. Good Cavalier breeders will only breed from dogs that have been carefully selected for health, temperament, physical shape and lineage. There are loads of good breeders out there, spend the time to find one.

Here's some advice from one experienced breeder in the US: "THE BAD: Shy away from the 'Puppy For Sale' internet sites that list multiple breed puppy sales, such as Puppyfind.com, Petfinder.com, nextdaypets and breeders.net. You know the sites; you click on a drop down menu to 'Select the breed you are looking for', then up pops 50 different listings of puppies from different kennels or individuals.

"These sites are used frequently by puppy millers, dog brokers and in general poor quality breeders with poor quality animals. It is a known fact that they 'bait/switch'. This means that they bait their ads with pictures of lovely puppies and/or dogs that are NOT the animal for sale and, in most cases, not even of an animal they own. Many steal pictures from reputable breeders' sites of darling pups and adults and place those pictures on their ad. Then, when someone makes a purchase, they are sent a dog that is the same breed/color and sex, but clearly NOT the one pictured!

"I have had my dogs and puppies pictures stolen on many occasions. I have even had these people say they have a litter sired by one of our Champion stud dogs with a direct link back to my stud's page. They are dishonest, so avoid at all cost.

"THE SHODDY: Now, let's say you type in 'Cavalier Breeders in Tennessee' or 'Georgia' or 'Florida'. What frequently pops up (for any state) is a website called (State)Cavalierbreeders.net or Purebredbreeder.com, etc. These are **dog broker sites.**

"A dog broker is someone who finds buyers (acts as a second party) for pups produced from puppy mills and bad breeders. These online sites are jammed packed full of poorly-bred pups, highly over-priced and in most cases they are known to use the same pictures to advertise hundreds of pups of the same color/sex/breed in different states. They mislead you into thinking the puppy is located in your state, only for you to later find out it was shipped in to you from five states away. Forget about warranties, forget about dealing with the breeder. By the time you get that puppy, he or she has changed hands several times and is exposed to many different pups that the broker hauls around. Not a good risk to take.

"THE WORST: pet stores, auctions and flea markets. No doubt you have heard: "Never purchase from a pet store as they are all puppy mill-bred puppies." IT IS TRUE! By the time they get to the store, they have been transformed from a feces/urine/flea-infested rag into the cutest puppy ever. Sickly, raised in cages, filth and more. Flea markets are full of Amish puppy mill pups. They are deplorable.

"Auctions are used for those pups a breeder can't find a home for. Don't fall victim to these people. I know how many of us want to reach out and save these puppies and give them a good home, but when you pay for them, you are just keeping these type of deplorable people in the breeding business and causing their dogs to suffer at the cost of being bred over and over until they die or are killed when they are no longer able to produce puppies.

"Just stay away from newspaper ads, Craigslist, eBay Pets, AKC online advertising. None of these are used by reputable breeders. Even AKC online ads are full of back yard breeders galore. Some terms you will not find on reputable breeder websites include: USDA Inspected - If you see these words run! It means they ARE NOT hobby breeders. They usually are high volume mass producers (puppy mills).

"Another is AKC Approved Breeder - There is no such thing! AKC does NOT approve breeders, they are just a registry body and AKC registration does not denote the quality of the breeder or the quality of the animals that are being produced! You should be looking for 'AKC Breeder of Merit. If you see Silver Cavaliers, White Cavaliers, Charcoal Cavaliers or Champagne Cavaliers advertised, run!"

UK breeder Julie Durham said: "I have had new owners come to me because they have seen puppy dealers first hand; some choosing to take on some poor little mite. Some are well-informed and walk away upset. There are various warning signs, but the main ones are lack of knowledge of the breed, lack of paperwork and either having a bitch brought in that's nervous and clearly not interested in the puppy and a definite lack of a milk bar (enlarged teats)."

Philip Lunt added: "The danger signs are when none of the parents can be seen - at least Mum should be. Look at where the where the puppies are kept and any other dogs sleep."

Here are some signs to help the savvy buyer spot a good breeder:

Top 10 Tips for Choosing a Good Breeder

1. Visit the Cavalier club and Kennel Club's websites in your country to find a good breeder in your area.

2. Choose a Cavalier breeder whose dogs are health tested with certificates to prove it.

3. Good breeders usually keep their Cavaliers in the home as part of the family - not permanently outside in kennel runs, garages or outbuildings. Check that the area where the puppies are kept is clean and that the puppies themselves look clean.

4. Their Cavaliers appear happy and healthy. Check that the pup has clean eyes, ears, nose and bum (butt) with no discharge. The pups are alert, excited to meet new people and don't shy away from visitors.

5. A good breeder will encourage you to spend time with the puppy's parents - or at least the mother - when you visit. They want your family to meet the puppy and are happy for you to visit more than once.

6. They are very familiar with Cavaliers, although some may also have other breed(s).

7. They feed their adults and puppies high quality dog food and give you some to take home and guidance on feeding and caring for your puppy. They will also be available for advice after you take your puppy home.

8. All responsible breeders should provide you with a written contract and health guarantee. They will also show you records of the puppy's visits to the vet, vaccinations, worming medication, etc. and explain what other vaccinations your puppy will need.

These pups are on their way to their eight-week vet check. Photo courtesy of Philippa Biddle, Hearthfriend Cavaliers, Norfolk.

9. They don't always have pups available, but keep a list of interested people for the next available litter. They don't over-breed, but do limit the number of litters from their dams. Over-breeding or breeding from older females can be detrimental to the female's health.

10. If you have selected a breeder and checked if/when she has puppies available, **go online to the Cavalier forums before you visit and ask if anyone already has a dog from this breeder.** If you are buying from a good breeder, the chances are someone will know her dogs or at least her reputation. If the feedback is negative, cancel your visit and start looking elsewhere.

11. A good breeder will, if asked, provide references from other people who have bought their puppies; call at least one before you commit. They will also agree to take a puppy back within a certain time frame if it does not work out for you, or if there is a health problem.

12. Good breeders have Puppy Contracts and provide you with a Going Home Bag with items to help the pup's transition.

13. And finally ... good Cavalier breeders want to know their beloved pups are going to good homes and will ask YOU a lot of questions about your suitability as owners. DON'T buy a puppy from a website or advert where a PayPal or credit card deposit secures you a puppy without any questions.

Important Questions to Ask a Breeder

Some of these points have already been covered, but here's a reminder and checklist of the questions you should be asking. The Kennel club also has a three-minute video entitled *The Dos and Don'ts of Buying a Puppy* on YouTube at: www.youtube.com/watch?v=1EhTu1TQcEc

Have the parents been health screened? Buy a Cavalier pup with health tested parents – see Chapter 12. Cavalier Health for what certificates to ask to see. Ask what guarantees the breeder or seller is offering in terms of genetic illnesses, and how long these guarantees last – 12 weeks, a year, a lifetime? It will vary, but good breeders will definitely give you some form of guarantee, and this should be stated in the Puppy Contract.

They will also want to be informed of any hereditary health problems with your puppy, as they may choose not to breed from the dam or sire (mother or father) again. Some breeders keep a chart documenting the full family health history of the pup – ask if one exists and if you can see it.

Can you put me in touch with someone who already has one of your puppies?

Are you registered with the Kennel Club (UK) or AKC (USA) or a member of a Cavalier breed club? Not all good Cavalier breeders are members, but this is a good place to start.

How long have you been breeding Cavaliers? You are looking for someone who has a track record with the breed.

How many litters has the mother had? Females should not have litters until they are two years old and then only have a few litters in their lifetime. The UK Kennel Club will not register puppies from a dam that has had more than four litters. Check the age of the mother; too young or too old is not good for her health.

What happens to the female(s) once she/they have finished breeding? Are they kept as part of the family, rehomed in loving homes or sent to animal shelters?

Do you breed any other types of dog? Buy from a Cavalier specialist, preferably one who does not breed lots of other types of dog - unless you know they have a good reputation.

What is so special about this litter? You are looking for a breeder who has used good breeding stock and his or her knowledge to produce healthy, handsome dogs with good temperaments, not just cute dogs in fancy colours. All Cavalier puppies look cute, don't buy the first one you see – be patient and pick the right one. If you don't get a satisfactory answer, look elsewhere.

What do you feed your adults and puppies? A reputable breeder will feed a top quality dog food and advise that you do the same.

Photo of three-year-old Zeta and her healthy litter of two pups courtesy of Sandra Coles.

What special care do you recommend? Your Cavalier will need regular grooming, trimming, teeth and ear cleaning.

What is the average lifespan of your dogs? Generally, pups bred from healthy stock tend to live longer.

How socialised and housetrained is the puppy? Good breeders will raise their puppies as part of the household and often start the socialisation and potty training process before they leave.

What healthcare have the pups had so far? Ask to see records of flea treatments, wormings and vaccinations.

Has the puppy been microchipped?

Why aren't you asking me any questions? A good breeder will be committed to making a good match between the new owners and their puppies. If the breeder spends more time discussing money than the welfare of the puppy and how you will care for her, you can draw your own conclusions as to what his or her priorities are – and they probably don't include improving the breed. Walk away.

Take your puppy to a vet to have a thorough check-up within 48 hours of purchase. If your vet is not happy with the health of the dog, no matter how painful it may be, return the pup to the breeder. Keeping an unhealthy puppy will only cause more distress and expense in the long run.

Puppy Contracts

Most good Cavalier breeders will provide you with an official Puppy Contract. This protects both buyer and seller by providing information on the puppy until he or she leaves the breeder. You should also have a health guarantee for a specified time period. A Puppy Contract will answer such questions as whether the puppy:

- 🐾 Is covered by breeder's insurance and can be returned if there is a health issue within a certain period of time
- 🐾 Was born by Caesarean section
- 🐾 Has been micro-chipped and/or vaccinated and details of worming treatments
- 🐾 Has been partially or wholly toilet trained
- 🐾 Has been socialised and where it was kept
- 🐾 And what health issues the pup and parents have been screened for
- 🐾 What the puppy is currently being fed by the breeder and if any food is being supplied
- 🐾 Details of the dam and sire

It's not easy for caring breeders to part with their puppies after they have lovingly bred and raised them for eight weeks or longer, and so many supply extensive care notes for new owners, which may include details such as:

- 🐾 The puppy's daily routine
- 🐾 Feeding schedule
- 🐾 Vet and vaccination schedule
- 🐾 General puppy care
- 🐾 Toilet training
- 🐾 Socialisation

Photo of this lively trio of eight-week-old Hearthfriend Cavaliers courtesy of Philippa Biddle.

New owners should do their research before visiting a litter as once there, the cute Cavalier puppies will undoubtedly be irresistible and you will buy with your heart rather than your head. If you have any doubts at all about the breeder, seller or the puppy, WALK AWAY.

Spend time beforehand to find a good Cavalier breeder with a proven track record and reduce the chances of health and behaviour problems later on. In the UK, The Royal Society for the Prevention of Cruelty to Animals (RSPCA) has a downloadable puppy contract endorsed by vets and animal welfare organisations; you should be looking for something similar from the breeder or seller of the puppy: https://puppycontract.rspca.org.uk/home

Top 10 Tips for Choosing a Healthy Cavalier

Once you've selected your breeder and a litter is available, you then have to decide WHICH puppy to pick, unless the breeder has already earmarked a pup for you after asking lots of questions. A good breeder will try and match you with a puppy to fit in with your household, lifestyle and schedule. Here are some signs to look for when selecting a puppy:

1. Your chosen puppy should have a well-fed appearance. He or she should not, however, have a distended abdomen (pot belly) as this can be a sign of worms - or other illnesses (such as Cushing's disease in adults). The ideal puppy should not be too thin either, you should not be able to see his ribs.

2. His or her nose should be cool, damp and clean with no discharge.

3. The pup's eyes should be bright and clear with no discharge or tear stain. Steer clear of a puppy that blinks a lot, this could be the sign of a problem.

4. Gums should be clean and pink.

5. The pup's ears should be clean with no sign of discharge, soreness or redness and no unpleasant smell.

6. Check the puppy's rear end to make sure it is clean and there are no signs of diarrhoea.

7. The pup's coat should look clean, feel soft, not matted - and puppies should smell good! The coat should have no signs of ticks or fleas. Red or irritated skin or bald spots could be a sign of infestation or a skin condition. Also, check between the toes of the paws for signs of redness or swelling.

8. Choose a puppy that moves freely without any sign of injury or lameness. It should be a fluid movement, not jerky or stiff, which could be a sign of joint problems.

9. When the puppy is distracted, clap or make a noise behind her - not so loud as to frighten her - to make sure she is not deaf.

10. Finally, ask to see veterinary records to confirm your puppy has been wormed and had her first injections.

If you are unlucky enough to have a health problem with your pup within the first few months, a reputable breeder will allow you to return the pup. Also, if you get the Cavalier puppy home and things don't work out for whatever reason, some breeders will also take the puppy back within a limited time frame. Check whether this is the case before you commit.

....

Advice From the Horse's Mouth

Choosing the right breeder and then the right puppy can be a minefield. Our breeders have plenty of advice for potential owners.

Sandra Coles, has bred Cavaliers for 45 years and says: "When visiting ask to see Mum and, if possible, Dad. Also to see other dogs that the breeder may have and how they are kept. See Mum with the puppies. I am careful because as a breeder there is also a risk of bringing in disease to the puppies and other dogs in the house. Puppies are more at risk when they start to lose their maternal antibodies.

"Obviously, look for nice clean conditions for Mum and pups and in the kennels generally. All my puppies are brought up indoors, where it's warm, dry and there's lots of social contact from family. Another good sign is the breeder taking time with the new owner and willing to answer any questions, not in a hurry to offload puppies because of some excuse. Other things to look for: the breeder vetting the new owner and getting references; pictures of house and garden and maybe a house visit, if practical.

"All of my puppies are first vaccinated, wormed several times and micro-chipped before leaving. They are registered with the Kennel Club. They all go with a comprehensive puppy pack and food to start with. This is read through with the owner before they have the puppy. New owners are given a book on caring for a puppy before they have it. They can ring or email me any time with any questions. Also, I allow visits to see their individual pup - which has been chosen by me.

"Ask to see certificates for Mum and Dad and check that they are clear for the condition tested. For Cavaliers this is hearts, eyes and DNA testing for dry eye, curly coat and episodic falling, scans for SM (Syringomyelia). Clear hearts in the parents means there is a better chance that the puppies will live a long and healthy life, and you know that the breeder has done all they can to ensure this. Hearts should be checked yearly."

Photo of this Twyforde trio courtesy of Sandra.

"I keep all of my oldies and therefore I have a very good idea of the lines that have good hearts and can make better informed decisions when breeding two parents together. SM is harder to pin down; we have MRI scans. Again, I use informed decisions and scanning when breeding and try to avoid lines that have had problems. Hearts are the biggest killer in Cavaliers. Definitely more research is needed.

"Puppy farms are a subject in themselves and yes, I have heard of horror stories from prospective owners about some of these places. Puppies being sold out of houses where they have not been born and developing major problems or dying in the first few weeks. Also breeders wanting to part with very young puppies because they are going on holiday!! A holiday would be lovely."

Philippa Biddle: "Firstly, research the health tests. Ring a breeder and ask if they have time to talk at that moment, or communicate by email. Buyers need to have some set questions prepared to ask in a conversational way and they need to prioritise those questions. That's what I do as a breeder and people don't get further with me if they don't pass the first few questions.

"Throw the questions into the conversation. Buyers need to interview the breeder just as the breeder will interview them through initial conversation. Be aware good breeders get calls daily and can't talk to everyone if they don't have puppies for sale. Never contact a breeder and say: "Have you got puppies how much are they?" Reticence in a breeder means they care who they sell the puppy to.

"Ask to see the health certificates and look at the health testing BEHIND the parents. Check out the Kennel Club health test pedigree of the parents. I always give buyers the pedigree name of the parents and ask them to look up the health test pedigree themselves. Be prepared for the fact that some tests are done as a guide and the result is not always black and white. Also, ask the breeder to explain her decision to mate those two dogs (to produce that litter).

"Always look for a confident, playful, bold yet calm and friendly puppy. Cavaliers should show no signs of nervousness, this is very important. Buyers should be aware of the age/stage the puppy is when they view it. I believe good breeders don't sell Cavaliers at eight weeks; 10 to 12 weeks is the right age. Look for the puppy interacting with the mother and check the mother's milk bar (teats) to ensure it really is the mother! Ask age of mother and how many litters she has had.

"In terms of the breeder the dogs should all be clean, happy and friendly, the environment spotless and suitable. Obviously mum and pups should be clean. Pups should be fat and have soft, shiny coats and clean ears, feet and bottoms, and smell sweet. In my opinion, once being weaned they should be in the process of being introduced to a variety of foods, not just kibble."

Kathy Hargest, Kathysgirls Cavaliers, Gloucestershire: "Look for a good solid-looking puppy with plenty of confidence that is inquisitive. Observe the mother and other dogs in house and living conditions. You must see the mother and other siblings. Please make sure "mother is mother" - I could write you a book on stories I've been told by people collecting pups. Puppies should have a clean run with food and water present. Are the living conditions appropriate? See all paperwork and microchip."

Dennis and Tina Homes, Leogem Cavaliers, Herefordshire: "Whenever a potential puppy buyer goes to view a litter, they should always be introduced to the mother. If the mother is not present then whatever excuse is made by the seller, we would suggest that you walk away. If the mother is around then you should be shown all the relevant health certificates of both the mother and father, and that includes certificates for hearts, eyes and DNA for hereditary conditions."

Pictured is the beautiful Ch Leogem Ginestra.

Julie Durham, Donrobby Cavaliers, Berkshire: "When first making contact with any breeder, ask lots of questions - any caring breeder will be happy to answer them. Visit puppy before it's ready to leave the breeder and get a feel for the environment it's coming from. Decide if you feel the breeder would help if you need help and support at any time in the future. Ask to see copies of health certificates that have been successfully completed."

American breeder Jina Ezell has had first-hand experience of bad breeders: "Unfortunately, there are far too many puppy farms out there in all breeds, which give those of us who are working hard to maintain high standards a bad name. Yes, many homes I have been in when searching for a new dog have terrible standards. The easy to spot issues can be seen through video chatting even before stepping foot on the property. I look for a clean and organized kennel, including an area for disposing the feces. Have the breeder show you: where the dogs run/play/exercise, where the feces are disposed of, and the records of health.

"Number one in my book is that the parents were health-tested before beginning to breed and that the Dam was over the age of two when delivering her first litter, and given adequate rest between litters and not breeding past seven and a half years. I have been in several breeders' yards/homes where there are 12 to 20 dogs in one place, not to mention how many puppies there were. The smell was horrid, the dirt and mess and the chaos was unbearable. I have left many homes that I had thought there was 'a possibility'. It's truly sad.

"Almost two years ago I was inquiring with a breeder in the mid-west over a few months period. We exchanged phone calls and emails. To cut a long story short, her husband called in the middle of our inquiries and said his wife died the night before! I let him know he must be in a bad spot to be reaching out to potential buyers the day after his wife died. I asked him some questions and was highly concerned for him and the dogs.

"The very next day my husband and I jumped in the car and drove straight through - 18 hours. Nothing could prepare us for what we found. What ended up happening is that I reached out to a local Cavalier breeder who, along with a local rescue group, removed approximately 18 dogs, six puppies, a horse, and a half dozen birds that day. You can only imagine the condition of the home, yard and kennels. There were at least a dozen dogs living in what looked like small carrying kennels."

 The fact that a breeder is listed with a local council or state does NOT necessarily mean that he or she is a good breeder. It simply means that they are breeding lots of puppies and are inspected yearly. In fact, when puppy farms have been uncovered, quite a number of them have been registered with their local authority.

Picking the Right Temperament

You've picked a Cavalier, presumably, because you love the way they look and you are attracted to the breed's traits: its close bond with humans, playfulness, gentle nature, eagerness to please, loyalty and ability to get on well with children and other animals. However, while Cavaliers may share many common characteristics and temperament traits, each puppy also has his own individual character, just like humans.

Visit the breeder to see how your chosen pup interacts and get an idea of his character in comparison to the littermates. Some puppies will run up to greet you, pull at your shoelaces and playfully bite your fingers.

Others will be more content to stay in the den sleeping. Watch their behaviour and energy levels. Are you an active person who enjoys lots of daily exercise or would a less energetic puppy be more suitable? Having said that, one of the attractions of Cavaliers is that they are very adaptable — happy to go for a long ramble in the countryside or snuggle up with you on the couch.

A submissive dog will by nature be more passive, less energetic and also possibly easier to train. A dominant dog will usually be more energetic and lively. He or she may also be more stubborn and need a firmer hand when training or socialising with other dogs. If you already have a dominant dog at home, you have to be careful about introducing a new dog into the household; two dominant dogs may not live together comfortably.

There is no good or bad, it's a question of which type of character will best suit you and your lifestyle. Here are a couple of quick tests to try and gauge your puppy's temperament; they should be carried out by the breeder in familiar surroundings so the puppy is relaxed. It should be pointed out that there is some controversy over temperament testing, as a dog's personality is formed by a combination of factors, which include inherited temperament, socialisation, training and environment (or how you treat your dog):

- ❧ The breeder puts the pup on his or her back on her lap and gently rests her hand on the pup's chest, or

- ❧ She puts her hands under the pup's tummy and gently lifts the pup off the floor for a few seconds, keeping the pup horizontal. A puppy that struggles to get free is less patient than one that makes little effort to get away. A placid, patient dog is likely to fare better in a home with young children than an impatient one.

Here are some other useful signs to look out for –

- ❧ Watch how he interacts with other puppies in the litter. Does he try and dominate them, does he walk away from them or is he happy to play with his littermates? This may give you an idea of how easy it will be to socialise him with other dogs

- ❧ After contact, does the pup want to follow you or walk away from you? Not following may mean he has a more independent nature

- ❧ If you throw something for the puppy is he happy to retrieve it for you or does he ignore it? This may measure willingness to work with humans

- ❧ If you drop a bunch of keys behind the puppy, does he act normally or does he flinch and jump away? The latter may be an indication of a timid or nervous disposition. Not reacting could also be a sign of deafness

Decide which temperament would fit in with you and your family and the rest is up to you. Whatever hereditary temperament your Cavalier has, it is true to say that dogs that have constant positive interactions with people and other animals during the first few months of life will generally be happier and more stable. In contrast, a puppy plucked from its family too early and/or isolated for long periods will be less happy, less socialised, needier, and may well display behaviour problems later on.

Puppies are like children. Being properly raised contributes to their confidence, sociability, stability and intellectual development. The bottom line is that a pup raised in a warm, loving environment with people is likely to be more tolerant and accepting, and less likely to develop behaviour problems.

For those of you who prefer a scientific approach to choosing the right puppy, we are including the full Volhard Puppy Aptitude Test (PAT). This test has been developed by the highly-respected Wendy and Jack Volhard who have built up an international reputation over the last 30 years for their invaluable contribution to dog training, health and nutrition. Their philosophy is: "We believe that one of life's great joys is living in harmony with your dog."

They have written several books and the Volhard PAT is regarded as an excellent method for evaluating the nature of young puppies. Jack and Wendy have also written the Dog Training for Dummies book. Visit their website at www.volhard.com for details of their upcoming dog training camps, as well as their training and nutrition groups.

The Volhard Puppy Aptitude Test

Here are the ground rules for performing the test: The testing is done in a location unfamiliar to the puppies. This does not mean they have to be taken away from home. A 10-foot square area is perfectly adequate, such as a room in the house where the puppies have not been.

- ✓ The puppies are tested one at a time. There are no other dogs or people, except the scorer and the tester, in the testing area
- ✓ The puppies do not know the tester
- ✓ The scorer is a disinterested third party and not the person interested in selling you a puppy
- ✓ The scorer is unobtrusive and positions herself so she can observe the puppies' responses without having to move

The puppies are tested before they are fed. The puppies are tested when they are at their liveliest. Do not try to test a puppy that is not feeling well.

Puppies should not be tested the day of or the day after being vaccinated. Only the first response counts! Tip: During the test, watch the puppy's tail. It will make a difference in the scoring whether the tail is up or down. The tests are simple to perform and anyone with some common sense can do them. You can, however, elicit the help of someone who has tested puppies before and knows what they are doing.

Social attraction - the owner or caretaker of the puppies places it in the test area about four feet from the tester and then leaves the test area. The tester kneels down and coaxes the puppy to come to him or her by encouragingly and gently clapping hands and calling. The tester must coax the puppy in the opposite direction from where it entered the test area. Hint: Lean backward, sitting on your heels instead of leaning forward toward the puppy. Keep your hands close to your body encouraging the puppy to come to you instead of trying to reach for the puppy.

Restraint - the tester crouches down and gently rolls the puppy on its back for 30 seconds. Hint: Hold the puppy down without applying too much pressure. The object is not to keep it on its back but to test its response to being placed in that position.

Following - the tester stands up and slowly walks away encouraging the puppy to follow. Hint: Make sure the puppy sees you walk away and get the puppy to focus on you by lightly clapping your hands and using verbal encouragement to get the puppy to follow you. Do not lean over the puppy.

Social Dominance - let the puppy stand up or sit and gently stroke it from the head to the back while you crouch beside it. See if it will lick your face, an indication of a forgiving nature. Continue stroking until you see a behaviour you can score. Hint: When you crouch next to the puppy avoid leaning or hovering over it. Have the puppy at your side, both of you facing in the same direction.

During testing maintain a positive, upbeat and friendly attitude toward the puppies. Try to get each puppy to interact with you to bring out the best in him or her. Make the test a pleasant experience for the puppy.

Elevation Dominance - the tester cradles the puppy with both hands, supporting the puppy under its chest and gently lifts it two feet off the ground and holds it there for 30 seconds.

Retrieving - the tester crouches beside the puppy and attracts its attention with a crumpled up piece of paper. When the puppy shows some interest, the tester throws the paper no more than four feet in front of the puppy encouraging it to retrieve the paper.

Touch Sensitivity - the tester locates the webbing of one the puppy's front paws and presses it lightly between his index finger and thumb.

The tester gradually increases pressure while counting to ten and stops when the puppy pulls away or shows signs of discomfort.

Sound Sensitivity - the puppy is placed in the center of the testing area and an assistant stationed at the perimeter makes a sharp noise, such as banging a metal spoon on the bottom of a metal pan.

Sight Sensitivity - the puppy is placed in the center of the testing area. The tester ties a string around a bath towel and jerks it across the floor, two feet away from the puppy.

Stability - an umbrella is opened about five feet from the puppy and gently placed on the ground. During the testing, make a note of the heart rate of the pup, this is an indication of how it deals with stress, as well as its energy level. Puppies come with high, medium or low energy levels. You have to decide for yourself, which suits your life style.

Dogs with high energy levels need a great deal of exercise, and will get into mischief if this energy is not channeled into the right direction.

Finally, look at the overall structure of the puppy. You see what you get at 49 days age (seven weeks). If the pup has strong and straight front and back legs, with all four feet pointing in the same direction, it will grow up that way, provided you give it the proper diet and environment. If you notice something out of the ordinary at this age, it will stay with puppy for the rest of its life. He will not grow out of it.

Scoring the Results

Following are the responses you will see and the score assigned to each particular response. You will see some variations and will have to make a judgment on what score to give them —

TEST	RESPONSE	SCORE
SOCIAL ATTRACTION	Came readily, tail up, jumped, bit at hands	1
	Came readily, tail up, pawed, licked at hands	2
	Came readily, tail up	3
	Came readily, tail down	4
	Came hesitantly, tail down	5
	Didn't come at all	6
FOLLOWING	Followed readily, tail up, got underfoot, bit at feet	1
	Followed readily, tail up, got underfoot	2
	Followed readily, tail up	3
	Followed readily, tail down	4
	Followed hesitantly, tail down	5
	Did not follow or went away	6
RESTRAINT	Struggled fiercely, flailed, bit	1
	Struggled fiercely, flailed	2

	Settled, struggled, settled with some eye contact	3
	Struggled, then settled	4
	No struggle	5
	No struggle, strained to avoid eye contact	6
SOCIAL DOMINANCE	Jumped, pawed, bit, growled	1
	Jumped, pawed	2
	Cuddled up to tester and tried to lick face	3
	Squirmed, licked at hands	4
	Rolled over, licked at hands	5
	Went away and stayed away	6
ELEVATION DOMINANCE	Struggled fiercely, tried to bite	1
	Struggled fiercely	2
	Struggled, settled, struggled, settled	3
	No struggle, relaxed	4
	No struggle, body stiff	5
	No struggle, froze	6
RETRIEVING	Chased object, picked it up and ran away	1
	Chased object, stood over it and did not return	2
	Chased object, picked it up and returned with it to tester	3
	Chased object and returned without it to tester	4
	Started to chase object, lost interest	5
	Does not chase object	6
TOUCH SENSITIVITY	8-10 count before response	1
	6-8 count before response	2
	5-6 count before response	3
	3-5 count before response	4
	2-3 count before response	5
	1-2 count before response	6
SOUND SENSITIVITY	Listened, located sound and ran toward it barking	1
	Listened, located sound and walked slowly toward it	2
	Listened, located sound and showed curiosity	3
	Listened and located sound	4
	Cringed, backed off and hid behind tester	5

		Ignored sound and showed no curiosity	6
SIGHT SENSITIVITY		Looked, attacked and bit object	1
		Looked and put feet on object and put mouth on it	2
		Looked with curiosity and attempted to investigate, tail up	3
		Looked with curiosity, tail down	4
		Ran away or hid behind tester	5
		Hid behind tester	6
STABILITY		Looked and ran to the umbrella, mouthing or biting it	1
		Looked and walked to the umbrella, smelling it cautiously	2
		Looked and went to investigate	3
		Sat and looked, but did not move toward the umbrella	4
		Showed little or no interest	5
		Ran away from the umbrella	6

The scores are interpreted as follows:

Mostly 1s - Strong desire to be pack leader and is not shy about bucking for a promotion.
Has a predisposition to be aggressive to people and other dogs and will bite.
Should only be placed into a very experienced home where the dog will be trained and worked on a regular basis.

Tip: Stay away from the puppy with a lot of 1's or 2's. It has lots of leadership aspirations and may be difficult to manage. This puppy needs an experienced home. Not good with children.

Mostly 2s - Also has leadership aspirations. May be hard to manage and has the capacity to bite.
Has lots of self-confidence. Should not be placed into an inexperienced home. Too unruly to be good with children and elderly people, or other animals. Needs strict schedule, loads of exercise and lots of training. Has the potential to be a great show dog with someone who understands dog behaviour.

Mostly 3s - Can be a high-energy dog and may need lots of exercise. Good with people and other animals. Can be a bit of a handful to live with. Needs training, does very well at it and learns quickly. Great dog for second-time owner.

Mostly 4s - The kind of dog that makes the perfect pet. Best choice for the first time owner.
Rarely will buck for a promotion in the family. Easy to train, and rather quiet.
Good with elderly people, children, although may need protection from the children.
Choose this pup, take it to obedience classes, and you'll be the star, without having to do too much work!

Tip: The puppy with mostly 3's and 4's can be quite a handful, but should be good with children and does well with training. Energy needs to be dispersed with plenty of exercise.

Mostly 5s - Fearful, shy and needs special handling. Will run away at the slightest stress. Strange people, strange places, different floor or surfaces may upset it. Often afraid of loud noises and terrified of thunderstorms. When you greet it upon your return, may submissively urinate. Needs a very special home where the environment doesn't change too much and where there are no children. Best for a quiet, elderly couple. If cornered and cannot get away, has a tendency to bite.

Mostly 6s – So independent that he doesn't need you or other people. Doesn't care if he is trained or not - he is his own person. Unlikely to bond to you, since he doesn't need you. A great guard dog for gas stations! Do not take this puppy and think you can change her into a lovable bundle - you can't, so leave well enough alone.

Tip: Avoid the puppy with several 6's. It is so independent it doesn't need you or anyone. He is his own person and unlikely to bond to you.

The Scores

Few puppies will test with all 2s or all 3s, there'll be a mixture of scores. For that first time, wonderfully easy to train, potential star, look for a puppy that scores with mostly 4s and 3s. Don't worry about the score on Touch Sensitivity - you can compensate for that with the right training equipment.

It's hard not to become emotional when picking a puppy - they are all so cute, soft and cuddly. Remind yourself that this dog is going to be with you for eight to 16 years. Don't hesitate to step back a little to contemplate your decision. Sleep on it and review it in the light of day. Avoid the puppy with a score of 1 on the Restraint and Elevation tests. This puppy will be too much for the first-time owner. It's a lot more fun to have a good dog, one that is easy to train, one you can live with and one you can be proud of, than one that is a constant struggle.

Getting a Dog From a Shelter - Don't overlook an animal shelter as a source for a good dog. Not all dogs wind up in a shelter because they are bad. After that cute puppy stage, when the dog grows up, it may become too much for its owner. Or, there has been a change in the owner's circumstances forcing him or her into having to give up the dog.

Most of the time these dogs are housetrained and already have some training. If the dog has been properly socialised to people, it will be able to adapt to a new environment. Bonding may take a little longer, but once accomplished, results in a devoted companion.

So you see, it's not all about the colour or the cutest face! When getting a puppy, your thought process should run something like this:

1. Decide to get a Cavalier.
2. Find a good breeder whose dogs are health tested.
3. Find one with a litter available when you are ready for a puppy – or wait.
4. Decide on a male or female.
5. Pick one with a suitable temperament to fit in with your family.

Some people pick a puppy based on how the dog looks. If coat colour, for example, is very important to you, make sure the other boxes are ticked as well.

5. A Puppy's Early Life

By Jina Ezell, AKC Bred with H.E.A.R.T. breeder

Good breeders very often have waiting lists for their puppies and by the time Washington State breeder Jina Ezell's Kalama Cavalier puppies are born, the new owners have already been vetted and approved. She emails them a weekly letter and photo/video album with news and images of the litter's progress, which helps the owners prepare for their puppies.

Jina has kindly given us permission to use extracts from these emails to give an insight into the life of a young puppy. They highlight the love and attention good breeders lavish on their litters, as well as the time spent socialising and training the pups in readiness for their new homes. Jina also provides links to some excellent resources for new Cavalier owners and tips for the homecoming.

Letter From The Litter

WEEK 1

Your sweet-breathed fur-babies weigh a little more than a half pound. They spend 90 per cent of the time sleeping and the remaining 10 per cent suckling, so there's really not much activity going on in the whelping box right now. For the first three weeks of life, a puppy is almost devoid of senses. Its eyes, ears and nose don't begin to work properly until the third week. During this period, puppies sleep most of the time and there's nothing wrong with that. Sleep is vital for a new-born puppy's development.

I try not to disturb them (too much) besides weighing them, we really keep the holding to a quick one to two minutes. You appreciate watching the changes: notice their sweet noses, pink and bright. The eyes and ears are closed and there's not much movement. In fact, the bedding hasn't needed to be changed. They don't make much noise... just a little hum/chirp ("that sounds like a guinea pig," says my daughter).

Between Days 3-17 I do a once-a-day 'Early Neurological Stimulation' exercise with the puppies: The workouts required handling them one at a time while performing a series of five exercises:

* Tactical stimulation between toes with Q-tip (cotton bud)
* Head held erect
* Head pointed down
* Supine position
* Thermal stimulation (on various surfaces)

Photo of four-day-old pups.

Five benefits have been observed in canines that were exposed to the Bio Sensor stimulation exercises:

* Improved cardio vascular performance (heart rate)
* Stronger heart beats
* Stronger adrenal glands

- 🐾 More tolerance to stress
- 🐾 Greater resistance to disease

Mercy (the mother) is doing extremely well. She is truly content. She just started coming out of the whelping box to try and play with all of us yesterday, ready for a little break.

WEEK 2

Some big changes have taken place during the last week.

From birth, puppies are able to use their sense of smell and touch, which helps them root about the nest to find their mother's scent-marked breasts. The first milk the mother produces is called colostrum. It is rich in antibodies that provide passive immunity and help protect the babies from disease during these early weeks of life.

Some of our puppies' eyes have begun to open. Ears should be open in the next few days, and your puppy will begin to hear. This gives our furry babies a new sense of their world. They learn what their mother and other dogs look and sound like, and begin to expand their own vocabulary from grunts and mews to yelps, whines and barks.

Puppies generally stand by Day 15 and take their first wobbly walk by Day 21, we will see if this is the case with your pups. Right now they are scooting all over the whelping box. By age three weeks, puppy development advances from the neonatal period to the transitional period. We have begun to handle the puppies more this week.

WEEK 3

Your fur babies are simply a delight! They are still sleeping a lot, but getting lots of snuggles and exercise when they are awake.

I have a puppy pad at the end of the box and they are already (randomly) going on the pad, trying to keep their bedding dry and unsoiled (not quite happening just yet). I will continue to layer pads and encourage the potty at the end of the box, keeping their den/sleeping area clean. So that when they progress - in the next seven to 10 days - to the floor, it will be a little easier to know where to potty and where to play/sleep. I added the reusable puppy potty training green mat - www.amazon.com/Puppy-Potty-Trainer-Indoor-Training/dp/B075X3VJ1Y but I'm not sure if they are using it yet... still.... with encouragement! It's amazing to see some already getting the idea of not soiling their bed...such smart pups!

In the next week or so, I will be introducing a play-mobile outside that we built, weather permitting, as well as the big (adult) dogs, bones and crates, and lots of movement time. This will begin training and help them prepare for you. As of yet, they are just getting strong enough to keep their head up (still pretty wobbly) and climbing over one another.

There are several cameras all around my puppy parlor areas so that I can keep watch anytime, anywhere with a click on an app on my phone. It's truly amazing!

I am sure each of you have begun to read books or websites to prepare your lives and homes for the training that will be taking place after these bundles of sweetness enter your homes. Many have asked about classes. I think it's wonderful to get your puppy trained as soon as they are fully inoculated (around three months). Look for AKC/Good Citizen Trainers.

Meanwhile, there are many wonderful articles and videos out there, just start somewhere. I would like each of you to read this and watch this video: www.akc.org/content/dog-training/articles/how-to-crate-train-a-puppy Hopefully, this will help us be on the same page with regard to potty/crate training. The key to a happy, smart puppy and family is (so similar to child-rearing): CONSISTENCY.

WEEK 4

Your puppies are getting their 'land legs', hopping, climbing, even running around the whelping box and now in their fenced Puppy Room area. Teeth have moved in this week and they are gnawing on everything, especially their litter mates!

Today, being their fourth-week birthday, they all got to celebrate by going outside as well as getting their first taste of kibble. I soaked the kibble with bone broth and had some help with the first bites...the puppies enjoy their new source of calories.

As some of you know, I make all my adult dog food, but in doing thorough research, I have decided to give Life's Abundance to the nursing Moms to have all they want, in addition to their two to three meals a day. This is what I am beginning your dogs on, as well as introducing them to raw bones

and a bit of the big boys' (raw) food in the next few weeks. I will send a small supply home of the food I am giving, feel free to do your own research, keeping the food as holistic as possible, without fillers.

By the time you receive your pup, I will have had them sleeping in a crate (three to four hours), taking them out, praising and, hopefully, very much on the way to being potty trained. When accidents do happen (aside from the puppy pads), clean the mess immediately. You will notice in some pictures, I layer the potty pads up so there is an obvious area for your puppy to 'go'. I did that while they were still in the whelping box and now that they are able to walk around, they 'go' to their pads most often. I have witnessed each of your pups initiate their constitution.

Some of you have been able to meet up this week, it's great that you now have your puppy named and face emblazoned into your mind. You'll be busy this next month preparing your lives and homes for these precious fur babies. If you are unable to meet the puppy in person, but would enjoy a live video feed, just let me know.

Between Weeks 4 and 5, Jina makes a "meet and greet" date when owners come to pick their individual puppy, with Jina's guidance. After that time, she makes the photos and videos more personalized and uses the puppy's call name.

WEEK 5

These are NOT the same puppies as you saw and experienced last week...these little doggies are experiencing so many things each day and growing in leaps and bounds. They aren't sleeping as much; taking time daily to be outside and play a lot in the Puppy Room with each other as well as the big dogs and their half siblings.

We will bring them to the kitchen (with baby gates) and even into the living room in baskets and on blankets into the living areas. We carry the puppies with us much of the time, so they don't have any issues (crying out) when they are being picked up, moved or carried.

It's been such a wonderful week - a week of transitions, explorations and awakening to all senses, they are looking and acting more like dogs than the babies they've been. Here are just a few changes:

Visually:

I've been adding items nearly each day to the puppy play area. This allows puppies to begin to be comfortable in a variety of arenas. They have been in nearly every part of our home with varying surfaces, smells and textures. The puppies will come with one or more items from the play yard, this way the familiar will be with them as they transition into your homes.

Tastes:

Sampling of the puppy food is still going on, no-one is truly hungry enough to eat too much. They LOVE their Mama's milk. Whenever Mercy is anywhere close, they begin to make a loud barking sound to try and get her to come and feed them (even though food is right there!) She's a very sweet and nurturing Mama...so weaning may be a little while yet.

Sensory/Feel:

All week we have been able to have short stints outside, the sun has been shining and getting them used to pottying outside (they do so good!) The puppies have had the big dogs and two-week-older half siblings around them a bit more inside and outside.

Hearing:

Not only am I NOT super quiet when I shut the gates and doors around the puppies, I have music on most of the day. I find the high megahertz binaural music (430hz and higher) calming and relaxing, there's also several desensitization playlists that I have begun to play for them; they have sirens, fireworks, saws, etc. in the background.

I have been saying "potty, kennel, outside", but now, when they bite each other or attempt to potty other than the pad, I do the "CHCHCH!" sound to associate with displeasure and show them what to do.

Photo shows two pups exploring Jina's kitchen and one using the puppy pad in the background.

Training:

I am layering the potty pads up and the puppies are running to the pad and going quite nicely. As you are preparing your home-kennel area, I hope you are deciding on the routine you will keep with your puppy - consistency is key.

An adorable puppy that has accidents is understandable, but one who is not trained will become a dog who is obnoxious.

This is your time to gather the tools and run. Sure, "Toy" dogs (the category Cavalier King Charles Spaniels are in) have a reputation for the lengthy time to potty train. So, get ready now... get motivated and gear up!

WEEK 6

Your pups are officially integrated out of the Puppy Area and into their big boy/girl area of the kennel with larger play, sleeping and potty areas. They are doing well: eating, sleeping, playing HARD and growing daily. Not only am I putting several tablespoons of the raw food into their kibble (adding less and less water - thus the kibble is constantly under foot), but they have also had a few chicken feet and necks as well - with supervision. As you can see, their tummies are quite full and happy...they have grown so much.

Mom has been taking long breaks, only nursing in the morning and once before bedtime. In the next week or so, I imagine Mom will be 'done' with nursing...but with their desire, little puppies don't break off the drink too easily! You'll see those freeloaders every now and again in the coming photo albums.

I have been changing the types of bowls and a variety of blankets and towels to lie on. Have you seen *Seven Rules by Seven Weeks?* www.thewholedog.org/ruleof7.html I attempt to expose the pups to seven things, such as floor textiles, bowls, people, music, toys... so much to share with them to and they are doing so well! None of the puppies jump or flinch when being handled, they are already so calm and relaxed. It would be helpful for you to embrace the idea to continue the socialization process in the first few months of your puppy's life.

They are in the 'learning and training mode', so run with it...you won't regret this!! We will be three-quarters of the way through the *100 Experiences in 100 Days*. You can continue working your way through the list after you have him in your arms:
www.nshoreanimalhospital.com/clients/18633/documents/Puppy%20Socialization.pdf

We have had a lot of dry weather, so the pups are being exposed to many ways to get their walks in. Your pups can let themselves out and down the step, into the puppy courtyard; holding his or her

bladder and toilet until the grass. I give lots of verbal cues ("Potty, potty") and affirmations to help associate and train. We have downsized the Potty Pad to about half the size. We added more chew-type toys and crates to the Puppy Play area now.

I open the portable fencing surrounding the play area almost as wide as it will go because there is so much running, jumping and tumbling going on. After they do their business, often times, I will bring them into the main area, kitchen, living room, etc. so they can run full speed ahead. It's gotta be illegal how much fun we all have!

It's been another week of play, lots of friends visiting and playing - they all love to be held and snuggled, run and tumble - eating (even in the Big Dog's Area), sleeping (maybe 70% of the time) and doing the puppy thing so beautifully. As soon as I see the pups getting sleepy, I am beginning to put them in separate kennels (crates) and shut the door (not too quietly, either). They are now up three to four hours at a time by themselves.

 I will continue to work on their kennel training until the day you have them in your arms. For you to prepare for crate training, here's a video and article for you: https://thedogtrainingsecret.com/crate-training/Crate-Training-Puppies

I want to assure you that when I hand over your puppy, it will be AFTER going over several things with you that I will have put together in their Puppy Packs. Included will be a Vaccination and Deworming Schedule. I will microchip and do the first, limited micro-vaccination within 48 hours of your pick-up. I am pro-vaccine, in a VERY limited amount, never double-triple vaccinating at one time.

This way, if there is a reaction, you can pinpoint it. I do have homeopaths on hand if there are reactions. As you begin looking for a veterinarian, look for one who thinks similarly (limited & micro vaccs). https://healthypets.mercola.com/sites/healthypets/archive/2017/12/20/canine-vaccine-guidelines.aspx

WEEK 7

It's been a week of transitions, new opportunities and excitement. Each morning we begin "running with the big dogs" as I let them in the big yard while straightening the puppy room and get breakfast out for them and change the potty pad. After eating, I let them outside once again and help them to adjust to the crates to nap in for several hours each day. Honestly, the pups have to be pretty tired for them to be super comfortable alone in their crates.

This week I will work much harder on their outside potty training and inside kennel training, preparing them to go home with you. They are up to about four hours in their sleeping crates, where they do NOT potty and usually are sleeping the entire time. This is the maximum length of time they should be left alone during the day.

As soon as I hear them up and playing/cooing, I open the door and watch as they run outside and give the cue: "Potty, potty" and when they do, I say "Good potty!" The pups will come in and usually eat some food, drink some water and are ready to BOUND everywhere. This routine of play until worn out will happen three to four times a day. You will do well to keep this routine as well.

Lots of new things were introduced this week, including the raw foods: chicken, steak and chicken feet and ribs (which they all adore!) I watched carefully, they mostly gnawed and suckled, but they do enjoy the raw bone - they're chewing anything they can sink their teeth into. There's been a variety of bones and hooves as well as a puppy Kong for them to test their milk teeth out on.

When the puppy tries to gnaw on a hand or finger it is important to let him or her know that this is NOT the place to chew. You can yelp out like the Mama does or say firmly "NO!" and then give a chew toy. By doing this immediately, your boundaries are established.

Training with a leash is happening, as are interactions with the big dogs and a variety of music and desensitization. These last few weeks are part of their socialization period where the puppies learn dog behavior. We begin this by training and surrounding them with other well-trained dogs - and humans.

Some puppy mills allow the puppies to leave between six to seven weeks, but I see such a difference that I have never let a puppy go before eight to 10 weeks.

We have given them leash-time as well; I just hook the leash onto their little collar, though you will need to provide a nice, adjustable harness, with an extra small collar. I keep my dogs in harnesses, especially if they are comfortable... it's much easier to quickly put your leash on for walks and training. I like the Eco Bark padded harness for pups, which you can find online.

Mama has been 100% separated (unless they are running and playing quickly together), so we are doing more and more individualized puppy socialization. Last week they all had their Well Puppy exams (all are perfectly fantastic!) and this week they will be micro-chipped and receive their first vaccination. I have homeopathies, should there be any concern or adverse reaction.

WEEK 8

This litter has the most adventurous, brilliant, beautiful puppies ever! I can stare at them and be mesmerized by them as they prance, dig, chew, brawl, coo, hop, and do all things puppy-related. I'm relishing these last few days with them all.

The microchips have been placed, their first puppy vaccinations given (with no adverse reactions), and their last deworming... these pups are ready for their fur-ever homes. All their Puppy Folders have been put together and their Going Home Bags are ready to go through when we meet.

There have been a few people asking about collars. The colored collars we use are not actual collars they are 'markers' for identification. If you will be using a collar, for tags, etc., you will need to purchase one that can loosen up, as these pups will grow two to three times larger in the next year.

Some of you will need to look into licensing your dog, and showing it with a tag. Lots of folks like to add their cell phone number on another tag. Some people advise against putting the dog's NAME on the tags, it's your choice. I don't have a recommendation about the type of collars, I just recommend using a harness for the leash when walking, not the collar.

Remember, NO pressure/pulling around the neck for these sensitive guys.

Foodstuffs: I am sending with your Puppy Pack about a week's supply of the Life's Abundance kibble that they have been eating along with their Mama.

Of course, by now you all have most likely seen and heard what a fan I am of the raw food diet for these sweet babies. I recommend it based on a lot of research and I am part of the Facebook group *Raw Fed Healthy Cavs* with lots of recipes and tons of support:
www.facebook.com/groups/505458656277685

I know it's not for everyone and I do NOT expect you to feed your dogs this way - though it would be amazing if you did. The puppies have all loved the raw food when I have given it to them. When feeding, it is helpful to have the Spaniel-style bowls (the inside is smaller) so that their ears don't get into the food; otherwise, you are cleaning up ears and floors!

Keeping your pup's diet as clean and whole as possible will help to eliminate many of the typical Cavalier King Charles Spaniel health issues. You are on the track to a long and wonderful relationship. Remember to keep your training and everyday treats whole and healthy as well, avoiding harsh chemicals and preservatives.

If you find there is a lot of tearing and staining happening in your sweet pup's face, this could indicate a leaching of yeast from his or her body. Take a quick inventory of what you are feeding, wipe down with a warm washcloth (sometimes twice a day, I hear) and sit back and read this article:
www.leospetcare.com/a-veterinary-guide-to-tear-stains

A few other recommendations: a: child's soft toothbrush works great - there's toothbrushes and toothpaste you can purchase together - anything works better than nothing... keep trying! I use a Pooper Scooper, it makes picking up after your dog so much easier. Shampoo/conditioners: anything sulphate-free. They really don't need bathing often, but it's good to have a nice, clean dog.

There are so many tips on bathing your puppy - some of which are not necessarily common sense – here are some:
https://healthypets.mercola.com/sites/healthypets/archive/2011/10/11/amp/mistakes-that-can-ruin-dogs-bath-time-for-his-lifetime.aspx

I hope you are all rested and ready for the amazing transition into your home and family. We're keeping two of the puppies ourselves, so I'll be training right alongside you! Now that the puppies will be in your arms very soon, there won't be many of these group updates.

What to Expect From Your Puppy

In the Week 7 letter, Jina gives her new puppy parents lots of tips on what to expect once back home.

Tip 1: Anticipate a shy start. He or she will need a very small world for a while. Don't plan on taking him or her out to play dates for a while. As hard as it will be, remember that your puppy has a limited amount of immunity in his or her system, so don't take him or her to public dog parks or on big walks for a few months.

Keep an indoor fenced kennel play area, similar to what I have, that he/she can stay in when not directly with you. I also love baby gates for the kitchen. This will help with 'accidents' as well as helping this pup feel like there is an area that is his or her complete domain.

The kennel (crate) will feel like a den and, if it is small, (enough to stand, turn around and lay down) they will not typically soil their bed. I put a cosy blanket and a little stuffed toy in, which I provide in their Going Home bag, which smells like all of us.

As your puppy grows, increase the sleeping area in size. Also, it's a nice calming effect to put a thin sheet or blanket over the kennel. Try and keep a rhythm/routine/schedule; his bladder will begin to rely on you to help!!

Some of my adoptive families find that putting the pup's sleeping crate on or near the parents' bed has helped for the first few nights. You can help him/her adjust to your new norm by:

- A good amount of exercise before bedtime
- Feeding and pottying
- Putting a bully stick or favorite chew toy in the crate.

When the puppy wakes, wait for the "I'm awake and need to potty" sound. Take him/her out and, after praising, bring back to the sleeping crate until morning. Your puppy will only take a few days to understand the normal routine and schedule, I am sure of this.

Tip 2: Don't be alarmed if your puppy squeals and flinches/jumps/shakes at first. This period, seven to 10 weeks, is a time of heightened awareness - very good for training, by the way. Stay extremely calm and begin setting patterns (boundaries) in a tone of voice and atmosphere to bring confidence and assurance to your puppy as well as yourself.

Don't always pick your puppy up, as hard as it will be, just calmly let your puppy know that "everything is alright!" Dogs first LISTEN and then LOOK, so make your tone calm and eyes warm. Soon your puppy will be running around, confidently exploring and seeking adventure around every corner. Hopefully by now you know what training method you will be using and will help him or her

work through the kinks together (you...and each one of the members of your family).

These dogs are extremely forgiving, loyal, and so loving that nothing is impossible. Set a goal. You have all he or she needs for success! May your puppy get his Canine Good Citizen certificate by six months. www.akc.org/products-services/training-programs/canine-good-citizen

Tip 3: Set your vet appointment within seven days of bringing your pup home, as per my Terms of Sale Agreement/Health Guarantee, to check for any genetic deformities, etc.

They will need to check him/her over and start a Health Schedule with you. Get all of them scheduled now so that you can have the next six to 12 months laid out (time, money, etc)..

Photo shows vet Amy Eilbeck, DVM, checking the puppies over before they leave Jina.

As you move forward with vaccines, please remember to ask for the ultra (micro) vaccine, this is a smaller dosage for our Toy breed: https://www.dogsnaturallymagazine.com/a-large-vaccine-problem-for-small-dogs

Once they hit the three-year mark, you will be able to skip a year or two of vaccines (yay!), but until then, I believe the limited amount of vaccine will be best.

AKC has a 30-day Pet Insurance Certificate that they have offered to each of my adoptive families because I have pre-registered this litter. In your new Puppy Pack I will give you the registration information and have attached the insurance certificate to this email. You can choose to complete this registration. Thus, you will have an official 'Registered Dog', or not - for Pet Quality vs. Show Quality, it does not matter to most. At that point, you can then go on to sign up for the insurance.

As well, I will have in your packet all the information for registering their microchip. This is very important. I will have taken the time to microchip, but YOU need to register this chip. There are so many dogs that are found each year, they happened to be chipped... but no one knows who they belong to. Thank you for doing your part in helping this sweet puppy start his/her life strong and well.

Tip 4: Be cautious about environmental poisons. There are so many people who unintentionally over-medicate their dogs, and the toxic issues can come from a variety of sources. I hope you have taken the time to read the ebook I sent you previously, 'Scared Poopless', or watched the 'Truth about Pet Cancer' series.

Now is the time to plan and prepare your home and yard and prepare for this sweet, but sensitive love bug. Go natural. That goes for all floor and surface cleaners (vinegar and water for us - don't forget about carpet cleaning too) where your pup will be, the air they breathe (avoid synthetic perfumes/sprays), and the food they eat (that's a book in itself).

Folks ask me all the time about managing fleas and ticks. Well, honestly, I really don't have to do much. My pack eats clean and the little buggers aren't attracted to a low alkaline state. If you see one when you are doing your weekly flea combing, then kill it and keep combing. I use a flea comb and vinegar/a drop of dish soap and water to lift the fur, pull the flea off and kill it. This is your best bet. In the case where I see a lot of fleas or flea poop (looks like pepper on their skin - I personally don't), then I will apply a tiny bit of essential oils - cedar/eucalyptus diluted when I wash and comb them.

Pictured: Jina with Ezell's Sir William. Photo by Andrea Bernard.

In my yard, I sprinkle Diatomaceous Earth all around (spring/summer/fall) which is non-toxic to humans and animals but will kill all kinds of little bugs. In the case where I might be going into someone else's environment and I want to really ensure my dog is protected I have found a few over the counter meds that seem to be safe(r) to use, such as Blue Bottle Advanced Flea Control, available from Amazon.

Research and apply with caution. I advise against the pills and once-a-month applications though, but feel free to do a thorough research, particularly with holistic veterinarians. Share your findings with me, I'm always eager to learn!

TIP 5: What to anticipate when you pick-up your puppy:

- 🐾 At least 45 minutes to adjust to you as I bring him/her to you and I step out of the picture

- 🐾 Go over your Puppy Pack and paperwork. If you have not done so, please do take the time to go over the Terms of Sale/Agreement (which includes the health guarantee) that I need to keep in my files. I will bring a copy with me to have you sign, but in all the excitement, it would be best for you to read ahead of time.

Some of the things you will find in your new Puppy Pack are: paperwork, a few toys, flea comb, a small blanket which I have been letting the pups and Mom lay with; it's full of their scent. This will be a BIG help when it comes to the first few nights alone. A small bag (should last you a few weeks) of the Life Abundance dog kibble, in addition to the raw feeding I have been using for Mom and Pups their entire lives.

One other item is a brochure from our favorite humanitarian relief agencies, which a portion (+100% of every 10th puppy) of each of your adoptions goes directly toward. We have interviewed the staff in person and believe that they are getting the most $$ on the ground for refuges, children, healthcare and the hungry. If you would like to partner with us, here is their website - we'd love to see and hear what you think! https://www.fh.org/our-work

If there are any issues that you are EVER concerned with, don't hesitate to write or call. I've gotten plenty of calls from the Vet Office "what do we do now!!" I will do my best to help walk you all through any challenges or concerns. I will always be available to you for the life of this amazing fur-baby (and beyond). This online page will be another good reminder of all things pertaining to bringing your puppy home: https://mysmartpuppy.com/bringing-puppy-home-first-days

I know there's a ton of things you are doing to prepare for your pups coming home. I hope these weekly emails with tips and reminders have helped you and your home and family prepare so that there is a sweet, smooth transition. Should you think of anything, please do not hesitate to call, text or email.

It has been a true joy to walk this journey with you and for you. I anticipate a smooth transition from my heart and arms to yours and I'm looking forward to hearing about how things are going for you.

Jina's Cavaliers kindly take a short break from watching their favourite TV show to pose for a photo:

All words and photos supplied by Jina Ezell

6. Bringing Your Puppy Home

Getting a new puppy is so exciting. You can't wait to bring your little bundle of joy home. Before that happens, you probably dream of all the things you and your fluffy little soul mate are going to do together; going for walks in the countryside, snuggling down by the fire, playing games together, setting off on holiday, maybe even taking part in competitions or shows.

Your pup has, of course, no idea of your big plans, and the reality when he or she arrives can be a bit of a shock for some owners! Puppies are wilful little critters with minds of their own and sharp teeth. They leak at both ends, chew anything in sight, constantly demand your attention, nip the kids or anything else to hand, often cry a lot for the first few days and don't pay a blind bit of notice to your commands. There is a lot of work ahead before the two of you develop a unique bond. Your pup has to learn what is required before he or she can start to meet some of your expectations - and you have to understand what your pup needs from you.

....

Once your new arrival lands in your home, your time won't be your own, but you can get off to a good start by preparing things before the big day. Here's a list of things to think about getting beforehand (your breeder may supply some of these):

Puppy Checklist

- ✓ A dog bed or basket
- ✓ Bedding – a Vetbed or Vetfleece would be a good choice, you can buy one online
- ✓ A towel or piece of cloth which has been rubbed on the puppy's mother to put in the bed
- ✓ A manufactured or home-made puppy gate and/or pen to contain the pup in one area of the house initially
- ✓ A collar or harness and lead (leash)
- ✓ An identification tag for the collar or harness
- ✓ Food and water bowls, preferably stainless steel
- ✓ Puppy food – find out what the breeder is feeding and stick with that initially
- ✓ Puppy treats, preferably healthy ones, like carrots or apple, not rawhide
- ✓ Lots of newspapers for housetraining
- ✓ Poo(p) bags
- ✓ Toys and chews suitable for puppies
- ✓ A puppy coat if you live in a cool climate
- ✓ A crate if you decide to use one
- ✓ Old towels for cleaning/drying your puppy and partially covering the crate

AND PLENTY OF TIME!

Later on you'll also need grooming tools, (see **Chapter 14. Grooming**), dog shampoo, flea and worming products, which you can buy from your vet, and maybe a travel crate.

Many good breeders provide Puppy Packs to take home; they contain some or all of the following items:

- ✓ Registration certificate
- ✓ Pedigree certificate
- ✓ Buyer's Contract
- ✓ Information pack with details of vet's visits, vaccinations and wormings, parents' health certificates, diet, breed clubs, etc.
- ✓ Puppy food
- ✓ ID tag/microchip info
- ✓ Blanket that smells of the mother and litter
- ✓ Soft toy that your puppy has grown up with, possibly a chew toy as well
- ✓ Collar or harness and lead (sometimes)
- ✓ Four or five weeks' free insurance

Puppy Proofing Your Home

Before your puppy arrives, you may have to make a few adjustments to make your home safe and suitable. Puppies are small bundles of instinct and energy when they are awake, with little common sense and even less self-control. Young Cavaliers love to play and have a great sense of fun. They may have bursts of energy before they run out of steam and spend much of the rest of the day sleeping. As one breeder says: They have two speeds – ON and OFF!

Make sure there are no poisonous plants which your pup might chew and check there are no low plants with sharp leaves or thorns which could cause eye or other injuries. There are literally dozens of plants which can harm a puppy if ingested, including azalea, daffodil bulbs, lily, foxglove, hyacinth, hydrangea, lupin, rhododendron, sweet pea, tulip and yew. The Kennel Club has a list of some of the most common ones here: http://bit.ly/1nCv1qJ and the ASPCA has an extensive list for the USA at: http://bit.ly/19xkhoG

If you have a garden or yard that you intend letting your puppy roam in, make sure that every little gap has been plugged. You'd be amazed at the tiny holes puppies can escape through - and Cavalier puppies don't have any road sense. Also, fence off any sharp plants, such as roses, which can injure a dog's eyes.

Avoid leaving your puppy unattended in the garden or yard, especially if you live near a road, as dognapping is on the increase, partly due to the high cost and resale value of purebred dogs. In the

UK, some 2,000 dogs are now being stolen each year. The figures are much higher for the US where the AKC reports that dog thefts are on the rise and warns owners against leaving their dog unattended – including tying them up outside a store.

Puppies are little chewing machines and puppy-proofing your home should involve moving anything sharp, breakable or chewable - including your shoes - out of reach of sharp little teeth. Lift electrical cords, mobile phones and chargers, remote controls, etc. out of reach and block off any off-limits areas of the house - such as upstairs or your bedroom - with a child gate or barrier, especially as he will probably be shadowing you for the first few days.

Laura and Mustapha are the proud owners of tricolour Alfred, aged two, and Bertie, a one-and-a-half-year-old Blenheim. Laura says: "We haven't had many instances of them chewing furniture, but have lost four pairs of flip-flops!"

Puppies are like babies and it's up to you to keep them safe and set the boundaries – both physically, in terms of where they can wander, and also in terms of behaviour – but gently and one step at a time. Create an area where the puppy is allowed to go, perhaps one or two rooms, preferably with a hard floor which is easy to clean, and keep the rest of the house off-limits, at least until housetraining (potty training) is complete.

The designated area should be near a door to the garden or yard for housetraining. Restricting the area also helps the puppy settle in. At the breeder's he probably had a den and an area to run around in. Suddenly having the freedom of the whole house can be quite daunting - not to mention messy.

You can buy a barrier specifically made for dogs or use a baby gate, which may be cheaper. Although designed for infants, they work perfectly well with dogs; you might even find a second-hand one on eBay. Choose one with narrow vertical gaps or mesh, and check that your puppy can't get his head stuck between the bars, or put a covering or mesh over the bottom of the gate initially. You can also make your own barrier, but bear in mind that cardboard and other soft materials will almost certainly get chewed.

Gates can be used to keep the puppy enclosed in a single room or specific area or put at the bottom of the stairs. A puppy's bones are soft, and recent studies have shown that if pups are allowed to climb or descend stairs regularly, they can develop joint problems later in life. This is worth bearing in mind, especially as some Cavaliers can be prone to hip or knee problems.

NOTE: The gaps between the bars of some safety gates and pens are sometimes too big to keep very small puppies contained. One UK breeder has recommended the Dreambaby Retractable Gate, which has mesh instead of bars. It can be bought at Argos in the UK or at Amazon.com in the USA.

Don't underestimate your puppy! Young Cavaliers can be lively and determined; they can jump and climb, so choose a barrier higher than you think necessary.

The puppy's designated area or room should not be too hot, cold or damp and it must be free from draughts. Little puppies can be sensitive to temperature fluctuations and don't do well in very hot or very cold conditions. If you live in a hot climate, your new pup may need air conditioning in the summertime.

Just as you need a home, so your puppy needs a den. This den is a haven where your pup feels safe, particularly in the beginning after the traumatic experience of leaving his or her mother and littermates. Young puppies sleep for 18 hours or longer a day at the beginning; this is normal.

You have a couple of options with the den; you can get a dog bed or basket, or you can use a crate. Crates have long been popular in North America and are becoming increasingly used in the UK, particularly as it can be quicker to housetrain a puppy using a crate.

It may surprise some American readers to learn that normal practice in the UK has often been to initially contain the puppy in the kitchen or utility room, and later to let the dog roam around the house. Some owners do not allow their dogs upstairs, but many do. The idea of keeping a dog in a cage like a rabbit or hamster is abhorrent to some animal-loving Brits.

However, a crate can be a useful aid if used properly. Using one as a prison to contain a dog for hours on end certainly is cruel, but the crate has its place as a sanctuary for your dog. It is the dog's own safe space and they know no harm will come to them in there. **See Chapter 7. Crate Training and Housetraining** for getting your Cavalier used to - and even to enjoy - being in a crate.

Most puppies' natural instinct is not to soil the area where they sleep. Put plenty of newspapers down in the area next to the den and your pup should choose to go to the toilet here if you are not quick enough to get outside. Of course, he or she may also decide to trash their designated area by chewing their blankets and shredding the newspaper – patience is the key!

Some owners prefer to create a safe penned area for their pup, rather than use a crate; while others use both a pen and a crate. You can make your own barriers or buy a manufactured playpen.

Playpens come in two types - mesh or fabric. A fabric pen is easy to put up and take down, but can be chewed so may not last long. A metal mesh pen is a better bet; it can be expanded and will last longer, but is not quite as easy to put up or take down.

One breeder said: "A play pen can be used in much the same way as a crate and has an advantage of being very versatile in separating eating, sleeping and - in the early days - toileting. They are ideal for the busy Mum or Dad who has other things on their mind and can't possibly watch the puppy, children and try and tidy the house or prepare dinner. Again, it is peace of mind for the owner, knowing the pup is safe and not chewing anything it shouldn't."

With initial effort on your part and a willing pupil, housetraining a Cavalier should not take long. One of the biggest factors influencing the success and speed of housetraining is your commitment. You may also want to remove your Oriental rugs, family heirlooms and other treasured possessions until your little darling is fully housetrained and has stopped chewing everything in sight.

If you have young children, the time they spend with the puppy should be limited to a few short sessions a day. Plenty of sleep is **essential** for the normal development of a young dog. You wouldn't wake a baby every hour or so to play, and the same goes for puppies. Wait a day or two - preferably longer – before inviting friends round to see your gorgeous little puppy. However excited you are, your new arrival needs a few days to get over the stress of leaving mother and siblings and to start bonding with you.

For puppies to grow into well-adjusted dogs, they have to feel comfortable and relaxed in their new surroundings and need a great deal of sleep. They are leaving the warmth and protection of their mother and littermates and for the first few days at least, most puppies may feel very sad. It is important to make the transition from the birth home to your home as easy as possible. Your pup's life is in your hands. How you react and interact with her in the first few days and weeks will shape your relationship and her character for the years ahead.

Chewing and Chew Toys

Like babies, most puppies are organic chewing machines and so remove anything breakable and/or chewable within the puppy's reach – including wooden furniture. Obviously, you cannot remove your kitchen cupboards, doors, sofas, fixtures and fittings, so don't leave your pup unattended for any length of time where he or she can chew something which is hard to replace. Chew toys are a must - don't give old socks, shoes or slippers or your pup will regard your footwear as fair game, and avoid rawhide chews as they can get stuck in the dog's throat or stomach.

A safe alternative to real bones or plastic chew bones are natural reindeer antler chew toys (pictured), which have the added advantage of calcium. Other natural chews preferred by some breeders include ears, dried rabbit pelt and tripe sticks – all excellent for teething puppies - once you have got over the gross factor! Other good choices include Kong toys, which are pretty indestructible, and you can put treats (frozen or fresh) or smear peanut butter inside to keep your dog occupied while you are out. Another good suggestion is a Lickimat (pictured), which you can also smear with a favourite treat. The inexpensive Lickimat, widely available online, will keep your Cavalier occupied for quite some time!

Dental bones are great for cleaning your dog's teeth, but many don't last for very long with a determined chewer; one that can is the Nylabone Dura Chew Wishbone, which is made of a type of plastic infused with flavours appealing to dogs. Get the right size and throw it away if it starts to splinter after a few weeks.

The Zogoflex Hurley and the Goughnut are both strong and float, so good for swimmers – and you'll get your money back on both if your Cavalier destroys them! For safety, the Goughnut has a green exterior and red interior, so you can tell if your dog has penetrated the surface - as long as the green is showing, you can let your dog "goughnuts."

A natural hemp or cotton tug rope is another option, as the cotton rope acts like dental floss and helps with teeth cleaning. It is versatile and can be used for fetch games as well as chewing.

 Puppies' stomachs are sensitive - so be careful what goes in. Even non-poisonous garden flora – like this pine cone - can cause intestinal blockages and vomiting. Like babies, pups can quickly dehydrate if they are being sick or have diarrhoea. If either continues for a couple of days, seek medical advice.

The First Few Days

Before you collect your puppy, let the breeder know what time you will arrive and ask him or her not to feed the pup for a couple of hours beforehand - unless you have a very long journey, in which case the puppy will need to eat something. He will be less likely to be car sick and should be hungry when he lands in his new home. The same applies to an adult dog moving to a new home.

When you arrive, ask for an old towel or toy which has been with the pup's mother – you can leave one on an earlier visit to collect with the pup. Or take one with you and rub the mother with it to collect her scent and put this with the puppy for the first few days. It will help him to settle in. In the US, some puppies are flown to their new homes; you can still ask for a toy or towel.

Make sure you get copies of any health certificates relating to the parents. Most good breeders will also have a Contract of Sale or Puppy Contract which outlines everyone's rights and responsibilities – **see Chapter 4. Finding Your Cavalier Puppy** for details of one breeder's contract. It should also state that you can return the puppy if there are health issues within a certain time frame – although if you have picked your breeder carefully, it will hopefully not come to this. The breeder will give you details of worming and any vaccinations. Most good breeders also supply information sheets and a puppy pack for new owners.

Find out exactly what the breeder is feeding and how much. You cannot suddenly switch a pup's diet; their digestive systems cannot cope with a sudden change. In the beginning, stick to whatever he or she is used to. Again, good breeders will send some food home with the puppy.

The Journey Home

Bringing a new puppy home in a car can be a traumatic experience. Your puppy will be devastated at leaving his or her mother, brothers and sisters and a familiar environment. Everything will be strange and frightening and he or she may well whimper and whine - or even bark - on the way home. If you can, take somebody with you on that first journey – some breeders insist on having somebody there to hold and cuddle the pup to make the journey less traumatic. Under no circumstances have the puppy on your lap while driving. It is simply too dangerous - a Cavalier puppy is extremely cute, often wriggly and far too distracting.

Have an old towel between your travel companion and the pup as (s)he may quite possibly urinate - the puppy, not the passenger!

If you have to go along, then take a crate – either a purpose-made travel crate or a wire crate which he will use at home. Travel crates can be soft (like this one pictured) or hard plastic. If you buy a plastic one, make sure there is a good air flow through. Put a comfortable blanket in the bottom - preferably rubbed with the scent of the mother.

If you have a journey of more than a couple of hours, make sure that you take water and offer the puppy a drink en route. She may need to eliminate or have diarrhoea (hopefully, only due to nerves), but don't let her outside on to the ground in a strange place as she is not yet fully vaccinated. Cover the bottom of the crate with a waterproof material and put newspapers in half of it, so the pup can eliminate without staining the car seats.

Dennis Homes, of Leogem Cavaliers, stresses the importance of getting pups used to car travel right from the beginning. It helps with the socialisation process and is less stressful when a trip to the vet or groomer is due.

He says: "Car travel should be enjoyable for you and your dog, so very early training is most important, with lots of little trips, and to return home with a small treat or their meal awaiting them. All this will only build the dog's mind into good things happening at the end of the journey. Never feed your dog before embarking on a car trip, having a full stomach will only increase the odds that what goes down can surely come up too.

"However, if your dog already has an aversion to the car, well then perhaps there could just be time for a little behaviour modification therapy. Put the dog's bed in the car with some of his favourite toys and sit him in there. You will, of course, need to keep him company, so take a good book to help pass the time! Seeing you calm and relaxed it should help him.

"Once you have gained his confidence and he appears to be a little less stressed, turn the ignition and let the engine idle for two to three minutes whilst calmly talking to and praising him. Do build up to taking him on very short journeys to the park or woods so that he knows there is something to look forward to. Hopefully, with time and patience he will learn to associate good things. Travelling in cars can be a nightmare if you and your dog are not properly prepared."

Our photo shows a Cavalier attached to the seatbelt by his harness.

"Never have your dog loose in the car. Get him used to travelling in a crate, and do make sure that it is properly anchored by seat belts and straps. Should you be unlucky to be involved in an accident your dog will not be thrown around and, of course, should you open a door, the dog cannot make a sudden dash out of the car.

"If you feel that a crate is not for you or your car there are some very good seat belts which are manufactured for dogs of all sizes; these are further secured via the car's own fitted seatbelts.

"Do make sure that your dog is wearing a collar and name tag, and do make sure that the lead is to hand in an emergency. Lastly, if you have to stop, never leave your dog unattended in the car. We have all heard of dogs dying by over-heating on hot summer days. But we also hear now that dogs have been stolen from parked cars."

Arriving Home

As soon as you arrive home, let your puppy into the garden or yard and when she 'performs,' praise her for her efforts. These first few days are critical in getting your puppy to feel safe and confident in her new surroundings. Spend time with the latest addition to your family, talk to her often in a reassuring manner. Introduce her to her den and toys, slowly allow her to explore and show her around the house — once you have puppy-proofed it.

Cavalier puppies are extremely curious - and amusing, you might be surprised at their reactions to everyday objects. Puppies explore by sniffing and mouthing, so don't scold for chewing. Instead, put objects you don't want chewed out of reach and replace them with chew toys. Some puppies can be more "mouthy" than others; if this is the case, make sure yours has safe toys to chew.

Almost all Cavalier owners say that theirs get on well with other animals. However, it is important that you introduce them to each other in the right conditions. Do it slowly and in supervised sessions on neutral territory or outdoors where there is space so neither feels threatened - preferably once the pup has got used to her new surroundings, not as soon as you walk through the door. Gentleness and patience are the keys to these first few days, so don't over-face your pup.

Have a special, gentle puppy voice and use her new name frequently - and in a pleasant, encouraging manner. **Never use her name to scold** or she will associate it with bad things. The sound of her name should always make her want to pay attention to you as something good is going to happen - praise, food, playtime, and so on.

Resist the urge to pick the puppy up – no matter how irresistible she is! Let her explore on her own legs, encouraging a little independence - this is important for Cavaliers. Cavalier pups are tiny and it is so tempting to pick them up and cuddle them all the time, but this will only encourage them to become "clingy."

One of the most important things at this stage is to ensure that your puppy has enough sleep – **which is nearly all of the time** - no matter how much you want to play with her, cuddle her or watch her antics when awake.

If you haven't decided what to call your new puppy yet, 'Shadow' might be a good suggestion, as he or she will follow you everywhere! Many puppies from different breeds do this, but Cavaliers like to stick close to their owners – both as puppies and adults. Our website receives many emails from worried new owners. Here are some of the most common concerns:

- 🐾 My puppy won't stop crying or whining
- 🐾 My puppy is shivering
- 🐾 My puppy won't eat
- 🐾 My puppy is very timid
- 🐾 My puppy follows me everywhere, she won't let me out of her sight
- 🐾 My puppy sleeps all the time, is this normal?

These behaviours are quite common at the beginning. They are just a young pup's reaction to leaving her mother and littermates and entering into a strange new world. It is normal for puppies to sleep most of the time, just like babies. It is also normal for some puppies to whine a lot during the first couple of days. A few puppies might not whine at all. If they are confident and have been well socialised and partly housetrained by the breeder, settling in will be much easier.

Make your new pup as comfortable as possible, ensuring she has a warm (but not too hot), quiet den away from draughts, where she is not pestered by children or other pets. Handle her gently, while giving her plenty of time to sleep. During the first couple of nights try your best to ignore the pitiful cries, but you should still get up in the middle of the night to take her into the garden or yard.

However, if you pick up or play with your pup every time she cries, she will learn that this behaviour gives her the reward of your attention.

A puppy will think of you as her new mother and it is quite normal for them to want to follow you everywhere, but after a few days start to leave your pup for short periods of a few minutes, gradually building up the time. A puppy unused to being left alone at all can grow up to have separation anxiety - see **Chapter 9. Cavalier Behaviour** for more information.

If your routine means you are normally out of the house for a few hours during the day, get your puppy on a Friday or Saturday so she has at least a couple of days to adjust to her new surroundings. A far better idea is to book time off work to help your puppy to settle in, if you can, or if you don't work, leave your diary free for the first couple of weeks.

Helping a new pup to settle in is virtually a full-time job. This can be a frightening time for some puppies. Is your puppy shivering with cold or is it nerves? Avoid placing your pup under stress by making too many demands. Don't allow the kids to pester the pup and, until they have learned how to handle a dog, don't allow them to pick her up unsupervised, as they could inadvertently damage her delicate little body.

If your pup won't eat, spend time gently coaxing. If she leaves her food, take it away and try it later. Don't leave it down all of the time or she may get used to turning her nose up at it. The next time you put something down, she is more likely to be hungry. If your puppy is crying, it is probably for one of the following reasons:

- ❧ She is lonely
- ❧ She is hungry
- ❧ She wants attention from you
- ❧ She needs to go to the toilet

If it is none of these, then physically check her over to make sure she hasn't picked up an injury. Try not to fuss too much! If she whimpers, just reassure her with a quiet word. If she cries loudly and tries to get out of her allotted area, she probably needs to go to the toilet. Even if it is the middle of the night, get up (yes, sorry, this is best) and take her outside. Praise her if she goes to the toilet.

The strongest bonding period for a puppy is between eight and 12 weeks of age. The most important factors in bonding with your puppy are TIME and PATIENCE, even when he or she makes a mess in the house or chews something. Remember, your Cavalier pup is just a baby (dog) and it takes time to learn not to do these things. Spend time with your pup and you will have a loyal friend for life. Cavaliers are very focused on their humans and that emotional attachment may grow to become one of the most important aspects of your life – and certainly his or hers.

Where Should the Puppy Sleep?

Where do you want your new puppy to sleep? You cannot simply allow a pup to wander freely around the house – at least not in the beginning. Ideally, she will be in a contained area, such as a pen or crate, at night. While it is not acceptable to shut a dog in a cage all day, you can keep your puppy in a crate at night until housetrained. Even then, some adult dogs still prefer to sleep in a crate.

You also have to consider whether you want the pup to permanently sleep in your bedroom or elsewhere. If it's the bedroom, do not allow her to jump on and off beds and/or couches or race up and down stairs until she has stopped growing, as this can cause joint damage.

 Some breeders recommend putting the puppy in a crate (or similar) next to your bed for the first two or three nights before moving her to the permanent sleeping place. Knowing you are close and being able to smell you will help overcome initial fears.

She may still cry when you move her further away or out of your bedroom, but that should soon stop - you just have to block your ears for a couple of nights! She will have had those few days to get used to her new surroundings and feeling safe with you.

Eight or nine-week-old puppies can't go through the night without needing to pee (and sometimes poo); their bladders simply aren't up to it. To speed up housetraining, consider getting up half way through the night from Day One for the first week or so to let your pup outside for a pee. Just pick her up, take her outside with the minimum of fuss, praise the pee and put her back into the crate. After that, set your alarm for an early morning wake-up call.

NOTE: While I and many breeders recommend getting up in the night, some breeders are firmly against it, as they don't believe it speeds up housetraining. Ask your own breeder's advice on this one.

We definitely don't recommend letting your new pup sleep on the bed. She will not be housetrained and also a puppy needs to learn her place in the household and have her own safe place. It's up to you whether you decide to let her on the bed when she's older.

If you do allow your dog to sleep in the bedroom but not on the bed, be aware that it is not unusual for some Cavaliers - like many other types of dog — to snuffle, snore, fart and - if not in a crate - pad around the bedroom in the middle of the night and come up to the bed to check you are still there! None of this is conducive to a good night's sleep.

While it is not good to leave a dog alone all day, it is also not healthy to spend 24 hours a day together. Cavaliers can become very clingy and while this is very flattering for you, it actually means that the dog is more nervous and less sure of herself when you are not there. She becomes too reliant on you and this increases the chances of separation anxiety when you do have to leave her. A Cavalier puppy used to being on her own every night is less likely to develop attachment issues, so consider this when deciding where she should sleep.

Unlike previous dogs, our current dog sleeps in our bedroom (in his own basket) and also has separation anxiety. Any future dogs we have will sleep in a separate room from us after the first couple of nights — no matter how hard that is in the beginning when the puppy whimpers.

If you decide you definitely do want your pup to sleep in the bedroom from Day One, put her in a crate or similar with a soft blanket covering part of the crate initially. Put newspapers inside and set your alarm clock.

Advice from Breeders

We asked a number of breeders what tips they have for new owners, and this is what they said, starting with Gloucestershire's Kathy Hargest, who has bred Cavaliers for 14 years: "Always try to collect the puppy early to allow time to settle in before the night-time. The puppy has left a warm family environment, so you should have a toy and blanket with the mother's and siblings' scent on.

"If the puppy is crying, use a heat pad or bottle to replicate the siblings and put the radio on quietly. The pup should sleep for in its own bed with a blanket from its old home, soft toys, heat and water. Explain to children that a puppy needs plenty of naps. If you take the puppy out to pee frequently, you avoid accidents and you may find them going to the exit themselves.

"Cavalier pups can get through the smallest spaces, so check all boundaries. They are also great chewers, so keep all electric and phone cables out of reach. Check for poisonous plants indoors and out. Avoid them coming downstairs at first or any jumps off heights."

"Introduce a new puppy to other animals carefully - remember they will probably want to play, which may not be appreciated. If a pup is biting, provide chewing toys under supervision and do what their siblings do when bitten: say Ouch! or whatever. One thing which surprises many new owners is how time-consuming their puppies are — and how quickly they can chew furniture!"

Pictured is Kathy's lovely black and tan puppy, Ebony, aged eight weeks. Ebony is the great-granddaughter of Tansy, who passed away earlier this year at the age of 14.

Julie Durham, of Donrobby Cavaliers, Berkshire, UK, has bred Cavaliers since 1985 and says: "Before puppy comes home, I always suggest new owners go around at knee height checking for gaps in the fence, and especially under any gate they may have. All gates should be locked when not in use to prevent intruders stealing puppy or someone inadvertently leaving the gate open. I also suggest that any steps should have bricks placed on them to make a large step small while puppy is young and these can be easily removed later. I also supply a list of known poisonous plants in their Puppy Pack.

"In terms of where the pup should sleep for the first few nights, the best place is where the owners want the dog to be long term. I think it is unfair to have the puppy with them in their bedroom at first and then change it again. If they are happy to share their bedroom, it is their rules - so long as they are consistent with their choices. It's important that puppy has a quiet place - either a crate with the door open or a quiet space they can retire to when tired - and he/she knows they will be left alone until they are rejuvenated and ready to rejoin the family. This is especially important in a family home."

Breeder of 24 years' standing, Philip Lunt, of Oaktreepark Cavaliers, Staffordshire, UK, added: "Before you bring the puppy home, make sure the garden is secure so that the puppy has no means of escape. Make sure there is no access to plants that could be harmful and be careful when using sprays like insecticide that may also be harmful.

"I provide a comfy blanket to go with each puppy. I recommend a Teddy that the puppy can snuggle to. A new puppy should sleep near to a rear exit where there is access to a garden/back yard as this helps in toilet training. Also, the place should be warm with a hard surface, in case of any accidents. He or she should be introduced to other animals with care to prevent any issues arising.

"One thing which surprises new owners about Cavaliers is their friendliness, affection and loyalty; they always want to be close to human contact."

Dennis and Tina Homes, of Leogem Cavaliers, Herefordshire, have been involved with Cavaliers for 40 years and have similar advice: "Check you have totally secure fencing and working gates around your property. Cables and electrical wiring should be shielded and kept out of reach of dogs in general. Always ensure that the dog is behind a closed door within the house before opening the front door if someone calls.

"A secure, private area away from heavy domestic traffic is important for the puppy. Also, a crate or penned-off area, preferably on a washable floor surface, so that the puppy can stay safe."

Philippa Biddle, of Heathfield Cavaliers, Norfolk, UK, has bred Cavaliers for 18 years ago and has these tips for new owners: "Be aware of what plants and foods are poisonous to dogs and instruct everyone in the household about it. The smallest holes in fences and gates will attract small puppies. So check boundaries and ensure gates to the rear garden have bolts that can't be undone from outside in case someone comes round and leaves the gate open. Teach the pup to sit behind you when answering the door; have a toy nearby to distract it. Always ensure you walk through gates, doors, openings before the dog. Teach that from the start.

"For the first few nights the pup should sleep somewhere near the family, but not in the human bed! A crate on the landing or in the bedroom is ideal. Once the pup goes through the night with toileting (circa four months), and has become familiar with the household and more settled in, you can gradually move them to the kitchen at night or wherever you want them to sleep."

Pictured is Philippa's Hearthfriend Katniss with her recent litter.

"The pup should have a familiar safe place of their own to rest in. Ideally, a crate with water, a soft bed, toys, chews and a puppy toilet pad or newspaper. Feed the pup in this place/crate so they feel safe eating, particularly if there are other animals in the house. Cavaliers are surprisingly confident and fearless for a small pup. They are also very tactile and friendly and like to be with you, following you EVERYWHERE."

Sandra Coles, of Twyforde Cavalier King Charles Spaniels, Devon, says: "Gardens should be fenced - I have one Cavalier that can jump over four feet and one can 'Houdini' through a fence. They will also dig, so fences do need to be secure. Theft is now a major problem, I would never leave a puppy outside and go out. You need to be aware where they are all the time, just like children. They will experiment and chew things.

"Lots of plants in the garden are poisonous. It is a good idea to check your plants before bringing a new puppy home to run free in the garden. There are also lots of foods that we eat that are also toxic to dogs. I name some of these to new owners, but also get them to research as well. Ponds should be cordoned off. Puppies, like children, can fall in and drown. When ponds ice over they are even more dangerous. Toys should be safe - never leave with a toy with a squeaker; this is one of the major obstruction operations that vets do.

"When you first arrive home with the puppy, put it straight into the garden to do a wee. It will then begin to associate this with where it needs to go and not on your best carpet. Take it indoors and if it is a meal time, feed it and give lots of cuddles. Let it find its way around the area you allow. A play pen is a good idea with a small run. It will regard this as a place of safety, like a den, and will be happier to sleep. A suitable bed can be put in this with some toys for comfort and the blanket that has come from the breeder with the smell of its Mum and litter mates for comfort.

"After feeding take puppy out again into the garden for a wee, etc. Let the puppy sleep and try to maintain the routine that the breeder has given you for the first few weeks. Also keep strictly to the diet and don't introduce anything else, unless advised. I phone new owners the next day and also later that week so see if there are any problems.

"Put the puppy into its intended sleeping area. If you start in the bedroom it is difficult to change this at a later date. Take out for a wee before bed. Some people use a ticking clock for company, this resembles the mother's heartbeat. Sleeping through the night is the main concern; you can never say exactly what will happen. I do say if they wake and cry: Go down. Take them out for a wee and then put them back to bed without too much fussing, lights out and then back to bed.

"Some new owners worry when the puppy doesn't cry and go down and wake them up. Some puppies will sleep right through. The worst I had was one that cried all night and I said it would get easier, it was worse the next night but after a week of this she did settle. Owners are surprised by how, on the whole, Cavalier puppies settle in. You would think they had never not been part of the family! They thrive on love, food and company."

Jina Ezell, of Kalama Cavaliers, Washington State, USA, has the distinction of being a member of the prestigious AKC (American Kennel Club) Bred with H.E.A.R.T. programme, which demands the highest standards in Health, Education, Accountability, Responsibility and Tradition. She says: "Prior to leaving my kennel, I begin putting the puppies into their own little bed kennels when it is nap and bed time. I encourage new owners to use the kennel as time to rest."

Photo of The Great Escape courtesy of Jina

"A kennel-trained puppy or dog finds their kennel a safe and comfortable place, does not potty in it and most new owners find the transition and potty training so much easier.

"For the first few nights I think the puppy should sleep in a crate near the bed of the new owner or in the room. This allows the puppy to wake, be comforted, but still continue the crate training. Ideally, the crate on top of or beside the bed will only be needed a night or two, if that. Most of my new owners know that giving the puppy a good hearty play/exercise time and wearing him/her out will help the puppy rest well."

"If the puppy is close, then after three to five hours he may wake up needing to relieve himself. A quick potty and back in the kennel with praise and a bully stick and this will be his routine. Usually this only takes three or four nights, then put the puppy where the permanent location of his sleeping kennel would be, i.e. living room, kitchen, etc. Again, consistency is key."

 Bully sticks (pictured) are dog treats made from ...a bull's penis or pizzle! If you can get the picture of their source out of your mind, you might want to consider buying some as a healthy treat for your dog.

Unlike rawhide, bully sticks are highly digestible, break down easily in the stomach and are generally considered safe for all dogs. They are made from 100% beef, normally contain no additives or preservatives, come in different sizes and dogs love 'em. Puppies should be supervised while eating bully sticks or any other treats.

Jina adds: "I send out a weekly email to the new owner or family in order to prepare for a smooth transition. I give the schedule that the puppies have been used to and tell them to keep things as consistent as they can." Jina has kindly given us permission to include these emails in **Chapter 5. A Puppy's Early Life.**

"In addition to the schedule, I give a New Puppy Adoption Bag which includes a hand-made blanket that the puppies and Mama have "scented" for a few days to help with the homesickness.

"I try and educate my new puppy owners of the high propensity toward all sorts of pet cancers that are avoidable. We can treat our home/yard with natural and safe things that are not causing our fur babies so many issues - for instance, diatomaceous earth for pesticides, and essential oils and herbs for fleas and ticks. Don't allow the pet access to any lawns unless you can confirm that no pesticides or herbicides have been used.

"The energy of these puppies always surprises their new owners, as well, how many naps they take until they are about four months old. They have two speeds, ON and OFF! My puppies have been worked with, and training them right off the bat is what they are used to - it does work. I am so excited when I get the emails and pictures of the four and five-month-olds just graduating from their AKC All Star Puppy Classes."

Vaccinations and Worming

It is always a good idea to have your Cavalier checked out by a vet within a few days of picking him up. Some Puppy Contracts even stipulate that the dog should be examined by a vet within a certain time frame – often 48 hours. This is to everyone's benefit and, all being well, you are safe in the knowledge that your puppy is healthy, at least at the time of purchase.

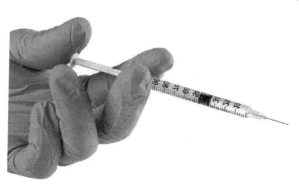

Keep your pup away from other dogs in the waiting room as he or she will not be fully protected against canine diseases until the vaccination schedule is complete.

All puppies need these injections; very occasionally a pup has a reaction, but this is very rare and the advantages of immunisation far outweigh the disadvantages.

Vaccinations

An unimmunised puppy is at risk every time he meets other dogs as he has no protection against potentially fatal diseases – another point is that it is unlikely a pet insurer will cover an unvaccinated dog. It should be stressed that vaccinations are generally quite safe and side effects are uncommon. If your Cavalier is unlucky enough to be one of the **very few** that suffer an adverse reaction, here are some signs to look out for; a pup may exhibit one or more of these:

MILD REACTION - Sleepiness, irritability and not wanting to be touched. Sore or a small lump at the place where he was injected. Nasal discharge or sneezing. Puffy face and ears.

SEVERE REACTION - Anaphylactic shock. A sudden and quick reaction, usually before leaving the vet's, which causes breathing difficulties. Vomiting, diarrhoea, staggering and seizures.

A severe reaction is rare. There is a far greater risk of your Cavalier either being ill and/or spreading disease if he does not have the injections.

The usual schedule is for the pup to have his first vaccination at eight or nine weeks of age, usually before he leaves the breeder. This will protect him from a number of diseases in one shot.

In the UK these are Distemper, Canine Parvovirus (Parvo), Infectious Canine Hepatitis (Adenovirus) and Leptospirosis. Most vets also recommend vaccinating against Kennel Cough (Bordetella). In the US this is known as DHPP.

Puppies in the US also need vaccinating separately against Rabies. There are optional vaccinations for Coronavirus and - depending on where you live and if your dog is regularly around woods or forests - Lyme Disease.

A puppy requires a second vaccination two to four weeks later. He or she is clear to mix with other animals two weeks after the second vaccinations.

- ❧ Boosters for Distemper, Parvo and Canine Hepatitis are every three years
- ❧ Boosters for Leptospirosis are every year

Leptospirosis is a bacterial infection which attacks the body's nervous system and organs. It is spread through infected rat pee and contaminated water, so dogs are at risk if they swim in or drink from stagnant water or canals. Outbreaks can often happen after flooding.

Diseases such as Parvo and Kennel Cough are highly contagious and you should not let your new arrival mix with other dogs - unless they are your own and have already been vaccinated - until two weeks after his last vaccination, otherwise he will not be fully immunised. Parvovirus can also be transmitted by fox faeces. The vaccination schedule for the USA is different, depending on which area you live in and what diseases are present. Full details can be found by typing "AKC puppy shots" into Google, which will take you to this page: www.akc.org/content/health/articles/puppy-shots-complete-guide

You shouldn't take your new puppy to places where unvaccinated dogs might have been, like the local park. This does not mean that your puppy should be isolated - far from it. This is an important time for socialisation. It is OK for the puppy to mix with another dog which you 100% know has been vaccinated and is up to date with its annual boosters. Perhaps invite a friend's dog round to play in your yard/garden to begin the socialisation process.

Once your puppy is fully immunised, you have a window of a few weeks when it's the best time to introduce him to as many new experiences as possible - dogs, people, traffic, noises, other animals, etc. This critical period before the age of four and a half to five months is when he is at his most receptive to socialisation. It is important that all of the experiences are **positive** at this stage of life; don't frighten or over-face your little puppy. Socialisation should not stop after a few months, but should continue for the rest of your dog's life.

The vet should give you a record card or send you a reminder when a booster is due, but it's also a good idea to keep a note of the date in your diary. Tests have shown that the Parvovirus vaccination gives most animals at least seven years of immunity, while the Distemper jab provides immunity for at least five to seven years. In the US, many vets now recommend that you take your dog for a 'titer' test once he has had his initial puppy vaccinations and one-year booster.

Titres (Titers in the USA)

Some breeders and dog owners feel very strongly that constantly vaccinating our dogs is having a detrimental effect on our pets' health. Many vaccinations are now effective for several years, yet some vets still recommend annual "boosters."

One alternative is titres. The thinking behind them is to avoid a dog having to have unnecessary repeat vaccinations for certain diseases as he or she already has enough antibodies present. Known as a VacciCheck in the UK, they are still relatively new here; they are more widespread in the USA.

Titres are a contentious issue. One English vet we spoke to commented that a titre is only good for the day on which it is carried out, and that antibody levels may naturally drop off shortly afterwards, possibly leaving the animal at risk. He added that the dog would still need vaccinating against Leptospirosis. His claim is strongly refuted by advocates of titre testing.

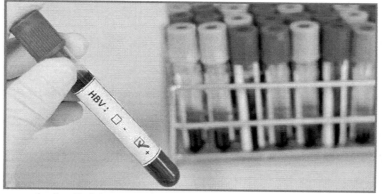

To 'titre' is to take a blood sample from a dog (or cat) to determine whether he or she has enough antibodies to guarantee immunity against a particular disease, usually Parvovirus, Distemper and Adenovirus (Canine Hepatitis). If so, then an annual injection is not needed. Titering is not recommended for Leptospirosis, Bordetella or Lyme Disease, as these vaccines provide only short-term protection. Many US states also require proof of a Rabies vaccination.

The vet can test the blood at the clinic without sending off the sample, thereby keeping costs down for the owner. A titre for Parvovirus and Distemper currently costs around $100 or less in the US, and a titre test in the UK costs as little as £40.

Titre levels are given as ratios and show how many times blood can be diluted before no antibodies are detected. So, if blood can be diluted 1,000 times and still show antibodies, the ratio would be 1:1000, which is a 'strong titre,' while a titre of 1:2 would be 'weak.'

A *strong (high) titre* means that your dog has enough antibodies to fight off that specific disease and is immune from infection. A **weak titre** means that you and your vet should discuss revaccination - even then your dog might have some reserve forces known as 'memory cells' which will provide antibodies when needed. (If you are going on holiday and taking your dog to kennels, check whether the kennel accepts titre records; many don't as yet).

One UK breeder said: "Most people don't realise that there are tests you can do to ensure that you don't over-vaccinate or over-worm your dog. It is well known that, although very rare, all vaccinations can have potential adverse reactions. These can range from mild problems such as cystitis to a severe autoimmune disease. There are also a lot of discussions going on as to whether the over-vaccination of dogs may be linked to the increased rates of cancers.

"When my puppies go to their new homes I tell all my owners to follow their vet's advice about worming and vaccinating, as the last thing new owners require is to be at odds with their vets. However, a few owners do express concern about all the chemicals we are introducing into our puppies' lives and if they do, I explain how I try to give my dogs a chemical-free life, if possible, as adult dogs. All dogs must have their puppy vaccinations.

"Instead of giving my adult dogs their core vaccinations for Canine Distemper, Parvovirus and Adenovirus (Hepatitis) every three years, I just take my dogs down to the local vet and ask them to do something called a titre test, also known as a VacciCheck.

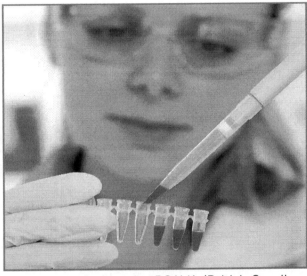

They take a small amount of blood and send it to a lab and the lab checks for antibodies to the diseases. If they have antibodies to the diseases, there is no reason to give dogs a vaccination. If a puppy has its puppy vaccinations, it is now thought that the minimum duration of immunity is between seven and 15 years.

"However, you should note that there is a separate vaccination for Leptospirosis and Canine Parainfluenza, which is given annually. Leptospirosis is recommended by the BSAVA (British Small Animal Veterinary Association). Leptospirosis is more common in tropical areas of the world and not that common in England. In order to make a decision about whether to give this to your dog annually, you need to talk to your vet and do some research yourself so you can make an informed decision. It may be that Leptospirosis is a problem in your area.

If you want to do some of your own research, then Ronald Schulz and Catherine O'Driscoll are some of the leading authorities on vaccinations and The Pet Welfare Alliance is also a good source of information."

She added: "We vaccinate our children up to about the age of 16. However, we don't vaccinate adults every one to three years, as it is deemed that the vaccinations they receive in childhood will cover them for a lifetime. This is what is being steadily proved for dogs and we are so lucky that we can titre test our dogs so we don't have to leave it to chance."

Philippa Biddle also uses titres: "A healthy Cavalier is dependent on the owner feeding, maintaining, training and exercising the dog. Some factors in ill health are considered to be environmental and this is beyond the control of the breeder. However, I do not vaccinate my dogs beyond the age of four to five years, I now have them titre tested. Every dog I have titre tested aged five to 10 years has been immune to the diseases vaccinated against when younger. I believe many vets over-vaccinate. Also, many dogs are given too many flu and worming chemicals."

The (UK) Kennel Club now includes titre testing information into its Assured Breeder Pack, but has yet to include it under its general information on vaccines on its website. The AKC (American

Worming

All puppies need worming (technically, deworming). A good breeder will give the puppies their first dose of worming medication at around two weeks old, then probably again at five and eight weeks before they leave the litter – or even more often. Get the details and inform your vet exactly what treatment, if any, your pup has already had.

The main worms affecting puppies are roundworm and tapeworm. In certain areas of the US, the dreaded heartworm can also pose a risk. If you live in an affected area, discuss the right time to start heartworm medication when you visit your vet for puppy vaccinations – it's usually from a few months old. The pill should be given every month when there is no heavy frost (frost kills mosquitos that carry the disease); giving it all year round gives the best protection. The heartworm pill is by prescription only and deworms the dog monthly for heart worm, round, hook, and whip worm.

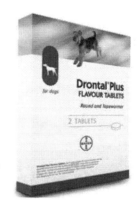

Roundworm can be transmitted from a puppy to humans – often children - and can in severe cases cause blindness, or miscarriage in women, so it's important to keep up to date with worming. Worms in puppies are quite common; they are often picked up through their mother's milk. If you have children, get them into the habit of washing their hands after they have been in contact with the puppy – lack of hygiene is the reason why children are most susceptible.

Most vets recommend worming a puppy once a month until he is six months old, and then around every two to three months. If your Cavalier is regularly out and about running through woods and fields, it is important to stick to a regular worming schedule, as he is more likely to pick up worms than one which spends less time in the Great Outdoors.

Fleas can pass on tapeworms to dogs, but a puppy would not normally be treated unless it is known for certain he has fleas - and then only with caution. You need to know the weight of your Cavalier and then speak to your vet about the safest treatment to rid your puppy of the parasites.

It is not usually worth buying a cheap worming or flea treatment from a supermarket, as they are usually far less effective than more expensive vet-recommended preparations, such as **Drontal.** Note that Drontal cannot be given to young puppies.

Many people living in the US have contacted our website claiming the parasite treatment **Trifexis** has caused severe side effects, and even death, to their dogs. Although this evidence is only anecdotal, you might want consider avoiding Trifexis to be on the safe side - even if your vet recommends it.

Breeders must worm their puppies as they are all born with worms picked up from the mother's milk. However, there are ways to reduce worming treatments for adult dogs.

Following anecdotal reports of some dogs experiencing side effects with chemical wormers, more owners are looking to use natural wormers on their dogs. If you go down this route, check exactly which worms your chosen herbal preparation deals with – it may not be all of them.

Also, in the UK, there is a company called Wormcount that tests your dog's stools. You send a small sample of your dog's poo(p) off in an envelope every two to three months. If the result is positive, your dog needs a worming treatment, but if negative, no treatment is necessary. This costs around £16 ($21) from www.wormcount.com

Similar options are available in the USA.

....

Top Tips For Working Cavalier Owners

We would not recommend getting a Cavalier if you are out at work all day. But if you're determined to get one when you're out for several hours at a time, here are some useful tips:

1. Either come home during your lunch break or employ a dog walker (or neighbour) to take him out for a walk in the middle of the day. If you can afford it, leave him at doggie day care where he can socialise with other dogs.

2. If not, do you know anybody you could leave your dog with during the day? Consider leaving your dog with a reliable friend, relative or neighbour who would welcome the companionship of a dog without the full responsibility of ownership.

3. Take him for a walk before you go to work – even if this means getting up at the crack of dawn – and spend time with him as soon as you get home. Exercise generates serotonin in the brain and has a calming effect. A dog that has been exercised will be less anxious and more ready for a good nap.

4. Leave him in a place of his own where he feels comfortable. If you use a crate, leave the door open. You may need to restrict access to other areas of the house to prevent him coming to harm or chewing things you don't want chewed. If possible, leave him in a room with a view of the outside world; this will be more interesting than staring at four blank walls.

5. Make sure that it does not get too hot during the day and there are no cold draughts.

6. Leave toys available to play with to prevent destructive chewing. Stuff a Kong toy (pictured) with treats or peanut butter to keep him occupied or buy a Lickimat.

7. Although most Cavaliers love their food, it is still generally a good idea to put food down at specific meal times and remove it after 15 or 20 minutes if uneaten to prevent your dog becoming fussy or 'punishing' you for leaving him alone by refusing to eat.

8. **Make sure he has access to water at all times.** Dogs cannot cool down by sweating; they do not have many sweat glands (which is why they pant, but this is much less efficient than perspiring) and can die without sufficient water.

9. Consider getting a companion for your Cavalier, bearing in mind that this will involve even more of your time and twice the expense.

10. Consider leaving a radio or TV on very softly in the background. The 'white noise' can have a soothing effect on some pets. If you do this, select your channel carefully – try and avoid one with lots of bangs and crashes or heavy metal music!

11. Stick to the same routine before you leave your dog home alone. This will help him to feel secure. Before you go to work, get into a daily habit of getting yourself ready, then feeding and exercising your Cavalier. Dogs love routine. But don't make a huge fuss of him when you leave as this can also stress the dog; just leave the house calmly.

Similarly, when you come home, your Cavalier may feel starved of attention and be pleased to see you. Greet him normally, but try not to go overboard by making too much of a fuss as soon as you walk through the door. Give him a pat and a stroke then take off your coat and do a few other things before turning your attention back to him.

Lavishing your Cavalier with too much attention the second you walk through the door may encourage needy behaviour or separation anxiety.

7. Crate Training and Housetraining

If you are unfamiliar with them, crates may seem like a cruel punishment for a lovable puppy. They are, however, becoming increasingly popular to help with housetraining (potty training), to give you and the puppy short breaks from each other and to keep the dog safe at night or when you are not there. Breeders, trainers, behaviourists and people who show and compete all use them.

Getting Your Dog Used to a Crate

If you decide to use a crate, then remember that it is not a prison to restrain the dog. It should only be used in a humane manner and time should be spent to make your puppy or adult dog feel like the crate is his own safe little haven. If used correctly and if time is spent getting the puppy used to the crate, it can be a godsend.

Crates may not be suitable for every dog. Cavaliers are not like hamsters or pet mice that can adapt to life in a cage; they are "Velcro" dogs that like sticking close to you. Our breeders say if they sit down on the sofa and one Cavalier jumps on to their lap, all the other Cavaliers jump on too. Similarly, if they are sleeping, Cavaliers like to sleep in piles just to be close to each other! Being caged all day is a miserable existence, and a crate should never be used as a means of confinement because you are out of the house all day. If the door is closed on the crate, your puppy must ALWAYS have access to water while inside.

If you do decide to use one - perhaps to put your dog in for short periods while you leave the house, or at night - the best place for it is in the corner of a room away from cold draughts or too much heat. And because Cavaliers like to be near their family, which is you and/or the other dogs, don't put the crate in a utility room or garage away from everybody else or your dog will feel lonely and isolated.

Photo of four-month-old Monty Hearthfriend Black Knight courtesy of Philippa Biddle.

Dogs with long coats like the Cavalier can overheat indoors. When you buy a crate, get a wire one (like the one pictured) which is robust and allows air to pass through, not a plastic one which may get very hot. If you cover the crate, leave the front open or you will restrict the flow of air.

The crate should be large enough to allow your dog to stretch out flat on his side without being cramped, and he should be able to turn round easily and to sit up without hitting his head on the top. A fully-grown Cavalier will probably require a 30" to 36" crate. If you only intend buying one, get the right size for an adult and divide it until your puppy grows into the full-sized crate. Here is Midwest Pet Products sizing guide for crates, based on the anticipated adult weight of your dog: www.midwestpetproducts.com/midwestdogcrates/dog-crate-sizes

You have a number of options when it comes to deciding where to put the crate. Perhaps consider leaving it in the kitchen or another room (preferably one with an easy-to-clean surface) where there are people during the day. If you have noisy children, you have to strike the balance between putting the crate somewhere where the pup won't feel isolated, yet is able to get some peace and quiet from the kids.

You could then bring it into your bedroom for the first one or two nights until the puppy settles. Some breeders advise putting the crate right next to the bed for the first couple of nights or so – even raised up next to the bed, so the puppy doesn't feel alone. A couple of nights with broken sleep is worth it if it helps the young pup to settle in, as he or she will often then sleep through the night quicker. After that, you could put the crate in a nearby place where the dog can hear or smell you at night-time, such as the landing, or you could leave it in the same place, e.g. the kitchen, 100% of the time. Ask your breeder for guidance.

It is only natural for any dog to whine in the beginning. He is not crying because he is in a cage. He would cry if he had the freedom of the room and he was alone - he is crying because he is separated from you. However, with patience and the right training, he will get used to it and some come to regard the crate as a favourite place. Some owners make the crate their dog's only bed, so he feels comfortable and safe in there. Crates aren't for every owner or every dog but, used correctly, they can:

- 🐾 Create a canine den
- 🐾 Be a useful housetraining tool
- 🐾 Give you a bit of a break
- 🐾 Limit access to the rest of the house while your dog learns the household rules
- 🐾 Be a safe way to transport your dog in a car

Admittedly, crates aren't the most attractive objects to have in your kitchen or living room; however, there are now some chic alternatives for the style-conscious pet owner. We particularly like the 36" Fido Studio Dog Crate from Omlet, pictured. Admittedly, it's not cheap, but not only does it look good, it also boasts *"the world's first doggie wardrobe"* (the closed section on the left) where you can store your dog's coats, toys, blankets, etc.

If you use a crate right from Day One, initially cover half of it with a blanket to help your puppy regard it as a den. He also needs bedding and it's a good idea to put a chew in as well. A large crate may allow your dog to eliminate at one end and sleep at the other, but this may slow down his housetraining. So, if you are buying a crate which will last for a fully-grown Cavalier, get adjustable crate dividers – or make them yourself (or put a box inside) - to block part of it off while he is small so that he feels safe and secure, which he won't do in a very big crate.

You can order a purpose-made crate mat or a *'Vet Bed'* (widely available) to cover the bottom of the crate and then put some bedding on top. Vet Beds are widely used by vets to make dogs feel warm, secure and cosy when receiving treatment, but they're just as good for using in the home. They are made from double-strength polyester with high fibre density to retain extra heat and allow air to permeate.

They also have drainage properties, so if your pup has an accident, he or she will stay dry, and they are a good choice for older dogs as the added heat is soothing for aging muscles and joints, and for any dogs recovering from surgery or treatment. Another added advantage of a Vet Bed is that you can wash it often and it shouldn't deteriorate. Bear in mind that a bored or lively Cavalier puppy is a little chew machine so, at this stage, don't spend a lot of money on a fluffy floor covering for the crate, as it is likely to get destroyed.

Many breeders recommend **not** putting newspapers in one part of the crate, as this encourages the pup to soil the crate. If you bought your puppy from a good breeder, she will probably already have started the housetraining process, and eight to 12-week-old pups should be able to last a couple of hours without needing the toilet. Some people say that a pup can last one hour or so without needing to urinate for every month of age. During the night, set your alarm clock to get up after four or five hours to let the pup out to do his or her business for the first week or so. You might not like it, but this, in our opinion, will speed up housetraining.

Once you've got your crate, you'll need to learn how to use it properly so that it becomes a safe, comfortable den for your dog. Here's a tried-and-tested method of getting your dog firstly to accept a crate, and then to actually want to spend time in there. Initially a pup might not be too happy about going inside, but he will be a lot easier to crate train than an adult dog which has got used to having the run of your house.

These are the first steps:

1. Drop a few tasty puppy treats around and then inside the crate.

2. Put your puppy's favourite bedding or toy in there.

3. Keep the door open.

4. Feed your puppy's meals inside the crate. Again, keep the door open.

Place a chew or treat INSIDE the crate and close the door while your puppy is OUTSIDE the crate. He will be desperate to get in there! Open the door, let him in and praise him for going in. Fasten a long-lasting chew inside the crate and leave the door open. Let your puppy go inside to spend some time eating the chew.

IMPORTANT: Always remove your dog's collar before leaving him unattended in a crate. A collar can get caught in the wire mesh.

After a while, close the crate door and feed him some treats through the mesh. At first just do it for a few seconds at a time, then gradually increase the time. If you do it too fast, he will become distressed. Slowly build up the amount of time he is in the crate. For the first few days, stay in the room, then gradually leave for a short time, first one minute, then three, then 10, 30 and so on.

Next Steps

5. Put your dog in his crate at regular intervals during the day - maximum two hours.

6. Don't crate only when you are leaving the house. Place the dog in the crate while you are home as well. Use it as a 'safe' zone.

7. By using the crate both when you are home and while you are gone, your dog becomes comfortable there and not worried that you won't come back, or that you are leaving him alone. This helps to prevent separation anxiety later in life.

8. Give him a chew and remove his collar, tags and anything else that could become caught in an opening or between the bars.

9. Make it very clear to any children that the crate is NOT a playhouse for them, but a 'special room' for the dog.

10. Although the crate is your dog's haven and safe place, it must not be off-limits to humans. You should be able to reach inside at any time.

The next point is important:

11. Do not let your dog immediately out of the crate if he barks or whines, or he will think that this is the key to opening the door. Wait until the barking or whining has stopped for at least 10 or 20 seconds before letting him out.

 One breeder puts a Smart Pet Love Snuggle Puppy in the crate with the new puppy. The Snuggle Puppy (available from Amazon) is a safe soft toy with a heartbeat. She added: "In their new home, the puppies have the heartbeat sound like they had from laying on mum. We've had really good feedback from families about the Snuggle Puppies."

A puppy should not be left in a crate for long periods except at night-time, and even then he has to get used to it first. Whether or not you decide to use a crate, the important thing to remember is that those first few days and weeks are a critical time for your puppy. Try and make him feel as safe and comfortable as you can. Bond with him, while at the same time gently and gradually giving him positive experiences with new places, humans and other animals.

Special travel crates are useful for the car, or for taking your dog to the vet's or a show. Choose one with holes or mesh in the side to allow free movement of air rather than a solid plastic one, in which your dog can soon overheat. Alternatively, you can buy a metal grille to keep your dog or dogs confined to the back on the car.

A crate is one way of transporting your Cavalier in the car. Put the crate on the shady side of the interior and make sure it can't move around; put the seatbelt around it. *Our photo shows breeder Philippa Biddle's crates fastened in the back of her car so they are unable to move in transit.*

If it's very sunny and the top of the crate is wire mesh, cover part of it so your dog has some shade and put the windows up and the air conditioning on. Never leave your Cavalier unattended in a vehicle for more than a few minutes; they can overheat very quickly - or be targeted by thieves.

Allowing your dog to roam freely inside the car is not a safe option, particularly if you - like me – are a bit of a 'lead foot' on the brake and accelerator! Don't let him put his head out of the window either, he can slip and hurt himself and the wind pressure can cause an ear infection or bits of dust, insects, etc. to fly into his big, unprotected eyes.

Breeders' Advice on Using Crates

Traditionally crates have been more popular in America than in the UK and the rest of Europe, but opinion is changing and more owners are using crates on both sides of the Atlantic. This is perhaps because people's perception of a crate is shifting from regarding it as a cage to thinking of it as a safe haven as well as a useful tool to help with housetraining and transportation, when used correctly.

Without exception, the breeders in this book believe that a crate should not be used for punishment or to imprison a dog all day while you are away from the house. This is cruel for any dog, but particularly a dog as intelligent and active as a Cavalier, who is extremely loyal and loves to be near you. The key to successful crate training is to spend time enticing the dog into the crate so that he or she starts to enjoy spending time in there - most puppies will not initially like being in a crate and patience, along with the right techniques, are required. If the breeder has already got your puppy used to a crate, then you're nearly there already.

Philippa Biddle: "Crate training is a long subject! Yes, I think crates are good, but they need to be initially set in a place where the pup can feel they are in with the family, not shut away on their own. They should be introduced gently and pups should never be left for long periods alone in the crate; it has to be a safe, pleasant place to be. Feed them in the crate, give chews in the crate. They will happily sleep in their crate for two hours, you can lengthen the time as they mature. I don't believe in regularly leaving a dog in a crate for more than four hours."

Kathy Hargest: "At six weeks the pups are normally in a crate in the run with lots of soft bedding so they get used to one. I also use crates if the dog needs confining for medical reasons."

Dennis and Tina Homes: "A secure, private area away from heavy domestic traffic is important for a puppy. Also, a crate or penned-off area so that the puppy can stay safe. A crate is a good idea as it imitates a den where a dog instinctively feels safe and also a place to go when a household is busy. An open door on the crate is also an encouragement for the puppy to find solace and a quiet space of its own."

Julie Durham: "I always strongly suggest that puppy has a quiet place, either a crate with the door open or a quiet space they can retire to when tired and he/she knows they will be left alone until they are rejuvenated and ready to rejoin the family. This is especially important in a family home. I suggest the crate is placed somewhere out of the busy walkway and draught-free. Owners should be guided by their dog, as some like to have a space that is theirs and feel secure and safe, so sleep well in there - so long as it is used as a safe place and not as a sin bin."

Philip Lunt, who has bred Cavaliers for 24 years: "I do not use crates and never have done. If you use one, you should never leave a dog in a crate for any longer than one hour. Crates can, however, provide a safe place for the dog to rest and get some peace with free movement whilst any human is in the house." *Pictured is Philip's Lola, aged 11 months.*

Sandra Coles: "I do use crates for sleeping and feeding. Otherwise, mine all run together around the house and garden. Bitches in season are kept apart at the other end of the house and let out separately."

US breeder Jina Ezell: "By the time my puppies are placed between eight to 10 weeks, the puppy will have had the experience of napping in the crate and sleeping approximately three to four hours in the crate. I will leave them for a few hours at a time in the crate after the age of six weeks to get them to adjust to this new norm. I try to prepare my new families so that the puppy can be left alone for up to four hours at a time between exercise and pottying, should the new family need to work outside the home. A crate-trained puppy or dog finds their crate a safe and comfortable place, does not potty in it and most new owners find the transition and potty training so much easier."

Top 12 Housetraining Tips

How easy are Cavaliers to housetrain?

Well, you will not be surprised to hear that... it varies! Toy breeds have a reputation of being slower than some other larger breeds to housetrain. As far as Cavaliers go, it depends very much on the individual dog, how much effort the breeder has put in and how vigilant you are prepared to be.

The dog is often only as good as his or her owners. In other words, the speed and success of housetraining often depends largely on one factor: the time and effort you put in - especially during the first few weeks. The more vigilant you are during the early days, the quicker your dog will be housetrained. It's as simple as that.

Taking the advice in this chapter and being consistent with your routines and repetitions is the quickest way to toilet train (potty train) your Cavalier pup.

You have five big factors in your favour when it comes to housetraining:

1. Cavaliers want to please their owners and love praise.

2. They are biddable (willing to learn).

3. Most would do anything for praise or a treat.

4. Dogs do not naturally soil their beds.

5. The Cavalier is a very clean breed.

From about the age of three weeks, a pup will leave his sleeping area to go to the toilet. Most good breeders will already have started the housebreaking process with their puppies, so when you pick up your little bundle of joy, all you have to do is ensure that you carry on the good work.

If you're starting from scratch when you bring your pup home, your new arrival thinks that the whole house is his den and may not realise that this is not the place to eliminate. Therefore, you need to gently and persistently teach him that it is unacceptable to make a mess inside the home. Cavaliers, like all dogs, are creatures of routine - not only do they like the same things happening at the same times every day, but establishing a regular routine with your dog also helps to speed up obedience and toilet training.

Dogs are tactile creatures, so they will pick a toilet area that feels good under their paws. Many dogs like to go on grass - but this will do nothing to improve your lawn, so you should think carefully about what area to encourage your puppy to use. You may want to consider a small patch of gravel crushed into tiny pieces in your garden, or a corner of the garden or yard away from any attractive flowerbeds.

Some breeders advise against using puppy pads at all, and certainly for weeks on end, as puppies like the softness of the pads, which can encourage them to eliminate on other soft areas - such as your carpets or bed. However, there are plenty breeders and owners that do use puppy pads, alongside regularly taking the puppy outside to eliminate. They gradually reduce the area covered by the pads over a period of a couple of weeks or so. Some people living in apartments allow their dogs to permanently use puppy pads.

Follow these tips to speed up housetraining:

1. **Constant supervision** is essential for the first week or two if you are to housetrain your puppy quickly. This is why it is important to book time off work when you bring him home, if you can. Make sure you are there to take him outside regularly. If nobody is there, he will learn to urinate or poo(p) inside the house.

2. **Take your pup outside at the following times:**

   ❖ As soon as he wakes – every time

   ❖ Shortly after each feed

   ❖ After a drink

   ❖ When he gets excited

   ❖ After exercise or play

   ❖ Last thing at night

   ❖ Initially every hour - whether or not he looks like he wants to go

You may think that the above list is an exaggeration, but it isn't! Housetraining a pup is almost a full-time job for the first few days. If you are serious about toilet training your puppy quickly, then clear your diary for a week or two and keep your eyes firmly glued on your pup...learn to spot that expression or circling motion just before he makes a puddle - or worse – on your floor.

3. Take your pup to **the same place** every time, you may need to use a lead (leash) in the beginning - or tempt him there with a treat. Some say it is better to only pick him up and dump him there in an emergency, as it is better if he learns to take himself to the chosen toilet spot. Dogs naturally develop a preference for going in the same place or on the same surface. Take or lead him to the same patch every time so he learns this is his toilet area. **No pressure – be patient.** You must allow your distracted little darling time to wander around and have a good sniff before performing his duties – but do not leave him, stay around a short distance away. Sadly, puppies are not known for their powers of concentration; it may take a while for him to select the perfect bathroom!

4. **Housetraining is reward-based.** Give praise or a treat immediately after he has performed his duties in the chosen spot. Cavaliers like to please you and love praise, and reward-based training is the most successful method for quick results with Cavs.

5. **Share the responsibility.** It doesn't have to be the same person who takes the dog outside all the time. In fact, it's easier if there are a couple of you, as housetraining is a very time-consuming business. Just make sure you stick to the same principles, command and patch of ground.

6. **Stick to the same routine.** Dogs understand and like routine. Sticking to the same one for mealtimes, short exercise sessions, playtime, sleeping and toilet breaks will help to not only housetrain him quicker, but also help him settle into his new home.

7. **Use the same word** or command when telling your puppy to go to the toilet – or while he is in the act. He will gradually associate this phrase or word with toileting and you will even be able to get him to eliminate on command after some weeks.

8. **Use your voice if you catch him in the act indoors.** A short sharp negative sound is best - NO! ACK! EH! It doesn't matter, as long as it is loud enough to make him stop. Then start running enthusiastically towards your door, calling him into the garden and the chosen place and patiently wait until he has finished what he started indoors. It is no good scolding your dog if you find a puddle or unwanted gift in the house but don't see him do it; he won't know why you are cross with him. Only use the negative sound if you actually catch him in the act.

9. **No punishment.** Accidents will happen at the beginning, do not punish your pup for them. He is a baby with a tiny bladder and bowels, and housetraining takes time - it is perfectly natural to have accidents early on. Remain calm and clean up the mess with a good strong-smelling cleaner to remove the odour, so he won't be tempted to use that spot again. Dogs have a very strong sense of smell; use a special spray from your vet or a hot solution of washing powder to completely eliminate the odour. Smacking or rubbing his nose in it can have the opposite effect - he will become afraid to do his business in your presence and may start going behind the couch or under the bed, rather than outside.

10. **Look for the signs.** These may be:

    a. Whining

    b. Sniffing the floor in a determined manner

    c. Circling and looking for a place to go

    d. Walking uncomfortably - particularly at the rear end!

Photo courtesy of Jina Ezell.

Take him outside straight away, and try not to pick him up all the time. He has to learn to walk to the door himself when he needs to go outside.

11. **If you use puppy pads, only do so for a short time** or your puppy will get used to them.

12. **Use a crate at night-time** and for the first couple of weeks, set your alarm clock. An eight-week-old pup should be able to last a few hours if the breeder has already started the process. Get up four hours after you go to bed and take the pup outside to eliminate. After a couple of days, gradually increase the time by 15 minutes. By the age of four or five months a Cavalier pup should be able to last through (a short night) without needing the toilet – provided you let him out last thing at night and first thing in the morning. Before then, you will have a lot of early mornings!

If using a crate, remember that during the day the door should not be closed until your pup is happy with being inside. At night-time it is acceptable to close the door. Consider keeping the pup close to you for the first two or three nights. He needs to believe that the crate is a safe place and not a trap or prison. If you don't want to use a crate, then section off an area inside one room or use a puppy pen to confine your pup at night. And finally, one British breeder added this piece of advice: "If you are getting a puppy, invest in a good dressing gown and an umbrella!"

Breeders on Housetraining

Most good breeders provide new owners with information to take home which helps them to understand their puppy's needs. In her Notes For Buyers one breeder says: "Your puppy has already started to ask to go out when she needs the toilet; in any case you will need to take her outside regularly. Typically, this would be every time she wakes up as well as after meals.

"Watch for the signs: searching the ground and sniffing is a good indication she needs to pass water. Puppies have relatively small bladders. Always choose the same place in the garden; remain with the puppy until she has performed and then give her plenty of praise. Remember, accidents will happen. If you catch her in the act, simply take her outside and then praise her for her efforts. Never shout at or hit your puppy as this will cause confusion and is likely to make matters worse.

"During the times when puppy has no access to the garden, it is a good idea to place some newspaper on the floor. The newspaper could be moved nearer and nearer to the outside door until puppy realises to go to the door to ask to go out. Puppy training pads are also available from pet shops, although we find that puppies prefer to rip them up rather than to use them for their correct purpose!"

If breeders have already started housetraining - either inside or outside the house — they may have a phrase that they already use, such as "Go toilet!" or "Go potty!" Ask your breeder if she has started the process and what phrase she uses to encourage the pups to eliminate.

Here is the routine from one breeder: "We have a pretty strict routine for toilet training which is a little intensive, but not unreasonable. It definitely works. They learn that 10pm till 6am is sleep time, which any new home could do. This matters as obviously they learn through conditioning. So, with a sleep routine, they know how long it is until they next can pee and near 10pm they know it's nearly bedtime, so learn quickly to pee then.

"Then, during the day, it's a case of taking them out every two hours on the hours so 6am, 8am, 10am and so on... I find that every time they go out, they pee so therefore they would probably struggle waiting longer. It's also important that they don't have free reign to go outside whenever they feel like it (unsupervised) which is tempting in summer months, but it's absolutely vital to notice every time they pee and when they do one to let them know what they're doing. "Go toilet" is what we use. Then reward immediately. Eventually, you'll be able to ask them to "Go toilet" as they've formed the association.

"This doesn't mean they categorically can't go longer than two hours, but it's better to set them up to win rather than fail. We then don't have a specified age where the length of time is extended as that's definitely an individual basis, so when they stop going every time you take them out, the time can be very gradually increased."

Here are some comments from other breeders: "I find they are fairly reliable by 11 to 12 weeks if taken out to the garden regularly when awake and always immediately after waking up or after a meal. I think Cavaliers can be a bit slower to grow up than breeds like Terriers, but I don't have much experience of other breeds. I expect them to know to ask to go out when needed by four to five months, but you need to respond consistently, reliably and fast! I find bitches can go backwards around the time they have their first season at six to eight months, but after that they seem to be much better." "They are housetrained by about six months of age. Take them out after food, every time they wake up and as often as possible. Accidents will happen, but if they have gone to the exit and done it, at least they are trying." "Each dog is individual, some are quicker than others. It is important that the new owner is aware that after waking or after a meal, the puppy should be taken out to a designated spot and encouraged to eliminate." "I always get asked how long it takes to housetrain a Cavalier puppy - if only there was a straight answer! Each dog is different. Some learn toilet rules early, some not. I always say stick with it and they do get that Eureka! moment and it all falls into place eventually."

"I start housetraining from about six-weeks-old when the puppy is getting stronger and can go outside in the garden. From the feedback I have had from new owners, they have said it has been quick and easy. I am unsure as to how this compares to other breeds." "Our first Cavalier was housetrained by four months. They are all different and I would expect them to be trained by six months. New owners do have to put the effort in, however. Take puppies out when they wake up and after feeding. But also, every couple of hours is a good idea."

"Some breeders do not advocate putting newspaper in the crate for the puppy to toilet. I agree, as by doing this it makes it much harder to get the puppy fully toilet trained. The idea of getting up in the night to toilet the puppy may not suit everyone. What we do is to use a fairly spacious puppy pen at night for a young puppy and not a crate. We have a bed at one end and newspaper at the far end where the puppy can eliminate. We still have a crate for the puppy to go in during the day if he so wishes and we leave the door open. This then becomes his own little den. But at night he is put in the playpen. By the time the puppy is about four-and-a-half to five months old we find that they can usually go all night without toileting and so we then put them in a crate at night."

"How can you tell the dogs need to go out?"

Jina Ezell adds: "My tip is actually for those breeding the puppy. At three weeks old, the puppy is now crawling out of the warmth of the dam; we can stimulate the bladder and take them to the potty pad and give special touch and affirmation. By four weeks, they are walking to the pad and going on their own. By five weeks, they are in a sleeping crate and let outside to do their business each time they wake. By six weeks they let themselves out through the puppy door to relieve themselves. By seven weeks, there are no accidents. It is my observation that these dogs are actually easy to train, although you need to get in there and train them right away, otherwise they find new, bad habits of pottying when they don't know the expectation.

"Praise, praise, praise - and treats for those who have a difficult time. I say that this is a Toy breed, and as such, it is similar in some ways to a premature human baby. Don't expect things to be done on the same timeframe as, say, a Labrador or Shepherd, but within a few months they will be able to do the same thing."

As you have read, housetraining varies from one breeder to another and one puppy to the next. The important thing as a new owner is to continue with the breeder's method, which your puppy has already part learned – and BE VIGILANT. Your Cavalier is very trainable and really wants to learn. Time spent housetraining during the first month will reap rewards with speedy results.

GENERAL HOUSETRAINING TIP: A trigger can be very effective to encourage your dog to perform his or her duties. Some people use a clicker or a bell - we used a word; well, two, actually. Within a week or so I trained our puppy to urinate on the command of "Wee wee!" Think very carefully before choosing the word or phrase, as I often feel an idiot wandering around our garden last thing at night shouting "WEE WEE!!" in an encouraging manner. (Although I'm not sure that the American expression "GO POTTY!!" sounds much better!

8. Feeding a Cavalier

To keep your dog's biological machine in good working order, it's important to supply the right fuel, as the correct diet is an essential part of keeping your dog fit and healthy. Feeding is a very important topic for Cavalier owners, perhaps more so than for owners of some other breeds.

Cavaliers are not like Labradors, which, although lovable, are almost without exception greedy dogs who would sell their own mothers for a treat. No, Cavaliers are more complex than that. Some are greedy dogs, while others are fussy eaters. Puppies are no different; some will gobble down anything put in front of them, while owners of other Cavalier puppies are at their wits' end trying to tempt them to eat.

The right diet is extremely important for Cavaliers. Not least because:

a) They can be prone to obesity - which causes all sorts of problems, and

b) The breed is prone to heart issues, so feeding a nutritious diet and maintaining a healthy weight can actually prolong the life of a Cavalier

The topic of feeding can be something of a minefield; owners are bombarded with endless choices as well as countless adverts from dog food companies, all claiming that theirs is best. There is not one food that will give every single dog the healthiest coat and skin, the brightest eyes, the most energy, the best digestion, the least gas, the longest life and stop her from scratching or having skin problems.

Dogs are individuals, just like people, which means that you could feed a quality food to a group of dogs and find that most of them thrive on it, some do not so well, while a few might get an upset stomach or even an allergic reaction. The question is: "Which food is best for **my** Cavalier?"

If you have been given a recommended food from a breeder, rescue centre or previous owner, stick to this as long as your dog is doing well on it. A good breeder knows which food her dogs thrive on. If you do decide - for whatever reason - to change diet, then this must be done gradually. There are several things to be aware of when it comes to feeding:

1. Food is a big motivator for many dogs, making a powerful training tool. You can use feeding time to reinforce a simple command on a daily basis.

2. Greedy dogs have no self-control when it comes to food, so it is up to you to control your dog's intake. Dogs of all breeds, including Cavaliers, can have food sensitivities or allergies - more on this topic later.

3. Some dogs do not do well on diets with a high grain content. There is enough anecdotal evidence from owners to know that that this is certainly true of some Cavaliers.

4. Excess gas is not uncommon, and one of the main reasons for flatulence is the wrong diet.

5. There is evidence that some dogs thrive on home-cooked or raw diets, particularly if they have been having skin issues with manufactured foods, but you need the time and money to stick to them.

6. With processed dried foods (kibble), you often get what you pay for, so a more expensive food is usually – but not always - more likely to provide better nutrition in terms of minerals, nutrients and high quality meats. Cheap foods often contain a lot of grain; read the list of ingredients to find out. Dried foods tend to be less expensive than some other foods. They have improved a lot over the last few years and some of the best ones are now a good choice for a healthy, complete diet. Dried foods also contain the least fat and most preservatives. Foods such as Life's Abundance dry formulas do not contain any preservatives.

7. Sometimes elderly dogs just get bored with their diet and go off their food. This does not necessarily mean that they are ill, simply that they have lost interest and a new food should be gradually introduced.

One of our dogs had inhalant allergies. He was fed a quality dried food which the manufacturers claimed was 'hypoallergenic,' i.e. good for dogs with allergies. Max did well on it, but not all dogs thrive on dried food. We tried several other foods first; it is a question of owners finding the best food for their dog. If you got your dog from a good breeder, they should be able to advise you.

Beware foods described as 'premium' or 'natural' or both, these terms are meaningless. Many manufacturers blithely use these words, but there are no official guidelines as to what they mean. However, **"Complete and balanced"** IS a legal term and has to meet standards laid down by AAFCO (Association of American Feed Control Officials) in the USA.

Always check the ingredients on any food sack, packet or tin to see what is listed first; this is the main ingredient and it should be meat or poultry, not grain. If you are in the USA, look for a dog food endorsed by AAFCO. In general, tinned foods are 60-70% water and often semi-moist foods contain a lot of artificial substances and sugar. Choosing the right food for your dog is important; it will influence health, coat, longevity and sometimes even temperament.

There are three stages of your dog's life to consider when feeding: *Puppy, Adult* and *Senior* (also called Veteran). Some manufacturers also produce a *Junior* feed for adolescent dogs. Each represents a different physical stage of life and you should choose the right food during each particular phase. (This does not necessarily mean that you have to feed Puppy, then Junior, then Adult, then Senior food; some owners switch their young dogs to Adult formulas fairly soon. Ask your breeder for his or her advice on the right time to switch.

A pregnant female will require a special diet to cope with the extra demands on her body; this is especially important as she nears the latter stages of pregnancy.

Many owners feed their Cavaliers twice a day; this helps to stop a hungry dog gulping food down in a mad feeding frenzy and also reduces the risk of Bloat although this is not a major concern for Cavaliers (see **Chapter 12. Cavalier Health**). Some owners of fussy eaters or older dogs who have gone off their food give two different meals each day to provide variety. One meal could be dried kibble, while the other might be home-made, with fresh meat, poultry and vegetables, or a tinned food - or a mix of the two for both meals. If you do this, make sure the combined meals provide a balanced diet and that they are not too rich in protein – especially with young or old dogs.

Food allergies are a growing problem in the canine world generally. Sufferers may itch, lick or chew their paws and/or legs, rub their face or get 'hot spots'. They may also get frequent ear infections as well as redness and swelling on their face. Switching to a grain-free diet can help to alleviate the symptoms, as your dog's digestive system does not have to work as hard. In the wild, a dog or wolf's staple diet would be meat with some vegetable matter from the stomach and intestines of the herbivores (plant-eating animals) that she ate – but no grains. Dogs do not efficiently digest corn or wheat, both of which are often staples of cheap commercial dog food). Grain-free diets provide carbohydrates through fruits and vegetables, so a dog still gets all the necessary nutrients.

20 Tips For Feeding Your Cavalier

1. If you do choose a manufactured food, don't pick one where meat or poultry content is NOT the first item listed on the bag or tin. Foods with lots of cheap cereals or sugar are not the best choice.

2. Some Cavaliers suffer from sensitive skin, 'hot spots' or allergies. A cheap food, often bulked up with grain, will only make this worse. If this is the case, bite the bullet and choose a high quality – usually more expensive – food, or consider a raw diet. You'll probably save money in vets' bills in the long run and your dog will be happier. A food described as 'hypoallergenic' on the sack means 'less likely to cause allergies.'

3. Consider feeding your dog twice a day, rather than once. Smaller feeds are easier to digest and reduce flatulence (gas). Puppies need to be fed more often; discuss exactly how often with your breeder.

4. Establish a feeding regime and stick to it. Dogs like routine. If you are feeding twice a day, feed once in the morning and then again at tea-time. Stick to the same times of day. Do not give the last feed too late, or your dog's body will not have chance to process or burn off the food before sleeping. She will also need a walk or letting out in the garden or yard after her second feed to allow her to empty her bowels. Feeding at the same times each day helps your dog establish a toilet regime.

5. Some owners practise 'free feeding,' which allows the dog to eat when he or she wants. However, some Cavaliers pups can be fussy eaters, so consider taking away any uneaten food between meals. Most Cavaliers enjoy their food, but any dog can become fussy if food is available all day. Imagine if your dinner was left on the table for hours. Returning to the table two or three hours later would not be such a tempting prospect, but coming back for a fresh meal would be far more appetising.

   Also, when food is left all day, some dogs take the food for granted and lose their appetite. They start leaving food and you are at your wits' end trying to find something they will actually eat. Put the food bowl down twice a day and take it up after 20 minutes – even if there is some left. If she is healthy and hungry, she'll look forward to her next meal and soon stop leaving food. If a Cavalier does not eat anything for a couple of days, it could well be a sign that she is unwell.

NOTE: The exception to this is with very young puppies – under three months – where the breeder might recommend free feeding so the dog can eat at will. Also, some fussy eaters do better with free feeding. Dishes must be washed daily and old uneaten food thrown away.

6. If your puppy is a fussy eater, don't be too quick to switch foods. Try removing the bowl between meals, so (s)he is hungry when it's time for the next meal. Switching foods too

quickly or tempting a young dog with treats can be a sure-fire way of encouraging fussy eating.

7. Some owners with fussy Cavaliers find that their dog eats better if the food is presented on a small plate.

8. If your dog is a fussy eater, try giving the teatime feed after a long walk when your dog is more likely to be hungry. (Wait until an hour after vigorous exercise).

9. Do not feed too many titbits (tidbits) and treats between meals. Extra weight will place extra strain on your Cavalier's heart, other organs and joints, causing a detrimental effect on health and even lifespan. It also throws a balanced diet out of the window if they are cheap and unhealthy. Try to avoid feeding your dog from the table or your plate, as this encourages attention-seeking behaviour, begging and drooling.

10. If you feed leftovers, feed them INSTEAD of a balanced meal, not as well as - unless you are feeding a raw diet. High quality commercial foods already provide all the nutrients, vitamins, minerals and calories that your dog needs. Feeding titbits or leftovers may be too rich for your Cavalier in addition to her regular diet and cause gas, scratching or other problems, such as obesity. You can feed your dog vegetables as a healthy low-calorie treat.

 Get your puppy used to eating raw carrots, pieces of apple, etc. as a treat and she will continue to enjoy them as an adult. If you wait until she's fully grown before introducing them, she may well turn her nose up.

11. Never give your dog cooked bones, as these can splinter and cause choking or intestinal problems.

12. Avoid rawhide, as dogs, particularly those that rush their food, have a tendency to chew and swallow without first nibbling it down into smaller pieces. Rawhide also contains glue and chemicals which are toxic in large quantities. Personally, I would never give rawhide to a dog.

13. If you switch to a new food, do the transition gradually. Unlike humans, dogs' digestive systems cannot handle sudden changes. Begin by gradually mixing some of the new food in with the old and increase the proportion so that after seven to eight days, all the food is the new one. The following ratios are recommended by Doctors Foster & Smith Inc: Days 1-3 add 25% of the new food, Days 4-6 add 50%, Days 7-9 add 75%, Day 10 feed 100% of the new food. By the way, if you stick to the identical brand, you can change flavours in one go.

NOTE: The exception is when switching to a raw diet as raw and processed or cooked food are digested at different rates, and the stomach produces different acids for the digestion of each. Raw takes around four hours to digest, whereas kibble takes 12 hours. To switch to raw, give the last bowl of kibble then start feeding raw the following day.

14. NEVER feed the following items to your dog: grapes, raisins, chocolate, onions, Macadamia nuts, any fruits with seeds or stones, tomatoes, avocadoes, rhubarb, tea, coffee or alcohol. All of these are poisonous to dogs.

15. Check your dog's faeces (aka stools, poo or poop!). If her diet is suitable, the food should be easily digested and produce dark brown, firm stools. If your dog produces soft or light stools, or has a lot of gas or diarrhoea, then the diet may not suit her, so consult your vet or breeder for advice.

16. Feed your dog in stainless steel or ceramic dishes. Plastic bowls don't last as long and can also trigger an allergic reaction around the muzzle in some sensitive dogs. Ceramic bowls are best for keeping water cold. We recommend using elevated bowls with narrow tops for your Cavalier – available on Amazon, eBay, etc. - to keep their ears out of food and drink.

17. If you have more than one dog, consider feeding them separately. Cavaliers normally get on well with other dogs, but feeding dogs together can sometimes lead to food aggression from one dog either protecting her own food or trying to eat the food designated for another.

18. Keep your dog's weight in check. Obesity can lead to the development of serious health issues, such as heart disease, diabetes and high blood pressure. Although weight varies from dog to dog, a good rule of thumb is that your Cavalier's tummy should be higher than her rib cage. If her belly is level or hangs down below it, she is overweight.

19. Many breeders feed vitamins and/or supplements to help keep their Cavaliers healthy. Check with your breeder or vet as to which, if any, to feed. These may include: L-Carnitine, CoQ10/ Ubiquinol, Taurine (for the heart) and fish oil for the coat and maybe a probiotic for digestion.

20. And finally, always make sure that your dog has access to clean, fresh water. Change the water and clean the bowl regularly – it gets slimy!

Many breeders feed their adult dogs twice a day, others feed just once, and yet others feed some dogs once a day and some dogs twice a day. As one US breeder put it: "They are not all made from the same cookie cutter." Start your dog on twice-daily feeds from four to six months old and, if he or she seems to be thriving on this regime, stick to it.

....

Types of Dog Food

We are what we eat. The right food is a very important part of a healthy lifestyle for dogs as well as humans. Here are the main options explained:

Dry dog food - also called kibble, is a popular and relatively inexpensive way of providing a balanced diet – look for *Complete and Balanced* on the packet in the UK. However, kibble was created for the convenience of owners, not dogs, and it doesn't suit all dogs. Kibble comes in a variety of flavours and with differing ingredients to suit the different stages of a dog's life. Cheap foods are often false economy, particularly if your Cavalier does not tolerate grain/cereal very well. You may also have to feed larger quantities to ensure she gets sufficient nutrients.

Canned food - another popular choice – and it's often very popular with dogs too. They love the taste and it generally comes in a variety of flavours. Canned food is often mixed with dry kibble, and a small amount may be added to a dog that is on a dry food diet if she has lost interest in food. It tends to be more expensive than dried food and many owners don't like the mess. These days there are hundreds of options, some are very high quality and made from natural, organic ingredients and contain herbs and other beneficial ingredients. A part-opened tin can sometimes smell when you open the fridge door. As with dry food, read the label closely. Generally, you get what you pay for and the origins of cheap canned dog food are often somewhat dubious. Some dogs can suffer from diarrhoea or soft stools and/or gas with too much tinned or soft food.

Freeze-Dried (pictured) - This is made by a special process which freezes the food, then removes the moisture before vacuum packing. The product is sealed with an oxygen-absorbing substance to increase shelf life. It doesn't need a fridge and can be kept at room temperature for up to six months. Usually with a very high meat content and no grain, many freeze-dried meals contain high quality, natural, human-grade ingredients. So what's the catch?

........Price! If you can afford it, freeze-dried will not only give you a quality, natural food, but your dog will love it. Many raw feeders use freeze-dried and it's also handy for those travelling with their dogs.

Home-Cooked - Some owners want the ability to be in complete control of their dog's diet, know exactly what their dog is eating and to be sure that his or her nutritional needs are being met. Feeding your dog a home-cooked diet of meat and vegetables can be time-consuming and more expensive than kibble, and the difficult thing is sticking to it once you have started out with the best of intentions. But many owners think the extra effort is worth it. If you decide to go ahead, spend the time to become proficient and learn about canine nutrition to ensure your dog gets all the vital nutrients and right amount of calories.

We have several friends with itchy dogs who are all now doing better having switched from a commercial, dried dog food to a home-cooked diet - usually involving chicken and vegetables.

Semi-Moist - These are commercial dog foods shaped like pork chops, salamis, bacon (pictured), burgers or other meaty foods and they are the least nutritional of all dog foods. They are full of sugars, artificial flavourings and colourings to help make them visually appealing. Cavaliers don't care two hoots what their food looks like, they only care how it smells and tastes; the shapes are designed to appeal to humans. While you may give your dog one as an occasional treat, they are not a diet in themselves and do NOT provide the nutrition your dog needs. Steer clear of them for regular feeding.

What the Breeders Say

All the UK breeders quoted here are Kennel Club Assured Breeders. Julie Durham says: "I brought my first Cavalier in 1982. I bred her in 1985 and have been in love with the breed ever since. All our dogs live happily together in our home, sharing everything from a toy to a bed and all are treated as individuals, whether on walks, cuddle time or playtime. They all have a good quality diet, which helps to keep them in tip-top condition. I use and recommend Royal Canin. I do not recommend raw at all as I used it many years ago and the results were poor then. I do not believe it would be different now."

As mentioned, every dog is different and if yours is not doing well on a particular food, you have to finds the diet which most suits the individual dog. Fellow Dennis and Tina Homes have had a different experience to Julie: "We have tried in the past to feed commercial kibble, but have found that raw meat and biscuit is more readily accepted. We have also found that they seem to suffer fewer teeth and gum problems on raw food and that their coats appear to be better - thicker and more lustrous. Dogs in the wild are omnivorous and have the gastric juices to digest a whole range of different foods. One of the ways of keeping your dog healthy is not to overfeed or allow the dog to become overweight."

Philippa Biddle agrees: "I give a very long lecture about diet. I feed raw and think there are many advantages; you know what your dog is eating for starters. They love it. Their coats and eyes are shining and mine hardly ever have health problems, allergies or weight problems. I do feed a little kibble for convenience at times and also tinned and cooked meals when on holiday, travelling and such times. I give raw bones and find they are marvellous for keeping the teeth clean and healthy and the dogs happy for hours. Feeding raw doesn't mean you can't use some kibble, tins and cooked trays.

"Don't buy titbits, treats, chews or food made in China, buy only stuff made in the UK. They don't need any manufactured treats, instead give gravy bones, bonio, real bones, fruit and veg slices, fried meat, tripe sticks, pigs' ears, hooves and rabbit ears, etc. Never mix or give foodstuffs when you don't know what they contain - like Dentastix; what the heck are they made of?"

Sandra Coles: "I feed both Forthglade cooked meats and a raw diet of minced beef and tripe with a wholemeal biscuit. I try to feed as natural a diet as possible. They have dried tripe sticks for teeth, carrots and other raw vegetables and the occasional bonio biscuit. They also love apple."

Kathy Hargest has bred Cavaliers for 14 years and has this advice: "Feed the best food you can afford, incorporate dry kibble, vegetables, tinned and fresh meat, and never let your dog get overweight." *Photo courtesy of Kathy.*

"Adults are fed twice a day; I do a mix of grain-free kibble, chopped veg, fruit and raw and tinned meat. The kibble is always grain-free, having had one that was grain intolerant. We have found some puppy foods to be too strong, causing diarrhoea. Beef can also be too strong."

Philip Lunt said: "I feed my dogs on Arden Grange, which is a gluten/wheat free kibble. It provides them with all the nutrients they need. I only feed dry food, which can have water added if needed; this helps with keeping teeth cleaner, I find." Philip also had a dog with a wheat/gluten allergy and added: "She was three years old and was scratching and had flaky skin. After a number of tests by the vet we opted to change foods." She was switched over to Arden Grange and did fine on it.

AKC Bred with H.E.A.R.T. breeder Jina Ezell, Kalama Cavaliers, Washington State, USA: "I have fed a variety of high quality kibble - Taste of the Wild and most recently, Life's Abundance. While researching how to get ahead of the health problems of the Cavalier, I began cooking for them a few years ago. I then began raw feeding about a year ago and have seen a decreased amount of yeast issues, scratching/itchy skin (which I believe were due to kibble allergens), halitosis, impacted anal glands and, I believe, an increase in energy and vitality.

"My puppies at birth have been strong and healthy as well. I begin raw feeding the puppies when they begin eating. Bella, a tricolor, came to me around nine months ago, her hair was coarse, she scratched (a lot!) and was nervous/aggressive. Since feeding an exclusive raw diet, her beautiful hair is SO soft and thick; she's much calmer and is quite the lovely girl."

The Raw Diet

If there is one thing which is guaranteed to divide opinion, it is the raw diet. There is anecdotal evidence that some dogs thrive on a raw diet, particularly those with food intolerances or allergies - although scientific proof is lagging behind. However, I also know several breeders who have tried feeding raw and say their dogs did badly on it. And some say their dogs actually dislike the taste of raw meat.

Given that our dog, Max, had allergies for many years, I would say that had he been younger, I would have tried him on a home-cooked or raw diet – but that's just personal opinion.

Most Cavaliers thrive on a high quality dried commercial dog food or a mix of cooked/raw and kibble. We are not suggesting that everybody rushes out and feeds their dog a raw diet. Due to various factors, the time and expense involved, the raw diet is certainly not for every dog, we are providing the information here for anyone considering feeding raw. They may be fans of a natural diet or have a Cavalier that is not doing well on a commercially-prepared diet or one that has skin issues. In these circumstances, a raw diet is one of the options for owners to consider.

Claims made by fans of the raw diet include:

- Reduced symptoms of - or less likelihood of - allergies, and less scratching
- Better skin and coats
- Easier weight management
- Improved digestion
- Less doggie odour and flatulence
- Higher energy levels
- Reduced risk of bloat
- Helps fussy eaters
- Fresher breath and improved dental health
- Drier and less smelly stools, more like pellets
- Overall improvement in general health and less disease
- Most dogs love a raw diet

Raw food emulates the way dogs ate before the existence of commercial dog foods, which may contain artificial preservatives and excessive protein and fillers – causing a reaction in some dogs. Dry, canned and other styles of processed food were mainly created as a means of convenience,

Some nutritionists believe that dogs fed raw whole foods tend to be healthier than those on other diets. They say there are inherent beneficial enzymes, vitamins, minerals and other qualities in meats, fruits, vegetables and grains in their natural forms that are denatured or destroyed when cooked. Many also believe dogs are less likely to have allergic reactions to the ingredients on this diet. Frozen food can be a valuable aid to the raw diet. The food is highly palatable and made from high quality ingredients. The downsides are that not all pet food stores stock it, it can be expensive and you have to remember to defrost it.

Many raw feeders actually buy prepared, balanced raw meals, made by companies such as such as Paleo Ridge or Naturaw, containing a frozen box of minced meat, bone and offal in the correct proportion. All owners just defrost the food and spoon it into a bowl, which is far easier than

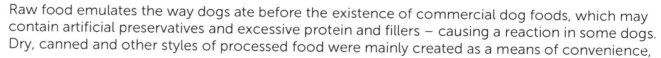

weighing out and organising quantities into the right proportions. There is also the freeze-dried option if you don't fancy handling raw meats and poultry.

Critics of a raw diet say that the risks of nutritional imbalance, intestinal problems and food-borne illnesses caused by handling and feeding raw meat outweigh any benefits. Owners must pay strict attention to hygiene when preparing a raw diet.

 A raw diet may not be a good option if you have young children in the house, due to the risk of bacterial infection from the raw meat. The dog may also be more likely to ingest bacteria or parasites such as Salmonella, E. Coli and Ecchinococcus.

There are two main types of raw diet, one involves feeding raw, meaty bones and the other is known as the BARF diet (*Biologically Appropriate Raw Food* or *Bones And Raw Food)*, created by Dr Ian Billinghurst.

Raw Meaty Bones

This diet is:

- 🐾 Raw meaty bones or carcasses, if available, should form the bulk of the diet
- 🐾 Table scraps both cooked and raw, such as vegetables, can be fed
- 🐾 As with any diet, fresh water should be constantly available. **NOTE: Do NOT feed cooked bones, they can splinter**

Australian veterinarian Dr Tom Lonsdale is a leading proponent of the raw meaty bones diet. He believes the following foods are suitable:

- 🐾 Chicken and turkey carcasses, after the meat has been removed for human consumption
- 🐾 Poultry by-products, including heads, feet, necks and wings
- 🐾 Whole fish and fish heads
- 🐾 Sheep, calf, goat, and deer carcasses sawn into large pieces of meat and bone
- 🐾 Other by-products, e.g. pigs' trotters, pigs' heads, sheep heads, brisket, tail and rib bones
- 🐾 A certain amount of offal can be included in the diet, e.g. liver, lungs, trachea, hearts, tripe

He says that low-fat game animals, fish and poultry provide the best source of food for pet carnivores. If you feed meat from farm animals (cattle, sheep and pigs), avoid excessive fat and bones that are too large to be eaten.

Some of it will depend on what's available locally and how expensive it is. If you shop around you should be able to source a regular supply of suitable raw meaty bones at a reasonable price. Start with your local butcher or farm shop. When deciding what type of bones to feed your Cavalier, one point to bear in mind is that dogs are more likely to break their teeth when eating large knuckle bones and bones sawn lengthwise than when eating meat and bone together.

You'll also need to think about WHERE you are going to feed your dog. A dog takes some time to eat a raw bone and will push it around the floor, so the kitchen may not be the most suitable or hygienic place. Outside is one option, but what do you do when it's raining?

Establishing the right quantity to feed your Cavalier is a matter of trial and error. You will reach a decision based on your dog's activity levels, appetite and body condition. High activity and a big appetite show a need for increased food, and vice versa. A very approximate guide, based on raw meaty bones, for the average dog is 15%-20% of body weight per week, or 2%-3% a day. So, if your Cavalier weighs 16lb (7.27kg), he or she will require 2.4lb-3.2lb (1kg-1.45kg) of carcasses or raw meaty bones weekly. Table scraps should be fed as an extra component of the diet. **These figures are only a rough guide** and relate to adult pets in a domestic environment.

Pregnant or lactating females and growing puppies may need much more food than adult animals of similar body weight. Dr Lonsdale says: "Wherever possible, feed the meat and bone ration in one large piece requiring much ripping, tearing and gnawing. This makes for contented pets with clean teeth. Wild carnivores feed at irregular intervals, in a domestic setting regularity works best and accordingly I suggest that you feed adult dogs and cats once daily. If you live in a hot climate I recommend that you feed pets in the evening to avoid attracting flies.

"I suggest that on one or two days each week your dog may be fasted - just like animals in the wild. On occasions you may run out of natural food. Don't be tempted to buy artificial food, fast your dog and stock up with natural food the next day. Puppies...sick or underweight dogs should not be fasted (unless on veterinary advice)."

Table scraps and some fruit and vegetable peelings can also be fed, but should not make up more than one-third of the diet. Liquidising cooked and uncooked scraps in a food mixer can make them easier to digest.

Things to Avoid:

- Excessive meat off the bone - not balanced
- Excessive vegetables - not balanced
- Small pieces of bone - can be swallowed whole and get stuck
- Cooked bones, fruit stones (pips) and corn cobs - get stuck
- Mineral and vitamin additives - create imbalance
- Processed food - leads to dental and other diseases
- Excessive starchy food - associated with Bloat
- Onions, garlic, chocolate, grapes, raisins, sultanas, currants - toxic to pets
- Milk - associated with diarrhoea. Animals drink it whether thirsty or not and can get fat

Points of Concern

- Old dogs used to processed food may experience initial difficulty when changed on to a natural diet. Discuss the change with your vet first
- Raw meaty bones are not suitable for dogs with dental or jaw problems
- This diet may not be suitable if your dog gulps her food, as the bones can become lodged internally, larger bones may prevent gulping

- ❧ The diet should be varied, any nutrients fed to excess can be harmful

- ❧ Liver is an excellent foodstuff, but should not be fed more than once weekly

- ❧ Weight bearing bones shouldn't be given as they damage teeth. One breeder added: "My general rule is that if I can cut it with poultry shears, they can eat it; anything harder should be avoided

- ❧ Other offal, e.g. ox stomachs, should not make up more than half of the diet

- ❧ Whole fish are an excellent source of food, but avoid feeding one species of fish constantly. Some species, e.g. carp, contain an enzyme which destroys thiamine (vitamin B1)

- ❧ If you have more than one dog, do not allow them to fight over the food, feed them separately if necessary

- ❧ Be prepared to monitor your dog while she eats the bones, especially in the beginning, and do not feed bones with sharp points

- ❧ Make sure that children do not disturb the dog when feeding or try to take the bone away

- ❧ Hygiene: Make sure the raw meaty bones are kept separate from human food and clean thoroughly any surface the uncooked meat or bones have touched. This is especially important if you have children. Feeding bowls are unnecessary, your dog will drag the bones across the floor, so feed them outside if you can, or on a floor that is easy to clean

- ❧ Puppies can and do eat diets of raw meaty bones, but you should consult the breeder or a vet before embarking on this diet with a young dog

You will need a regular supply of meaty bones - either locally or online - and you should buy in bulk to ensure a consistency of supply. For this you will need a large freezer. You can then parcel up the bones into daily portions. You can also feed frozen bones; some dogs will gnaw them straight away, others will wait for them to thaw. More information is available from the website www.rawmeatybones.com and I would strongly recommend discussing the matter with your breeder or vet first before switching to raw meaty bones.

The BARF diet

A variation of the raw meaty bones diet is the BARF created by Dr Ian Billinghurst, who owns the registered trademark 'Barf Diet'. A typical BARF diet is made up of 60%-75% of raw meaty bones (bones with about 50% meat, such as chicken neck, back and wings) and 25%-40% of fruit and vegetables, offal, meat, eggs or dairy foods. Bones must not be cooked or they can splinter inside the dog. There is a great deal of information on the BARF diet on the internet.

 Only start a raw diet if you have done your research and are sure you have the commitment and money to keep it going. There are numerous websites and canine forums with information on switching to a raw diet and everything it involves.

Food Allergies

Dog food allergies affect about one in 10 dogs. They are the third most common canine allergy for dogs after atopy (inhaled or contact allergies) and flea bite allergies. While there's no scientific evidence of links between specific breeds and food allergies, there is anecdotal evidence from owners that some Cavaliers can be sensitive to, and suffer a reaction from, certain foods.

Food allergies affect males and females in equal measure as well as neutered and intact pets. They can start when your dog is five months or 12 years old - although the vast majority start when the dog is between two and six years old. It is not uncommon for dogs with food allergies to also have other types of allergies. If your dog is not well, how do you know if the problem lies with her food or not? Here are some common symptoms to look out for:

- Itchy skin (this is the most common). Your dog may lick or chew her paws or legs and rub her face with her paws or on the furniture, carpet, etc.

- Excessive scratching

- Ear infections (pictured)

- Hot patches of skin – 'hot spots'

- Hair loss

- Redness and inflammation on the chin and face

- Recurring skin infections

- Increased bowel movements (maybe twice as often as usual)

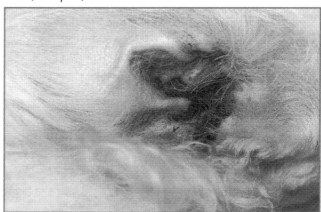

- Skin infections that clear up with antibiotics but recur when the antibiotics run out

Allergies or Intolerance?

There's a difference between dog food **allergies** and dog food **intolerance (sensitivity)**:

Typical reactions to allergies are skin problems and/or itching

Typical reactions to intolerance are diarrhoea and/or vomiting

Dog food intolerance can be compared to people who get diarrhoea or an upset stomach from eating spicy food. Both can be cured by a change to a diet specifically suited to the individual, although a food allergy may be harder to get to the root cause of. As they say in the canine world: "One dog's meat is another dog's poison." With dogs, certain ingredients are more likely to cause allergies than others. In order of the most common triggers across the canine world in general they are: **Beef, dairy products, chicken, wheat, eggs, corn, and soy.**

There is also increasing evidence that some dogs cannot tolerate the preservatives and other chemicals in dried dog food.

Unfortunately, these most common offenders are also the most common ingredients in dog foods! Dogs were often put on a rice and lamb kibble diet, which were thought to be less likely to cause allergies. However, the reason was simply because they were not traditionally included in many dog food recipes - therefore fewer dogs had reactions to them.

It is also worth noting that a dog is allergic or sensitive to an **ingredient**, not to a particular brand of dog food, so it is very important to read the ingredients label on the sack or tin. If your Cavalier has a reaction to beef, for example, she will react to any food containing beef, regardless of how expensive it is or how well it has been prepared.

Food intolerances frequently start when a dog is less than one year old. If your Cavalier starts scratching, has diarrhoea, ear infections or other symptoms, don't think that because she has always had this food that it can't be the food that's causing the problem. It may simply be that she has developed an intolerance to the food as her body changes and matures.

Symptoms of food allergies are well documented. Unfortunately, the problem is that these conditions may also be symptoms of other issues such as environmental or flea bite allergies, intestinal problems, mange, and yeast or bacterial infections. You can have a blood test on your dog for food allergies, but many veterinarians now believe that this is not accurate enough.

The only way to completely cure a food allergy or intolerance is total avoidance. This is not as easy as it sounds. First you have to be sure that your dog does have a food allergy, and then you have to discover which food is causing the reaction. Blood tests are not thought to be reliable and, as far as I am aware, the only true way to determine exactly what your dog is allergic to, is to start a food trial. If you don't or can't do this for the whole 12 weeks, then you could try a more amateurish approach, which is eliminating ingredients from your dog's diet one at a time by switching diets – remember to do this over a period of a week.

A food trial is usually the option of last resort, due to the amount of time and attention that it requires. It is also called *an exclusion diet* and is the only truly accurate way of finding out if your dog has a food allergy and what is causing it. Before embarking on one, try switching dog food.

If you wish to stick with commercial dog food, try switching to a grain-free, hypoallergenic one – preferably with natural (not chemical) preservatives. Although usually more expensive, hypoallergenic dog food ingredients do not include common allergens such as wheat protein or soya, thereby minimising the risk of an allergic reaction. Many may have less common ingredients, such as venison, duck or types of fish.

Here are some things to look for in a high-quality food:

- Meat or poultry as the first ingredient
- Vegetables
- Natural herbs such as rosemary or parsley
- Oils such as rapeseed (canola) or salmon.

Here's what to avoid if your dog is showing signs of a food intolerance:

- Corn, corn meal, corn gluten meal
- Meat or poultry by-products (as you don't know exactly what these are or how they have been handled)
- Artificial preservatives including BHA, BHT, Propyl Gallate, Ethoxyquin, Sodium Nitrite/Nitrate and TBHQBHA
- Artificial colours, sugars and sweeteners like corn syrup, sucrose and ammoniated glycyrrhizin
- Powdered cellulose
- Propylene glycol

If you can rule out all of these and you've tried switching diet without much success, then a food trial may be your only option.

Here is a list of Dog Food Advisor's best commercial dried food available in the USA: https://www.dogfoodadvisor.com/best-dog-foods/best-dry-dog-foods)or type *"Dog Food Advisor best Dry Dog Foods'* into Google. If you are in the UK, go to www.allaboutdogfood.co.uk and read their Dog Food directory, which ranks food out of five.

Food Trials

Before you embark on one of these, you need to know that they are a real pain-in-the-you-know-what to monitor. You have to be incredibly vigilant and determined, so only start one if you 100% know you can see it through to the end, or you are wasting your time. It is important to keep a diary during a food trial to record any changes in your dog's symptoms, behaviour or habits.

A food trial involves feeding one specific food for 12 weeks, something the dog has never eaten before, such as rabbit and rice or venison and potato. Surprisingly, dogs are typically NOT allergic to foods they have never eaten before. The food should contain no added colouring, preservatives or flavourings.

There are a number of these commercial diets on the market, as well as specialised diets that have proteins and carbohydrates broken down into such small molecular sizes that they no longer trigger an allergic reaction. These are called *'limited antigen'* or *'hydrolysed protein'* diets.

Home-made diets are another option as you can strictly control the ingredients. The difficult thing is that this must be the **only thing** the dog eats during the trial. Any treats or snacks make the whole thing a waste of time. During the trial, you shouldn't allow your dog to roam freely, as you cannot control what she is eating or drinking when out of sight outdoors. Only the recommended diet must be fed. Do NOT give:

- Treats
- Rawhide
- Pigs' ears
- Cows' hooves
- Flavoured toothpastes
- Flavoured medications (including heartworm treatments) or supplements
- Flavoured plastic toys

If you want to give a treat, use the recommended diet. (Tinned diets can be frozen in chunks or baked and then used as treats). If you have other dogs, either feed them all on the trial diet or feed the others in an entirely different location. If you have a cat, don't let the dog near the cat litter tray. And keep your dog out of the room when you are eating — not easy with a hungry Cav! But even small amounts of food dropped on the floor or licked off of a plate can ruin a food trial, meaning you'll have to start all over again.

Although beef is the food most likely to cause allergies in the general dog population, there are plenty of stories to suggest that the ingredient most likely to cause a problem in many dogs is grain — just visit any canine internet forum to see that this is true. *'Grain'* is wheat or any other cultivated cereal crop. Some dogs also react to starch, which is found in grains and potatoes (also bread, pasta, rice, etc)..

Some breeds (especially the Bully breeds, e.g. Bulldogs, Boxers, Pugs, Bull Terriers and French Bulldogs) can be prone to a build-up of yeast in the digestive system. Foods that are high in grains and sugar can cause an increase in unhealthy bacteria and yeast in the stomach. This crowds out the good bacteria in the stomach and can cause toxins to occur that affect the immune system. And when the immune system is not functioning properly, the itchiness related to food allergies can cause secondary bacterial and yeast infections, which, in Cavaliers, may show as ear infections, hot spots, reddish or dark brown tear stains or other skin disorders. Symptoms of a yeast infection also include:

- ❧ Itchiness

- ❧ A musty smell

- ❧ Skin lesions or redness on the underside of the neck, the belly or paws

Although drugs such as antihistamines and steroids will temporarily help, they do not address the root cause. Wheat products are also known to produce flatulence, while corn products and feed fillers may cause skin rashes or irritations. Switching to a grain-free diet may help to get rid of yeast and bad bacteria in the digestive system.

Introduce the new food over a week or so and be patient, it may take two to three months for symptoms to subside – but you will definitely know if it has worked after 12 weeks. Some owners also feed their dogs a daily spoonful of natural or live yoghurt, as this contains healthy bacteria and helps to balance the bacteria in your dog's digestive system - by the way, it can work for humans too! Others have switched their dogs to a home-cooked or raw diet.

It is also worth noting that some of the symptoms of food allergies - particularly the scratching, licking, chewing and redness - can also be a sign of inhalant or contact (environmental) allergies, which are caused by a reaction to such triggers as pollen, grass or dust. Some dogs are also allergic to flea bites - see **Chapter 13. Skin and Allergies** for more details.

If you suspect your dog has a food allergy, the first port of call should be to the vet to discuss the best course of action. However, many vets' clinics promote specific brands of dog food, which may or may not be the best for your dog. Don't buy anything without first checking every ingredient on the label.

The website www.dogfoodadvisor.com provides useful information with star ratings for grain-free and hypoallergenic dogs' foods, or www.allaboutdogfood.co.uk if you are in the UK, or www.veterinarypartner.com/Content.plx?P=A&S=0&C=0&A=2499 for more details about canine food trials. We have no vested interest in these sites or their recommended products, but have found them to be good sources of unbiased information.

How Much Food?

This is another question I am often asked. The answer is ... there is no easy answer! The correct amount of food for a dog depends on a number of factors:

- ❧ Breed

- ❧ Gender

- ❧ Age

- ❧ Health

- ❧ Environment

- ❧ Number of dogs in the house or kennel

- Quality of the food
- Natural energy levels
- Amount of daily exercise
- Whether your dog is working, competing, performing a service or simply a pet

Some breeds have a higher metabolic rate than others, and energy levels vary tremendously from one dog to the next. Some individual Cavaliers are energetic, while others are more laid back. Generally:

- Smaller dogs have faster metabolisms so require a higher amount of food per pound of body weight
- Dogs that have been spayed may be more prone to putting on weight
- Growing puppies and young dogs need more food than senior dogs with a slower lifestyle

Every dog is different; you can have two Cavaliers with different energy levels, body shapes and capacity for exercise. The energetic dog will burn off more calories.

Maintaining a healthy body weight for dogs – and humans – is all about balancing what you take in with how much you burn off. If your dog is exercised two or three times a day or has regular play sessions with other dogs, she will need more calories than a couch potato. Certain health conditions such as heart disease - which many Cavaliers suffer from - an underactive thyroid, diabetes and arthritis can all lead to dogs gaining weight, so their food has to be adjusted accordingly.

Just like us, a dog kept in a very cold environment will need more calories to keep warm than a dog in a warm climate, as they burn extra calories to keep themselves warm. Here's an interesting fact: a dog kept on her own is more likely to be overweight than a dog kept with other dogs, as she receives all of the food-based attention.

Manufacturers of cheaper foods usually recommend feeding more to your dog, as much of the food is made up of cereals, which are not doing much except bulking up the weight of the food – and possibly triggering allergies in your Cavalier. The daily recommended amount listed on the dog food sacks or tins is generally too high – after all, the more your dog eats, the more they sell!

Because there are so many factors involved, there is no simple answer. However, below we have listed the recommended feeding amount for dogs for James Wellbeloved's hypoallergenic kibble, which we feed.

Adult Cavaliers, both male and female, can be expected to weigh between 13lb to 18lb (5.9kg to 8.2kg) when fully grown.

In the chart, the number on the left is the dog's adult weight. The numbers on the right are the amount of daily food that an average dog with average energy levels requires.

NOTE: The following Canine Feeding Chart gives only very general guidelines; your dog may need more or less than this. Use the chart as a guideline only and if your dog loses or gains weight, adjust meals accordingly.

PUPPY

Size type	Expected adult body weight in kg (lb)	Daily serving in grams (ounces)					
		2 mths	3 mths	4 mths	5 mths	6 mths	> 6 mths
Small	5kg (11lb)	95g (3.5oz)	110g (3.9oz)	115g (4oz)	115g (4oz)	110g (3.9oz)	Change to Adult or Small Breed Junior
Small	10kg (22lb)	155g (5.5oz)	185g (6.5oz)	195g (6.9 oz)	190g (6.7oz)	185g (6.5oz)	Change to Adult or Small Breed Junior

JUNIOR

Size type	Expected adult body weight in kg (lb)	Daily serving in grams (ounces)						
		6 mths	7 mths	8 mths	10 mths	12 mths	14 mths	16 mths
Small	10kg (22lb)	195g (6.9 oz)	185g (6.5oz)	175g (6.2oz)	160g (5.6oz)	Change to Adult		

ADULT

Size type	Bodyweight in kg (lb)	Daily serving in grams (ounces)		
		High activity	Normal activity	Low activity
Small	5-10kg (11-22lb)	115-190g (4-6.7oz)	100-170g (3.5-6oz)	85-145g (3-5.1oz)
Medium	10-15 (22-33lb)	190-255g (6.7-9oz)	170-225g (6-7.9oz)	145-195g (5.1-6.9oz)

SENIOR

Size type	Bodyweight in kg (lb)	Daily serving in grams (ounces)	
		Active	Normal
Small	5-10kg (11-22lb)	105-175g (3.7-6.2oz)	90-150g (3.2-5.3oz)
Medium	10-15kg (22-33lb)	175-235g (6.2-8.3oz)	150-205g (3.2-7.2oz)

Canine Bloat

Bloat is known by several different names: twisted stomach, gastric torsion or Gastric Dilatation-Volvulus (GDV). It occurs mainly in larger breeds, however, there have been cases of Cavaliers getting Bloat. It is one reason why owners often feed their dogs twice a day - particularly if he or she gulps food.

Tips to avoid Bloat:

- Buy an elevated feeding bowl, which will not only keep your Cav's ears out of the food, but many people believe helps to prevent bloat. If you have a gulper, consider buying a bowl with nobbles in (pictured) and moisten your dog's food — both of these will slow her down

- Feed twice a day rather than once

- Diet - avoid dog food with high fats or which use citric acid as a preservative, also avoid tiny pieces of kibble

- Don't let your dog drink too much water just before, during or after eating. Remove the water bowl just before mealtimes, but be sure to return it soon after

- Stress can possibly be a possible trigger, with nervous (and aggressive) dogs being more susceptible; maintain a peaceful environment for your dog, particularly around mealtimes

- IMPORTANT: Avoid vigorous exercise before or after eating, allow one hour either side of mealtimes before strenuous exercise

Bloat can kill a dog in less than one hour. If you suspect your Cavalier has bloat, get her into the car and off to the vet IMMEDIATELY. Even with treatment, mortality rates range from 10% to 60%. With surgery, this drops to 15% to 33%.

Overweight Dogs

Due to the prevalence of heart and other issues within the breed, the Cavalier is most definitely a dog that benefits from maintaining a healthy weight. Any dog can become overweight given too much food, too many treats and not enough exercise. It is far easier to regulate your dog's weight and keep it at a healthy level than to try and slim down a voraciously hungry Cavalier when she becomes overweight. Sadly, overweight and obese dogs are susceptible to a range of illnesses. According to James Howie, Veterinary Advisor to Lintbells, some of the main ones are:

Heart and lung problems — fatty deposits within the chest cavity and excessive circulating fat play important roles in the development of cardio-respiratory and cardiovascular disease.

Joint disease — excessive body weight may increase joint stress, which is a risk factor in joint degeneration (arthrosis), as is cruciate disease (knee ligament rupture). Joint disease tends to lead to a reduction in exercise that then increases the likelihood of weight gain which reduces exercise further. A vicious cycle is created. Overfeeding growing dogs can lead to various problems, including the worsening of hip dysplasia. Weight management may be the only measure required to control clinical signs in some cases.

Diabetes – resistance to insulin has been shown to occur in overweight dogs, leading to a greater risk of diabetes mellitus.

Tumours – obesity increases the risk of mammary tumours in female dogs.

Liver disease – fat degeneration may result in liver insufficiency.

Reduced Lifespan - one of the most serious proven findings in obesity studies is that obesity in both humans and dogs reduces lifespan.

Exercise intolerance – this is also a common finding with overweight dogs, which can compound an obesity problem as fewer calories are burned off and are therefore stored, leading to further weight gain. Obesity also puts greater strain on the delicate respiratory system of Cavaliers, making breathing even more difficult for them.

Most Cavaliers are extremely loyal companions and very attached to their humans. However, beware of going too far in regarding your dog as a member of the family. It has been shown that dogs regarded as 'family members' (i.e. anthropomorphosis) by the owner are at greater risk of becoming overweight. This is because attention given to the dog often results in food being given as well.

The important thing to remember is that many of the problems associated with being overweight are reversible. Increasing exercise increases the calories burned, which in turn reduces weight. If you do put your dog on a diet, the reduced amount of food will also mean reduced nutrients, so she may need a supplement during this time.

Feeding Puppies

Feeding your Cavalier puppy the right diet is important to help her young body and bones grow strong and healthy. Puppyhood is a time of rapid growth and development, and puppies require different levels of nutrients to adult dogs.

Initially, pups get all their nutrients from their mother's milk and then they are gradually weaned from three or four weeks of age. Many owners prefer to stick with the food provided and recommended by the breeder. If your pup is doing well on this, there is no reason to change. However, if you do change food, it should be done very gradually by mixing in a little more of the new food each day over a period of seven to 10 days.

If at any time your puppy starts being sick, has loose stools or is constipated, slow the rate at which you are switching him over. If she continues vomiting, seek veterinary advice quickly - within a day or two - as she may have a problem with the food you have chosen. Puppies quickly dehydrate if they are vomiting or have diarrhoea.

Because of their special nutritional needs, you should only give your puppy a food that is approved either just for puppies or for all life stages. If a feed is recommended for adult dogs only, it won't have enough protein, and the balance of calcium and other nutrients will not be right for a pup. Puppy food is very high in calories and nutritional supplements, so you want to switch to a junior or adult food once she leaves puppyhood, which is at about six months old. Feeding puppy food too long can result in obesity and orthopaedic problems.

Getting the amount and type of food right for your pup is important. Feeding too much will cause him to put on excess pounds, and overweight puppies are more likely to grow into overweight adults. As a very broad guideline, Cavaliers normally mature (physically) into fully developed adults at around 18 months to two years old- females tend to mature slightly earlier than males - although both sexes can behave like puppies for much longer!

DON'T:

- Feed table scraps from the table. Your Cavalier will get used to begging for food, it will also affect a puppy's carefully balanced diet

- Feed food or uncooked meat that has gone off. Puppies have sensitive stomachs

DO:

- Check the weight of your growing puppy to make sure she is within normal limits for her age. There are charts available on numerous websites, just type *"puppy weight chart"* into Google – you'll need to know the exact age and current weight of your puppy

- Take your puppy to the vet if she has diarrhoea or is vomiting for two days or more

- Remove her food after it has been down for 15 to 20 minutes. Food available 24/7 encourages fussy eaters

How Often?

Most puppies have small stomachs but big appetites, so feed them small amounts on a frequent basis. Establishing a regular feeding routine with your puppy is good, as this will also help to toilet train her. Get her used to regular mealtimes and then let her outside to do her business straight away when she has finished. Puppies have fast metabolisms, so the results may be pretty quick!

Don't leave food out for the puppy so that she can eat it whenever she wants, as you need to be there for the feeds because you want her and her body on a set schedule. Smaller meals are easier for her to digest and energy levels don't peak and fall so much with frequent feeds. There is some variation between recommendations, but as a general rule of thumb:

- Up to the age of three or four months, feed your puppy three or four times a day

- Then three times a day until she is four to six months old

- Twice a day until she is one year old

- Then once or twice a day for the rest of her life

 Tip Cavaliers are very loving companions. If your dog is not responding well to a particular family member, a useful tactic is to get that person to feed the dog every day. The way to a dog's heart is often through his or her stomach!

Feeding Seniors

Once your adolescent dog has switched to an adult diet she will be on this for several years. However, as a dog moves towards old age, her body has different requirements to those of a young dog. This is the time to consider switching to a senior diet.

Dogs, generally, are living longer than they did 30 years ago. There are many factors that contribute to a longer life, including better immunisation and veterinary care, but one of the most important factors is better nutrition. Generally, a dog is considered to be older or senior if she is in the last third of her normal life expectancy. Some owners of large breeds, such as Great Danes (with an average lifespan of nine years) switch their dogs from an adult to a senior diet when they are only six or seven years old.

A Cavalier's average lifespan is around 10 years, but this can vary from nine to 14; genetics and general health play a role. Look for signs of your dog slowing down or having joint problems. If you wish to discuss it with your vet, you can describe any changes at your dog's vaccination appointment, rather than having the expense of a separate consultation.

As a dog ages her metabolism slows, her joints stiffen, her energy levels decrease and she needs less exercise, just as with humans. An adult diet may be too rich and have too many calories, so it may be the time to move to a senior diet. Having said that, some dogs stay on a normal adult diet all of their lives – although the amount is usually decreased and supplements added, e.g. for joints.

Even though she is older, keep her weight in check, as obesity in old age only puts more strain on the body - especially joints and organs - and makes any health problems even worse. Because of lower activity levels, many older dogs will gain weight and getting an older dog to slim down can be very difficult. It is much better not to let your Cavalier get too chunky than to put her on a diet. But if she is overweight, put in the effort to shed the extra pounds. This is one of the single most important things you can do to increase your Cavalier's quality AND length of life.

Other changes in canines are again similar to those in older humans and as well as stiff joints or arthritis, they may move more slowly and sleep more. Hearing and vision may not be so sharp and organs don't all work as efficiently as they used to; teeth may have become worn down or decayed. When this starts to happen, it is time to consider feeding your old friend a senior diet, which will take these changes into account. Specially formulated senior diets are lower in protein and calories but help to create a feeling of fullness.

Older dogs are more prone to develop constipation, so senior diets are often higher in fibre - at around 3% to 5%. Wheat bran can also be added to regular dog food to increase the amount of fibre - but do not try this if your Cavalier has a low tolerance or intolerance to grain. If your dog has poor kidney function, then a low phosphorus diet will help to lower the workload for the kidneys.

Ageing dogs have special dietary needs, some of which can be provided in the form of supplements, such as glucosamine and chondroitin, which help joints. Two popular joint supplements in the UK are GWF Joint Aid for dogs, used by several breeders, and Lintbell's Yumove. If your dog is not eating a complete balanced diet, then a vitamin/mineral supplement is recommended to prevent any deficiencies. Some owners also feed extra antioxidants to an older dog – ask your vet's advice on your next visit. Antioxidants are also found naturally in fruit and vegetables.

While some older dogs suffer from obesity, others have the opposite problem – they lose weight and are disinterested in food. If your old dog is getting thinner and not eating well, firstly get her checked out by the vet to rule out any possible diseases. If she gets the all-clear, your next challenge is to tempt her to eat. She may be having trouble with her teeth, so if she's on a dry food, try smaller kibble or moistening it with water or gravy.

Our old dog loved his twice daily feeds until he got to the age of 10 when he suddenly lost interest in his hypoallergenic kibble. We tried switching flavours within the same brand, but that didn't work. After a short while we mixed his daily feeds with a little gravy and a spoonful of tinned dog food – Bingo! He started wolfing it down again and was as lively as ever. At 12 he started getting some diarrhoea, so we switched again and for the last year of his life he was mainly on home-cooked chicken and rice diet with some senior kibble, which worked well.

Some dogs can tolerate a small amount of milk or eggs added to their food, and home-made diets of boiled rice, potatoes, vegetables and chicken or meat with the right vitamin and mineral supplements can also be good. See **Chapter 17. Caring for Senior Cavaliers** for more information on looking after an ageing Cavalier.

....

Reading Dog Food Labels

A NASA scientist would have a hard job understanding some manufacturers' labels, so it's no easy task for us lowly dog owners. Here are some things to look out for on the manufacturers' labels:

🐾 The ingredients are listed by weight and the top one should always be the main content, such as chicken or lamb. Don't pick one where grain is the first ingredient; it is a poor-quality feed. Some dogs can develop grain intolerances or allergies, and often it is specifically wheat they have a reaction to

Ingredients
Chicken, brewers rice, poultry by-product meal (source of glucosamine), whole grain corn, wheat flour, corn gluten meal, whole grain wheat, corn germ meal, animal fat preserved with mixed-tocopherols (form of Vitamin E), fish meal (source of glucosamine), animal digest, wheat bran, calcium carbonate, salt, potassium chloride, Vitamin E supplement, calcium phosphate, choline chloride, zinc sulfate, ferrous sulfate, L-ascorbyl-2-polyphosphate (source of Vitamin C), manganese proteinate, niacin, and Vitamin A supplement

Ingredients
High quality protein and thoughtfully sourced ingredients.
Whole Grain Corn, Chicken By-Product Meal, Flaxseed, Soybean Mill Run, Brewers Rice, Soybean Meal, Pork Fat, Powdered Cellulose, Chicken Liver Flavor, Fish Oil, Lactic Acid, Potassium Chloride, L-Lysine, Calcium Carbonate, Iodized Salt, Choline Chloride, DL-Methionine, vitamins (Vitamin E Supplement, L-Ascorbyl-2-Polyphosphate (source of Vitamin C), Niacin Supplement, Thiamine Mononitrate, Vitamin A Supplement, Calcium Pantothenate, Vitamin B12 Supplement, Pyridoxine Hydrochloride, Riboflavin Supplement, Biotin, Folic Acid, Vitamin D3 Supplement), L-Threonine, minerals (Ferrous Sulfate, Zinc Oxide, Copper Sulfate, Manganous Oxide, Calcium Iodate, Sodium Selenite), Taurine, Glucosamine Hydrochloride, L-Tryptophan, L-Carnitine, Mixed Tocopherols for freshness, Chondroitin Sulfate, Natural Flavors, Beta-Carotene

NOTE: On the top label, the first ingredients are chicken, brewer's rice and poultry by-product, with no artificial preservatives. Despite the claim of 'high quality protein' on the second label, this is a cheap food bulked up with corn containing virtually no meat, but lots of chemicals.

🐾 High on the list should be meat/poultry or meat/poultry by-products, these are clean parts of slaughtered animals, not including meat. They include organs, blood and bone, but not hair, horns, teeth or hooves

🐾 Chicken meal (dehydrated chicken) has more protein than fresh chicken, which is 80% water. The same goes for beef, fish and lamb. So, if any of these meals are number one on the ingredient list, the food should contain enough protein

🐾 A certain amount of flavourings can make a food more appetising for your dog. Choose a food with a specific flavouring, like *'beef flavouring'* rather than a general *'meat flavouring'*, where the origins are not so clear

🐾 Guaranteed Analysis – This guarantees that your dog's food contains the labelled percentages of crude protein, fat, fibre and moisture. Keep in mind that wet and dry dog

Crude Protein (min)	32.25%
Lysine (min)	0.43%
Methionine (min)	0.49%
Crude Fat (min)	10.67%
Crude Fiber (max)	7.3%
Calcium (min)	0.50%
Calcium (max)	1.00%
Phosphorus (min)	0.44%
Salt (min)	0.01%
Salt (max)	0.51%

foods use different standards. (It does not list the digestibility of protein and fat and this can vary widely depending on their sources).

While the Guaranteed Analysis is a start in understanding the food quality, be wary about relying on it too much. One pet food manufacturer made a mock product with a guaranteed analysis of 10% protein, 6.5% fat, 2.4% fibre, and 68% moisture (similar to what's on many canned pet food labels) – the ingredients were old leather boots, used motor oil, crushed coal and water!

- ❧ Find a food that fits your dog's age, breed and size. Talk to your breeder, vet or visit an online Cavalier forum and ask other owners what they are feeding their dogs

- ❧ If your Cavalier has a food allergy or intolerance to wheat, check whether the food is gluten free; all wheat contains gluten

- ❧ Natural is best. Food labelled *'natural'* means that the ingredients have not been chemically altered, according to the FDA in the USA. However, there are no such guidelines governing foods labelled *'holistic'* – so check the ingredients and how it has been prepared

- ❧ In the USA, dog food that meets minimum nutrition requirements has a label that confirms this. It states: *"[food name] is formulated to meet the nutritional levels established by the AAFCO Dog Food Nutrient Profiles for [life stage(s)]"*

Even better, look for a food that meets the minimum nutritional requirements *'as fed'* to real pets in an AAFCO-defined feeding trial, then you know the food really delivers the nutrients that it is *'formulated'* to. AAFCO feeding trials on real dogs are the gold standard. Brands that do costly feeding trials (including Nestlé and Hill's) indicate so on the package.

NOTE: Look for the words *'Complete and Balanced'* on a commercial food. Dog food labelled *'supplemental'* isn't complete and balanced. Check with your vet if in doubt.

If it all still looks a bit baffling, you might find the following websites, mentioned earlier, very useful. The first is www.dogfoodadvisor.com run by Mike Sagman. He has a medical background and analyses and rates hundreds of brands of dog food based on the listed ingredients and meat content. You might be surprised at some of his findings. The second is www.allaboutdogfood.co.uk run by UK canine nutritionist David Jackson.

To recap: no one food is right for every dog; you must decide on the best for yours. If you have a puppy, initially stick to the same food that the breeder has been feeding the litter, and only change diet later and gradually. Once you have decided on a food, monitor your puppy or adult. The best test of a food is how well your dog is doing on it.

If your Cavalier is happy and healthy, interested in life, has enough energy, is not too fat and not too thin, doesn't scratch a lot and has healthy-looking stools, then...

Congratulations, you've got it right!

9. Cavalier Behaviour

Just as with humans, a dog's personality is made up of a combination of temperament and character.

Temperament is the nature – or inherited characteristics - a dog is born with; a predisposition to act or react in a certain way. This is why getting your puppy from a good breeder is so important. Committed Cavalier breeders not only produce puppies from physically healthy dams and sires (mothers and fathers), but they also look at the temperament of the dogs and only breed from those with good traits.

Character varies from one dog to the next. It develops through the dog's life and is formed by a combination of temperament and environment. How you treat your dog will have a huge effect on his or her personality and behaviour. Starting off on the right foot with good routines for your puppy is very important; so treat your dog well, spend time with him or her and make time for plenty of socialisation and exercise.

All dogs need different environments, scents and experiences to keep them stimulated and well-balanced. Despite being classed as a Toy breed, Cavaliers are still Spaniels and enjoy running free off the lead (leash) with their noses to the ground.

Praise good behaviour, use positive methods and keep training short and fun. At the same time, all dogs should understand the "No" (or similar) command. Just as with children, a dog has to learn boundaries to adapt successfully and be content with his or her environment. Be consistent so your dog learns the guidelines quickly. All of these measures will help your dog grow into a happy, well-adjusted and well-behaved adult that is a delight to be with.

If you adopt a Cavalier from a rescue centre, you may need a little extra patience. These eager-to-please people-loving dogs may arrive with some baggage. They have been abandoned by their previous owners for a variety of reasons - or perhaps forced to produce puppies in a puppy mill - and may very well still carry the scars of that trauma. They may feel nervous and insecure, needy or aloof, and may not know how to behave in a house or interact with a loving owner. Your time and patience is needed to teach these poor animals to trust again and to become happy in their new forever homes.

Understanding Canine Emotions

As pet lovers, we are all too keen to ascribe human characteristics to our dogs; this is called *anthropomorphism* – "the attribution of human characteristics to anything other than a human being." Most of us dog lovers are guilty of that, as we come to regard our pets as members of the family - and Cavaliers certainly regard themselves as members of the family! An example of anthropomorphism might be that the owner of a male dog might not want to have him neutered because he will "miss sex", as a human might if he or she were no longer able to have sex.

This is simply not true. A male dog's impulse to mate is entirely governed by his hormones, not emotions. If he gets the scent of a bitch on heat, his hormones (which are just body chemicals) tell him he has to mate with her. He does not stop to consider how attractive she is or whether she is 'the one' to produce his puppies. No, his reaction is entirely physical, he just wants to dive in there and get on with it!

It's the same with females. When they are on heat, a chemical impulse is triggered in their brain making them want to mate — with any male, they aren't at all fussy. So don't expect your little princess to be all coy when she is on heat, she is not waiting for Prince Charming to come along - the tramp down the road or any other scruffy pooch will do! It is entirely physical, not emotional.

Food is another example. A dog will not stop to count the calories of that lovely treat (you have to do that). No, he or she is driven by food and just thinks about getting the treat. Most non-fussy eaters will eat far too much, given the opportunity.

Cavaliers are very loving, incredibly loyal and extremely eager to please you, and if yours doesn't make you laugh from time to time, you must have had a humour by-pass. All of this adds up to one thing: an extremely endearing and loving family member that it's all too easy to reward - or spoil.

It's fine to treat your dog like a member of the family - as long as you keep in mind that she is a dog and not a human. Understand her mind, patiently train her to learn her place in the household and that there are household rules she needs to learn — like not jumping on the couch when soaking wet or covered in mud - and you will be rewarded with a companion who is second to none and fits in beautifully with your family and lifestyle.

Dr Stanley Coren is a psychologist well known for his work on canine psychology and behaviour. He and other researchers believe that in many ways a dog's emotional development is equivalent to that of a young child. Dr Coren says: "Researchers have now come to believe that the mind of a dog is roughly equivalent to that of a human who is two to two-and-a-half years old. This conclusion holds for most mental abilities as well as emotions.

"Thus, we can look to human research to see what we might expect of our dogs. Just like a two-year-old child, our dogs clearly have emotions, but many fewer kinds of emotions than found in adult humans. At birth, a human infant only has an emotion that we might call excitement. This indicates how excited he is, ranging from very calm up to a state of frenzy. Within the first weeks of life the excitement state comes to take on a varying positive or a negative flavour, so we can now detect the general emotions of contentment and distress.

"In the next couple of months, disgust, fear, and anger become detectable in the infant. Joy often does not appear until the infant is nearly six months of age and it is followed by the emergence of shyness or suspicion. True affection, the sort that it makes sense to use the label "love" for, does not fully emerge until nine or ten months of age."

So, our Cavaliers can truly love us — but we knew that already!

A Study of Canine Emotion

According to Dr Coren, dogs can't feel shame, so if you are housetraining your puppy, don't expect him to be ashamed if he makes a mess in the house, he can't; he simply isn't capable of feeling shame. But he will not like it when you ignore him when he's behaving badly, and he will love it when you praise him for eliminating outdoors. He is simply responding to your reaction with his simplified range of emotions.

Dr Coren also believes that dogs cannot experience guilt, contempt or pride. I'm no psychology expert, but I'm not sure I agree. Take a Cavalier to a show, obedience class or agility competition, watch him perform and maybe win a rosette and applause - is the dog's delight something akin to pride? Cavaliers can certainly experience joy. They love your attention and praise; is there a more joyful sight for you both than when your Cavalier runs towards you, tail wagging like crazy, with those big, loving eyes that say you're the best person in the world?

If you want to see a happy dog, just watch Cavaliers running free with their noses to the ground, or snuggling up on the sofa with you. And when they trot around a show ring, run through the countryside or jump into water and return with the ball, isn't there a hint of pride there? Of all the dog breeds, the Cavalier is one of the most gentle and they can certainly show empathy - "the

ability to understand and share the feelings of another." They can pick up people's moods and emotions, which is one reason why some make excellent therapy dogs.

One emotion that all dogs can experience is jealousy. It may display itself by possessive or aggressive behaviour over food, a toy or a person, for example. An interesting article was published in the PLOS (Public Library of Science) Journal in 2014 following an experiment into whether dogs get jealous.

Building on research that shows that six-month old infants display jealousy, the scientists studied 36 dogs in their homes and video recorded their actions when their owners displayed affection to a realistic-looking stuffed canine (pictured).

Over three-quarters of the dogs were likely to push or touch the owner when they interacted with the decoy. The envious mutts were more than three times as likely to do this for interactions with the stuffed dog compared to when their owners gave their attention to other objects, including a book. Around a third tried to get between the owner and the plush toy, while a quarter of the put-upon pooches snapped at the dummy dog!

"Our study suggests not only that dogs do engage in what appear to be jealous behaviours, but also that they were seeking to break up the connection between the owner and a seeming rival," said Professor Christine Harris from University of California in San Diego.

The researchers believe that the dogs understood that the stuffed dog was real. The authors cite the fact that 86% of the dogs sniffed the toy's rear end during and after the experiment!

"We can't really speak of the dogs' subjective experiences, of course, but it looks as though they were motivated to protect an important social relationship. Many people have assumed that jealousy is a social construction of human beings - or that it's an emotion specifically tied to sexual and romantic relationships," said Professor Harris.

"Our results challenge these ideas, showing that animals besides ourselves display strong distress whenever a rival usurps a loved one's affection."

Typical Cavalier Traits

Every dog is different, of course. But within the breeds, there are some similarities. Here are some typical Cavalier characteristics - some of them also apply to other breeds of dog, but put them all together and you have a blueprint for the Cavalier.

1. Cavaliers are one of the most gentle of all breeds.

2. They were bred for companionship and are "Velcro" dogs; they like to stick close to you and do not do well when left alone for long periods.

3. They like to be close to their Cavalier friends as well as humans and – if you have several, they will all pile up on top of each other – or you!

4. It is not uncommon for Cavaliers to suffer from separation anxiety if left on their own too much.

5. They are friendly with everyone and love to be petted or made a fuss of.

6. They are sensitive dogs and can pick up on emotions.

7. Some can be a bit "wimpy", so socialisation is important to give the dog self-confidence.

8. Cavaliers are extremely keen to please and "biddable", meaning they can be easily trained - provided the owner puts in the time.

9. Praise, praise and praise is the way to train a Cavalier; they do not respond well to rough treatment or loud, harsh voices, which can lead to fear and timidity.

10. Toy breeds have a reputation for being slow to housetrain, but a Cavalier can get the hang of it pretty quickly, provided you are vigilant in the beginning.

11. Cavaliers are extremely patient and gentle with children – it is often the dog that needs protecting from the kids!

12. Provided they are fully socialised, Cavaliers are non-aggressive with other dogs and do particularly well with other Cavaliers.

13. Many Cavaliers have an instinctive love of water – although some don't. **Photo courtesy of Kathy Hargest.**

14. Cavaliers often love playing in the snow – although they may need their feet gently "de-icing" after an exercise session in the snow.

15. The Cavalier was originally bred down from the Spaniel and some still retain sporting instincts, with a strong prey drive, leading them to chase small mammals and birds when outdoors.

16. However, they often live happily with cats and other animals inside the house if introduced at a young age.

17. They do not respond well to rough treatment or loud, harsh voices, which can lead to neurotic habits.

18. Cavaliers are adaptable when it comes to exercise. They can go hiking for hours or snuggle up on the sofa all day.

19. All Cavaliers love running off the lead (leash) with their noses to the ground.

20. Bred from sporting origins, Cavaliers are playful and enjoy a mental challenge, such as games or retrieving, to keep their brains active.

21. An under-exercised, under-stimulated Cavalier will display poor behaviour, as will any dog.

22. They enjoy being the centre of attention and can sulk or be demanding if they think they are not getting enough attention from their owner(s).

23. Some Cavaliers can be a little nervous around new people, dogs and situations. Again, socialisation from an early age is the key. The more varied **positive** experiences a dog has when young, the more comfortable and relaxed he or she will be as an adult. DON'T pick your Cavalier up unless there is a real danger of injury; panicky owners trigger a fear response in their dogs.

24. They are supremely loyal to their human and canine companions and highly affectionate, forming deep bonds. Unlike some breeds, they often bond with the entire family, rather than just one person.

25. A Cavalier will 100% steal your heart - OK, that's not very scientific, but ask anyone who owns one!

Cause and Effect

As you've read, properly socialised and trained, well-bred Cavaliers make devoted canine companions. They are sweet-natured, affectionate and loyal, and love being around people or other dogs, Cavaliers in particular. Once you've had one, no other dog seems quite the same.

But any dog can develop behaviour problems given a certain set of circumstances. There are numerous reasons for this; every dog is an individual with his or her own temperament and environment, both of which influence the way the dog interacts with the world. Poor behaviour can result from a number of factors, including:

- Poor breeding
- Lack of socialisation

- 🐾 Lack of training
- 🐾 Lack of exercise or mental challenges
- 🐾 Being left alone too long
- 🐾 Being badly treated
- 🐾 A change in living conditions
- 🐾 Anxiety or insecurity
- 🐾 Fear
- 🐾 Being spoiled

Bad behaviour may show itself in a number of different ways, e.g.:

- 🐾 Nervousness/neurotic behaviour
- 🐾 Chewing or destructive behaviour
- 🐾 Jumping up
- 🐾 Constantly demanding attention
- 🐾 Being over-protective or jealous
- 🐾 Incessant barking
- 🐾 Biting or nipping
- 🐾 Growling
- 🐾 Soiling or urinating inside the house
- 🐾 Aggression towards humans or other dogs

Another issue which may arise is one dog mounting another. Of course, if a female is on heat, other dogs will try to mount her. But there are also behavioural issues which can lead to dogs - even females – mounting other dogs.

Dennis Homes has some insight into this: "Through writing our *Cavaliers as Companions* page for the Cavalier King Charles Spaniel Club, we often receive emails from pet owners. I remember receiving a message from a lady who had two Cavalier bitches and was quite alarmed by the fact that one would sometimes mount the other.

"Having a house full of dogs and bitches, we see this quite a lot and it has absolutely nothing to do with sex. It's purely a pecking order trait and is often done by the alpha female to assert her dominance. In the 40 years that we have kept Cavaliers of both sexes, we have always found that it's a female who is the alpha of the pack. With many other breeds, particularly Terriers and Bull breeds, it's usually the male that's top dog."

This chapter looks at some familiar behaviour problems. Although every dog is different, some common causes of unwanted behaviour are covered, along with tips to help improve the situation. The best way to avoid poor behaviour is to put in the time early on to socialise and train your dog, and nip any potential problems in the bud. If you are rehoming a Cavalier, you'll need extra time and patience to help your new arrival unlearn some bad habits.

Dennis added: "Socialization is of utmost importance. A properly socialized puppy is well-adjusted and makes a good companion. It is neither frightened by nor aggressive towards anyone or anything that it would normally meet in an everyday situation.

"An unsocialized dog is untrustworthy and can be a liability. They often become fear-biters and may have a tendency to fight with other dogs. They are difficult to train and are generally unpleasant to be around. Dogs that have not been properly socialized cannot adapt to new situations and a simple routine visit to the vet is a nightmare not only for the dog itself, but for everyone involved.

"Even before it has had its vaccinations I believe that you should carry the young puppy to places where there is lots of activity, such as a shopping area or outside a school playground. Make a fuss of the puppy and he would become oblivious to all of the hubbub and simply think that it's all fun.

"It is also very important to take the puppy on short car rides, even if it is a quick drive around the block. One of the main reasons why dogs suffer from car sickness is because they were not introduced to car journeys as young puppies."

NOTE: More detailed information on can be found on **Page 144 Socialisation** and further information on dealing with chewing and puppy biting can be found in **Chapter 11. Training.**

10 Ways to Avoid Bad Behaviour

Different dogs have different reasons for exhibiting bad behaviour. There is no simple cure for everything. Your best chance of ensuring your dog does not become badly behaved is to start out on the right foot and follow these simple guidelines:

1. **Buy from a good breeder**. They use their expertise to match suitable breeding pairs, taking into account factors such as good temperament, health, appearance and being "fit for function."

2. **Start socialisation right away**. We now realise the vital role that early socialisation plays in developing a well-rounded adult dog. Lack of socialisation is one of the major causes of unwanted behaviour or timidity. It is essential to expose your puppy to other people, places, animals and experiences as soon as possible; it will go a long way towards him or her becoming a stable, happy and trustworthy companion.

IMPORTANT: Socialisation does not end at puppyhood. Cavaliers are social creatures that thrive on sniffing, seeing, hearing and even licking. While the foundation for good behaviour is laid down during the first few months, good owners reinforce social skills and training throughout a dog's life.

Cavaliers like to be involved and sometimes the centre of attention and it is important they learn when young that they are not also the centre of the universe! Socialisation helps them to learn their place in that universe and to become comfortable with it.

3. **Start training early** - you can't start too soon. Like babies, puppies have incredibly enquiring minds that quickly absorb a lot of new information. You can start

teaching your puppy to learn his own name as well as some simple commands a couple of days after you bring him home.

4. **Basic training should cover several areas:** housetraining, chew prevention, puppy biting, simple commands like 'sit', 'come' or 'here', 'stay' and familiarising him with a collar or harness and lead. Adopt a gentle approach and keep training sessions short.

    Cavaliers are sensitive to you and your mood and do not respond well to harsh words or treatment. Start with five or 10 minutes a day and build up. Puppy classes or adult dog obedience classes are a great way to start, but make sure you do your homework afterwards. Spend a few minutes each day reinforcing what you have both learned in class - owners need training as well as dogs!

5. **Reward your dog for good behaviour.** All behaviour training should be based on positive reinforcement; so praise and reward your dog when he does something good. Cavaliers love to please their owners; this trait and their intelligence speeds up the training process. The main aim of training is to build a good understanding between you and your dog.

6. **Ignore bad behaviour**, no matter how hard this may be. If, for example, your dog is chewing his way through your shoes, the couch or toilet rolls or eating things he shouldn't, remove him from the situation and then ignore him. For some dogs even negative attention is some attention. Or if he is constantly demanding your attention, ignore him.

Remove yourself from the room so he learns that you give attention when you want to give it, **not** when he demands it. The more time you spend praising and rewarding good behaviour, while ignoring bad behaviour, the more likely he is to respond to you. If your pup is a chewer – and most are - make sure he has plenty of durable toys to keep him occupied.

7. **Take the time to learn what sort of temperament your dog has.** Is (s)he by nature a nervous or confident boy/girl? What was he like as a puppy, did he rush forward or hang back? Does he fight to get upright when on his back or is he happy to lie there? Is he a couch potato or a ball of fire?

    Your puppy's temperament will affect his behaviour and how he responds to the world around him. A timid Cavalier will certainly not respond well to a loud approach on your part, whereas an energetic, strong-willed one will require more patience and exercise.

8. **Exercise and stimulation.** A lack of either is another major reason for dogs behaving badly. Regular daily exercise, indoor or outdoor games and toys are all ways of stopping your dog from becoming bored or frustrated.

9. **Learn to leave your dog.** Just as leaving your dog alone for too long can lead to problems, so can being with her 100% of the time. The dog becomes over-reliant on you and then gets stressed when you leave; this is called *separation anxiety*. When your dog first arrives at your house, start by leaving him for a few minutes every day (after the first few days) and gradually build it up so that after a few weeks you can leave him for up to four hours.

10. **Love your Cavalier – but don't spoil him,** however difficult that might be. You don't do your dog any favours by giving him too many treats, constantly responding to his demands for attention or allowing him to behave as he wants inside the house.

Separation Anxiety

It's not just dogs that experience separation anxiety - people do too. About 7% of adults and 4% of children suffer from this disorder. Typical symptoms for humans are:

- Distress at being separated from a loved one
- Fear of being left alone

Our canine companions aren't much different to us. When a dog leaves the litter, her owners become her new family or pack. It's estimated that as many as 10% to 15% of dogs suffer from separation anxiety. It is an exaggerated fear response caused by separation from their owner. Toy Cavaliers can be more clingy than Miniatures and Standards.

Separation anxiety is on the increase and recognised by behaviourists as the most common form of stress for dogs. Millions of dogs suffer from separation anxiety.

It can be equally distressing for the owner - I know because our dog, Max, suffers from this. He howls whenever we leave home without him. Fortunately his problem is only a mild one.

If we return after only a short while, he's usually quiet. Although if we silently sneak back home and peek in through the letterbox, he's never asleep. Instead he's waiting by the door looking and listening for our return. It can be embarrassing.

Whenever I go to the Post Office, I tie him up outside and even though he can see me through the glass door, he still barks his head off - so loud that the people inside can't make themselves heard.

Luckily the lady behind the counter is a dog lover and, despite the large **'GUIDE DOGS ONLY'** sign outside, she lets Max in. He promptly dashes through the door and sits down beside me, quiet as a mouse!

Tell-Tale Signs

Does your Cavalier do any of the following?

- Get anxious or stressed when you're getting ready to leave the house?
- Howl, whine or bark when you leave?
- Tear up paper or chew furniture or other objects?
- Dig, chew, or scratch at the carpet, doors or windows trying to join you?
- Soil or urinate inside the house, even though she is housetrained? (This **only** occurs when left alone)
- Exhibit restlessness - such as licking her coat excessively, pacing or circling?
- Greet you ecstatically every time you come home – even if you've only been out to empty the bins?
- Wait by the window or door until you return?

- Dislike spending time alone in the garden or yard?
- Refuses to eat or drink if you leave her?
- Howl or whine when one family member leaves - even though others are still in the room or car?

If so, she or he may suffer from separation anxiety. Fortunately, in many cases this can be cured.

NOTE: Cavaliers are known as "shadow dogs" or "Velcro dogs." In other words, it is quite normal for them to stick close and follow their favourite human from room to room. In other dogs this would be a sign of separation anxiety, but not in the Cavalier, unless he or she gets distressed when you leave the house.

Causes

Dogs are pack animals and being alone is not a natural state for them. Puppies should be patiently taught to get used to short periods of isolation slowly and in a structured way if they are to be comfortable with it. It is also important for them to have a den where they feel safe - this may be a crate or dog bed where the pup can sleep in peace and quiet. A puppy will emotionally latch on to her new owner, who has taken the place of mother and siblings.

She will want to follow you everywhere initially and, although you want to shower her with love and attention, it's important to leave your new puppy alone for short periods in the beginning to avoid her becoming totally dependent on you.

In our case, I was working from home when we got Max. With hindsight, we should have regularly left him alone for short periods more often in the critical first few weeks and months. Adopted Cavaliers may be particularly susceptible to separation anxiety. They may have been abandoned once already and fear it happening again.

There are several causes, one or more of which can trigger separation anxiety. These include:

- Not being left alone for short periods when young
- Poor socialisation with other dogs and people resulting in too much focus and dependence on the owner
- Boredom - Cavaliers are intelligent dogs and need physical and mental exercise
- Being left for too long by owners who are out of the house for much of the day
- Leaving a dog too long in a crate or confined space
- Being over-indulgent with your dog; giving her too much attention
- Making too much of a fuss when you leave and return to the house
- Mistreatment in the past; a dog from a rescue centre may have insecurities and feel anxious when left alone
- Wilful behaviour due to a lack of training

Symptoms are not commonly seen in middle-aged dogs, although dogs that develop symptoms when young may be at risk later on. Separation anxiety is, however, common in elderly dogs. Pets age and - like humans - their senses, such as hearing and sight, deteriorate. They become more dependent on their owners and may then become more anxious when they are separated from them - or even out of view.

It may be very flattering and cute that your dog wants to be with you all the time, but insecurity and separation anxiety are forms of panic, which is distressing for your Cavalier. If she shows any signs, help her to become more self-reliant and confident; she will be a happier dog.

So what can you do if your dog is showing signs of canine separation anxiety? Every dog is different, but here are some tried and tested techniques that have proved effective for some dogs.

....

12 Tips to Combat Separation Anxiety

1. After the first two or three days, practise leaving your new puppy or adult dog for short periods, starting with a minute or two and gradually lengthening the time you are out of sight.

2. Tire your dog out before you leave her alone. Take her for a walk or play a game before leaving and, if you can, leave her with a view of the outside world, e.g. in a room with a patio door or low window.

3. Keep arrivals and departures low key and don't make a big fuss. Don't say hello or goodbye – either in words or body language, and don't sneak in and out of the house either.

For example, when I come home, Max is hysterically happy and runs round whimpering with a toy in his mouth. I make him sit and stay and then let him out into the garden without patting or acknowledging him. I pat him several minutes later.

4. Leave your dog a 'security blanket,' such as an old piece of clothing you have recently worn that still has your scent on it, or leave a radio on - not too loud - in the room with the dog. Avoid a heavy rock station! If it will be dark when you return, leave a lamp on a timer. One breeder leaves a TV on low, on the same channel, so her dogs become familiar with the same programmes! This also cuts out background noise such as traffic, people and barking dogs.

5. Associate your departure with something good. As you leave, give your dog a rubber toy, like a Kong filled with a tasty treat, a frozen treat, or spread her favourite treat over a Lickimat (available on Amazon). This may take her mind off your departure - some dogs may refuse

to touch the treat until you return home! Give her the treat when you are at home as well, so she doesn't just associate it with being left.

6. If your dog is used to a crate, try crating her when you go out. Many dogs feel safe there, and being in a crate can also help to reduce destructiveness. Always take the collar off first. Pretend to leave the house, but listen for a few minutes. NEVER leave a dog in a crate with the door closed all day; two or three hours are long enough during the day.

Warning: if your dog starts to show major signs of distress, remove her from the crate immediately as she may injure herself.

7. Structure and routine can help to reduce anxiety in your dog. Carry out regular activities, such as feeding and exercising, at the same time every day.

8. Dogs read body language very well; many Cavaliers are intuitive. They may start to fret when they think you are going to leave them. One technique is to mimic your departure routine when you have no intention of leaving. So put your coat on, grab your car keys, go out of the door and return a few seconds later. Do this randomly and regularly and it may help to reduce your dog's stress levels when you do it for real.

9. Some dogs show anxiety in new places; get her better socialised and used to different environments, dogs and people.

10. However lovable your Cavalier is, if she is showing early signs of anxiety when separating from you, do not shower her with attention all the time when you are there. She will become too dependent on you.

11. If you have to leave the house for a few hours at a time, ask a neighbour or friend to call in - or drop the dog off with them.

12. Getting another dog to keep the first one company can help, but first ask yourself whether you have the time and money for two or more dogs. Can you afford double the vet's and food bills?

Sit-Stay-Down

Another technique for helping to reduce separation anxiety is to practise the common "sit-stay" or "down-stay" exercises using positive reinforcement. The goal is to be able to move briefly out of your dog's sight while she is in the "stay" position.

Through this your dog learns that she can remain calmly and happily in one place while you go about your normal daily life. You have to progress slowly with this. Get your dog to sit and stay and then walk away from her for five seconds, then 10, 20, a minute and so on. Reward your dog with a treat every time she stays calm.

Then move out of sight or out of the room for a few seconds, return and give her the treat if she is calm, gradually lengthen the time you are out of sight. If you're watching TV with your Cavalier snuggled up at your side and you get up for a snack, say "stay" and leave the room.

When you come back, give her a treat or praise her quietly. It is a good idea to practise these techniques after exercise or when your dog is a little sleepy (but not exhausted), as she is likely to be more relaxed.

Canine separation anxiety is NOT the result of disobedience or lack of training. It's a psychological condition; your dog feels anxious and insecure.

NEVER punish your dog for showing signs of separation anxiety – even if she has chewed your best shoes. This will only make her worse.

NEVER leave your dog unattended in a crate for long periods or if she is frantic to get out, it can cause physical or mental harm. If you're thinking of leaving an animal all day in a crate while you are out of the house, get a rabbit or a hamster - not a dog.

....

Excessive Barking

Dogs, especially youngsters and adolescents, sometimes behave in ways you might not want them to, until they learn that this type of unwanted behaviour doesn't earn any rewards. Cavaliers are not known for being yappy dogs, although some can develop into annoying barkers. Like any dog, especially ones in the Toy Group, a Cavalier can get into the habit of barking too much if you don't put a stop to it.

Some puppies start off by being noisy from the outset, while others hardly bark at all until they reach adolescence or adulthood. Some may be triggered by other, noisier dogs in the household.

On our website we get emails from dog owners worried that their young dogs are not barking enough. However, we get far more from owners whose dogs are barking too much!

Some Cavaliers will bark if someone comes to the door – and then welcome them like best friends - while others remain quiet. Cavaliers do not make good guard dogs, as they are friendly with everyone.

There can be a number of reasons a dog barks too much. She may be lonely, bored or demanding your attention. She may be possessive and over-protective and so barks (or howls) her head off when others are near you. She may have picked up the habit from other dogs.

Excessive, habitual barking is a problem best corrected early on before it gets out of hand and drives you and your neighbours nuts. The problem often develops during adolescence or early adulthood (before the age of two or three) as your dog becomes more confident.

If your barking dog is an adolescent, she is probably still teething, so get a good selection of hardy chews, and stuff a Kong toy with a treat or peanut butter to keep her occupied and gnawing. But give her these when she is quiet, not when she is barking.

Your behaviour can also encourage excessive barking. If your dog barks non-stop for several seconds or minutes and then you give her a treat to quieten her, she associates barking with getting a nice treat.

A better way to deal with it is to say in a firm voice: **"Quiet"** after she has made a few barks. When she stops, praise her and she will get the idea that what you want her to do is stop. The trick is to nip the bad behaviour in the bud before it becomes ingrained.

If she's barking to get your attention, ignore her. If that doesn't work, leave the room and don't allow her to follow you, so you deprive her of your attention. Do this as well if her barking and attention-seeking turns to nipping. Tell her to **"Stop"** in a firm voice - not shouting - remove your hand or leg and, if necessary, leave the room.

As humans, we can use our voice in many different ways: to express happiness or anger, to scold, to shout a warning, and so on. Dogs are the same; different barks and noises give out different messages. **Listen** to your dog and try and get an understanding of Cavalier language. Learn to recognise the difference between an alert bark, an excited bark, a demanding bark, a nervous, high pitched bark, an aggressive bark or a plain "I'm barking 'coz I can bark" bark!

If your dog is barking at other dogs, arm yourselves with lots of treats and spend time calming your dog down. With Cavaliers, this is rarely pure aggression, it is more likely a fear response – especially if they are on a lead (leash) as they know they cannot escape so are trying to make themselves look and sound fierce to the other dog or dogs.

Listen to the tone of the bark, a high-pitched bark is usually a sign of fear or nervousness.

When she starts to bark wildly at another dog while on the lead, distract her by letting her sniff a treat in your hand. Make your dog sit down and give a treat. Talk in a gentle manner and keep showing and giving her a treat for remaining calm and not barking. There are several videos on YouTube that show how to deal with this problem in the manner described here.

Speak and Shush!

Cavaliers are not good guard dogs, most of them couldn't care less if somebody breaks in and walks off with the family silver – they are more likely to approach the burglar for a treat or a pat. But if you do have a problem with excessive barking when somebody visits your home, the Speak and Shush technique is one way of getting a dog to quieten down.

If your Cavalier doesn't bark and you want her to, a slight variation of this method can also be used to get her to bark as a way of alerting you that someone is at the door.

When your dog barks at an arrival at your house, gently praise her after the first few barks. If she persists, gently tell her that that is enough. Like humans, some dogs can get carried away with the sound of their own voice, so try and discourage too much barking from the outset. The Speak and Shush technique teaches your dog or puppy to bark and be quiet on command.

Get a friend to stand outside your front door and say "Speak" - or "Woof" or "Alert". This is the cue for your accomplice to knock or ring the bell – don't worry if you both feel like idiots, it will be worth the embarrassment!

When your dog barks, praise her profusely. You can even bark yourself in encouragement! After a few good barks, say "Shush" and then dangle a tasty treat in front of her nose. She will stop barking as soon as she sniffs the treat, because it is physically impossible for a dog to sniff and woof at the same time.

Praise your dog again as she sniffs quietly and then give her the treat. Repeat this routine a few times a day and your Cavalier will quickly learn to bark whenever the doorbell rings and you ask her to speak.

"Yes, I live on the third floor ...
but I have never heard any howling sounds."

Eventually your dog will bark after your request but BEFORE the doorbell rings, meaning she has learned to bark on command. Even better, she will learn to anticipate the likelihood of getting a treat following your "Shush" request and will also be quiet on command.

With Speak and Shush training, progressively increase the length of required shush time before offering a treat - at first just a couple of seconds, then three, five, 10, 20, and so on. By alternating instructions to speak and shush, the dog is praised and rewarded for barking on request and also for stopping barking on request.

If you want your dog to be more vocal, you need to have some treats at the ready, waiting for that rare bark. Wait until she barks - for whatever reason - then say "Speak" or whatever word you want to use, praise her and give her a treat.

At this stage, she won't know why she is receiving the treat. Keep praising her every time she barks and give her a treat. After you've done this for several days, hold a treat in your hand in front of her face and say "Speak".

Your dog will probably still not know what to do, but will eventually get so frustrated at not getting the treat that she will bark.

At which point, praise her and give her the treat. We trained a Labrador to do this in a week or so and he barked his head off when anybody came to the door or whenever we give him the command: "Speak".

Always use your 'encouraging teacher voice' when training; speak softly when instructing your dog to Shush, and reinforce the Shush with whisper-praise.

The more softly you speak, the more your dog will be likely to pay attention. Cavaliers respond very well to training when it is fun, short and reward-based.

Dealing with Aggression

Some breeds are more prone to aggression than others. Fortunately, this is a problem not often seen in Cavaliers. However, given certain situations, any dog can growl, bark or even bite.

Sometimes a dog learns unwanted behaviour from another dog or dogs, but often it is because the dog either feels insecure or has become too territorial or protective of her owner, toys or food. By the way, puppy biting is not aggression; all puppies bite; they explore the world with their noses and mouths. But it is important to train your cute little pup not to bite, as he may cause injury if he continues as an adult. **Any dog can bite** when under stress and, however unlikely it may seem, so can Cavaliers. Here are some different types of aggressive behaviour:

- Growling at you or other people

- Snarling or lunging at other dogs

- Growling or biting if you or another animal goes near his food

- Being possessive with toys

- Growling if you pet or show attention to another animal

- Marking territory by urinating inside the house

- Growling and chasing other small animals

- Growling and chasing cars, joggers or strangers

- Standing in your way, blocking your path

- Pulling and growling on the lead

Aggression is often due to the fact that the dog has not been properly socialised, and so feels threatened or challenged. Rather than being comfortable with new situations, other dogs or intrusions, she responds using "the best form of defence is attack" philosophy and displays aggressive behaviour to anything or anyone he perceives as a threat.

As well as snarling, lunging, barking or biting, you should also look out for other physical signs, such as: raised hackles, top lip curled back to bare teeth, ears up and tail raised.

Cavaliers love your attention, but they can sometimes become possessive of you, their food or toys, or territorial, which in itself can lead to bullying behaviour. Aggression may be caused by a lack of socialisation, an adolescent dog trying to see how far he or she can push the boundaries, nervousness, being spoiled by the owner, jealousy or even fear.

This fear may come from a bad experience the dog has suffered or from lack of proper socialisation. Another form of fear-aggression is when a dog becomes over-protective/possessive of her owner, which can lead to barking and lunging at other dogs or humans.

An owner's treatment of a dog can be a further reason. If the owner has been too harsh with the dog, such as shouting, using physical violence or reprimanding the dog too often, this in turn causes poor behaviour. Aggression breeds aggression. Dogs can also become aggressive if they are consistently left alone, cooped up, under-fed or under-exercised. A bad experience with another dog or dogs can also trigger aggressive behaviour.

Many dogs are more combative on the lead. This is because once on a lead, they cannot run away. Fight or flight. They know they can't escape, so they make themselves as frightening as possible and bark or growl to warn off the other dog or person. Train your dog from an early age to be comfortable walking on the lead. And socialisation is, of course vital — the first four to five months of a puppy's life is the critical time.

If your dog **suddenly** shows a change of behaviour and becomes aggressive, have her checked out by a vet to rule out any underlying medical reason for the crankiness, such as earache or toothache. Raging hormones can be another reason for aggression.

Another reason for dogs to display aggression is because they have been spoiled by their owners and have come to believe that the world revolves around them. Not spoiling your dog and teaching her what is acceptable behaviour in the first place is the best preventative measure. Early training, especially during puppyhood and adolescence - before he or she develops unwanted habits - can save a lot of trouble in the future.

Professional dog trainers employ a variety of techniques with a dog that has become aggressive. Firstly they will look at the causes and then they almost always use reward-based methods to try and cure aggressive or fearful dogs. **Counter conditioning** is a positive training technique used by many professional trainers to help change a dog's aggressive behaviour towards other dogs.

A typical example would be a dog that snarls, barks and lunges at other dogs while on the lead. It is the presence of other dogs that is triggering the dog to act in a fearful or anxious manner.

Every time the dog sees another dog, he or she is given a tasty treat to counter the aggression. With enough steady repetition, the dog starts to associate the presence of other dogs with a tasty treat.

Properly and patiently done, the final result is a dog that calmly looks to the owner for the treat whenever he or she sees another dog while on the lead. Whenever you encounter a potentially aggressive situation, divert your Cavalier's attention by turning her head away from the other dog and towards you, so that she cannot make eye contact with the other dog.

Aggression Towards People

Desensitisation is the most common method of treating aggression. It starts by breaking down the triggers for the behaviour one small step at a time. The aim is to get the dog to associate pleasant things with the trigger, i.e. people or a specific person whom she previously feared or regarded as a threat.

This is done through using positive reinforcement, such as praise or treats. Successful desensitisation takes time, patience and knowledge. If your dog is starting to growl at people, there are a couple of techniques you can try to break her of this bad habit before it develops into full-blown biting.

One method is to arrange for some friends to come round, one at a time. When they arrive at your house, get them to scatter kibble on the floor in front of them so that your dog associates the arrival of people with tasty treats. As they move into the house, and your dog eats the kibble, praise your dog for being a good boy or girl. Manage your dog's environment. Don't over-face him.

Most Cavaliers love children, but if yours is at all anxious around them, separate them or carefully supervise their time together in the beginning. Children typically react enthusiastically to dogs and some dogs may regard this as frightening or an invasion of their space.

Some dogs, particularly spoiled ones, may show aggression towards people other than the owner. Several people have written to our website on this topic and it usually involves a partner or husband. Often the dog is jealous of the attention the owner is giving to the other person, or it could be that the dog feels threatened by him; this is more common with Toy breeds.

If it happens with your Cavalier, the key is for the partner to gradually gain the trust of the dog. He or she should show that they are not a threat by speaking gently to your dog and giving treats for good behaviour. Avoid eye contact, as the dog may see this as a challenge. If the subject of the aggression lives in the house, then try letting this person give the dog his daily feeds. The way to a Cavalier's heart is often through his stomach.

A crate is also a useful tool for removing an aggressive dog from the situation for short periods of time, allowing him out gradually and praising good behaviour. As with any form of aggression, the trick is to take steps to deal with it **immediately.**

In extreme cases, when a dog exhibits persistent bad behaviour that the owner is unable to correct, a canine professional may be the answer. However, this is not an inexpensive option. Far better to spend time training and socialising your dog as soon as you get him or her.

Coprophagia (Eating Faeces)

It is hard for us to understand why a dog would want to eat his or any other animal's faeces (stools, poop or poo, call it what you will), but it does happen. There is plenty of anecdotal evidence that some dogs love the stuff.

Nobody fully understands why dogs do this, it may simply be an unpleasant behaviour trait or there could be an underlying reason. It is also thought that the inhumane and useless housetraining technique of "sticking the dog's nose in it" when he has eliminated inside the house can also encourage coprophagia.

If your dog eats faeces from the cat litter tray - a problem several owners have contacted us about - the first thing to do is to place the litter tray somewhere where your dog can't get to it — but the cat can. Perhaps on a shelf or put a guard around it, small enough for the cat to get through, but not your Cavalier.

Our dog sometimes eats cow or horse manure when out in the countryside. He usually stops when we tell him to and he hasn't suffered any after effects — so far. But again, this is a very unpleasant habit as the offending material sticks to the fur around his mouth and has to be cleaned off.

Sometimes he rolls in the stuff and then has to be washed down. You may find that your Cavalier will roll in fox poo to cover the fox's scent. Try and avoid areas you know are frequented by foxes if you can, as their faeces can transmit several diseases, including Canine Parvovirus or worms — neither of these should pose a serious health risk if your dog is up to date with vaccinations and worming treatments.

Vets have found that canine diets with low levels of fibre and high levels of starch increase the likelihood of coprophagia. If your dog is exhibiting this behaviour, first check that the diet you are feeding is nutritionally complete.

Look at the first ingredient on the dog food packet or tin – is it corn or meat? Does he look underweight? Check that you are feeding the right amount. If there is no underlying medical reason, you will have to try and modify your dog's behaviour. Remove cat litter trays, clean up after your dog and do not allow him to eat his own faeces. If it's not there, he can't eat it.

One breeder told us of a dog that developed the habit after being allowed to soil his crate as a pup, caused by the owners not being vigilant in their housetraining. The puppy got used to eating his own faeces and then continued to do it as an adult, when it became quite a problem.

Don't reprimand the dog for eating faeces. A better technique is to cause a distraction while he is in the act and then remove the offending material.

NOTE: Coprophagia is sometimes seen in pups aged between six months to a year and often disappears after this age.

Important: This chapter provides just a general overview of canine behaviour. If your Cavalier exhibits persistent behavioural problems, particularly if he or she is aggressive towards people or other dogs, you should consider seeking help from a reputable canine behaviourist, such as those listed the Association of Professional Dog Trainers, at: http://www.apdt.co.uk (UK) or https://apdt.com (USA).

Check they use positive reinforcement techniques - the old Alpha dominance theories of forcefully imposing your will on a dog have largely been discredited and, even if they hadn't, a Cavalier will not respond positively to this type of treatment.

10. Exercise

One thing all dogs have in common – including every Cavalier ever born - is that they need daily exercise. Even if you have a large garden or back yard where your dog can run free, there are still lots of benefits to daily walks.

One of the great things about Cavs is that they are so adaptable. They love going for long walks, but are equally happy to lounge around at home if you have to skip a walk. But don't think that because yours is happy to snuggle up on the sofa with you that they don't need exercise – THEY DO. Start regular exercise patterns early so your dog gets used to a routine. **Dogs love routine.** Daily exercise helps to keep your Cavalier happy, healthy and free from disease. It:

- ❧ Strengthens respiratory and circulatory systems
- ❧ Helps get oxygen to tissue cells
- ❧ Helps keep a healthy heart (very important for Cavaliers)
- ❧ Wards off obesity
- ❧ Keeps muscles toned and joints flexible
- ❧ Aids digestion
- ❧ Releases endorphins that trigger positive feelings
- ❧ Helps to keep dogs mentally stimulated and socialised

Surprisingly, the AKC (American Kennel Club) advises against letting your Cavalier off the leash (lead): *"Cavaliers should not be allowed off leash because they retain scenting and hunting instincts, and they may not come when called if they've found an interesting trail to follow or a creature to pursue. A fenced yard is recommended."*

We disagree! It is true, given the slightest opportunity, most Cavaliers will be off on a scent as fast as you can shout "Here Boy" in vain – but it only falls on deaf ears if your dog hasn't learned the recall. Spend time training your dog to come back to you, as regular off-lead (leash) exercise and games should be part of your normal routine. Breeders and owners interviewed for this book said that their Cavaliers ran all over the place and out of sight when off the lead, but virtually all of them came back to the call or whistle. The key is training. Do you really want to keep a Cavalier on a lead for a decade or more?

Photo courtesy of Philippa Biddle, Hearthfriend Cavaliers, Norfolk.

Another way of keeping your dog exercised and happy is to take part in an activity, such as Obedience, Agility, therapy work, Canine Freestyle/Heelwork to Music (dancing) or other canine activities which challenge dogs physically and mentally. And even if you don't do any official competitions, all Cavaliers love to show off by learning new tricks.

Lapdogs or Hunters?

The answer is a mixture of both! How much hunter and how much lapdog depends largely on bloodlines - and it's another question to ask the breeder if you haven't got your puppy yet. The Cavalier has been bred down from larger Spaniels, which are hardy sporting dogs bred to flush birds such as pheasant, partridge and woodcock from dense undergrowth and then retrieve the game for the guns. A working Spaniel can run all day long.

However, the Cavalier was developed not for sport, but to be a companion - originally for the aristocracy - and the breed is much less demanding mentally and physically than a sporting dog. The Cavalier is the only Spaniel to be classed in the Toy Group; all other Spaniels are classed in the Gundog Group in the UK and Sporting Group in the USA.

As the breed developed, dogs with more gentle and placid dispositions were chosen as breeding stock. So, the modern Cavalier retains some sporting instincts, but is also happy to be with you at home. Cavaliers are different in one other respect - they are far more dependent on humans for their happiness than sporting and working dogs.

Owner Nicola Byam-Cook, of Hampshire, is the proud owner of 18-month-old Ruby, her first Cavalier. She says: "Ruby is part lapdog, part hunter. She loves to sit on our lap, but loves chasing birds and going shooting as well and has even caught a baby rabbit.

"On the shoots, Ruby is the only Cavalier there amongst the Labs and the Spaniels. She is good on the peg, sits quietly and doesn't bark. She is good at flushing and finding birds on the ground, but is too small to actually pick up partridge or pheasant. She also doesn't seem too interested in picking up birds, but she has a good nose." *Photos of Ruby courtesy of India Brown Photography..*

"She runs around similar to a Spaniel and just gets stuck in, but always comes back to her whistle. She isn't trained to move to the whistle so she just hunts on her own. When my husband wears his shooting gear, she gets very excited! She enjoys the whole day out."

Here are some breeders' answers to the lapdog or hunter question, starting with Kathy Hargest: "As with all dogs, my Cavaliers would kill a running rabbit, but then be very happy on your lap for the rest of the day. I do not think they have a strong prey drive as do some other breeds, thankfully. As long as they are properly socialised when young, they get on with all animals."

Philippa Biddle: "They are both and that's what's so nice about them. They are lapdogs with go and attitude! Some have more hunting instinct than others, but they all enjoy searching hedgerows for birds and rabbits, mice and rats. They enjoy a hunt, but I can always call them back. I walk them in groups of four to six off-lead in the country and they are very obedient.

"They tend to love meeting other Cavaliers and Spaniels - they recognise their breed. They tend to ignore other dogs unless they know them well. They are very biddable and don't respond to aggressive dogs - "What's your problem?" and walk away is their usual response."

Dennis and Tina Homes: "In the 39 years of keeping and breeding Cavaliers, we have never encountered a hunting temperament. They may love to chase birds for fun, but when they sometimes catch up with one they invariably just stand and stare!"

Jina Ezell: "Ours are typical lapdogs: I will be working inside or outside and as soon as I sit down (anywhere), they will all pile up on me. I have my 'Morning Coffee Chair' and, thankfully it's wide enough and has arms, so that when I pull the feet out, I have room enough for all five to pile on! In my experience, Cavaliers don't have a strong prey drive. They will bark and enjoy a little hunt and chase, but will adapt to any/all animals."

Julie Durham: "The Cavalier is adaptable, meaning they love to go for a walk or short run if the weather is kind, but equally happy to snuggle up on a lap in front of the TV. Cavaliers are not brave and are happy to chase a fly or even the odd spider. They will even bark at the post entering the home or the doorbell going, but not at something that will bark back; they are not good with confrontation."

Philip Lunt: "Cavaliers are more lapdogs, but can have a tendency to be hunters. If in a pack they will chase sometimes anything. They are outgoing dogs that get on well with other animals."

Sandra Coles: "They will walk miles as adults and are very sporting, although they are just as content to be a lapdog. Mine will hunt and often find the pheasants or rabbits in the hedges. I have to be careful that they come back and do not get too focused on the hunting.

Owners Laura and Mustafa Rakla: "Ours are more lapdogs and enjoy a lot of attention. We have two and they are very happy to be docile and sleeping or resting, but Bertie does have a more rigorous temperament to chase birds and other small animals. We have never had any problems with other dogs. They do like to chase cats and birds - they have been surprisingly energetic and jumped to catch birds in mid-air!"

How Much Exercise?

The amount of exercise each adult Cavalier needs varies tremendously from one dog to the next. It depends on various factors, including:

* Temperament
* Natural energy levels
* Bloodline
* Your living conditions
* Whether your dog is kept with other dogs
* What he or she gets used to

The UK Kennel Club says: "Up to an hour a day" and the AKC describes the breed as being calm with moderate energy levels. One of the great advantages of Cavaliers is that they are happy to fit in with your lifestyle; they enjoy short and long walks but are not bouncing off the walls if they miss a walk. They are playful and enjoy games and retrieving, which help to stop them getting bored and keep them mentally stimulated.

Take the lead from your dog. Some of your dog's natural temperament and energy level will depend on the bloodline - ask the breeder how much exercise he or she recommends. But the good news is that even active Cavaliers love nothing more than snuggling up on the couch with you.

As a rule of thumb with adult dogs, two walks of around half an hour a day would keep your dog exercised and stimulated. Owners of competition or show dogs may train and exercise their Cavaliers in short, high energy sessions. Owning more than one dog - or having friends with dogs - is a great way for your dog to get more exercise. A couple of dogs running round together will get far more exercise than one on her own. If you already have a Cavalier and are looking for a second dog, consider another Cavalier. Several of our breeders have said that Cavs seem to recognise, and have an affinity with, their own breed.

Cavaliers are natural retrievers, i.e. they love fetching things back to you. As well as throwing a toy or ball, you can make it more interesting by hiding the object and training your dog to retrieve it – he or she will love the challenge. Try and avoid sticks, which can splinter in a dog's mouth. Playing in the garden or yard with toys or balls is also a good way to let off steam. If you play Frisbee, don't overdo it - especially with young, growing dogs, as this can lead to joint damage.

A fenced garden or yard is a MUST for a Cavalier - but should not be seen as a replacement for daily exercise away from the home, where a dog can experience new places, scents, other people and dogs. Your Cavalier will enjoy going for walks on the lead (leash), but will enjoy it far more when (s)he is allowed to run free, following a scent, chasing a ball or going for a swim. .

 Make sure you plug any and every gap in the fence. You will be surprised what tiny spaces they can wriggle through, and Cavaliers have absolutely NO road sense.

If your Cav is happy just to amble along beside you, think about playing some games, such as retrieving, to raise her heartbeat, build muscle and get her fit. If you want to hike or hunt with your dog, build up the distance gradually. This loyal breed WILL want to keep up with you, regardless of how fit he or she is, and you don't want your beloved pooch to have a heart attack.

The Cavalier also loves to follow her instincts to run free. You must, however, make sure it is safe to let your dog off the lead, away from traffic and other hazards - and don't let your dog off the lead until she has learned the recall. Also, there are reports in both the UK and North America about dog attacks in public parks and dog parks. If you are at all worried about this, avoid popular dog walking areas and find woodlands, fields, beaches or open countryside where your dog can exercise safely.

Cavaliers and Water

Cavaliers are Spaniels and Spaniels were bred to flush and retrieve game from land and water. Many Cavaliers enjoy swimming. If your dog enjoys it, swimming is an excellent way for dogs to exercise; many veterinary clinics now use water tanks, not only for remedial therapy, but also for canine recreation.

Remember that swimming is a lot more strenuous for a dog than walking or even running. Don't constantly throw that ball into the water for long periods - your Cavalier will fetch it back until she drops. Your dog should exercise within her limits; overstretching could place a strain on the heart. We also advise gently drying under your Cavalier's ear flaps after swimming to reduce the risk of ear infections.

Not all Cavaliers like water and not all are natural swimmers – yours might not have inherited 'the water gene'! Some dogs have a natural fear of water. Never force a dog into water that doesn't want to go; you will only make your dog even more fearful. If you live near water and/or want your dog to enjoy it, introduce him or her while still a puppy.

Start off by getting the feet wet, NOT by throwing a ball into water. Allow a young dog to build up confidence. Once used to getting wet feet, throw an object (preferably not one that will float into deep water) into the shallows and encourage your Cavalier to fetch. You can even get into the shallow water yourself to give encouragement. Then gradually throw the object into slightly deeper water. All of this should be done over a period of time on separate visits, not in a single day.

Avoid very cold weather and choppy water. Like a child, if a young dog gets frightened of water or loses confidence, he or she is unlikely to want to go near water as an adult. If you are regularly near water, you might want to get a life vest, which will keep your dog afloat even when exhausted.

Establish a Routine

Establish an exercise regime early in your dog's life. If possible, get your dog used to a walk or walks at the same time every day, at a time that fits in with your daily routine. For example, take your dog out after her morning feed, then again in the afternoon and a toilet trip last thing at night. Whatever routine you decide on, stick to it. To those owners who say their dog is happy and getting enough exercise playing in the yard or garden, just show her the lead (leash) and see how she reacts. Do you think she is excited at the prospect of leaving the home environment and going for a walk? Of course she is. Nothing is quite as exciting as investigating interesting new scents and places. Why do you think they would escape given half the chance?!

Older dogs still need exercise to keep their body, joints and systems functioning properly. They need a less strenuous regime – they are usually happier with shorter walks, but still enough to keep them physically and mentally active. Again, every dog is different, some are willing and able to keep on running to the end of their lives. The exception is if your old or sick dog is struggling – she will show you that she doesn't feel well enough to walk far by stopping and looking at you or sitting down and refusing to move.

Regular exercise can add months or even years to a dog's life.

Many Cavaliers love snow, but it can sometimes present problems with clumps of snow and ice building up on paws, ears, legs and tummy. Salt or de-icing products on roads and pathways can also cause irritation – particularly if he or she tries to lick it off - as they can contain chemicals that are poisonous to dogs. If your dog gets iced up, you can bathe paws and anywhere else affected in lukewarm - NOT HOT - water. If your dog spends a lot of time in snow, you might invest in a quality paw wax (pictured) or a pair of canine snow boots, which are highly effective in preventing snow and ice balls forming on paws – provided you can get the boots to stay on!

Dennis and Tina Homes added this advice: "Whilst in icy conditions and where rock salt has been laid, do make sure when you return from your walks you immerse your dog's feet in warm water to wash out the salt, which can be toxic if ingested. After every walk you should also check their feet to make sure there are no cuts, grazes or grass seeds that have penetrated the soft tissue between the pads, which is a common cause of distress in dogs during hot dry summer months. Small stones and grit can also become lodged between their pads, as can discarded chewing gum, and again in warmer weather, molten tar deposits can also be a hazard."

Mental Stimulation

Without mental challenges, a dog can become bored, unresponsive, destructive, attention-seeking and/or needy. You should factor in play time with your dog – even gentle play time for old dogs. If your dog's behaviour deteriorates or she suddenly starts chewing things he's not supposed to or barking a lot, the questions you should ask yourself are: "Is she getting enough exercise?" and "Am I leaving her alone for too long?"

Boredom through lack of exercise or mental stimulation - such as being alone and staring at four walls a lot - leads to bad behaviour or depression, and it's why some dogs end up in rescue centres, through no fault of their own. On the other hand, a Cavalier at the heart of the family getting regular exercise and mental stimulation is a happy dog and a loyal companion second to none.

Exercising Puppies

There are strict guidelines to stick to with puppies, as it is important not to over-exercise young pups as their bones and joints are still soft and cannot tolerate a lot of stress. Too much impact can cause permanent damage. So, playing Fetch or Frisbee for hours on end with your young Cavalier is definitely not a good plan, nor is allowing a pup to freely run up and down stairs in your home.

You'll end up with a damaged dog and a pile of vet's bills.

We are often asked how much to exercise a pup. Just like babies, puppies have different temperaments and energy levels; some will need more exercise than others. Start slowly and build it up. The worst danger is a combination of over-exercise and overweight when puppy is growing.

Don't take your pup out of the yard or garden until the all-clear after the vaccinations - unless you carry him or her around to start the socialisation process. Begin with daily short walks on the lead. Puppies have enquiring minds. Get yours used to being outside the home environment and experiencing new situations as soon as possible. The general guideline is:

Five minutes of on-lead exercise per month of age

* So, a total of 15 minutes when three months (13 weeks)

* 30 minutes when six months (26 weeks) old, etc.

This applies until around one year to 18 months old, when most of their growing has finished. Slowly increase the time as (s)he gets used to being exercised and this will gradually build up muscles and stamina. It is OK for your young pup to have free run of your garden or yard, once you have plugged any gaps in the fence, provided it has a soft surface such as grass, not concrete. It is also fine for your pup to run freely around the house to burn off energy - although not up and down stairs.

A pup will take things at her own pace and stop to sniff or rest. If you have other dogs, restrict the time the pup is allowed to play with them, as (s)he won't know when (s)he's had enough. When older, your dog can go out for much longer walks.

And when your little pup has grown into a beautiful adult Cavalier with a skeleton capable of carrying him or her through a long and healthy life, it will have been worth all the effort. Remember:

A long, healthy life is best started slowly

Cavalier Exercise Tips

- Don't over-exercise puppies or allow them to race up and down stairs

- Aim for at least one walk away from the house every day

- Vary your exercise route – it will be more interesting for both of you

- Triple check the fencing around your garden or yard to prevent The Great Escape

- If you want your dog to retrieve, don't fetch the ball or toy back yourself or he will never learn. Train him when young by giving praise or a treat when he brings the ball or toy back to your feet

- Do not throw a ball or toy repeatedly for a dog if he shows signs of over-exertion. Your Cavalier will fetch to please you and because it's great fun. Stop the activity after a while - no matter how much he begs you to throw it again

- The same goes for swimming, which is an exhausting exercise for a dog. Ensure any exercise is within your dog's capabilities – look out for heavy panting. Gentle swimming, if your dog enjoys it, is a good activity for all dogs, and particularly beneficial for older dogs as it is low impact on joints

- Don't strenuously exercise your dog straight after or within an hour of a meal as this can cause Bloat. More normally seen in deep-chested dogs, Canine Bloat can affect any breed and is extremely serious, if not fatal. See **Chapter 12. Cavalier Health** for details

- Cavaliers need play time as well as walk time. It keeps their minds exercised – and they love the interaction with their beloved owner

- Exercise old dogs more gently - especially in cold weather when it is harder to get their bodies moving. Have a cool-down period after exercise to reduce stiffness and soreness; it helps to remove lactic acids from the dog's body. Our 13-year-old loves a body rub

- If you throw a stick, try not to let your dog chew it to bits, as splinters can get lodged in the mouth – or worse

- Make sure your dog has constant access to fresh water. Dogs can only sweat a tiny amount through the pads of their paws, they need to drink water to cool down

Admittedly, when it is pouring down with rain, freezing cold (or scorching hot), the last thing you want to do is to venture outdoors with your dog. And in all likelihood, your Cavalier may not be too keen either! But make the effort; the lows are more than compensated for by the highs. Exercise helps you bond with your dog, keep fit, see different places and meet new companions - both canine and human. In short, it enhances both your lives.

Socialisation

Your adult dog's character will depend largely on two things. The first is her temperament, which she is born with, and presumably one of the reasons you have chosen a Cavalier. (The importance of picking a good breeder who selects breeding stock based on temperament, physical characteristics and health cannot be over-emphasised). The second factor is environment – or how you bring her up and treat her. In other words, it's a combination of **nature and nurture**. And one absolutely essential aspect of nurture is socialisation.

Scientists have come to realise the importance that socialisation plays in a dog's life. We also now know that there is a fairly small window that is the optimum time for socialisation - and this is up to the age of around four or five months. Most young animals, including dogs, are naturally able to get used to their everyday environment until they reach a certain age. When they reach this age, they become much more suspicious of things they haven't yet experienced. This is why it often takes longer to train an older dog.

The age-specific natural development allows a puppy to get comfortable with the normal sights, sounds, people and animals that will be a part of her life. It ensures that she doesn't spend her life jumping in fright or growling at every blowing leaf or sudden noise. The suspicion that dogs develop later also ensures that they react with a healthy dose of caution to new things that could really be dangerous - Mother Nature is clever!

Socialisation means 'learning to be part of society', or 'integration'. When we talk about socialising puppies, it means helping them learn to be comfortable within a human society that includes many different types of people, environments, buildings, traffic, sights, noises, smells, animals, other dogs, etc. It is essential that your dog's introductions to new people, animals, places, etc. are all **positive**, as negative experiences lead to a dog becoming fearful and untrusting.

Your dog may already have a wonderful temperament, but she still needs socialising to avoid her thinking that the world is tiny and it revolves around her - which in turn leads to unwanted adult behaviour traits. Cavaliers can be demanding enough of your attention without developing a 'Little Emperor' complex as well!

Good socialisation helps puppies – whether bold or timid - to learn their place in society and become more relaxed and integrated adults. It will give your dog confidence and teach her not to be afraid of new experiences. The ultimate goal of socialisation is to have a happy, well-adjusted dog that you can take anywhere.

Ever seen a therapy Cavalier in action and noticed how incredibly well-adjusted to life they are? This is no coincidence. These dogs have been extensively socialised and are ready and able to deal in a calm manner with whatever situation they encounter. They are relaxed and comfortable in their own skin - just like you want your dog to be.

Start socialising your puppy as soon as you bring her home; start around the house and garden and, if it is safe, carry her out of the home environment. Regular socialisation should continue until your dog is around 18 months of age. After that, don't just forget about it; socialisation isn't only for puppies, it should continue throughout your dog's life. As with any skill, if it is not practised, your dog will become less proficient at interacting with other people, animals and environments.

Developing the Well-Rounded Adult Dog

Well-socialised puppies usually develop into safer, more relaxed and enjoyable adult dogs. This is because they're more comfortable in a wider variety of situations than poorly socialised canines. Dogs that have not been properly integrated are much more likely to react with fear or aggression to unfamiliar people, dogs and experiences. Cavaliers that are relaxed about other dogs, honking horns, cats, farm animals, cyclists, veterinary examinations, traffic, crowds and noise are easier to live with than dogs who find these situations challenging or frightening.

And if you are planning on showing your dog or taking part in canine competitions, get her used to the buzz of these events early on. Well-socialised dogs also live more relaxed, peaceful and happy lives than dogs that are constantly stressed by their environment. Socialisation isn't an "all or nothing" project. You can socialise a puppy a bit, a lot, or a whole lot. The wider the range of positive experiences you expose her to when young, the better her chances are of becoming a more relaxed adult. Don't over-face your little puppy.

Socialisation should never be forced, but approached systematically and in a manner that builds confidence and curious interaction. If your pup finds a new experience frightening, take a step back, introduce her to the scary situation much more gradually, and make a big effort to do something she loves during the situation or right afterwards.

For example, if your puppy seems to be frightened by noise and vehicles at a busy road, a good method would be to go to a quiet road, sit with the dog away from - but within sight of - the traffic. Every time she looks towards the traffic say "YES" and reward her with a treat. If she is still stressed, you need to move further away.

When your dog takes the food in a calm manner, she is becoming more relaxed and getting used to traffic sounds, so you can edge a bit nearer - but still just for short periods until she becomes totally relaxed. Keep each session short and **positive.**

Meeting Other Dogs

When you take your gorgeous and vulnerable little pup out with other dogs for the first few times, you are bound to be a little nervous. To start with, introduce your puppy to just one other dog — one that you know to be friendly, rather than taking her straight to the park where there are lots of dogs of all sizes racing around, which might frighten the life out of your timid little darling.

Always make the initial introductions on neutral ground, so as not to trigger territorial behaviour. You want your Cavalier to approach other dogs with confidence, not fear. From the first meeting, help both dogs experience good things when they're in each other's presence. Let them sniff each other briefly, which is normal canine greeting behaviour. As they do, talk to them in a happy, friendly tone of voice; never use a threatening tone. Don't allow them to sniff each other for too long as this may escalate to an aggressive response. After a short time, get the attention of both dogs and give each a treat in return for obeying a simple command, such as "Sit" or "Stay." Continue with the "happy talk", food rewards and simple commands.

Of course, if you have more than one dog, your puppy will learn to socialise within the pack. However, you should still spend time introducing her to new sights, sounds and animals. Here are some signs of fear to look out for when your dog interacts with other canines:

- Running away
- Freezing on the spot
- Frantic/nervous behaviour, e.g. excessive sniffing, drinking or playing frenetically with a toy
- A lowered body stance or crouching
- Lying on her back with paws in the air – this is a submissive gesture
- Lowering of the head, or turning the head away
- Lips pulled back baring teeth and/or growling
- Hair raised on her back (hackles)
- Tail lifted in the air
- Ears high on the head

Some of these responses are normal. A pup may well crouch on the ground or roll on to her back to show other dogs she is not a threat. Try not to be over-protective, your puppy has to learn how to interact with other dogs, but if the situation looks like escalating into something more aggressive, calmly distract the dogs or remove your puppy – don't shout or shriek. The dogs will pick up on your fear and this in itself could trigger an unpleasant situation.

Another sign to look out for is eyeballing. In the canine world, staring a dog in the eyes is a challenge and may trigger an aggressive response. This is more relevant to adult dogs, as a young pup will soon be put in her place by bigger or older dogs; it is how they learn. The rule of thumb with puppy socialisation is to keep a close eye on your pup's reaction to whatever you expose her to so that you can tone things down if she seems at all frightened.

Always follow up a socialisation experience with praise, petting, a fun game or a special treat. One positive sign from a dog is the play bow, when she goes down on to her front elbows but keeps her backside up in the air. This is a sign that she is feeling friendly towards the other dog and wants to play.

Although Cavaliers are not naturally aggressive dogs, aggression is often grounded in fear, and a dog that mixes easily is less likely to be aggressive. Similarly, without frequent and new experiences, some Cavaliers can become timid and nervous. Take your new dog everywhere you can. You want her to feel relaxed and calm in any situation, even noisy and crowded ones. Take treats with you and praise her when she reacts calmly to new situations.

Once settled into your home, introduce her to your friends and teach her not to jump up. If you have young children, it is not only the dog that needs socialising! Youngsters also need training on how to act around dogs, so both parties learn to respect the other.

An excellent way of getting your new puppy to meet other dogs in a safe environment is a puppy class. Ask around about local classes. Some vets and dog trainers run classes for very junior pups who have had all their vaccinations. These help pups get used to other dogs of a similar age.

Breeders and Owners on Exercise

"Little and often is the rule for pups. To begin with, make it a simple training and socialisation exercise. Just aim to get a little way up the road and back, but walking nicely on a lead. Take the pup to a safe fenced place and allow off lead exploring. Teach the pup to come to call in the garden, then call the pup back to you regularly, praise and let them go off again. A small pup will not want to go very far, so get them used to being off lead and coming back at this young age and then they will do it for life."

"When you have several dogs they will invariably interact and play among themselves. Single dogs, however, will need a regular time to be walked and played with."

"Ours can do a half-day walk or not be walked at all; she is very easy. She is very good with other dogs, but will chasing deer, rabbits, birds, etc. She does not like water or swimming. She was quick to learn to be trained, but not good at self-preservation in terms of avoiding cars and vehicles. They like to explore, so get a fence, as they are bad with vehicles and have no sense of danger."

"I probably exercise all my dogs for one to two hours each day, this does not change with energy levels or age. They all get two to three good walks of approximately one mile plus a lot of play time and training time each day."

"Exercise is something that must be done carefully and slowly and built up over a year, but it must be to a level that will be maintained. You can't suddenly stop as the dog will not understand why and risks him thinking he has disappointed you in some way because his daily walks have ceased." "When young we only exercise puppies for 10 minutes two to three times a day, then gradually increase the time." "Ours have 30 to 40 minutes at a gentle pace twice a day. This seems to enough to manage energy and keep them excited, although a friend's Cavalier only needs one walk per day."

"Cavaliers are devoted and easy to train. They can go on a five-mile walk, but don't go crazy if they don't get walked every day. They are a great dog for those with busy lives and fab with kids." "I exercise my dogs twice a day for 30 minutes with free access to the garden throughout the day."

11. Training

Training a young dog is like bringing up a child. Put in the effort early on to teach him or her some rules and you will be rewarded with a well-adjusted, sociable individual who will be a joy to live with and take anywhere. Cavaliers have a reputation for a gentle temperament and a desire to be with and please their owners.

Dogs are not clones and you can get some more stubborn or independent-minded Cavaliers, but generally the breed is relatively easy to train. However, YOU have to put in the time too. Cavaliers make wonderful companions, but let yours behave exactly how he or she wants and you may well finish up with an attention-seeking adult who rules your life.

The secret of good training can be summed up quite simply:

* Consistency
* Praise
* Patience
* Reward

Cavaliers are highly motivated by reward – especially praise as well as treats - and this is a big bonus when it comes to training. Your dog WANTS to please you and enjoys learning. All you have to do is spend the time teaching her what you want her to do, then repeat the actions so it becomes second nature.

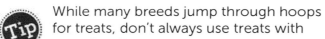 While many breeds jump through hoops for treats, don't always use treats with your Cavalier, as your praise is often enough reward. If you do use treats, try getting your pup used to a small piece of carrot or apple as a healthy, low-calorie alternative to traditional dog treats.

Many owners would say that Cavaliers are gentle, sensitive and have empathy (the ability to pick up on the feelings of others); some are even a bit wimpy. All of them respond well to your encouragement and a positive atmosphere, they do not respond well to shouting or heavy-handed training methods. Cavaliers are certainly 'biddable', i.e. it is not difficult to teach them commands, provided you make it clear exactly what you want them to do; don't give conflicting signals. They can be trained in a number of different fields.

The Intelligence of Dogs

Psychologist and canine expert Dr Stanley Coren has written a book called **The Intelligence of Dogs** in which he ranks the breeds. He surveyed dog trainers to compile the list and used *Understanding of New Commands* and *Obeying First Command* as his standards of intelligence. He says there are three types of dog intelligence:

* Adaptive Intelligence (learning and problem-solving ability). This is specific to the individual animal and is measured by canine IQ tests

* Instinctive Intelligence. This is specific to the individual animal and is measured by canine IQ tests

🐾 Working/Obedience Intelligence. This is breed-dependent

He divides dogs into six groups and the brainboxes of the canine world are the 10 breeds ranked in the 'Brightest Dogs' section of his list. It will come as no surprise to anyone who has ever been into the countryside and seen sheep being worked by a farmer and his right-hand man (his dog) to learn that the Border Collie is the most intelligent of all dogs. The other nine are, in order: Poodle, German Shepherd Dog, Golden Retriever, Doberman Pinscher, Shetland Sheepdog, Papillon, Rottweiler, Australian Cattle Dog. All dogs in this class:

🐾 Understand New Commands with Fewer than Five Repetitions

🐾 Obey a First Command 95% of the Time or Better

Fans of Cavaliers may be disappointed to learn that, along with the Akita, their beloved breed is languishing at Number 73 in the table out of 138 in the fourth group, described as 'Average Working/Obedience Intelligence, Understanding of New Commands: 25 to 40 repetitions. Obey First Command: 50% of the time or better.' The full list can be seen here: https://en.wikipedia.org/wiki/The_Intelligence_of_Dogs

By the author's own admission, the drawback of this rating scale is that it is heavily weighted towards obedience-related behavioural traits, which are often found in working dogs, rather than understanding or creativity (found in hunting dogs). As a result, some dogs, such as the Bully breeds – Bulldogs, Mastiffs, Bull Terriers, Pugs, French Bulldogs, etc. - are ranked quite low on the list, due to their independent or stubborn nature.

However, as far as Cavaliers are concerned, it's true to say that you are starting out with a dog that has the intelligence to pick up new commands quickly and really wants to please you. You just have to convince her that good things will happen when she obeys your commands!

Most of the breeders thought that Dr Coren's verdict on Cavaliers was about right. One said: "It's probably fair. Cavaliers have plenty of intelligence to train for Obedience, Rally, Agility, etc. but not so much that they think for themselves too much, like a working breed might do." Another added: "I think they should be higher up the list they are very obedient and are known to be good working/assistance dogs." One breeder strongly disagreed with Dr Coren, saying: "I do not think this is a fair assessment of the breed. In my opinion, the Cavaliers they judged had probably not been worked with, I have seen my fair share of spoiled Cavaliers whose owners have not worked with the dogs. On the most part, I see Cavaliers as pretty easy to train, from three weeks on, and they want to please."

Five Golden Rules

Five golden rules when training a Cavalier are:

1. Training must be reward-based, not punishment based.
2. Keep sessions short or your dog will get bored.
3. Never train when you are in a rush or a bad mood.
4. Training after exercise is fine, but never train when your dog is exhausted.
5. Keep sessions fun; give your Cavalier a chance to shine!

Energetic or independent Cavaliers may try to push the boundaries when they reach adolescence, i.e. as they come out of puppyhood and before they mature into adults, and some may act like spoiled children if allowed to. If you have a high spirited, high energy dog, you have to use your brain to think of ways that will make training challenging and to persuade your dog that what you want her to do is actually what SHE wants to do!

She will come to realise that when she does what you ask of her, something good happens – verbal praise, pats, play time, healthy treats, etc. You need to be firm with a strong-willed or stubborn dog, but all training should still be carried out using positive techniques.

Establishing the natural order of things is not something forced on a dog through shouting or violence; it is brought about by mutual consent and good training.

Cavaliers are happiest and behave best when they are familiar and comfortable with their place in the household. If you have adopted an older dog, you can still train her, but it will take a little longer to get rid of bad habits and instil good manners. Patience and persistence are the keys here.

Socialisation is a very important aspect of training. Your puppy's breeder should have already begun this process with the litter and then it's up to you to keep it going when the pup arrives home. Young pups can absorb a great deal of information, but they are also vulnerable to bad experiences. They need exposing – in a positive manner - to different people, other animals and situations; if not, they can find them very frightening when they do finally encounter them later. They may react by cowering, urinating, barking, growling or even snapping. If they have a lot of good experiences with other people, places, noises, situations and animals before four or five months old, they are less likely to: a) be timid or nervous, or b) try to establish dominance later.

Don't just leave your dog at home in the early days, take her out and about with you, get her used to new people, places and noises. Dogs that miss out on being socialised can pay the price later.

All young Cavaliers are chewers. If you are not careful, some young pups and adolescents will chew through anything – wires, phone chargers, remote controls, bedding, rugs, etc. Young dogs are not infrequent visitors to veterinary clinics to have 'foreign objects' removed from their stomachs.

Train your young Cavalier only to chew the things you give her – so don't give her your old slippers, an old piece of carpet or anything that resembles something you don't want her to chew, she won't know the difference between the old and the new. Buy purpose-made long-lasting chew toys.

Breeder Philippa Biddle says: "One puppy I sold got into a habit of picking up a stone from the driveway every time they went out for a walk. The owner got very upset and fussed and tried to remove it. I am sure this dog saw it as an attention seeking activity. One day she did swallow it and had to have an operation to have it removed.

"All puppies, like babies, will firstly explore the world around them by taste and texture and put everything in their mouths. Usually, they roll it round and spit it out. It's important to resist the urge to grab things they have got in their mouths. In the dog kingdom the rule i: "If it's in my mouth, it's mine." They will nearly always give it up if offered something better, like a biscuit or a treat or a toy or a bit of tissue or paper from your pocket, if that's all you have to hand - and it's safer than what they have got!"

Jumping up is another common issue. Cavaliers are generally enthusiastic about life, so it's often a natural reaction when they see somebody. You don't, however, want your dog to jump up on

Granny when she has just come back from a romp through the muddy woods and a swim in a dirty pond. Teach her while still small not to jump up!

A puppy class is one of the best ways of getting a pup used to being socialised and trained. This should be backed up by short sessions of a few minutes of training a day back home.

Cavaliers are a good choice for first-time dog owners, and anybody prepared to put a bit of time in should be able to train one. But if you do need some extra one-on-one tuition (for you and the dog!) from a professional, make sure you choose a trainer registered with the Association of Professional Dog Trainers (APDT) - you can find details at the back of this book — who uses positive reward-based training methods, as the old alpha-dominance theories have largely been discredited.

When you train your dog, it should never be a battle of wills; it should be a positive learning experience for you both. Bawling at the top of your voice or smacking should play NO part in training any dog, but especially one as sensitive and loving as the Cavalier.

12 Training Tips

1. Start training and socialising straight away. Like babies, puppies learn quickly and it's this learned behaviour that stays with them through adult life. Puppy training should start with a few minutes a day two or three days after he has arrived home, even if he's only a few weeks old. The critical window is up to four or five months.

2. Your voice is a very important training tool. Your dog has to learn to understand your language and you have to understand him. Commands should be issued in a calm, authoritative voice - not shouted. Praise should be given in a happy, encouraging voice, accompanied by stroking or patting. If your dog has done something wrong, use a stern voice, not a harsh shriek. This applies even if your Cavalier is unresponsive at the beginning.

3. Avoid giving your dog commands you know you can't enforce. Every time you give a command that you don't enforce, she learns that commands are optional. One command equals one response. Give your dog only one command - twice maximum - then gently enforce it.

   Repeating commands or nagging will make her tune out, and teach her that the first few commands are a bluff. Telling your dog to **"SIT, SIT, SIT, SIT!!!"** is neither efficient nor effective. Give your dog a single "SIT" command, gently place her in the sitting position and then praise her.

4. Train your dog gently and humanely. Cavaliers are sensitive by nature and do not respond well to being shouted at or hit. Keep training sessions short and upbeat so the whole experience is enjoyable for you and for her. If obedience training is a bit of a bore, pep things up a bit by 'play training' by using constructive, non-adversarial games.

5. Begin your training around the house and garden or yard. How well your dog responds to you at home affects his behaviour away from the home as well. If she doesn't respond well at home, she certainly won't respond any better when she's out and about where there are 101 distractions, such as interesting scents, food scraps, other dogs, people, cats, etc.

6. Cavaliers usually love their food and mealtimes are a great time to start training. Teach your dog to sit and stay at breakfast and dinnertime, rather than just putting the dish down and letting her dash over immediately. In the beginning, she won't know what you mean, so gently place her into the sit position while you say "Sit." Place a hand on her chest during the "Stay" command - gradually letting go — and then give her the command to eat her dinner, followed by encouraging praise - she'll soon get the idea.

7. When you bring your pup or new dog home, use her name often and in a positive manner so she gets used to the sound of it. She won't know what it means in the beginning, but it won't take her long to realise you're talking to her.

8. DON'T use her name when reprimanding, warning or punishing. She should trust that when she hears her name, good things happen. She should always respond to her name with enthusiasm, never hesitancy or fear. Use words such as "No," "Ack!" or "Bad Girl/Boy" in a stern (not shouted) voice instead.

   Some parents prefer not to use "No" with their dog, as they use it so often around the kids that it can confuse the pup! When a puppy is corrected by her mother, e.g. – if she bites her – she growls to warn her not to do it again. Using a short sharp sound like **"Ack!"** can work surprisingly well; it does for us.

9. Don't give your dog lots of attention (even negative attention) when she misbehaves. Dogs like attention. If yours gets lots when she jumps up on you, her bad behaviour is being reinforced. If she jumps up, push her away, use the command "No" or "Down" and then ignore her.

10. Timing is critical. When your puppy does something right, praise her immediately. If you wait a while, she will have no idea what she has done right. Similarly, when she does something wrong, correct her straight away. For example, if she eliminates in the house, don't shout and certainly don't rub her nose in it; this will only make things worse. If you catch her in the act, use your "No" or "Ack" sound and immediately carry her out of the house. Then use your toilet command and praise your pup or give her a treat when she performs. If your pup is constantly eliminating indoors, you are not keeping a close enough eye on her.

11. In the beginning, give your dog attention when YOU want to – not when she wants it. When you are training, give your puppy lots of positive attention when she is good. But if she starts jumping up, nudging you constantly or barking to demand your attention, ignore her. Don't give in to her demands. Wait a while and pat her when you want and after she has stopped demanding your attention.

12. Start as you mean to go on. In other words, in terms of rules and training, treat your cute little pup as though she were a fully-grown Cavalier; introduce the rules you want her to live by as an adult. If you don't want your dog to take over your couch or bed or jump up at people when she is an adult, train her not to do it when she is small. You can't have one set of rules for a pup and one set for a fully-grown dog; she won't understand. Also make sure that

everybody in the household sticks to the same set of rules. Your dog will never learn if one person lets him jump on the couch and another person doesn't.

Philippa added: "Dogs like to know what their job is, so give them a job before they choose one for themselves! They look to the leader for instruction and guidance, so the most important first thing is to get them to look at you and reward that. You will find them just standing watching you.

"Catch their eye and say "Good dog", give them a pat and sometimes a treat. If you can get them looking at you and giving you their attention, ready for the next command, the training will be much, much easier. To that end, give plenty of kind commands like Come Here, Sit, Down, Lie down, Go to Bed - even when it is not really necessary .

Teaching Basic Commands

Sit - Teaching the Sit command to your Cavalier is relatively easy. Teaching a young pup to sit still for a few seconds is a bit more difficult! In the beginning you may want to put your protégé on a lead (leash) to hold his attention.

Stand facing each other and hold a treat between your thumb and fingers just an inch or so above his head. Don't let your fingers and the treat get much further away or you might have trouble getting him to move his body into a sitting position. In fact, if your dog jumps up when you try to guide him into the Sit, you're probably holding your hand too far away from his nose. If your dog backs up, you can practise with a wall behind him.

As he reaches up to sniff it, move the treat upwards and back over the dog towards his tail at the same time as saying "Sit." Most dogs will track the treat with their eyes and follow it with their noses, causing their snouts to point straight up.

As his head moves up toward the treat, his rear end should automatically go down towards the floor. TaDa! (drum roll!)

As soon as he sits, say "Yes!" Give him the treat and tell your dog (s)he's a good boy or girl. Stroke and praise him for as long as he stays in the sitting position. If he jumps up on his back legs and paws you while you are moving the treat, be patient and start all over again. Another method is to put one hand on his chest and with your other hand, gently push down on his rear end until he is sitting, while saying "Sit." Give him a treat and praise, even though you have made him do it, he will eventually associate the position with the word 'sit'.

Once your dog catches on, leave the treat in your pocket (or have it in your other hand). Repeat the sequence, but this time your dog will just follow your empty hand. Say "Sit" and bring your empty hand in front of your dog's nose, holding your fingers as if you had a treat. Move your hand exactly as you did when you held the treat.

When your dog sits, say "Yes!" and then give him a treat from your other hand or your pocket.

Gradually lessen the amount of movement with your hand. First, say "Sit" then hold your hand eight to 10 inches above your dog's face and wait a moment. Most likely, he will sit. If he doesn't, help him by moving your hand back over his head, like you did before, but make a smaller movement this time. Then try again. Your goal is to eventually just say "Sit" without having to move or extend your hand at all.

Once your dog reliably sits on cue, you can ask him to sit whenever you meet and talk to people (admittedly, it may not work straight away, but it might help to calm him down a bit). The key is anticipation. Give your dog the cue before he gets too excited to hear you and before he starts jumping up on the person just arrived. Generously reward him the instant he sits. Say "Yes" and give treats every few seconds while he holds the Sit.

Whenever possible, ask the person you're greeting to help you out by walking away if your dog gets up from the sit and lunges or jumps towards him or her. With many consistent repetitions of this exercise, your dog will learn that lunging or jumping makes people go away, and polite sitting makes them stay and give him attention.

You can practise training your bouncy Cavalier not to jump up by arranging for a friend to come round, then for him or her to come in and out of the house several times. Each time, show the treat, give the Sit command (initially, don't ask your dog to hold the sit for any length of time), and then allow him to greet your friend. Ask your friend to reach down to pat your dog, rather than standing straight and encouraging the dog to jump up for a greeting.

If your dog is still jumping up, you can use a harness and lead inside the house to physically prevent him from jumping up at people, while still training him to sit when someone arrives. Treats and praise are the key. (You can also use the "Off" command - and reward with praise or a treat for success - when you want your dog NOT to jump up at a person, or not to jump up on furniture). 'Sit' is a useful command and can be used in a number of different situations. For example, when you are putting his lead on, while you are preparing his meal, when he returned the ball you have just thrown, when he is jumping up, demanding attention or getting over-excited.

Come - This is known as "the recall" and is a basic command that you can teach right from the beginning. Teaching your dog to come to you when you call is an important lesson. A dog who responds quickly and consistently can enjoy freedoms that other dogs cannot. Although you might spend more time teaching this command than any other, the benefits make it well worth the investment. Despite what the AKC (American Kennel club) says, Cavaliers love to run free, but you can't allow that in open spaces until your dog has learned the recall.

Tip "Come" or a similar word is better than "Here" if you intend using the "Heel" command, as Here and Heel sound too similar.

Whether you're teaching a young puppy or an older Cavalier, the first step is always to establish that coming to you is the best thing he can do. Any time your dog comes to you whether you've called him or not, acknowledge that you appreciate it. You can do this with praise, affection, play or treats. This consistent reinforcement ensures that your dog will continue to "check in" with you frequently.

1. Say your dog's name followed by the command "Come!" in an enthusiastic voice. You'll usually be more successful if you walk or run away from him while you call. Dogs find it hard to resist chasing after a running person, especially their owner.

2. He should run towards you. NOTE: Dogs tend to tune us out if we talk to them all the time. Whether you're training or out for an off-lead walk, refrain from constantly chattering to your dog - no matter how much of a brilliant conversationalist you are! If you're quiet much of the time, he is more likely to pay attention when you call him. When he does, praise him.

3. Often, especially outdoors, a young dog will start running towards you but then get distracted and head off in another direction. Pre-empt this situation by praising your puppy and cheering him on when he starts to come to you and **before** he has a chance to get distracted. Your praise will keep him focused so that he'll be more likely to come all the way to you. If he stops or turns away, you can give him feedback by saying "Uh-uh!" or "Hey!" in a different tone of voice (displeased or unpleasantly surprised). When he looks at you again, smile, call him and praise him as he approaches you.

4. When your puppy comes to you, give him the treat BEFORE he sits down or he may think that the treat was earned for sitting, not coming to you.

Progress your dog's training in baby steps. If he's learned to come when called in your kitchen, you can't expect him to be able to do it straight away at the park or on the beach when he's surrounded by distractions. When you first try this outdoors, make sure there's no one around to distract your dog. It's a good idea to consider using a long training lead - or to do the training within a safe, fenced area. Only when your dog has mastered the recall in a number of locations and in the face of various distractions can you expect him to come to you regularly.

....

Down - There are a number of different ways to teach this command, which here means for the dog to lie down. (If you are teaching this command, then use the **"Off"** command to teach your dog not to jump up). This does not come naturally to a young pup, so it may take a little while for him to master the Down command. Don't make it a battle of wills and, although you may gently push him down, don't physically force him down against his will. This will be seen as you asserting dominance in an aggressive manner and your Cavalier will not like it.

1. Give the 'Sit' command.

2. When your dog sits, don't give him the treat immediately, but keep it in your closed hand. Slowly move your hand straight down toward the floor, between his front legs. As your dog's nose follows the treat, just like a magnet, his head will bend all the way down to the floor.

3. When the treat is on the floor between your dog's paws, start to move it away from him, like you're drawing a line along the floor. (The entire luring motion forms an L-shape).

4. At the same time say "Down" in a firm manner.

5. To continue to follow the treat, your dog will probably ease himself into the Down position. The instant his elbows touch the floor, say "Yes!" and immediately let him eat the treat. If your dog doesn't automatically stand up after eating the treat, just move a step or two away to encourage him to move out of the Down position. Then repeat the sequence above several times. Aim for two short sessions of five minutes per day.

If your dog's back end pops up when you try to lure him into a Down, quickly snatch the treat away. Then immediately ask your dog to sit and try again. It may help to let your dog nibble on the treat as you move it toward the floor. If you've tried to lure your dog into a Down, but he still seems confused or reluctant, try this trick:

1. Sit down on the floor with your legs straight out in front of you. Your dog should be at your side. Keeping your legs together and your feet on the floor, bend your knees to make a 'tent' shape.

2. Hold a treat right in front of your dog's nose. As he licks and sniffs the treat, slowly move it down to the floor and then underneath your legs. Continue to lure him until he has to crouch down to keep following the treat.

3. The instant his belly touches the floor, say "Yes!" and let him eat the treat. If your dog seems nervous about following the treat under your legs, make a trail of treats for him to eat along the way.

Some dogs find it easier to follow a treat into the Down from a standing position.

🐾 Hold the treat right in front of your dog's nose, and then slowly move it straight down to the floor, right between his front paws. His nose will follow the treat

🐾 If you let him lick the treat as you continue to hold it still on the floor, your dog will probably plop into the Down position

🐾 The moment he does, say "Yes!" and let him eat the treat (some dogs are reluctant to lie on a cold, hard surface. It may be easier to teach yours to lie down on a carpet). The next step is to introduce a hand signal. You'll still reward him with treats, though, so keep them nearby or hidden behind your back.

1. Start with your dog in a Sit.

2. Say "Down."

3. Without a treat in your fingers, use the same hand motion you did before.

4. As soon as your dog's elbows touch the floor, say "Yes!" and immediately get a treat to give him. Important: Even though you're not using a treat to lure your dog into position, you must still give him a reward when he lies down. You want your dog to learn that he doesn't have to see a treat to get one.

5. Clap your hands or take a few steps away to encourage him to stand up. Then repeat the sequence from the beginning several times for a week or two. When your dog readily lies down as soon as you say the cue and then use your new hand signal, you're ready for the next step.

    You probably don't want to keep bending all the way down to the floor to make your Cavalier lie down. To make things more convenient, you can gradually shrink the signal so that it becomes a smaller movement. To make sure your dog continues to understand what you want him to do, you'll need to progress slowly.

6. Repeat the hand signal, but instead of guiding your dog into the Down by moving your hand all the way to the floor, move it almost all the way down. Stop moving your hand when it's an inch or two above the floor. Practise the Down exercise for a day or two, using this slightly smaller hand signal. Then you can make your movement an inch or two smaller, stopping your hand three or four inches above the floor.

7. After practising for another couple of days, you can shrink the signal again. As you continue to gradually stop your hand signal farther and farther from the floor, you'll bend over less and less. Eventually, you won't have to bend over at all. You'll be able to stand up straight, say "Down," and then just point to the floor.

Your next job is a bit harder - it's to practise your dog's new skill in many different situations and locations so that he can lie down whenever and wherever you ask him to. Slowly increase the level of distraction; for example, first practise in calm places, like different rooms in your house or in your garden, when there's no one else around. Then increase the distractions; practise at home when family members are moving around, on walks and then at friends' houses, too.

....

Stay - This is a very useful command, but it's not so easy to teach a lively and distracted young Cavalier pup to stay still for any length of time. Here is a simple method to get your dog to stay; if you are training a young dog, don't ask him to stay for more than a few seconds at the beginning.

 This requires some concentration from your dog, so pick a time when he's relaxed and well exercised, or just after a game or mealtimes - but not exhausted when he is too tired to concentrate.

1. Tell your dog to sit or lie down, but instead of giving a treat as soon as he hits the floor, hold off for one second. Then say "Yes!" in an enthusiastic voice and give him a treat. If your dog bounces up again instantly, have two treats ready. Feed one right away, before he has time to move; then say "Yes!" and feed the second treat.

2. You need a release word or phrase. It might be "Free!" or "Here!" or a word that you only use to release your dog from this command. Once you've given the treat, immediately give your release cue and encourage your dog to get up. Then repeat the exercise, perhaps up to a dozen times in one training session, gradually wait a tiny bit longer before releasing the treat. (You can delay the first treat for a moment if your dog bounces up).

3. A common mistake is to hold the treat high and then give the reward slowly. As your dog doesn't know the command yet, he sees the treat coming and gets up to meet the food. Instead, bring the treat toward your dog quickly - the best place to deliver it is right between his front paws. If you're working on a Sit-Stay, give the treat at chest height.

4. When your dog can stay for several seconds, start to add a little distance. At first, you'll walk backwards, because your dog is more likely to get up to follow you if you turn away from him. Take one single step away, then step back towards your dog and say "Yes!" and give the treat. Give him the signal to get up immediately, even if five seconds haven't passed. The stay gets harder for your dog depending on how long it is, how far away you are, and what else is going on around him.

5. Trainer shorthand is **"distance, duration, distraction."** For best success in teaching a Stay, work on one factor at a time. Whenever you make one factor more difficult, such as distance, ease up on the others at first, then build them back up. So, when you take that first step back from your dog, adding distance, you should cut the duration of the stay.

6. Now your dog has mastered the Stay with you alone, move the training on so that he learns to do the same with distractions. Have someone walk into the room, or squeak a toy or bounce a ball once. A rock-solid stay is mostly a matter of working slowly and patiently to start with. Don't go too fast - the ideal scenario is that your Cavalier never breaks out of the Stay position until you release him.

If he does get up, take a breather and then give him a short refresher, starting at a point easier than whatever you were working on when he cracked. If you think he's tired or had enough, leave it for the day and come back later – just finish off on a positive note by giving one very easy command you know he will obey, followed by a treat reward.

Don't use the Stay command in situations where it is unpleasant for your dog. For instance, avoid telling him to stay as you close the door behind you on your way to work. Finally, don't use Stay to keep a dog in a scary situation.

Cavaliers can do so much more than sit and stay! They are biddable and their great desire to please their owners means that they can be trained in different fields. Their gentle nature makes then suitable for therapy work; they can also be trained for showing, agility, canine freestyle (dancing with dogs), rallying, obedience and other canine competitions.

The Cavalier may be a Toy breed with a reputation for a sweet disposition, but it is still a Spaniel with a sporting background. Some have more hunting instinct than others and love nothing more than going back to their roots to flush out game on a shoot - which is why some Cavaliers love to chase anything smaller than themselves!

Puppy Biting and Chewing

All Cavalier puppies spend a great deal of time chewing, playing, and investigating objects. And it's natural for them to explore the world with their mouths and needle-sharp teeth.

When puppies play with people, they often bite, chew, nip and mouthe on people's hands, limbs and clothing. Play biting is normal for puppies; they do it all the time with their littermates. They also bite moving targets with their sharp teeth; it's a great game.

But when they arrive in your home, they have to be taught that human skin is sensitive and body parts are not suitable biting material. Biting is not acceptable, not even from a puppy, and can be a real problem initially, especially if you have children.

When your puppy bites you or the kids, she is playing and investigating; she is NOT being aggressive. Even though the breed has a reputation for being sweet, lively young Cavaliers can easily get carried away with energy and excitement. This is when puppy biting can develop into a problem if it isn't checked.

Make sure every time you have a play session, you have a soft toy nearby and when she starts to chew your hand or feet, clench your fingers (or toes!) to make it more difficult and distract her with a soft toy in your other hand.

Keep the game interesting by moving the toy around or rolling it around in front of her. (She may be too young to fetch it back if you throw it). She may continue to chew you, but will eventually realise that the toy is far more interesting and lively than your boring hand.

If she becomes over-excited and too aggressive with the toy, if she growls a lot, stop playing with her and walk away. When you walk away, don't say anything or make eye or physical contact with your puppy. Simply ignore her, this is extremely effective and often works within a few days.

If your pup is more persistent and tries to bite your legs as you walk away, thinking this is another fantastic game, stand still and ignore her. If she still persists, say "No!" in a very stern voice, then praise her when she lets go. If you have to physically remove her from your trouser leg or shoe, leave her alone in the room for a while and ignore her demands for attention if she starts barking.

Although you might find it quite cute and funny if your puppy bites your fingers or toes, it should be discouraged at all costs. You don't want your Cavalier doing this as an adolescent or adult, when she can inadvertently cause real injury.

Here are some tips to deal with puppy biting:

- Puppies growl and bite more when they are excited. Don't allow things to escalate, so remove your pup from the situation before she gets too excited by putting her in a crate or pen

- Don't put your hand or finger into your pup's mouth to nibble on; this promotes puppy biting

- Limit your children's play time with pup - and always supervise the sessions in the beginning. Teach them to gently play with and stroke your puppy, not to wind her up

- Don't let the kids (or adults) run round the house with the puppy chasing – this is an open invitation to nip at the ankles

- If your puppy does bite, remove her from the situation and people – never smack her

Many Cavaliers are sensitive and another method that can be very successful is to make a sharp cry of **"Ouch!"** when your pup bites your hand – even when it doesn't hurt.

This worked very well for us. Your pup may well jump back in amazement, surprised that he has hurt you. Divert your attention from your puppy to your hand. He will probably try to get your attention or lick you as a way of saying sorry. Praise him for stopping biting and continue with the game. If he bites you again, repeat the process. A sensitive dog should soon stop biting you.

You may also think about keeping the toys you use to play with your puppy separate from other toys. That way he will associate certain toys with having fun with you and will work harder to please you. Cavaliers are playful and you can use this to your advantage by teaching your dog how to play nicely with you and the toy and then by using play time as a reward for good behaviour.

As mentioned, puppies explore the world by putting things into their mouths. Other reasons for chewing is that it is a normal part of the teething process, and some adolescent and adult dogs chew because they are bored - usually due to lack of exercise and/or mental stimulation.

If puppy chewing is a problem it is because your pup is chewing on something you don't want him to. So, the trick is to keep him, his mouth and sharp little teeth occupied with something he CAN chew on, such as a durable toy – see **Chapter 6. Bringing Your Puppy Home** for more information.

You might also consider freezing peanut butter and/or a liquid inside a Kong toy (pictured). Put the Kong into a mug, plug the small end with peanut butter and fill it with gravy before putting it into the freezer. (Check the peanut butter doesn't contain the sweetener xylitol as this can is harmful to dogs). Don't leave the Kong and your Cavalier on your precious Oriental rug!

This will keep your pup occupied for quite a long time. It is also worth considering giving the dog a frozen Kong or Lickimat when you leave the house if your dog suffers from separation anxiety. There are lots of doggie recipes for frozen Kongs online.

Clicker Training

Clicker training is a method of training that uses a sound - a click - to tell an animal when she does something right. The clicker is a tiny plastic box held in the palm of your hand, with a metal tongue that you push quickly to make the sound. The clicker creates an efficient language between a human trainer and a trainee.

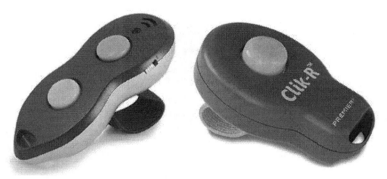

First, a trainer teaches a dog that every time she hears the clicking sound, she gets a treat. Once the dog understands that clicks are always followed by treats, the click becomes a powerful reward. When this happens, the trainer can use the click to mark the instant the animal performs the right behaviour. For example, if a trainer wants to teach a dog to sit, he'll click the instant her rump hits the floor and then deliver a tasty treat. With repetition, the dog learns that sitting earns rewards.

So, the 'click' takes on huge meaning. To the animal it means: "What I was doing the moment my trainer clicked, that's what he wants me to do." The clicker in animal training is like the winning buzzer on a game show that tells a contestant he's just won the money! Through the clicker, the trainer communicates precisely with the dog, and that speeds up training.

Although the clicker is ideal because it makes a unique, consistent sound, you do need a spare hand to hold it. For that reason, some trainers prefer to keep both hands free and instead use a one-syllable word like **"Yes!"** or **"Good!"** to mark the desired behaviour. In the steps below, you can substitute the word in place of the click to teach your pup what the sound means.

It's easy to introduce the clicker to your Cavalier. Spend half an hour or so teaching her that the sound of the click means "Treat!" Here's how:

1. Sit and watch TV or read a book with your dog in the room. Have a container of (healthy) treats within reach.

2. Place one treat in your hand and the clicker in the other. (If your dog smells the treat and tries to get it by pawing, sniffing, mouthing or barking at you, just close your hand around the treat and wait until he gives up and leaves you alone).

3. Click once and immediately open your hand to give your dog the treat. Put another treat in your closed hand and resume watching TV or reading. Ignore your dog.

4. Several minutes later, click again and offer another treat.

5. Continue to repeat the click-and-treat combination at varying intervals, sometimes after one minute, sometimes after five minutes. Make sure you vary the time so that your dog doesn't know exactly when the next click is coming. Eventually, she'll start to turn toward you and look expectantly when she hears the click - which means she understands that the sound of the clicker means a treat is coming her way.

If your dog runs away when she hears the click, you can make the sound softer by putting it in your pocket or wrapping a towel around your hand that's holding the clicker. You can also try using a different sound, like the click of a retractable pen or the word "Yes!"

Clicker Training Basics

Once your dog seems to understand the connection between the click and the treat, you're ready to get started.

1. Click just once, right when your pup does what you want her to do. Think of it like pressing the shutter of a camera to take a picture of the behaviour.

2. Remember to follow every click with a treat. After you click, deliver the treat to your puppy's mouth as quickly as possible.

3. It's fine to switch between practising two or three behaviours within a session, but work on one command at a time. For example, say you're teaching your dog to sit, lie down and raise her paw. You can do 10 repetitions of sit and take a quick play break. Then do 10 repetitions of down and take another quick break. Then do 10 repetitions of stay, and so on. Keep training sessions short and stop before you or your dog gets tired of the game.

 When training, always set your dog up to succeed, not fail. If she has been struggling with a new command, end training sessions on a good note with something she can do.

Collar, Harness and Lead (Leash) Training

You have to train your dog to get used to a collar and/or harness and lead (leash), and then she has to learn to walk nicely beside you. Teaching these manners can be challenging because young Cavaliers are lively and don't necessarily want to walk at the same pace as you! All dogs will pull on a lead initially. This isn't because they want to show you who's boss, it's simply that they are excited to be outdoors and are forging ahead.

You might prefer to use a body harness instead. Harnesses work very well with Cavaliers; they take the pressure away from the dog's sensitive neck area and distribute it more evenly around the body. Many owners use harnesses, although the dogs may also have a collar with an ID tag. Harnesses with a chest ring for the lead can be effective for training. When your dog pulls, the harness turns her around.

Another option is to start your dog on a small lightweight collar and then change to a harness once she has learned some lead etiquette. Some dogs don't mind collars, some will try to fight them, while others will slump to the floor! You need to be patient and calm and proceed at a pace comfortable to her; don't fight your dog and don't force the collar on.

1. If you start your puppy off with a collar, you need a small, lightweight one - not one she is going to grow into. You can buy one with clips to start with, just put it on and clip it together, rather than fiddling with buckles, which can be scary when she's wearing a collar for the first time. Stick to the principle of positive reward-based training and give a treat or praise once the collar is on, not after you have taken it off. Then gradually increase the length of time you leave the collar on.

IMPORTANT: If you leave your dog in a crate, or leave her alone in the house, take off the collar. She is not used to it and it may get caught on something, causing panic or injury to your dog.

2. Put the collar on when there are other things that will occupy her, like when she is going outside to be with you, or in the home when you are interacting with her. Or put it on at mealtimes or when you are doing some basic training. Don't put the collar on too tight, you

want her to forget it's there; you should be able to get two fingers underneath. Some pups may react as if you've hung a two-ton weight around their necks, while others will be more compliant. If yours scratches the collar, get her attention by encouraging her to follow you or play with a toy to forget the irritation.

3.   Once your puppy is happy wearing the collar, introduce the lead. Many owners prefer an extending or retractable lead for their Cavalier, but you might want to consider a fixed-length lead to start training her to walk close to you. Start off in the house or garden; don't try to go out and about straight away.

Think of the lead as a safety device to stop her running off, not something to drag her around with. You want a dog that doesn't pull, so don't start by pulling her around; you don't want to get into a tug-of-war contest.

This photo shows how NOT to do it.

4.   Attach the lead to the collar and give her a treat while you put it on. The minute it is attached, use the treats (instead of pulling on the lead) to lure her beside you, so that she gets used to walking with the collar and lead. As well as using treats you can also make good use of toys to do exactly the same thing - especially if your dog has a favourite. Walk around the house with the lead on and lure her forwards with the toy.

It might feel a bit odd but it's a good way for your pup to develop a positive relationship with the collar and lead with the minimum of fuss. Act as though it's the most natural thing in the world for you to walk around the house with your dog on a lead – and just hope that the neighbours aren't watching! Some dogs react the moment you attach the lead and they feel some tension on it – a bit like when a horse is being broken in for the first time. Drop the lead and allow her to run round the house or yard, dragging it after her, but be careful she doesn't get tangled and hurt herself.

Try to make her forget about it by playing or starting a short fun training routine with treats. Treats are a huge distraction for most young dogs. While she is concentrating on the new task, occasionally pick up the lead and call her to you. Do it gently and in an encouraging tone.

5.   The most important thing is not to yank on the lead. If it gets tight, just lure her back beside you with a treat or a toy while walking. All you're doing is getting her to move around beside you. Remember to keep your hand down (the one holding the treat or toy) so your dog doesn't get the habit of jumping up at you.

If you feel she is getting stressed when walking outside on a lead, try putting treats along the route you'll be taking to turn this into a rewarding game: good times are ahead... That way she learns to focus on what's ahead of her with curiosity and not fear.

Take collar and lead training slowly, give your pup time to process all this new information about the lead. Let her gain confidence in you, and then in the lead and herself. Some dogs can sit and decide not to move! If this happens, walk a few steps away, go down on one knee and encourage her to come to you using a treat, then walk off again.

For some pups, the collar and lead can be restricting and they will react with resistance. Some dogs are perfectly happy to walk alongside you off-lead, but behave differently when they have one on. Proceed in tiny steps if that is what your puppy is happy with, don't over face her, but stick at it if you are met with resistance. With training and patience, your puppy will learn to walk nicely on a lead; it is a question of when, not if.

Harnesses

These are very popular with owners of Cavaliers as they do not put any strain on the neck. There are several different options:

- **Front-clip or training harness -** this has a lead attachment in front of the harness at the centre of your dog's chest. Dog trainers often choose this type as it helps to discourage your dog from pulling on the lead by turning her around

- **Back-clip –** this is generally the easiest for most dogs to get used to and useful for small dogs with delicate throats that are easily irritated by collars. This type is for calm dogs or ones that have already been trained not to pull on the lead

- **Comfort wrap or step-in harness -** lay the harness on the ground, have your dog step in, pull the harness up and around her shoulders and then clip her in; simple!

- **Soft or vest harness -** typically made of mesh and comes in a range of colours and patterns. Some slip over the head and some can be stepped into

- **No-pull harness -** similar to a training harness, designed to help discourage your dog from pulling. The lead attachment ring is at the centre of the dog's chest and the harness tightens pressure if the dog pulls, encouraging him to stay closer to you. Some styles also tighten around the dog's legs

- **Auto or car harness -** these are designed for car travel and have an attachment that hooks into a seat belt

When choosing a harness, decide what its primary purpose will be – is it instead of or in addition to a collar? Do you need one that will help to train your dog, or will a back-clip harness do the job?

You want to make sure that it is a snug fit for your dog, and if it's a front clip, that it hangs high on your dog's chest. If it dangles too low, it can't help control forward momentum.

Make sure the harness isn't too tight or too difficult to get on. It shouldn't rub under your dog's armpits or anywhere else. If possible, take your dog to try on a few options before buying one for the first time.

 If you've never used a harness before, it's easy to get tangled up while your pup is bouncing around, excited at the prospect of a walk. It's a good idea to have a few "dry runs" without the dog!

Lay the harness on the floor and familiarise yourself with it. Learn which bits the legs go through, which parts fit where and how it clicks together once the dog is in. If you can train your Cavalier to step into the harness, then even better...!

Walking on a Lead

There are different methods, but we have found the following one to be successful for quick results. Initially, the lead should be kept fairly loose. Have a treat in your hand as you walk, it will encourage your dog to sniff the treat as she walks alongside. She will not pull ahead as she will want to remain near the treat.

Give her the command **"Walk"** or **"Heel"** and then proceed with the treat in your hand, keep giving her a treat every few steps initially, then gradually extend the time between treats. Eventually, you should be able to walk with your hand comfortably at your side, periodically (every minute or so) reaching into your pocket to grab a treat to reward your dog.

If your dog starts pulling ahead, first give her a warning, by saying "No" or "Steady," or a similar command. If she slows down, give her a treat. But if she continues to pull ahead so that your arm becomes fully extended, stop walking and ignore your dog. Wait for her to stop pulling and to look up at you. At this point reward her for good behaviour before carrying on your walk.

A very tall breeder has this tip: "Constantly bending down to lead train can be difficult, so I put liver paste in the ball end of a ball thrower. It means I can use that to reward the dog when they're in the right place at my side without bending down!"

If your pup refuses to budge, DON'T drag her. This will ultimately achieve nothing as she will learn to resent the lead. Coax her along with praise and, if necessary, treats so that when she moves forward with you, it is because SHE wants to and not because she has been dragged by somebody 10 or 20 times bigger.

Be sure to quickly reward your dog any time she doesn't pull and walks with you with the lead slack. If you have a lively young pup who is dashing all over the place on the lead, try starting training when she is already a little tired, after a play or exercise session – but not exhausted.

Another method is what dog trainer Victoria Stillwell describes as the Reverse Direction Technique. When your dog pulls, say **"Let's Go!"** in an encouraging manner, then turn away from her and walk off in the other direction, without jerking on the lead. When she is following you and the lead is slack, turn back and continue on your original way.

It may take a few repetitions, but your words and body language will make it clear that pulling will not get your dog anywhere, whereas walking calmly by your side - or even slightly in front of you - on a loose lead will get her where she wants to go.

There is an excellent video (in front of her beautiful house!) which shows Victoria demonstrating this technique and highlights just how easy it is with a dog that's keen to please. It only lasts three minutes and is worth watching:

https://positively.com/dog-behavior/basic-cues/loose-leash-walking

Breeders on Training

Sandra Coles: "They are intelligent and can be trained easily. They love reward, whether it is by treat or word. They love the praise. I have one called Adam that can do 'high fives', sometimes it turns into ten! Another loves to dance and she is a natural. With more time and training, she would have been very good.

"There are amazing facilities to help with training today: puppy training classes, obedience and agility, dancing with dogs. These experts would help train you and your dog. One of my Cavaliers called Oddy has done agility and he loved it. My boys would often set up a training ring on the lawn for the older ones. The dogs are not allowed to take part until they are a certain age and most of their growing has been completed. The technique is lots of praise for reward, repeating the trick and then rewarding when they do it properly - but make it fun and don't let them become bored."

Philippa Biddle: "Firstly, ALWAYS BE GENTLE. Cavaliers hate to be reprimanded; they are very, very willing to please. The first thing is to train them to look at your eye for the command/communication. Then reward always works well - not always food or they can get too obsessed with the treat and forget the 'work' they are supposed to be doing! Affection and attention works just as well as a reward.

"They get bored training for too long. They don't have the attention span of some working dogs, so little and often and keep them busy. If they have to wait, for example in a training class, they just switch off and doze!!"

Dennis and Tina Homes: "Before we start putting a lead on a young puppy, we first get them use to wearing a collar (but they should not be left in a crate unattended with one on).

Pictured is Dennis and Tina's Leogem Glad News

"Although they cannot walk in the street before they have had all their injections, it's wise to get them used to a lead by walking them around the garden or house with one on. The best thing is to attach the lead and hold it, but let the puppy walk around with it on **leading you** and not you leading the dog. Just go wherever the dog takes you.

"Once the puppy is older and can go for walks they often start pulling on the lead. When you have your dog on a lead and you are about to step out of the door, DO NOT allow the dog to go first. Although the dog will accept you as pack leader inside your house or garden, they often want to assume the role of pack leader once they step outside into open territory, and whoever leads the way is pack leader.

"If you are out walking and the dog is on your left and begins to pull, call his name and give a deliberate: "NO!" Then do an about-turn to the right, so taking the lead and take the dog round in a full circle. This will probably confuse the dog, but that is the idea; you are reinforcing the notion that you are in charge. As soon as he starts to pull again, repeat the tactic. You will probably end up quite dizzy! But with a lot of patience it should eventually work."

Other breeders added: "Cavaliers love to learn things, but one should always keep it simple. To set a dog up to fail is not necessary or fair as they are born to please - and if you are wanting more from your dog, you did not do your homework when choosing a breed!"

"Training starts with the breeder. I find that Cavaliers are obedient and can be easily trained."

"You must be consistent and have a good routine; I treat-train. Having so many, I find that mine learn quickly from each other."

"What motivates Cavaliers is praise, praise, praise, petting and, of course, treats. A calm consistency is key to getting the Cavalier to obedience as well as tricks."

TREATS!!...Who's got the treats? Photo courtesy of Kathy Hargest.

We strongly recommend that all new owners book their puppy or rescue dog on to a basic training course.

Your Cavalier will really enjoy the experience and, as well as learning basic obedience, he or she will learn how to socialise with other dogs. It is also the best, least expensive way for owners to learn how to train their dog properly. Many local veterinary clinics now run puppy training classes.

Once you have mastered the basics, you can go on to learn more and win certificates on the Canine Good Citizen Dog Scheme.

More details are at: www.thekennelclub.org.uk/training/good-citizen-dog-training-scheme For the USA, AKC training clubs are listed here: http://webapps.akc.org/obedience-training-club/#/

GENERAL NOTE: If your puppy is in a hyperactive mood or extremely tired, he is not likely to be very receptive to training.

CREDIT: With thanks to the American Society for the Prevention of Cruelty to Animals for assistance with parts of this chapter. The ASPCA has a lot of good advice and training tips on its website at: www.aspca.org

Once you have a Cavalier, the world's your oyster!

12. Cavalier Health

Health has a major impact on an animal's quality of life and should always be a major consideration when choosing and raising a dog. The first step is to select a puppy from a breeder who produces Cavalier King Charles Spaniels that are sound in both body and temperament – and this involves health screening - and secondly, to play your part in keeping your dog healthy throughout his or her life.

NOTE: This chapter is intended to be used as a medical encyclopaedia to help you to identify potential health issues and act promptly in the best interests of your dog. Please don't read it thinking your Cavalier will get lots of these ailments – he or she WON'T!

....

It is becoming increasingly evident that genetics can have a huge influence on a person's health and life expectancy – which is why so much time and money is currently being devoted to genetic research. A human is more likely to suffer from a hereditary illness if the gene - or genes - for that disorder is passed on from parents or grandparents. That person is said to have a 'predisposition' to the ailment if the gene(s) is in the family's bloodline. Well, the same is true of dogs.

There is not a single breed without the potential for some genetic weakness. For example, German Shepherd Dogs are more prone to hip problems than many other breeds, and 30% of Dalmatians have problems with their hearing. If you get a German Shepherd or a Dalmatian, your dog will not automatically suffer from these issues, but if he or she comes from unscreened parents, the dog will statistically be more likely to have them than a dog from a breed with no history of the complaint.

In other words, 'bad' genes can be inherited along with good ones.

The average lifespan of Cavaliers is anything from nine to 14 years; a handful live longer. The Cavalier King Charles Spaniel Club (CKCSC) in America says: "Breed-wide, the average lifespan of a Cavalier is about 9-10 years." The UK Kennel Club carried out a study involving nearly 1,500 Cavaliers and found that the *median longevity* for the breed was 10 years. This means that 50% of the dogs died before this age and 50% after.

Of the dogs in the study, nearly one in five (19.73%) died of heart failure, 12.11% died of old age, 10.76% of cardiomyopathy (disease of the heart muscle), 7.17% of Syringomyelia, 6.73% of kidney failure and 4.04% of mitral valve disease (another heart condition).

A further study by UK veterinary practices involving 3,624 Cavaliers found that: "The most common specific disorders recorded during the study period were heart murmur (541 dogs, representing 30.9% of study group), diarrhoea of unspecified cause (193 dogs, 11.0%), dental disease (166 dogs, 9.5%), otitis externa - ear infections - (161, 9.2%), conjunctivitis (131, 7.4%) and anal sac infection (129, 7.4%). The five most common disorder categories were cardiac (affecting 31.7% of dogs), dermatological (22.2%), ocular (20.6%), gastrointestinal (19.3%) and dental/periodontal disorders (15.2%)." In other words: heart, skin, eyes, tummy and teeth.

Importance of Health Certificates

The Cavalier King Charles Spaniel was one of the breeds highlighted in the BBC documentary **Pedigree Dogs Exposed** which investigated health issues caused by the breeding of some purebred dogs. It was aired in the UK in 2008 and caused a stir around the world. In it, the UK Kennel Club was criticized for allowing breed standards, judging standards and breeding practices to compromise the health of pedigree (purebred) dogs.

A Cavalier was shown to be in agony with SM (Syringomyelia), due to the skull being too small for the brain. Cavaliers have a relatively small head and short muzzle - unlike other Spaniels which all have long noses - and are in fact classed as a *brachycephalic* (flat-faced) breed.

In the documentary, veterinary Neurologist Dr Claire Rusbridge described the Cavalier brain as: "A size 10 foot that's been shoved into a size 6 shoe", and estimated that up to one-third of the breed suffered from this problem. Cardiologist Simon Swift added that about half of all Cavaliers aged five would have heart murmurs and that by the age of 10 to 11, almost all Cavaliers would have a heart condition.

After the documentary, three separate health reports were commissioned. They concluded that current breeding practices were detrimental to the welfare of pedigree dogs and steps were taken to improve the health of breeds across the board. The Kennel Club took action by rolling out new health plans and reviewing the Breed Standard for every single breed.

As well as the relatively small skull and short muzzle, there is another reason why the Cavalier is not among the list of the healthiest dog breeds. There were very few examples of the breed left after World War II and all modern Cavalier King Charles Spaniels are descended from a tiny gene pool that, unfortunately, passed on some inheritable diseases as well as good genes.

The good news is that anyone thinking of getting a Cavalier puppy today can reduce the chance of their dog having a genetic disease by choosing a puppy from healthy bloodlines – and asking to see the parents' relevant health certificates.

If you've not got your puppy yet, you might be considering choosing your breeder based on the look or colour of her dogs, or their success in the show ring or other events, but you would be well advised to consider the health of the puppy's parents and ancestors as well.

Could they have passed on unhealthy genes to the puppy along with the good genes for all those features you are attracted to?

 Just because the puppy and parents are registered with the Kennel Club in the UK or AKC in the USA and have pedigree certificates, **it does not necessarily mean that they have passed any health tests**. All a pedigree certificate guarantees is that the puppy's parents can be traced back several generations and the ancestors were all purebred Cavalier King Charles Spaniels. Many pedigree (purebred) dogs have indeed passed health tests, but prospective buyers should always find out **exactly** what health screening the sire and dam (mother and father) have undergone - ask to see original certificates - and what, if any, health guarantees the breeder is offering with the puppy. **NOTE: "Vet Checked" does NOT mean health tested.**

If you're buying a puppy, ask to see these certificates for the parents:

USA:

- 🐾 **Heart** - CKCSC recommends a minimum of a cardiology clearance at age 2.5 years by a board-certified veterinary cardiologist
- 🐾 **Eyes** – CERF certificate by a board-certified veterinary ophthalmologist
- 🐾 **Patella Luxation** - from an evaluation by a licensed veterinarian
- 🐾 **Hip Dysplasia** - OFA certificate

UK:

- 🐾 **Eyes -** BVA/KC/ ISDS Eye Scheme or ECVO Scheme for various eye diseases. This is **mandatory** for KC Assured Breeders

The following certificates are recommended by the Kennel Club for all breeding Cavaliers:

- 🐾 **Heart -** breed club test for mitral valve dysplasia
- 🐾 **Chiari-like Malformation/Syringomyelia –** the KC recommends that dogs showing early onset of this skull disorder should not be used for breeding. As yet the only test is an MRI scan
- 🐾 **Episodic Falling (EF)** – a neurological disease
- 🐾 **Curly Coat Dry Eye (CC/DE)** – also called Dry Eye Curly Coat, this affects a Cavalier's skin and eyes

Tip Ideally you are looking for a five-star breeder who can provide all the relevant certificates for the puppy's parents. However, as an *absolute bare minimum*, you should be looking for heart and eye certificates for both parents, whichever country you live in, and you would be well advised to get a Cav puppy from a litter whose dam and sire have also both been screened for the distressing disease Syringomyelia (SM).

If you have already got your dog, don't worry! There is plenty of advice in this book on how to take good care of your dog. Feeding a quality food, monitoring your dog's weight, regular grooming and check-overs, plenty of exercise, socialisation and stimulation will all help to keep him or her in tiptop condition. Good, responsible owners can certainly help to extend the life of their Cavalier.

Breeders on Health

Our breeders have some advice for owners both before and after getting their puppy. Sandra Coles: "Ask to see certificates for the puppy's Mum and Dad and check that they are clear for the condition tested. For Cavaliers this is hearts, eyes and DNA testing for Dry Eye, Curly Coat and Episodic Falling, scans for SM and clear hearts in the parents." There is a better chance that the puppies will live a long and healthy life and you know that the breeder has done all they can to ensure this. Hearts should be checked yearly.

"Diet is very important and both my husband and I impress on new owners not to let their Cavalier become overweight. I see a lot of the puppies I have bred; new and old owners are often visiting and get reprimanded if that happens. Obesity is linked to heart disease, as can be bad teeth. Teeth should be cleaned throughout the dog's life. Hearts should be checked annually and most vets do this as routine when you visit. Losing weight, coughing, a build-up of fluid, exercise intolerance and collapse can all be signs of heart disease. Vets will grade a murmur and medicate if necessary."

Philippa Biddle, Hearthfriend Cavaliers, Norfolk: "Look at the health testing BEHIND the parents. Check out the Kennel Club health test pedigree of the parents. I always give buyers the pedigree name of the parents and ask them to double check the health test pedigree themselves."

Dennis and Tina Homes, Leogem Cavaliers, Herefordshire: "As with humans, dogs also have a number of inherent health problems and most breeds are prone to breed-specific ailments. The main ones with Cavaliers are Mitral Valve Disease of the heart (MVD), Syringomyelia (SM), Episodic Falling (EF), Dry Eye/Curly Coat (DE/CC) and Multifocal Retinal Dysplasia (MRD).

"There is now in place a DNA test for both EF and DE/CC and all breeding stock should be tested for these diseases. As they are recessive genes it is OK to breed a Carrier to a dog that tested Clear, but not two Carriers together, nor two Affected dogs.

"We always litter screen a litter of puppies at around eight or nine weeks for eye problems. As the pigment behind the retina is not fully filled in at this age, any retinal folds are clearly seen. We always have our dogs eye tested prior to breeding. MRI scanning for SM is recommended for potential breeding stock by the time they are two and a half, and we have our dogs heart tested annually.

"When we first became involved with the breed nearly 40 years ago, Slipping (Luxating) Patella was a major problem, as too was Juvenile Cataract. But with careful breeding both these diseases are hardly ever seen among Cavaliers from show lines these days. In fact, we've encountered show breeders who have only been involved during the past 10 years and didn't even know that Cavaliers ever had these problems. Most cases of Slipping Patella seem to be mainly from puppy farm-bred stock. However, it's very important that Cavalier owners should be aware of these diseases."

Julie Durham, Donrobby Cavaliers, Berkshire: "Cavaliers have a longer nose, unlike their cousins the King Charles Spaniel, so the brachycephalic traits are minimal or not evident. They do, however, have a soft palate so a sleeping Cavalier can be quite a noisy experience."
Photo of Louise courtesy of Julie.

"I always emphasise the fact that a fat, unexercised Cavalier is a recipe for heart problems. My hard work trying to eliminate heart problems is an ongoing exercise."

Philip Lunt, Oaktreepark Cavaliers, Staffordshire: "A puppy should always come from fully-heath tested parents which are clear of all known issues in the breed. Ask to see the certificates; you can also check on the Kennel Club or Cavalier King Charles Spaniel websites. Once you have your Cavalier, heart checks can be done every year at the time of booster vaccinations by any good vet. A more specialist test can be done if the owner desires. Signs of a heart issue tend to be coughing - reduced activity and an increase in weight all contribute to this."

Cavalier Insurance

Insurance is another point to consider for a new puppy or adult dog. The best time to get pet insurance is BEFORE you bring your Cavalier home and before any health issues develop. Don't wait until you need to seek veterinary help - bite the bullet and take out annual insurance. If you can afford it, take out life cover. This may be more expensive, but will cover your dog throughout his or her lifetime - including for chronic (recurring and/or long term) ailments, such as eye, heart or joint problems, ear infections and cancer.

Insuring a healthy puppy or adult dog is the only sure-fire way to ensure vets' bills are covered before anything unforeseen happens - and you'd be a rare owner if you didn't use your policy at least once during your dog's lifetime. According to the UK's Bought By Many, monthly cover for a healthy eight-week-old Cavalier varies from around £29 to £49, depending on where you live, how much excess you are willing to pay and the amount of total vets' bills covered per year.

In the UK, Bought By Many offers policies from insurers More Than at: https://boughtbymany.com/offers/cavalier-king-charles-spaniel-pet-insurance They get groups of single breed owners together, so you have to join the Cavalier King Charles Spaniel Group, but it claims you'll get a 10% saving on normal insurance. We are not on commission - just trying to save you some money! There are numerous companies out there offering pet insurance. Read the small print and the amount of excess; a cheap policy may not always be the best long-term decision.

I ran a few examples for US pet insurance on an eight-week-old Cavalier pup and came back with quotes from $31 to $51, depending on location, amount of coverage in dollars and deductible. With advances in veterinary science, there is so much more vets can do to help an ailing dog - but at a cost. Surgical procedures can rack up bills of thousands of pounds or dollars.

According to www.PetInsuranceQuotes.com these are some of the most common ailments affecting Cavaliers and typical treatment costs: Mitral Valve Disease $15,000-$20,000, Heart Murmur $100-$20,000, Degenerative Valve Disease $8,000-$15,000, Progressive Retinal Atrophy (PRA) $2,000-$3,000 per eye, Luxating Patella $1,500-$3,000, Hip Dysplasia $3,000-$6,000 and Epilepsy $500-$15,000. ($1.30 = approximately £1 at the time of writing).

PetInsuranceQuotes rated insurance companies based on coverage, cost, customer satisfaction and the company itself and came up with a top dozen: 1.Healthy Paws, 2.Petplan, 3.Pets Best, 4.Embrace, 5.Nationwide, 6.Trupanion, 7.Figo, 8.ASPCA, 9.Pet Premium, 10.PetFirst, 11.AKC Pet Insurance, 12.24PetWatch.

Of course, if you make a claim, your monthly premium will increase, but if you have a decent insurance policy BEFORE a recurring health problem starts, your dog should continue to be covered if the ailment returns. You'll have to decide whether the insurance is worth the money. On the plus side, you'll have peace of mind if your beloved Cavvie falls ill and you'll know just how much to fork out every month.

Another point to consider is that dogs are at increasing risk of theft by criminals, including organised gangs. With the purchase price of puppies rising, dognapping has shot up. More than 1,900 dogs were stolen in the UK in 2017. Some 49% of dogs are snatched from owners' gardens and 13% from people's homes. Check that theft is included on the policy. Although nothing can ever replace your favourite companion, good insurance will ensure you are not out of pocket.

Three Health Tips

1. **Buy a well-bred puppy** - A responsible breeder selects their stock based on:

   🐾 General health and DNA testing of the parents

   🐾 Conformation (physical structure)

   🐾 Temperament

   Although well-bred puppies are not cheap, believe it or not, committed Cavalier breeders are not in it for the money, often incurring high bills for health screening, stud fees, veterinary costs, specialised food, etc. The main concern of a good breeder is to produce healthy, handsome puppies with good temperaments and instincts that are "fit for function."

   Better to spend time beforehand choosing a good puppy than to spend a great deal of time and money later when your wonderful pet bought from an online advert or pet shop develops health problems due to poor breeding, not to mention the heartache that causes. **Chapter 4. Finding Your Cavalier Puppy** has detailed information on how to find him or her and the questions to ask.

   🐾 Don't buy from a pet shop - no reputable breeder allows her pups to end up in pet shops

   🐾 Don't buy a puppy from a small ad on a general website

   🐾 Don't buy a pup or adult dog unseen with a credit card - you are storing up trouble and expense for yourself. (If you have selected a reputable breeder located many states away in the USA and can't travel to see the puppy, make sure you ask lots of questions)

2. **Get pet insurance as soon as you get your dog** - Don't wait until your dog has a health issue and needs to see a vet. Most insurers will exclude all pre-existing conditions on their

   policies. When choosing insurance, check the small print to make sure that all conditions are covered and that if the problem is recurring, it will continue to be covered year after year. When working out costs, factor in the annual or monthly pet insurance fees and trips to a vet for check-ups, annual vaccinations, etc. Some breeders provide free insurance for the first few weeks in their Puppy Pack - ask yours if this is the case.

3. **Find a good vet** - Ask around your pet-owning friends, rather than just going to the first one you find. A vet that knows your dog from his or her puppy vaccinations and then right through their life is more likely to understand your dog and diagnose quickly and correctly when something is wrong. If you visit a big veterinary practice, ask for the vet by name when you make an appointment.

We all want our dogs to be healthy - so how can you tell if yours is? Well, here are some positive things to look for in a healthy Cavalier King Charles Spaniel:

Signs of a Healthy Cavalier

1. **Eyes -** A Cavalier's eyes should not be too prominent or too close together. They should be round in shape and dark brown with very dark rims. Paleness around the eyeball (conjunctiva) could be a sign of underlying problems. A red swelling in the corner of one or both eyes could be cherry eye. Sometimes the dog's third eyelid (the nictating membrane) is visible at the eye's inside corner - this is normal. There should be no thick, green or yellow discharge from the eyes. A cloudy eye could be a sign of cataracts.

2. **Nose –** A dog's nose is an indicator of health symptoms. Normal nose colour is black, although some Cavalier pups are born with pink patches that usually turn black during the first year, sometimes called a 'butterfly nose'. Regardless of colour, the nose should be moist and cold to the touch as well as free from clear, watery secretions.

   Any yellow, green or foul smelling discharge is not normal - in younger dogs this can be a sign of canine distemper. A pink nose or 'snow nose' may appear in winter due to a lack of Vitamin D, but the nose usually returns to a darker colour during summer – it happens more often with lighter coloured Cavaliers. A 'Dudley nose' or 'putty nose' is one where the nose, the area around the eyes and the feet lack any pigment from birth to old age and appear pink. Some dogs' noses turn pinkish with age; this is because their bodies are producing less pigment and is not a cause for concern. Avoid getting a Cavalier puppy with small, pinched nostrils, as these may cause breathing difficulties.

3. **Ears –** If you are choosing a puppy, gently clap your hands behind the pup (not so loud as to frighten him) to see if he reacts. If not, this may be a sign of deafness. Also, ear infections – sometimes known as "otitis" - can be a problem with Cavaliers and other breeds with floppy, hairy ears. A pricked-up ear allows air to circulate, while a folded ear flap creates a warm, moist haven for mini horrors such as bacteria and mites. The ear flap can also trap dirt and dust and should be inspected during your regular grooming routine. An unpleasant smell, redness or inflammation are all signs of infection. Some wax inside the ear – usually brown or yellowy - is normal; excessive wax or crusty wax is not. Tell-tale signs of an infection are scratching the ears, rubbing them on the floor or furniture, or shaking the head a lot, often accompanied by an unpleasant smell.

4. **Mouth –** Gums should be a healthy pink or black colour, or a mixture. A change in colour can be an indicator of a health issue. Paleness or whiteness can be a sign of anaemia or lack of oxygen due to heart or breathing problems (this is hard to tell with black gums). Blue gums or tongue are a sign that your Cavvie is not breathing properly. Red, inflamed gums can be a sign of gingivitis or other tooth disease. Again, your dog's breath should smell OK. Young dogs will have sparkling white teeth, whereas older dogs will have darker teeth, but they should not have any hard white, yellow, green or brown bits.

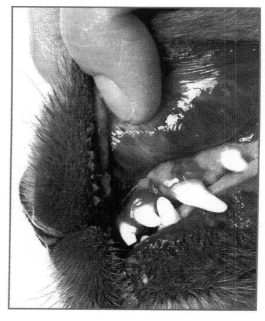

5. **Coat and Skin –** These are easy-to-monitor indicators of a healthy dog. A Cavalier has a double layer coat with silky soft hair that sheds. Any dandruff, bald spots, a dull lifeless coat, a discoloured

or oily coat, or one that loses excessive hair, can all be signs that something is amiss. Skin should be smooth without redness. If a puppy or adult dog is scratching, licking or biting himself a lot, he may have a condition that needs addressing before he makes it worse. Open sores, scales, scabs, red patches or growths can be a sign of a problem. Signs of fleas, ticks and other external parasites should be treated immediately. Check there are no small black specks, which may be fleas, on the coat or bedding.

6. **Weight** – A general rule of thumb is that your dog's stomach should be above the bottom of his rib cage when standing, and you should be able to feel his ribs beneath his coat without too much effort. If the stomach is level or hangs below, your dog is overweight - or may have a pot belly, which can also be a symptom of other conditions.

7. **Temperature** – The normal temperature of a dog is 101°F to 102.5°F. (A human's is 98.6°F). Excited or exercising dogs may run a slightly higher temperature. Anything above 103°F or below 100°F should be checked out. The exceptions are female dogs about to give birth that will often have a temperature of 99°F. If you take your dog's temperature, make sure he or she is relaxed and **always** use a purpose-made canine thermometer.

8. **Stools** - Poo, poop, business, faeces - call it what you will - it's the stuff that comes out of the less appealing end of your Cavalier on a daily basis! It should be firm and brown, not runny, with no signs of worms or parasites. Watery stools or a dog not eliminating regularly are both signs of an upset stomach or other ailments. If it continues for a couple of days, consult your vet. If puppies have diarrhoea they need checking out much quicker as they can quickly dehydrate.

9. **Energy** – Cavaliers retain some of their sporty ancestry and are lively, engaged dogs. Yours should have good amounts of energy with fluid and pain-free movements. Lack of energy or lethargy – if it is not the dog's normal character – could be a sign of an underlying problem.

10. **Smell** – If there is a musty, 'off' or generally unpleasant smell coming from your Cavalier's body, it could be a sign of a yeast infection. There can be a number of reasons for this; often the ears require attention or it can sometimes be an allergy to a certain food. Another not uncommon cause with this breed is that one of the anal glands has become blocked and needs expressing, or squeezing - a job best left to the vet or groomer unless you know what you are doing! Whatever the cause, you need to get to the root of the problem as soon as possible before it develops into something more serious.

11. **Attitude** – A generally positive attitude is a sign of good health. Cavaliers are lively and playful, so symptoms of illness may include one or all of the following: a general lack of interest in his or her surroundings, tail not wagging, lethargy, not eating food and sleeping a lot (more than normal). The important thing is to look out for any behaviour that is out of the ordinary for your individual dog.

So now you know some of the signs of a healthy dog – what are the signs of an unhealthy one? There are many different symptoms that can indicate your canine companion isn't feeling great. If you don't yet know your dog, his habits, temperament and behaviour patterns, then spend some time getting acquainted with them.

What are his normal character and temperament? Lively or calm, playful or serious, a joker or an introvert, bold or nervous, happy to be left alone or loves to be with people, a keen appetite or a fussy eater? How often does he empty his bowels, does he ever vomit? (Dogs will often eat grass to make themselves sick, this is perfectly normal and a natural way of cleansing the digestive system).

You may think your Cavalier can't talk, **but he can!** If you really know your dog, his character and habits, then he CAN tell you when he's not well. He does this by changing his patterns. Some symptoms are physical, some emotional and others are behavioural. It's important for you to be able to recognise these changes as soon as possible. Early treatment can be the key to keeping a simple problem from snowballing into something more serious.

If you think your dog is unwell, it is useful to keep an accurate and detailed account of his symptoms to give to the vet, perhaps even take a video of him on your mobile phone. This will help the vet to correctly diagnose and effectively treat your dog.

Four Vital Signs of Illness

1. **Temperature** - A new-born puppy will have a temperature of 94-97°F. This will reach the normal adult body temperature of 101°F at about four weeks old. As stated, anything between 100°F and 102.5°F is regarded as normal for an adult dog.

   The temperature is normally taken via the rectum. If you do this, be very careful. It's easier if you get someone to hold your dog while you do this. Digital thermometers are a good choice, but **only use one specifically made for rectal use,** as normal glass thermometers can easily break off in the rectum. Ear thermometers are available (pictured) - from Amazon and Walmart among others - making the task much easier, although they can be expensive and don't suit all dogs' ears.

   Ear Thermometer

   Remember that exercise or excitement can cause the temperature to rise by 2°F to 3°F when your dog is actually in good health, so wait until he is relaxed before taking his temperature. If it is above or below the norms and he seems off-colour, give your vet a call.

2. **Respiratory Rate** - Another symptom of canine illness is a change in breathing patterns. This varies a lot depending on the size and weight of the dog. An adult dog will have a respiratory rate of 15-25 breaths per minute when resting. You can easily check this by counting your dog's breaths for a minute with a stopwatch handy. Don't do this if he is panting; it doesn't count.

3. **Heart Rate** - You can feel your Cavalier's heartbeat by placing your hand on his lower ribcage – just behind the elbow. Don't be alarmed if the heartbeat seems irregular compared to that of a human; it IS irregular in some dogs. Your dog will probably love the attention, so it should be quite easy to check his heartbeat. Just lay him on his side and bend his left front leg at the elbow, bring the elbow in to his chest and place your fingers on this area and count the beats.

   - Tiny dogs have a heartbeat of up to 160 or 180 beats per minute
   - Small to medium dogs have a normal rate of 90 to 140 beats per minute. (A Cavalier's heartbeat should be between 70 and 120 beats per minute)

- Dogs weighing more than 30lb have a heart rate of 60 to 120 beats per minute; the larger the dog, the slower the normal heart rate

- A young puppy has a heartbeat of around 220 beats per minute

- An older dog has a slower heartbeat

4. **Behaviour Changes -** Classic symptoms of illness are any inexplicable behaviour changes. If there has NOT been a change in the household atmosphere, such as another new pet, a new baby, moving home, the absence of a family member or the loss of another dog, then the following symptoms may well be a sign that all is not well:

- Depression

- Anxiety and/or trembling

- Falling or stumbling

- Loss of appetite

- Walking in circles

- Being more vocal - grunting, whining and/or whimpering

- Aggression

- Tiredness - sleeping more than normal and/or not wanting to exercise

- Abnormal posture

Your dog may normally show some of these signs, but if any of them appear for the first time or worse than usual, you need to keep him under close watch for a few hours or even days. Quite often he will return to normal of his own accord. Like humans, dogs have off-days too.

If he is showing any of the above symptoms, then don't over-exercise him, and avoid stressful situations and hot or cold places. Make sure he has access to clean water. There are many other signals of ill health, but these are four of the most important. Keep a record for your vet, if your dog does need professional medical attention, most vets will want to know:

WHEN the symptoms first appeared in your dog

WHETHER they are getting better or worse, and

HOW FREQUENT the symptoms are. Are they intermittent, continuous or increasing?

This chapter highlights ailments which can affect the breed. However, this should not put you off the Cavalier King Charles Spaniel. They are the most loving, loyal, attractive, biddable and characterful dogs; no other breed is quite like the Cavalier.

But it does mean that if you have or are considering getting one, you'd be well advised to take extra care regarding health. Once you've got your dog, getting to know his or her character, habits and temperament will go a long way towards spotting the early signs of ill health.

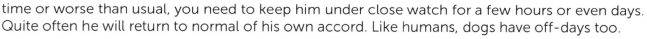

The Heart

Just as with humans, heart problems are fairly common among the canine population in general. However, **Mitral Valve Disease (MVD)** is the biggest killer of Cavaliers. While MVD affects about 10% of older dogs of other breeds, it affects a huge percentage of Cavaliers - and at an earlier age. One study suggests that half of all Cavaliers have a heart murmur (usually the first indication of MVD) by the age of five and nearly 100% have one by 10 years old. The Kennel Club says that it "affects more than 40% of the breed in the UK alone."

Of course, the best advice is to get a puppy whose parents have tested clear of heart issues. But if you already have your dog, don't worry, there is plenty you can do to prolong his or her life. A heart murmur does NOT mean that your dog will die of a heart attack - our dog had a murmur for six or seven years and died of old age at 13. In fact, dogs don't have sudden heart attacks like humans, they experience a gradual onset of symptoms.

The heart muscle is a pump that moves blood through the four chambers using involuntary contractions. Blood is pumped around the body via a one-way system. The valves between the chambers form a tight seal that prevent the blood from flowing backwards into the chamber it has just come from, so the blood is always flowing forwards.

When the valves degenerate over time, they become thickened and deformed, losing their tight seal and causing some blood to seep backwards. When the valve between the left atrium and left ventricle – i.e. the mitral valve - no longer forms a tight seal, blood moves back into the left atrium. This means the heart has to work harder to pump the volume of blood the body needs for normal functions.

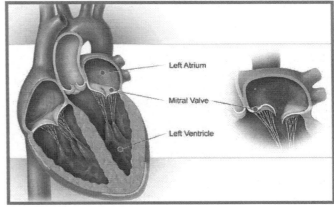

Symptoms

- Heart murmur
- Tiredness
- Decreased activity levels
- Restlessness, pacing around instead of settling down to sleep
- Intermittent coughing, especially during exertion or excitement. This tends to occur at night, sometimes about two hours after the dog goes to bed or when he wakes up in the morning. This coughing is an attempt to clear fluid in the lungs and is often the first clinical sign of MVD

If the condition worsens, other symptoms may appear:

- Shallow, rapid breathing
- Laboured, harsh-sounding breaths
- A panicky or unfocussed look as the dog struggles for breath
- Fainting (syncope)
- Abdominal swelling (due to fluid)
- Noticeable loss of weight
- Lack of appetite
- Paleness around the gums and eyes

If your dog has some of the above symptoms, the vet may suspect a heart problem, so ask to be referred to a cardiologist, who will carry out further tests. These may include listening to the heart, chest X-rays, blood tests, electrocardiogram (a record of your dog's heartbeat) or an echocardiogram (ultrasound of the heart). A cardiologist will be familiar with the condition and the wide range of medications and other available options - and when and how to adjust them to best suit your dog.

Treatment

If the heart problem is due to valve disease or an enlarged heart (dilated cardiomyopathy - DCM), the condition cannot be reversed. However, the vast majority of affected dogs don't require any treatment at all until they show symptoms, and then they generally do well on medication. Only in very severe cases do dogs die from the disease. The only way to prevent the disease is to remove affected dogs from the breeding pool.

Treatment focuses on managing the symptoms with various medications. Diuretics may be prescribed to reduce fluid around the lungs and coughing — these will make your dog pee a lot. A special low salt diet may also be prescribed, as sodium (found in salt) determines the amount of water in the blood.

The amount of exercise your dog has will have to be managed; it could be controlled exercise or complete rest. The treatment and medication may change as the condition develops. There is some evidence that vitamins and other supplements may be beneficial, discuss this with your vet or cardiologist. It is ESSENTIAL that the dog does not become overweight, as this places increased stress on the heart.

The prognosis (outlook) for dogs with heart problems depends on the cause and severity, as well as their response to treatment. Once diagnosed, many dogs can live a long, comfortable life with the right medication and regular check-ups.

The MDV Breeding Protocol

This is a set of guidelines introduced with the aim of eliminating, or greatly reducing, this hereditary disease. It was introduced following extensive studies by scientists in Europe and the USA who concluded:

- 🐾 MVD is the leading cause of death in Cavaliers

- 🐾 It is a hereditary, genetic disorder

- 🐾 There has been no statistical improvement in Cavaliers' mitral valves in the 11 years since the first studies

- 🐾 The disease can be decreased and the age of onset delayed by following guidelines of only breeding Cavaliers who are over the age of 2.5 years, have hearts free from MVD murmurs, and have parents whose hearts were MVD murmur-free at the age of five years. No Cavaliers which have murmurs before the age of five years should be bred

The MVD Breeding Protocol states:

- Every breeding CKCS should be examined annually by a board-certified veterinary cardiologist

- No Cavalier diagnosed with an MVD murmur under the age of five years should be bred

- No Cavalier should be bred before the age of 2.5 years

- If breeding from Cavaliers aged less than five years, both of his or her parents should be free of MDV murmurs at the age of five years

This Protocol is the gold standard for breeders and, while it is compulsory in Denmark, the uptake has been poor in the UK and North America - much to the scientists' disappointment. According to the UK Kennel Club (KC): "The Danish scheme has seen a 73% reduction in risk of having Mitral Valve murmurs in dogs whose parents were on the breeding scheme. The scheme is widely recognised and established, being the only Cavalier heart scheme which has been validated by scientific evidence over a 10-year period."

A new Doppler (ultrasound-type) system of checking hearts is now being rolled out in the UK. It is a collaboration between the KC and Veterinary Cardiovascular Society (VCS) in consultation with Cavalier King Charles Spaniel breed clubs.

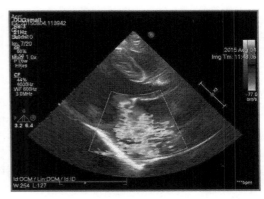

Compared with a vet or cardiologist simply listening to the heart through a stethoscope, a Doppler shows so much more and should be a guide for breeding for better hearts. *Photo shows a Doppler scan.*

The dog has wired pads placed on different parts of his or her body and – this is the difficult part - has to lie very still for around 20 minutes. Dogs are given a Green, Amber or Red result, with Green being the best. Dogs with a Red test result should not be used for breeding, and only Ambers that are otherwise fit and have passed other health screens should be bred. The intention is that the scheme will become widely available to Cavalier breeders and owners.

Heart Murmurs

Heart murmurs are not uncommon in dogs. When our dog was diagnosed with a Grade 1-2 murmur, my heart sank when the vet gave us the bad news. But once the shock is over, it's important to realise that there are several different severities of the condition and, at its mildest, it is no great cause for concern. The murmur did slightly develop, but never affected his quality of life.

Literally, a heart murmur is a specific sound heard through a stethoscope. It results from the blood flowing faster than normal within the heart itself or in one of the two major arteries. Instead of the normal 'lubb dupp' noise, an additional sound can be heard that can vary from a mild 'pshhh' to a loud 'whoosh'. Murmurs are caused by a number of factors, including MVD. Other reasons include hyperthyroidism, anaemia and heartworm. The different grades of heart murmurs are:

- **Grade I -** barely audible

- **Grade II -** soft, but easily heard with a stethoscope

- **Grade III -** intermediate loudness; most murmurs that are related to the mechanics of blood circulation are at least grade III

- **Grade IV -** loud murmur that radiates widely, often including opposite side of chest

❖ **Grades V and Grade VI** - very loud, audible with stethoscope barely touching the chest; the vibration is also strong enough to be felt through the animal's chest wall

In puppies, there are two major types of heart murmurs, and they will probably be detected by your vet at the first or second vaccinations. The most common type is called an innocent 'flow murmur.' This type of murmur is soft (typically Grade II or less) and is not caused by underlying heart disease. An innocent flow murmur typically disappears by four to five months of age.

However, if a puppy has a loud murmur (Grade III or louder), or if the heart murmur is still easily heard with a stethoscope after four or five months of age, the likelihood of the puppy having an underlying congenital (from birth) heart problem becomes much higher. The thought of a puppy having lifelong heart disease is extremely worrying, but it is important to remember that the disease will not affect all puppies' life expectancy or quality of life.

A heart murmur can also develop suddenly in an adult dog with no prior history of the problem. This is typically due to heart disease that develops with age. In Toy and small breeds, a heart murmur may develop in middle-aged to older dogs due to an age-related thickening and degeneration of one of the valves in the heart, the mitral valve.

Eyes

According to Cavalierhealth.org: "A 2008 study of cavaliers conducted by the Canine Eye Registration Foundation showed that an average of 28% of all CKCSs evaluated had eye problems." There is a range of eye conditions which can affect Cavaliers, many of which can be carefully managed with medication and extra care from the owner. All breeding stock should be examined annually by certified veterinary ophthalmologists, so ask to see the parents' up-to-date certificates if you are buying a Cavalier puppy.

Retinal Dysplasia

This is an inherited disease which affects some Spaniels in which the cells and layer of retinal tissue at the back of the eye do not develop properly. One or both eyes may be affected. It can be detected by a vet using an ophthalmoscope when the puppy is six weeks old or even younger. Most

cases of retinal dysplasia do get worse after puppyhood. *Our photo shows a young dog with healthy eyes.*

Retinal Dysplasia occurs when the two layers of the retina do not form together, causing folds. The disorder causes small blind spots which are probably not even noticed by the dog.

However, the more serious geographic dysplasia may lead to large blanks in the visual field, and Cavaliers with retinal detachments are completely blind. Severely affected puppies may have symptoms such as a reluctance to walk into dark areas, bumping into things and obvious sight problems.

There is sadly no treatment for the condition. Ask the breeder if there is any history of retinal dysplasia in his or her bloodlines.

Juvenile Cataracts

The Cavalier can develop one of two forms of hereditary cataracts. The most common is Juvenile Hereditary Cataract (JHC), sometimes also referred to as Early Onset Hereditary Cataract (EHC). It may be seen as early as eight weeks old or as late as six months old, when owners might notice small white flecks in their dog's eye or eyes - both eyes will develop the disease, but it may be at different rates.

The purpose of the transparent lens is to focus the rays of light form an image on the retina. A cataract occurs when the lens becomes cloudy. Less light enters the eye, images become blurry and the dog's sight diminishes as the cataract becomes larger. The mutated gene has been identified by scientists as the HSF4, and the DNA test, called 'Juvenile Hereditary Cataract HC-HSF4' (HSF4 in the USA) is available both in the UK and USA. The gene is recessive, which means that both parents have to carry it for the puppy to inherit the disease.

Unfortunately, most untreated dogs with JHC are completely blind by two to four years old. The good news is that surgery is often an (expensive) option in severe cases, often involving lens replacement, which is 90% successful. Eye drops have also been shown to be effective in improving vision in some cases. Very occasionally, puppies born with congenital cataracts can sometimes improve as they mature. That's because the lens inside the puppy's eye grows along with the dog. When the area of cloudiness on the lens remains the same size, by the time the puppy becomes an adult, the affected portion of the lens is relatively small.

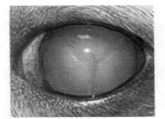 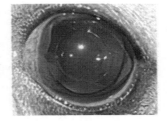

Left: eye with cataracts. Right: same eye with artificial lens

By adulthood, some dogs born with cataracts are able to compensate and see 'around' the cloudiness. The other type of hereditary cataracts affects dogs later in life, up to the age of around seven years.

Progressive Retinal Atrophy (PRA)

PRA is the name for several progressive diseases that lead to blindness. First recognised at the beginning of the 20th century in Gordon Setters, this inherited condition has been documented in over 100 breeds. It can develop any time from as early as one year old to middle age. PRA causes cells in the retina at the back of the eye to degenerate and die, even though the cells seem to develop normally early in life.

A dog's rod cells operate in low light levels and are the first to lose normal function, and so the first sign of PRA is night blindness. Then the cone cells gradually lose their normal function in full light situations. As yet there is no treatment and most affected dogs will eventually go blind. However, dogs do not rely on sight as much as humans. PRA develops slowly, allowing the dog to gradually adjust to life without sight, when the other senses, such as hearing and smell, will be heightened.

If your dog has PRA, you may first notice that he lacks confidence in low light; he is perhaps reluctant to go down stairs or along a dark hallway. If you look closely into his eyes, you may see the pupils dilating (becoming bigger) and/or the reflection of greenish light from the back of his eyes. As the condition worsens, he might then start bumping into things, first at night and then in the daytime too. The condition is not painful and the eyes often appear normal - without redness, tearing or squinting. The lenses may become opaque or cloudy in some dogs.

Dry Eye (Keratoconjunctivitis sicca)

Keratoconjunctivitis sicca is the technical term for a fairly common condition known as Dry Eye which can affect any breed of dog. KCS is caused by not enough tears being produced. With insufficient tears, a dog's eyes can become irritated and the conjunctiva appears red. It's estimated that as many as one in five dogs can suffer from Dry Eye at one time or another in their lives.

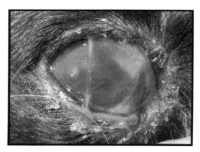

NOTE: Dry Eye Curly Coat (congenital Keratoconjunctivitis sicca and Ichthyosiform Dermatosis) is a rarer but very much more severe syndrome, which can be inherited by Cavaliers. It is a combination of extreme Dry Eye and a congenital skin condition called "Curly Coat" or "Rough Coat."

Dry Eye causes a Cavalier to blink a lot, the eye or eyes typically develop a thick, yellowy discharge and the cornea develops a film. Infections are common as tears also have anti-bacterial and cleansing properties, and inadequate lubrication allows dust, pollen and other debris to accumulate. The nerves of these glands may also become damaged.

The most common cause is an immune disease that damages the tear glands. Dry eye may also be caused by injuries to the tear glands, eye infections, disease such as distemper or reactions to drugs. Left untreated, the dog will suffer painful and chronic eye infections, and repeated irritation of the cornea results in severe scarring, and ulcers may develop which can lead to blindness.

Early treatment is essential to save the cornea and usually involves drugs: cyclosporine, ophthalmic ointment or drops. In some cases, another eye preparation – Tacrolimus - is also used and may be effective when cyclosporine is not. Sometimes artificial tear solutions are also prescribed. Treating Dry Eye involves commitment from the owner. Gently cleaning the eyes several times a day with a warm, wet cloth helps a dog feel better and may also help stimulate tear production. In very severe and rare cases, an operation can be performed to transplant a salivary duct into the upper eyelid, causing saliva to drain into and lubricate the eye.

Eyelash Disorders

Distichiasis, trichiasis and **ectopic cilia** are canine eyelash disorders that can affect any breed. They are included here to help you recognise the signs. *Distichiasis* is an eyelash that grows from an abnormal spot on the eyelid, *trichiasis* is ingrowing eyelashes and *ectopic cilia* are single or multiple hairs that grow through the inside of the eyelid ('cilia' are eyelashes).

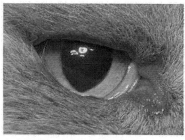

With distichiasis (pictured, also called distichia), small eyelashes abnormally grow on the inner surface or the very edge of the eyelid, and both upper and lower eyelids may be affected. The affected eye becomes red, inflamed, and may develop a discharge. The dog will typically squint or blink a lot, just like a human with a hair or other foreign matter in the eye.

The dog can make matters worse by rubbing the affected eye against furniture, other objects or the carpet. In severe cases, the cornea can become ulcerated and it looks blue. If left, the condition usually worsens and severe ulcerations and infections develop, which can lead to blindness.

Treatment usually involves electro- or cryo-epilation where a needle is inserted into the hair follicle emitting an ultra-fast electric current that produces heat to destroy the stem cells responsible for hair growth. This procedure may need to be repeated after several months because all of the abnormal hairs may not have developed at the time of the first treatment - although this is not common with dogs older than three years.

Sometimes surgery may be required and here the lid is split to remove the areas where the abnormal hairs grow. Both treatments require anaesthesia and usually result in a full recovery. After surgery, the eyelids are swollen for several days and the eyelid margins turn pink. Usually they return to their normal colour within four months. Antibiotic eye drops are often used following surgery to prevent infections. All three conditions are straightforward to diagnose.

Entropion

This is a condition in which the edge of the lower eyelid rolls inward, causing the dog's fur to rub the surface of the eyeball, or cornea. In rare cases the upper lid can also be affected, and one or both eyes may be involved. This painful condition is thought to be hereditary and is more commonly found in dog breeds with a wrinkled face, like the Bulldog.

The affected dog will scratch at the painful eye with his paws and this can lead to further injury. If your Cavalier is to suffer from Entropion, he will usually show signs at or before his first birthday. You will notice that his eyes are red and inflamed and they will produce tears. He will probably squint. The tears typically start off clear and can progress to a thick yellow or green mucus.

If the Entropion causes Corneal Ulcers, you might also notice a milky-white colour develop. This is caused by increased fluid which affects the clarity of the cornea. For the poor dog, the irritation is constant. It's important to get your dog to the vet as soon as you suspect Entropion, before the cornea gets scratched. The condition can cause scarring around the eyes or other issues which can jeopardise a dog's vision if left untreated. A vet will make the diagnosis after a painless and relatively simple inspection, but they will have to rule out other issues, such as allergies, which might also be making your dog's eyes red and itchy.

In young dogs, some vets may delay surgery and treat the condition with medication until the dog's face is fully formed to avoid having to repeat the procedure at a later date. In mild cases, the vet may successfully prescribe eye drops, ointment or other medication. However, the most common treatment for more severe cases is a fairly straightforward surgical procedure to pin back the lower eyelid. Discuss the severity of the condition and all possible options with your vet before proceeding to surgery.

Chiari-like Malformation/Syringomyelia

Syringomyelia (SM) is an extremely serious hereditary disease affecting Cavaliers and is caused by the brain being too big for the skull or an abnormal skull shape. This restricts the normal flow of fluids between the brain and the spine, which are squeezed into cavities and eventually destroy the spinal cord.

SM is a very painful disease, also known as "neck scratcher's disease", because one of the common signs is scratching the air near the neck. The Cavalier King Charles Spaniel Club in the US says: "The most common sign of this condition is shoulder/neck/ear scratching (with no evidence of skin or ear disease), especially when excited or walking on a lead – typically to one side only but may become bilateral. Affected dogs may also be sensitive around the head, neck and forelimbs and often cry/yelp/scream for apparently no reason. Pain may be related to head posture and some dogs prefer to sleep or eat with their heads up.

"Some severely affected young dogs develop a neck scoliosis, i.e. their neck is twisted. Some dogs may develop a wobbling hind limb gait and/or a forelimb weakness. Signs are usually recognised between six months and three years, however dogs of any age may begin showing symptoms. The only definite way to diagnose Syringomyelia and the associated skull malformation is by a MRI scan. Unfortunately, this expensive test, usually performed by a neurologist, is only available at specialist veterinary centers."

There is a hole at the base of the skull where the brain stem exits and becomes the spinal cord. Chiari-like Malformation (CM) occurs when this space is too small or there is some other malformation. The CM forces the brain and spine fluids to be squeezed into places they shouldn't go, causing Syringomyelia.

SM and CM are widespread among Cavaliers, and screening is recommended by the UK Kennel Club (KC). The KC says: "While some dogs show no or only mild symptoms, unfortunately, in some cases the condition progresses and deteriorates causing the dog pain and neurological problems. Medical interventions can help to alleviate health problems, but very sadly in some cases this is not possible. Unfortunately, - although some show no symptoms at all; it all depends on the severity of the malformation. There is no cure and in severe cases, the dog is put to sleep.

Hip Dysplasia

Hip Dysplasia (HD) - or Canine Hip Dysplasia (CHD) as it is also called - is the most common inherited orthopaedic problem in dogs of all breeds and the biggest cause of hind leg lameness. The hips are the uppermost joints on the rear legs of a dog, either side of the tail, and 'Dysplasia' means 'abnormal development.' Dogs with this condition develop painful degenerative arthritis of the hip joints.

According to America's OFA (Orthopedic Foundation for Animals), of the 1,426 Cavalier King Charles Spaniels born between 2011 and 2015 that were tested, some 17.2% suffered from abnormal hips: www.ofa.org/diseases/breed-statistics#detail Unlike other breeds where the condition is reducing, the figures have actually got worse for Cavaliers. Only 13.8% of the 8,055 Cavaliers tested since records began showed signs of dysplasia.

The hip is a ball and socket joint. Hip dysplasia is caused when the head of the femur (thigh bone) fits loosely into a shallow and poorly developed socket in the pelvis. Most dogs with dysplasia are born with normal hips, but due to their genetic make-up, and sometimes caused by or worsened by other factors, such as over-exercising young dogs, diet or obesity, the soft tissues that surround the joint develop abnormally.

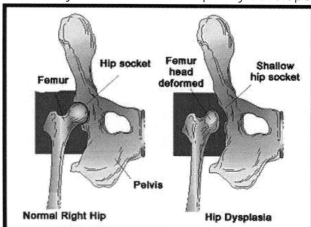

The joint carrying the weight of the dog becomes loose and unstable, muscle growth lags behind normal growth and is often followed by degenerative joint disease, or osteoarthritis, which is the body's attempt to stabilise the loose hip joint. Symptoms often start to show at five to 18 months of age. Occasionally, an affected dog will display no symptoms at all, while others may experience anything from mild discomfort to extreme pain.

Early diagnosis gives a vet the best chance to tackle the problem, minimising the chance of arthritis developing. If your dog shows any of the following symptoms, it's time to get him to a vet:

- Lameness in the hind legs, particularly after exercise
- Difficulty or stiffness when getting up or climbing uphill
- A 'bunny hop' gait
- Dragging the rear end when getting up
- Waddling rear leg gait
- A painful reaction to stretching the hind legs, resulting in a short stride
- A side-to-side sway of the croup (area above the tail) with a tendency to tilt the hips down if you push down on the croup
- A reluctance to jump, exercise or climb stairs
- Wastage of the thigh muscle(s)

While hip dysplasia is usually inherited, other factors can trigger or worsen the condition, including:

- Too much exercise, especially while the dog is still growing
- Extended periods without exercise
- Overfeeding, especially on a diet high in protein and calories
- Excess calcium, also usually due to overfeeding
- Obesity, which places excess stress on joints
- As with humans, damp or cold weather can worsen arthritic symptoms

Diet can play a role in the development of hip dysplasia. Feeding a high-calorie diet to growing dogs can trigger a predisposition to HD, as the rapid weight gain places increased stress on the hips. During their first year or so of life, it is particularly important that puppies are fed a diet that contains the right amount of calories, minerals and protein, thereby reducing the risk of hip dysplasia. Ask your breeder or vet for advice.

Dogs that have a predisposition to the disease may have an increased chance of getting it if they are over-exercised at a young age. See **Chapter 10. Exercise** for more information. The key is *moderate, low impact exercise for young dogs.* Activities that strengthen the gluteus muscles, such as running (preferably on grass) and swimming, are probably a good idea. Whereas high impact activities that apply a lot of force to the joint - such as jumping and catching Frisbees, are not recommended with young Cavaliers, however energetic they are. For more information, visit www.bva.co.uk/Canine-Health-Schemes/Hip-Scheme

Prevention and Treatment

The most common cause of hip dysplasia is genetic. There is, however, a system called 'hip scoring,' which is run by the British Veterinary Association and Kennel Club in the UK and OFA in the USA. The dog's hips are X-rayed when the dog reaches a minimum of 12 months of age. (Dogs must be 24 months of age in the USA before they can receive their final hip certification).

In the UK, the X-rays are submitted to a specialist panel at the BVA who assess nine features of each hip, giving each feature a score. **The lower the score, the better the hips,** so the range can be from 0 (clear) to 106 (badly dysplastic). A hip certificate has a number written as 6:5 or 6/5, giving a total of 11 and indicating the score for each hip. (The section of BVA certificate, right, shows a low combined hip score of 10).

It is also far better if the dog has evenly matched hips, rather than a low score for one and a high score for the other. The Kennel Clubs advise breeders to only breed from dogs that score below the breed average. In the USA, dogs are given a rating, listed below, the equivalent BVA score is in brackets:

Excellent (0-4, with no hip higher than 3)

Good (5-10, with no hip higher than 6)

Fair (11-18)

Borderline (19-25)

Mild (26-35)

Moderate (36-50)

Severe (51-106)

The Breed Mean Score (BMS) is currently 16 for Cavaliers. Dogs with 0:0 hips are very much the exception rather than the rule.

Section C _TO BE COMPLETED BY SCRUTINEERS_

CERTIFICATE OF SCORING

HIP JOINT	Score Range	Right	Left
Norberg angle	0-6	O	1
Subluxation	0-6	2	3
Cranial acetabular edge	0-6	2	2
Dorsal acetabular edge	0-6	—	
Cranial effective acetabular rim	0-6	—	
Acetabular fossa	0-6	—	
Caudal acetabular edge	0-5	—	
Femoral head/neck exostosis	0-6	—	
Femoral head recontouring	0-6	—	
TOTALS (max possible 53 per column)		4	6	10

 If you live in the USA, always ask to see certificates for both dam and sire, ideally looking for parents with below average hip scores; avoid buying a puppy from parents with high combined or individual hip scores.

There is no 100% guarantee that a puppy from low scoring parents will not develop hip dysplasia, as the condition is caused by a combination of genes, rather than just a single gene. However, the chances of it happening are significantly reduced. As with most conditions, early detection leads to a better outcome.

Treatment is geared towards preventing the hip joint getting worse as well as decreasing pain, and various medical and surgical treatments are now available to ease the dog's discomfort and restore some mobility. It depends upon several factors, such as age, how bad the problem is and, sadly, sometimes how much money you can afford for treatment – another reason for taking out early insurance.

Management of the condition usually consists of restricting exercise, keeping body weight down and then managing pain with analgesics and anti-inflammatory drugs. As with humans, cortisone injections may sometimes be used to reduce inflammation and swelling. Cortisone can be injected directly into the affected hip to provide almost immediate relief for a tender, swollen joint. In severe cases, surgery may be an option.

Luxating Patella

Luxating patella, also called 'floating kneecap' or 'slipped stifle' can be a painful condition akin to a dislocated knee cap in humans; the most common cause is genetic.

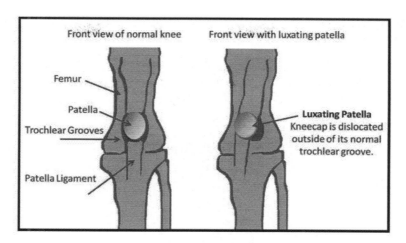

Front view of normal knee   Front view with luxating patella

Femur

Patella

Trochlear Grooves

Patella Ligament

Luxating Patella
Kneecap is dislocated outside of its normal trochlear groove.

A groove in the end of the femur (thigh bone) allows the knee cap to glide up and down when the knee joint is bent, while keeping it in place at the same time. If this groove is too shallow, the knee cap may luxate − or dislocate. It can only return to its natural position when the quadriceps muscle relaxes and increases in length, which is why a dog may have to hold his leg up for some time after the dislocation. Patellar luxation typically affects Toy and miniature breeds.

The condition ranges from Grade 1 to Grade 4. In mild cases (Grade 1) the kneecap may pop back into its socket of its own accord, or be manipulated back into place by a vet. In severe cases the patella is permanently out of place and the dog has extreme difficulty extending the knees. He or she walks with bent knees virtually all the time - often with the whole leg angled and rotated out.

Severe cases are usually dealt with by surgery. Sometimes the problem can be caused − and is certainly worsened - by obesity, the excess weight putting too much strain on the joint − another good reason to keep your Cavalier's weight in check.

Symptoms - A typical sign would be if your dog is running across the park when he suddenly pulls up short and yelps with pain. He might limp on three legs and then after a period of about 10 minutes, drop the affected leg and start to walk normally again. Another sign is that you might notice him stretching out a rear leg quite often or 'skipping' once in a while when walking or running. If the condition is severe, he may hold up the affected leg up for a few days.

Dogs that have a luxating patella on both hind legs may change their gait completely, dropping their hindquarters and holding the rear legs further out from the body as they walk. In the most extreme cases they might not even use their rear legs, but walk like a circus act by balancing on their front legs so their hindquarters don't touch the ground.

There is a DNA test that can tell if the parents are clear of the disease. It's run by the OFA in the USA and by qualified veterinary clinics in the UK. If you are in the USA, ask to see screening certificates for the parents. Typically, many sufferers are middle-aged dogs with a history of intermittent lameness in the affected rear leg or legs, although the condition may appear as early as four to six months old.

Treatment - If moderate to severe cases are left untreated, the groove will become even shallower and the dog will become progressively lamer, with arthritis prematurely affecting the joint. This will cause a permanently swollen knee and reduce your dog's mobility. It is therefore important to get your dog in for a veterinary check-up ASAP if you suspect he or she may have a luxating patella.

Surgery is often required for Grade III and IV luxation. In these cases, known as a **trochlear modification**, the groove at the base of the femur is surgically deepened to better hold the knee cap in place. The good news is that dogs generally respond well, whatever the type of surgery, and are usually completely recovered within two months.

Curly Coat Dry Eye (CC/DE)

This is a serious inherited condition for which, sadly, there is no cure and dogs which suffer from it are often put to sleep. It is different from Dry Eye (Keratoconjunctivitis Sicca), which usually develops later in life and can affect dogs of all breeds. If you are thinking of buying a puppy in the UK, you can check if the parents have been tested for CC/DE in one of two ways:

1. Go to the Kennel Club's Mate Select: www.thekennelclub.org.uk/services/public/mateselect and *"Find a Dog's Health Test Results."* Then type in the Registered Name or Registration/Studbook Number of the puppy's parents.

2. Go to the Kennel Club's page for Cavalier health tests at: https://bit.ly/2E9NCe5 and search the list of Clear, Affected and Carrier dogs to see if the potential parents are listed.

If the parents of the puppy aren't listed, it means they haven't been tested. You should then ask the breeder if there is any history of the disease in her bloodlines. Ideally, only dogs tested **CLEAR** should be used for breeding. However, if bred, a **CARRIER** should only ever be mated with a **CLEAR** dog or bitch.

The gene is *Autosomal Recessive;* here are all possible outcomes; they are the same for all other conditions caused by autosomal recessive traits:

PARENT CLEAR + PARENT CLEAR = pups clear
PARENT CLEAR + PARENT CARRIER = 50% will carry the disease, 50% will be clear
PARENT CLEAR + PARENT AFFECTED = 100% will be carriers
PARENT CARRIER + PARENT CLEAR = 50% will carry disease, 50% will be clear
PARENT CARRIER + PARENT CARRIER = 25% clear, 25% affected and 50% carry disease
PARENT CARRIER + PARENT AFFECTED = 50% affected and 50% carry disease
PARENT AFFECTED + PARENT CLEAR = 100% will carry disease
PARENT AFFECTED + PARENT CARRIER = 50% affected and 50% carry disease
PARENT AFFECTED + PARENT AFFECTED = 100% affected

Fortunately, only a very tiny percentage of Cavaliers are currently affected by CC/DE. This could be because affected animals have been put to sleep. However, in the UK nearly one in nine (10.8%) Cavaliers actually carry the disease, according to the UK's Animal Health Trust. As you can see from the above outcomes, this means that they can pass it on to puppies if mated with another Carrier or an Affected dog.

Symptoms —A curly or rough coat is present from birth. The puppy also suffers from an extreme version of Dry Eye, and as the affected dog matures, it develops a deterioration of the skin which results in seborrhoea, consisting of skin inflammation and excessive oiliness. Also, the dog's teeth, gums, and other connective tissues may be adversely affected. The form of dry eye associated with curly coat also is distinctive in that it is of congenital origin.

Reverse Sneezing

Although Cavaliers are technically classed as a brachycephalic (flat-faced) breed, they are only border line and do not exhibit many of the brachycephalic traits, such as struggling for breath, overheating, pinched nostrils, etc. Breeds such as the Bulldog, French Bulldog, Pug, Pekingese and King Charles Spaniels are far more prone to these and other disorders. However, Cavaliers can suffer from Reverse Sneezing.

Pharyngeal Gag Reflex, more commonly known as Reverse Sneezing, is a rapid inhalation of air through the nose which causes the dog to make repetitive snorting sounds, almost as if he is choking. This often causes great alarm the first time an owner sees and hears it, but in the majority of cases there is absolutely nothing to worry about.

A reverse sneeze can last from just a few seconds or up to a minute or so. It is smaller breeds with that are more prone to this condition - especially breeds with shorter muzzles, as they often have an overlong soft palate (the soft fleshy extension of the hard palate at the roof of the mouth), which is sometimes sucked across the entrance to the larynx and this in turn makes the dog snort.

Various things may trigger an incident, most commonly pulling on a lead when out walking - another reason to consider attaching the lead to a harness instead of the collar. Foreign bodies and even pollens in the nasal passage may cause a reaction.

The best way to stop the dog from snorting is to hold him still and briefly close his nostrils until he swallows or gently rub his throat. Usually the dog is quickly back to normal. It is only in cases where a dog has an excessively long soft palate that veterinary treatment is needed and, fortunately, this is not common in Cavaliers. Dogs who are afflicted by Reverse Sneezing this usually pant and snort quite a lot of the time.

....

Hemorrhagic Gastroenteritis (HGE)

HGE is a sudden—onset episode of diarrhoea, often very bloody in nature. Dennis Homes says: "Last year one of our dogs went down with the condition and it was only prompt, urgent action that saved him. We have heard of quite a few Cavaliers that have developed HGE."

If you suspect your dog is having an episode of HE, get him or her to the vet straight away; it is a potentially life-threatening condition. The dog usually recovers very quickly with early intervention, but the mortality rate is high for dogs that go untreated.

This is a condition characterized by the sudden onset of vomiting (sometimes bloody) and bloody diarrhoea. As large amounts of fresh blood are passed in the vomit and diarrhoea, it leaves the dog weak, depressed, and reluctant to eat. As the disease progresses, the dog rapidly deteriorates, going into shock and then collapsing. This is a life—threatening situation that requires immediate treatment.

HGE typically lasts about two to three days. If a vet suspects HGE, the dog should be hospitalized and treated aggressively. Fluid therapy is the mainstay of treatment. IV fluids, and occasionally blood transfusions, are used to replace lost blood, maintain adequate heart function, and correct any electrolyte deficits. Antibiotics and steroids are also recommended. Dogs should receive nothing to eat or drink during the acute stage of the disease. As they recover, they should be started on a bland, easily digestible diet for at least a week before resuming their normal diet.

The actual cause of Hemorrhagic Gastroenteritis is unknown. Toy breeds and small dogs tend to be more affected and the average age at onset of disease is two to four years old, both males and females. There are theories that it may be caused by a viral infection, bacterial infection, bacterial toxins, reaction to an intestinal parasite, etc. – but nothing has ever been proven.

The disease usually occurs in healthy animals, often young adults, with no history of concurrent illness. It is estimated that 15% of dogs that have had an episode of HGE will suffer a relapse.

Dennis adds: "As with the case of our dog and also of the other Cavaliers we have heard about, no other dogs in the household were affected, so it does not necessarily mean that it is contagious."

Chronic Pancreatitis

This condition is being increasingly diagnosed in Cavaliers. The pancreas is a V-shaped organ located behind the stomach and the first section of the small intestine, the duodenum. It has two main functions: it aids the metabolism of sugar in the body by producing insulin, and it helps the digestion of nutrients by producing enzymes that help the body digest and absorb nutrients from food.

Acute pancreatitis is a sudden onset of pancreatic inflammation. Chronic pancreatitis means recurring, and this is the type which can affect some Cavaliers. In effect, dogs with chronic pancreatitis have multiple attacks of acute pancreatitis. It is a complicated illness more common in older dogs, overweight dogs and females. There are many factors which can contribute to its development, such as:

- Genetics
- Certain medications
- Liver disease
- Metabolic disorders including hyperlipidaemia (high amounts of fatty acids in the blood) and hypercalcaemia (high amounts of calcium in the blood)
- Hormonal diseases such as Cushing's Disease, hypothyroidism and diabetes mellitus
- Obesity - overweight dogs appear to be more at risk
- Nutrition: dogs with high fat diets, dogs who have recently eaten rubbish or have been fed table scraps and dogs who 'steal' or are fed greasy 'people food' appear to have a higher incidence of the disease

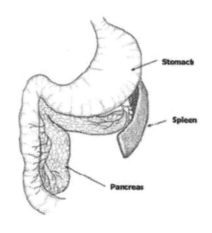

- Infection
- Toxins
- Abdominal surgery, trauma to the abdomen (e.g. being hit by a car), shock or other conditions that could affect blood flow to the pancreas

Symptoms range from mild to very severe, some are similar to those of other diseases, and include:

- Not eating or drinking
- Upset stomach and abdominal pain/swollen abdomen
- Unusual posture, such as arching of the back
- Vomiting
- Diarrhoea
- Restlessness
- Gagging
- Fever
- Depression

It can be difficult to diagnose mild cases as the symptoms are similar to many other diseases. Severe disease can lead to diabetes mellitus, heart problems or other issues.

Diagnosis and Treatment - Pancreatitis is a degenerative, self-fuelling illness that can eventually cause irreversible damage to your dog's system. Since the symptoms of pancreatitis will usually begin long before serious damage, it is important to identify the symptoms and start treatment as soon as possible.

The vet will ask for a history of your dog, make a thorough physical exam and take a complete blood count to check for infection, anaemia and other blood issues. He will probably also do the following tests: electrolytes, specific pancreas tests, X-ray, Ultrasound and urinalysis. He may also do a biopsy. The goals of treatment are to rehydrate the dog, provide pain relief, control vomiting, provide nutritional support and prevent complications.

Dehydration and electrolyte imbalances are common, so extra fluids are often given either by the injection or intravenously, depending on how severe the condition is. If vomiting is severe, food, water and oral medications are stopped for at least 24 hours.

Depending upon the dog's response, food can be started again after a day or more. The dog is generally fed small meals of a bland, easily digestible, high-carb, low-fat food. In some cases, it may be necessary to use tube feeding.

The vet may also prescribe painkillers and will put your dog on a bland diet.

Good habits can go a long way in preventing pancreatitis, as well as many other health conditions.

Pancreatitis is often found in dogs that have eaten foods with a high fat content. The best way to ensure that your dog is a lower risk is to feed him a healthy, low fat diet. Since obese dogs are commonly afflicted with pancreatitis, a **regular exercise** routine is also important.

Hypothyroidism

Hypothyroidism (underactive thyroid) is a hormonal disorder that can affect many breeds. This gland, located on either side of the windpipe in the dog's throat, does not produce enough of the hormone thyroid, which controls the speed of the metabolism. Dogs with very low thyroid levels have a slow metabolic rate.

Hypothyroidism occurs in both males and females that are usually over five years old. The symptoms are often non-specific and quite gradual in onset; they may vary depending on breed and age. Most forms of hypothyroidism are diagnosed with a blood test.

Symptoms - listed in order, with the most common ones being at the top of the list:

- High blood cholesterol
- Lethargy
- Hair loss
- Weight gain or obesity
- Dry coat or excessive shedding
- Hyper pigmentation or darkening of the skin, seen in 25% of cases
- Intolerance to cold, seen in 15% of dogs with the condition

Treatment - Although Hypothyroidism is a type of auto-immune disease and cannot be prevented, the good news is that symptoms can usually be easily diagnosed and treated. Most affected dogs can be well-managed on oral thyroid hormone replacement therapy (tablets), often a daily dose of a synthetic thyroid hormone called thyroxine (levothyroxine).

A dog is usually given a standard dose for his weight and then blood samples are taken periodically to check the dog's response and the dose is adjusted accordingly. The medication can also be given in liquid form or as a gel that can be rubbed into ears. Once treatment has started, the dog will have to be on it for life.

In some less common situations, surgery may be required to remove part or all of the thyroid gland. Another treatment is radioiodine, where radioactive iodine is used to kill the overactive cells of the thyroid. While this is considered one of the most effective treatments, not all animals are suitable for the procedure and a lengthy hospitalisation is often required.

Happily, once the diagnosis has been made and treatment has started, whichever treatment your dog undergoes, the majority of symptoms disappear.

NOTE: Some dogs may suffer from **Hyper**thyroidism (as opposed to **Hypo**thyroidism). This is caused by the thyroid gland producing **too much** thyroid hormone. It is quite rare in dogs, being more often seen in cats. A common symptom is the dog being ravenously hungry all the time, but actually losing weight.

Epilepsy

Epilepsy means repeated seizures (also called fits or convulsions) due to abnormal electrical activity in the brain. It can affect any breed of dog and in fact affects around four or five dogs in every 100. A study carried out in Sweden (Heske et al. 2014), based on data on 35 breeds from insurance companies, found that the Boxer emerged as the breed most likely to be affected by epilepsy, with the Cavalier being ranked third out of 35. The full results are at:
www.instituteofcaninebiology.org/blog/epilepsy-incidence-and-mortality-in-35-dog-breeds

The type of epilepsy that can affect Cavalier King Charles Spaniels is called *Idiopathic Epilepsy*, which means there is no detectable injury, disease or abnormality. Although yet to be proven, scientists believed that some forms of epilepsy are genetic and that the type which affects Cavaliers is **autosomal recessive** – i.e. both parents need a copy of the faulty gene(s) for the disease to be passed on. The majority of epileptic dogs have their first seizure between one and five years old.

Affected dogs behave normally between seizures. In some cases, the gap between seizures is relatively constant, in others it can be very irregular with several occurring over a short period of time, but with long intervals between 'clusters'. If they occur because of a problem somewhere else in the body, such as heart disease (which stops oxygen reaching the brain), this is not epilepsy.

Anyone who has witnessed their dog having a seizure knows how frightening it can be. Seizures are not uncommon, and many dogs only ever have one. If your dog has had more than one, it may be that he or she is epileptic. The good news is that, just as with people, there are medications to control epilepsy in dogs, allowing them to live relatively normal lives with normal lifespans.

There is another condition that can affect Cavaliers which has been linked to epilepsy, as it is caused by a disturbance in the brainwaves. Called **Flycatcher's Syndrome**, the affected Cavalier snaps at imaginary flies buzzing in front of its face. Some affected dogs may compulsively chase their tails or act as if their ears or paws are irritated for hours on end. There are various videos of Cavaliers with Flycatcher's Syndrome on YouTube.

Symptoms of Epilepsy

Some dogs seem to know when they are about to have a seizure and may behave in a certain way. You will come to recognise these signs as meaning that an episode is likely. Often dogs just seek out their owner's company and come to sit beside them.

There are two main types of seizure: **Petit Mal**, also called a Focal or Partial Seizure, which is the lesser of the two as it only affects one half of the brain. This may involve facial twitching, staring into space with a fixed glaze and/or upward eye movement, walking as if drunk, snapping at imaginary flies, and/or running or hiding for no reason. Sometimes this is accompanied by urination and the dog is conscious throughout.

Grand Mal, or Generalised Seizure affects both hemispheres of the brain and is more often what we think of when we talk about a seizure. Most dogs become stiff, fall onto their side and make running movements with their legs. Sometimes they will cry out and may lose control of their bowels, bladder or both. The dog is unconscious once the seizure starts – he cannot hear or respond to you. While it is distressing to watch, **the dog is not in any pain** - even if howling.

It's not uncommon for an episode to begin as a focal seizure, but progress into a generalized seizure. Sometimes, the progression is pretty clear - there may be twitching or jerking of one body part that gradually increases in intensity and progresses to include the entire body – other times the progression happens very fast.

Most seizures last between one and three minutes - it is worth making a note of the time the seizure starts and ends – or record it on your phone because it often seems that it goes on for a lot longer than it actually does. If you are not sure whether or not your dog has had a seizure, look on YouTube, where there are many videos of dogs having epileptic seizures. Afterwards dogs behave in different ways.

Some just get up and carry on with what they were doing, while others appear dazed and confused for up to 24 hours afterwards. Most commonly, dogs will be disorientated for only 10 to 15 minutes before returning to their old self. They often have a set pattern of behaviour that they follow - for example going for a drink of water or asking to go outside to the toilet. If your dog has had more than one seizure, you may well start to notice a pattern of behaviour which is typically repeated.

Most seizures occur while the dog is relaxed and resting quietly, often in the evening or at night; it rarely happens during exercise. In a few dogs, seizures seem to be triggered by particular events or stress. It is common for a pattern to develop and, should your dog suffer from epilepsy, you will gradually recognise this as specific to your dog.

The most important thing is to **stay calm**. Remember that your dog is unconscious during the seizure and is not in pain or distressed. It is likely to be more distressing for you than for him. Make sure that he is not in a position to injure himself, for example by falling down the stairs, but otherwise do not try to interfere with him. Never try to put your hand inside his mouth during a seizure or you are very likely to get bitten.

It is very rare for dogs to injure themselves during a seizure. Occasionally they may bite their tongue and there may appear to be a lot of blood, but it's unlikely to be serious; your dog will not swallow his tongue. If it goes on for a very long time (more than 10 minutes), his body temperature will rise, which can cause damage to other organs such as liver, kidneys and brain.

In very extreme cases, some dogs may be left in a coma after severe seizures. Repeated seizures can cause cumulative brain, which can result in early senility (with loss of learned behaviour and housetraining, or behavioural changes).

When Should I Contact the Vet?

Generally, if your dog has a seizure lasting more than five minutes, or is having more than two or three a day, you should contact your vet. When your dog starts fitting, make a note of the time. If he comes out of it within five minutes, allow him time to recover quietly before contacting your vet. It is far better for him to recover quietly at home rather than be bundled into the car and carted off to the vet right away.

However, if your dog does not come out of the seizure within five minutes, or has repeated seizures close together, contact your vet immediately, as he or she will want to see your dog as soon as possible. If this is his first seizure, your vet may ask you to bring him in for a check-up and some routine blood tests. Always call the vet clinic before setting off to be sure that there is someone there who can help when you arrive.

There are many things other than epilepsy that cause seizures in dogs. When your vet first examines your dog, he or she will not know whether your dog has epilepsy or another illness. It's unlikely that the vet will see your dog during a seizure, so it is **vital** that you're able to describe in some detail just what happens. Your vet may need to run a range of tests to ensure that there is no other cause of the seizures. These may include blood tests, possibly X-rays, and maybe even an MRI scan of your dog's brain. If no other cause can be found, then a diagnosis of epilepsy may be made.

If your Cavalier already has epilepsy, remember these key points:

- Don't change or stop any medication without consulting your vet
- See your vet at least once a year for follow-up visits
- Be sceptical of 'magic cure' treatments

Treatment

It is not usually possible to remove the cause of the seizures, so your vet will use medication to control them. Treatment will not cure the disease, but it will manage the signs – in some cases even a well-controlled epileptic may have occasional seizures. As yet there is no cure for epilepsy, so don't be tempted with 'instant cures' from the internet.

There are many drugs used in the control of epilepsy in people, but very few of these are suitable for long-term use in a dog. Two of the most common are Phenobarbital and Potassium Bromide (some dogs can have negative results with Phenobarbital).

There are also a number of holistic remedies advertised, but we have no experience of them or any idea if any are effective. Other factors that have proved useful in some cases are avoiding dog food containing preservatives, adding vitamins, minerals and/or enzymes to the diet and ensuring drinking water is free of fluoride.

Each epileptic dog is an individual and a treatment plan will be designed specifically for him. It will be based on the severity and frequency of the seizures and how he responds to different medications. Many epileptic dogs require a combination of one or more types of drug to achieve the most effective control of their seizures.

You need patience when managing an epileptic pet. It is important that medication is given at the same time each day. Once your dog has been on treatment for a while, he will become dependent on the levels of drug in his blood at all times to control seizures. If you miss a dose of treatment, blood levels can drop and this may be enough to trigger a seizure.

Keep a record of events in your dog's life, note down dates and times of episodes and record when you have given medication. Each time you visit your vet, take this diary along with you so he or she can see how your dog has been since his last check-up. If seizures are becoming more frequent, it may be necessary to change the medication. The success or otherwise of treatment may depend on YOU keeping a close eye on your Cavalier King Charles Spaniel to see if there are any physical or behavioural changes.

It is not common for epileptic dogs to stop having seizures altogether. However, provided your dog is checked regularly by your vet to make sure that the drugs are not causing any side effects, **there is a good chance that he will live a full and happy life.**

Remember, live **with** epilepsy not **for** epilepsy. With the proper medical treatment, most epileptic dogs have far more good days than bad ones. Enjoy all those good days.

Thanks to www.canineepilepsy.co.uk for assistance with this article. If your Cavalier has epilepsy, we recommend reading this website to gain a greater understanding of the illness.

....

Canine Diabetes

Diabetes can affect dogs of all breeds, sizes and both genders, as well as obese dogs. There are two types: d**iabetes mellitus** and **diabetes insipidus. Diabetes insipidus** is caused by a lack of vasopressin, a hormone that controls the kidneys' absorption of water.

Diabetes mellitus occurs when the dog's body does not produce enough insulin and cannot successfully process sugars. Dogs, like us, get their energy by converting the food they eat into sugars, mainly glucose. This glucose travels in the dog's bloodstream and individual cells then remove some of that glucose from the blood to use for energy. The substance that allows the cells to take glucose from the blood is a protein called **insulin.**

Insulin is created by beta cells that are located in the pancreas, next to the stomach. Almost all diabetic dogs have Type 1 diabetes; their pancreas does not produce any insulin. Without it, the cells have no way to use the glucose that is in the bloodstream, so the cells "starve" while the glucose level in the blood rises. Your vet will use blood samples and urine samples to check glucose concentrations in order to diagnose diabetes. Early treatment helps to prevent further complications developing.

Diabetes mellitus (sugar diabetes) is the most common form and, according to UFAW, affects one in 294 dogs in the UK. According to a study of 180,000 insured dogs, Cavaliers ranked 18th out of 46 breeds for the disorder, with the average age being 7.8 years when the condition was reported. Both males and females can develop it; unspayed females have a slightly higher risk. The typical canine diabetes sufferer is middle-aged, female and overweight, with unspayed females being at slightly higher risk, but there are also juvenile cases.

The condition is now treatable and need not shorten a dog's lifespan or interfere greatly with his quality of life. Due to advances in veterinary science, diabetic dogs undergoing treatment now have the same life expectancy as non-diabetic dogs of the same age and gender.

Symptoms of Diabetes Mellitus

- Extreme thirst
- Excessive urination
- Weight loss
- Increased appetite
- Coat in poor condition
- Lethargy
- Vision problems due to cataracts

If left untreated, diabetes can lead to cataracts and even blindness, increasing weakness in the legs (neuropathy), other ailments and

even death. Cataracts may develop due to high blood glucose levels causing water to build up in the eyes' lenses. This leads to swelling, rupture of the lens fibres and the development of cataracts.

In many cases, the cataracts can be surgically removed to bring sight back to the dog. However, some dogs may stay blind even after the cataracts are gone, and some cataracts simply cannot be removed. Blind dogs are often able to get around surprisingly well, particularly in a familiar home.

Treatment and Exercise

Treatment starts with the right diet. Your vet will prescribe meals low in fat and sugars. He or she will also recommend medication. Many cases of canine diabetes can be successfully treated with a combination of diet and medication, while more severe cases may require insulin injections. In the newly-diagnosed dog, insulin therapy begins at home.

Normally, after a week of treatment, you return to the vet for a series of blood sugar tests over a 12-14 hour period to see when the blood glucose peaks and when it hits its lows. Adjustments are then made to the dosage and timing of the injections. Your vet will explain how to prepare and inject the insulin. You may be asked to collect urine samples using a test strip of paper that indicates the glucose levels in urine.

If your dog is already having insulin injections, beware of a 'miracle cure' offered on some internet sites. It does not exist. There is no diet or vitamin supplement which can reduce your dog's dependence on insulin injections, because vitamins and minerals cannot do what insulin does in the dog's body. If you think that your dog needs a supplement, discuss it with your vet first to make sure that it does not interfere with any other medication.

Managing your dog's diabetes also means managing his activity level. Exercise burns up blood glucose the same way that insulin does. If your dog is on insulin, any active exercise on top of the insulin might cause him to have a severe low blood glucose episode, called 'hypoglycaemia.'

Keep your dog on a reasonably consistent exercise routine. Your usual insulin dose will take that amount of exercise into account. If you plan to take your dog out for some demanding exercise, such as running round with other dogs, you may need to reduce his usual insulin dose.

Tips

- 🐾 You can usually buy specially formulated diabetes dog food from your vet
- 🐾 You should feed the same type and amount of food at the same time every day
- 🐾 Most vets recommend twice-a-day feeding for diabetic pets (it's OK if your dog prefers to eat more often). If you have other pets, they should also be on a twice-a-day feeding schedule, so that the diabetic dog cannot eat from their bowls
- 🐾 Help your dog to achieve the best possible blood glucose control by not feeding table scraps or treats between meals

🐾 Watch for signs that your dog is starting to drink more water than usual. Call the vet if you see this happening, as it may mean that the insulin dose needs adjusting

Remember these simple points:

Food raises blood glucose - Insulin and exercise lower blood glucose - Keep them in balance

For more information on canine diabetes visit **www.caninediabetes.org**

....

Canine Cancer

This is the biggest single killer and will claim the lives of one in four dogs, regardless of breed. It is the cause of nearly half the deaths of all dogs aged 10 years and older, according to the American Veterinary Medical Association. There are many different types of cancer and a study of more than 15,000 dogs of different breeds found that the Cavalier isn't any more prone to many types of cancer than other breeds.

However, one unusual disease that can affect Cavaliers is anal sac gland carcinoma. On a positive note, they are less likely than most breeds to get mast cell tumours.

Detailed cancer statistics involving the Cavalier King Charles Spaniel can be found at the NCBI (National Center for Biotechnology Information) website: www.ncbi.nlm.nih.gov/pmc/articles/PMC3658424 (Go to the top right of your screen in Google, click the three vertical dots, then click *Find* and type in *"Cavalier"* - all the references will be highlighted in yellow).

Common Cancer Symptoms

Early detection is critical, and some things to look out for are:

🐾 Swellings anywhere on the body or around the anus

🐾 Lumps in a dog's armpit or under the jaw

🐾 Sores that don't heal

🐾 Weight loss

🐾 Laboured breathing

🐾 Changes in exercise or stamina level

🐾 Change in bowel or bladder habits

🐾 Increased drinking or urination

🐾 Bad breath, which can be a sign of oral cancer

🐾 Poor appetite, difficulty swallowing or excessive drooling

🐾 Vomiting

If your dog has been spayed or neutered, there is evidence that the risk of certain cancers decreases. These cancers include uterine and breast/mammary cancer in females, and testicular cancer in males (if the dog was neutered before he was six months old).

However, recent studies also show that some dogs may have a higher risk of certain cancers after early neutering. Spaying prevents mammary cancer in female dogs, which is fatal in about 50% of all cases.

Diagnosis and Treatment

Just because your dog has a skin growth doesn't mean that it's cancerous. Your vet will probably confirm the tumour using X-rays, blood tests or a biopsy. Often these are benign (harmless), but if you discover one you should get it checked out by a vet, as they can sometimes be malignant (cancerous).

Many older dogs develop fatty lumps, or *lipomas*, which are often benign, but still need checking out by a vet to make sure.

If your dog is diagnosed with cancer, there is hope. Advances in veterinary medicine and technology offer various treatment options, including chemotherapy, radiation and surgery. Unlike with humans, a dog's hair will not fall out with chemotherapy. Canine cancer is growing at an ever-increasing rate, and one of the difficulties is that your dog cannot tell you when a cancer is developing. However, if cancers can be detected early enough through a physical or behavioural change, dogs often respond well to treatment.

Over recent years, we have all become more aware of the risk factors for human cancer. Responding to these by changing our habits is having a significant impact on human health. Stopping smoking, protecting ourselves from over-exposure to strong sunlight and eating a healthy, balanced diet all help to reduce cancer rates. We know to keep a close eye on ourselves, go for regular health checks and report any lumps and bumps to our doctors as soon as they appear. **The same is true with your dog.**

Reducing the Risk

The success of treatment depends on the type of cancer, the treatment used and, importantly, how early the tumour is found. The sooner treatment begins, the greater the chances of success. One of the best things you can do for your dog is to keep a close eye on him for any tell-tale signs. This shouldn't be too difficult and can be done as part of your regular handling and grooming sessions. If you notice any new bumps, for example, monitor them over a period of days to see if there is a change in their appearance or size. If there is, then make an appointment to see your vet as soon as possible. It might only be a cyst, but better to be safe than sorry.

While it is impossible to completely prevent cancer from occurring, the following points may help to reduce the risk:

- Feed a healthy diet with little or, preferably, no preservatives
- Consider adding a dietary supplement, such as antioxidants, Vitamins, A, C, E, beta carotene, lycopene or selenium, or coconut oil – check compatibility with any other treatments
- Don't let your Cavalier Spaniel get overweight
- Give pure, filtered or bottled water (fluoride-free) for drinking
- Give your dog regular daily exercise
- Keep your dog away from chemicals, pesticides, cleaning products, etc. around the garden and home
- Avoid passive smoking
- Consider using natural flea remedies (check they are working) and avoid unnecessary vaccinations
- If your dog has light skin, don't leave him in the blazing sunshine for extended periods

❧ Check your dog regularly for lumps and bumps and any other physical or behavioural changes

❧ If you are buying a puppy, ask whether there is a history of cancer among the parents and grandparents

Research into earlier diagnosis and improved treatments is being conducted at veterinary schools and companies all over the world. Advances in biology are producing a steady flow of new tests and treatments that are now becoming available to improve survival rates and canine cancer care.

One of our dogs was diagnosed with T-cell lymphoma - a particularly aggressive form of cancer - when he was four years old. We had noticed a small lump on his anus, which grew to the size of a small grape within a couple of days.

We rushed him down to the vet and he had surgery the following day. He died last year, aged 13, having lived a further nine very happy and energetic years.

If your dog is diagnosed with cancer, do not despair, there are many options and new, improved treatments are constantly being introduced.

Disclaimer: The author is not a vet. This chapter is intended to give owners an outline of some of the health issues and symptoms that may affect their dog(s). If you have any concerns regarding your dog's health, our advice is always the same: consult a veterinarian. There is an excellent website with very detailed information on all aspects of Cavalier health at: www.cavalierhealth.org

13. Skin and Allergies

Allergies are a growing concern for owners of many breeds. Visit any busy veterinary clinic these days — especially in spring and summer — and it's likely that one or more of the dogs is there because of some type of sensitivity. A study by UK vets revealed that of the 1,875 King Charles Cavalier Spaniels attending their clinics, some 388 (22%) were suffering from skin issues. The full report is at: https://cgejournal.biomedcentral.com/articles/10.1186/s40575-015-0016-7

Any individual dog can have issues. Skin conditions, allergies and intolerances are on the increase in the canine world as well as the human world. How many children did you hear of having asthma or a peanut allergy when you were at school? Not many, I'll bet, yet allergies and adverse reactions are now relatively common — and it's the same with dogs. The reasons are not clear; it could be connected to breeding or feeding — or both, but as yet, there is no clear scientific evidence to back this up.

The skin is a complicated topic and a whole book could be written on this subject alone. While many dogs have no problems at all, some suffer from sensitive skin, dry or oily skin, allergies, yeast infections and/or skin disorders, causing them to scratch, bite or lick themselves excessively. Symptoms may vary from mild itchiness to a chronic reaction.

In common with other breeds with long, floppy ears, ear infections can be a cause for concern with Cavaliers — more on these later. There is also a hereditary disease known by a various names: Curly Coat Dry Eye (CC/DE), Dry Eye Curly Coat or Congenital Keratoconjunctivitis Sicca and Ichthyosiform Dermatosis, to give the condition its scientific name. Whatever it's called, the fact is that the Cavalier King Charles Spaniel is the only breed known to suffer from this serious disease, which is covered in **Chapter 12. Cavalier Health.**

Canine Skin

As with humans, the skin is the dog's largest organ. It acts as the protective barrier between your dog's internal organs and the outside world; it also regulates temperature and provides the sense of touch. Surprisingly, a dog's skin is actually thinner than ours, and it is made up of three layers:

1. **Epidermis** or outer layer, the one that bears the brunt of your dog's contact with the outside world.

2. **Dermis** is the extremely tough layer mostly made up of collagen, a strong and fibrous protein. This where blood vessels deliver nutrients and oxygen to the skin, and it also acts as your dog's thermostat by allowing his body to release or keep in heat, depending on the outside temperature and your dog's activity level.

3. **Subcutis** is a dense layer of fatty tissue that allows your dog's skin to move independently from the muscle layers below it, as well as providing insulation and support for the skin.

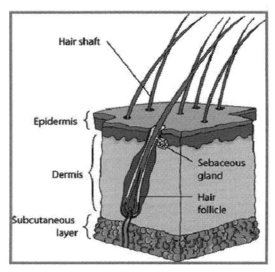

Human allergies often trigger a reaction within the respiratory system, causing us to wheeze or sneeze, whereas *allergies or hypersensitivities in a dog often cause a reaction in his or her skin.*

Skin can be affected from the **inside** by things that your dog eats or drinks.

Skin can be affected from the **outside** by fleas, parasites, inhaled or contact allergies triggered by grass, pollen, man-made chemicals, dust, mould, etc. and like all dogs, Cavaliers can suffer from food allergies or intolerances as well as environmental allergies. Canine skin disorders are a complex subject. Some dogs can run through fields, digging holes and rolling around in the grass with no after-effects at all. Others may spend a lot of time indoors and have an excellent diet, but still experience severe itching and/or bald spots.

It's by no means possible to cover all of the issues and causes in this chapter. The aim here is to give a broad outline of some of the ailments most likely to affect your Cavalier and how to deal with them. We have also included remedies tried with some success by ourselves (we had a dog with skin issues) and other owners of affected dogs, as well as advice from a holistic specialist. This information is not intended to take the place of professional help. We are not animal health experts and you should always contact your vet as soon as your dog appears physically unwell or uncomfortable. This is particularly true with skin conditions:

If a vet can find the source of the problem early on, there is more chance of successfully treating it before it has chance to develop into a more serious condition with secondary issues and infections.

One of the difficulties with skin ailments is that the exact cause is often difficult to diagnose, as the symptoms may also be common to other issues. If environmental allergies are involved, some specific tests are available costing hundreds of pounds or dollars. You will have to take your vet's advice on this, as the tests are not always conclusive and if the answer is dust or pollen, it can be difficult to keep your lively dog away from the triggers while still having a normal life - unless you and your Cavalier spend all your time in a spotlessly clean city apartment! It is often a question of managing a skin condition, rather than curing it.

Another issue reported by some dog owners is food allergy or intolerance - there is a difference – often to grain. There is anecdotal evidence that switching to a raw diet or raw meaty bones diet can significantly help in some (but not all) cases. See **Chapter 8. Feeding a Cavalier** for more information on dealing with food intolerances and allergies.

Skin issues and allergies often develop in adolescence or early adulthood, which is often anything from a few months to two or three years old. Our affected dog was perfectly normal until he reached two when he began scratching, triggered by environmental allergies - most likely pollen. Over the years he was on various different remedies which all worked for a time. As his allergies were seasonal, he normally did not have any medication between

October and March. But come spring and as sure as daffodils are daffodils, he started scratching again. Luckily, they were manageable and he lived a happy, active life until he passed away aged 13.

Allergies and their treatment can cause a lot of stress for dogs and owners alike. The number one piece of advice is that if you suspect your Cavalier has an allergy or skin problem, try to **deal with it right away** - either via your vet or natural remedies – before the all-too-familiar scenario kicks in and it develops into a chronic (long term) condition.

Whatever the cause, before a vet can diagnose the problem you have to be prepared to tell him or her all about your dog's diet, exercise regime, habits, medical history and local environment. The vet will then carry out a thorough physical examination, possibly followed by further (expensive) tests, before a course of treatment can be prescribed. You'll have to decide whether these tests are worth it and whether they are likely to discover the exact root of the problem.

Types of Allergies

'*Canine dermatitis*' means inflammation of a dog's skin and it can be triggered by numerous things, but the most common by far is allergies. Vets estimate that one in four dogs at their clinics is there because of some kind of allergy. Symptoms are:

- Chewing his or her feet
- Rubbing the face on the carpet
- Scratching the body
- Scratching or biting the anus
- Itchy ears, head shaking
- Hair loss
- Mutilated skin with sore or discoloured patches or hot spots

NOTE: Scratching near the head, neck and/or shoulders can also be a sign of Syringomyelia (SM) in Cavaliers.

A Cavalier who is allergic to something will show it through skin problems and itching; your vet may call this '*pruritus*'. It may seem logical that if a dog is allergic to something inhaled, like certain pollen grains, his/her nose will run; if (s)he's allergic to something he eats, (s)he may vomit, or if allergic to an insect bite, (s)he may develop a swelling. But in practice this is seldom the case. In dogs, the skin is the organ most affected by allergies, often resulting in a mild to severe itching sensation over the body and possibly a chronic ear infection.

Dogs with allergies often chew their feet until they are sore and red. You may see yours rubbing his or her face on the carpet or couch or scratching the belly and flanks. Because the ear glands produce too much wax in response to the allergy, ear infections can occur - with bacteria and yeast (which is a fungus) often thriving in the excessive wax and debris. Cavaliers don't have to suffer from allergies to get an ear infection; the lack of air flow under the floppy hairy ears makes them prone to the condition.

Digestive health can also play an important role. If your dog does develop a yeast infection and you switch to a grain-free diet, avoid those that are potato-based, as these contain high levels of starch. Holistic vet Dr Jodie Gruenstern says: "It's estimated that up to 80% of the immune system resides within the gastrointestinal system; building a healthy gut supports a more appropriate immune response. The importance of choosing fresh proteins and healthy fats over processed, starchy diets (such as kibble) can't be overemphasized. Grains and other starches have a negative impact on gut health, creating insulin resistance and inflammation."

An allergic dog may cause skin lesions or 'hot spots' by constant chewing and scratching. Sometimes he or she will lose hair, which can be patchy, leaving a mottled appearance. The skin itself may be dry and crusty, reddened, swollen or oily, depending on the dog. It is very common to get secondary bacterial skin infections due to these self-inflicted wounds. An allergic dog's body is reacting to certain molecules called 'allergens.' These may come from:

- Trees

- Grass

- Pollens

- Foods and food additives, such as specific meats, grains or colourings

- Milk products

- Fabrics, such as wool or nylon

- Rubber and plastics

- House dust and dust mites

- Mould

- Flea bites

- Chemical products used around the house

These allergens may be **inhaled** as the dog breathes, **ingested** as the dog eats or caused by **contact** with the dog's body when (s)he walks or rolls. However they arrive, they all cause the immune system to produce a protein (IgE), which causes irritating chemicals like histamine to be released. In dogs these chemical reactions and cell types occur in sizeable amounts **only within the skin**, hence the scratching.

Inhalant Allergies (Atopy)

The most common allergies in dogs are inhalant and seasonal - at least at first; some allergies may develop and worsen. Substances that can cause an allergic reaction in dogs are similar to those causing problems for humans, and dogs of all breeds can suffer from them. A clue to diagnosing these allergies is to look at the timing of the reaction. Does it happen all year round? If so, this may be mould, dust or some other trigger that is permanently in the environment. If the reaction is seasonal, then pollens may well be the culprit. A diagnosis can be made by one of three methods of **allergy testing.**

The most common is a blood test for antibodies caused by antigens in the dog's blood, and there are two standard tests: a RAST test (radioallergosorbent) and an ELISA test (enzyme-linked immunosorbent assay). According to the Veterinary and Aquatic Services Department of Drs. Foster and Smith, they are very similar, but many vets feel that the ELISA test gives more accurate results.

The other type of testing is intradermal skin testing where a small amount of antigen is injected into the skin of the animal and after a short period of time, the area around the injection site is inspected to see if the dog has had an allergic reaction. This method has been more widely used in the USA than the UK to date. Here is a link to an article written by the owner of a Boxer dog with severe inhalant allergies: www.allergydogcentral.com/2011/06/30/dog-allergy-testing-and-allergy-shots

This photo shows a Golden Retriever that has undergone intradermal skin testing. In this particular case, the dog has been tested for more than 70 different allergens, which is a lot. In all likelihood, your vet would test for fewer. The injections are in kits. If you consider this option, ask the vet or specialist how many allergens are in the kit.

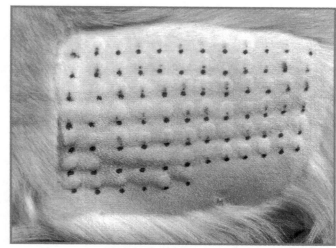

Intradermal skin testing is regarded as 'the gold standard' of allergy testing for atopy. The dog is sedated and an area on the flank is shaved down to the skin. A small amount of antigen is injected into the skin on this shaved area. This is done in a specific pattern and order. After a short time, the shaved area is examined to detect which antigens, if any, have created a reaction. It may look pretty drastic, but reactions – the visible round bumps - are only temporary and the hair grows back.

Intradermal skin testing works best when done during the season when the allergies are at their worst. The good news is that it is not necessarily much more expensive than blood testing and after a while the dog is none the worse for the ordeal. The procedure is normally carried out by a veterinary dermatologist or a vet with some dermatological experience, and dogs need to be clear of steroids and antihistamines for around six weeks beforehand.

While allergy testing is not particularly expensive, the intradermal method usually requires your dog to be sedated. And there's also no point doing it if you are not going to go along with the recommended method of treatment afterwards - which is immunotherapy, or **'hyposensitisation'**, and this can be an expensive and lengthy process. It consists of a series of injections made specifically for your dog and administered over months (or even years) to make him or her more tolerant of specific allergens. Vets in the US claim that success rates can be as high as 75%.

But before you get to the stage of considering allergy testing, your vet will have had to rule out other potential causes, such as fleas or mites, fungal, yeast or bacterial infections and hypothyroidism. Due to the time and cost involved in skin testing, vets treat most mild cases of allergies with a combination of avoidance, fatty acids, tablets, and sometimes steroid injections for flare-ups. Many owners of dogs with allergies also look at diet change and natural alternatives to long-term use of steroids, which can cause other health issues.

Environmental or Contact Irritations

These are a direct reaction to something the dog physically comes into contact with. It could be as simple as grass, specific plants, dust or other animals. If the trigger is grass or other outdoor materials, the allergies are often seasonal. The dog may require treatment (often tablets, shampoo or localised cortisone spray) for spring and summer, but be perfectly fine with no medication for the other half of the year. This was the case with our dog.

If you suspect your Cavalier may have outdoor contact allergies, here is one very good tip guaranteed to reduce scratching: get him or her to stand in a tray or large bowl of water on your return from a walk. Washing the feet and under the belly will get rid of some of the pollen and other allergens, which in turn will reduce the scratching and biting. This can help to reduce the allergens to a tolerable level.

Other possible triggers include dry carpet shampoos, caustic irritants, new carpets, cement dust, washing powders or fabric conditioners. If you wash your dog's bedding or if he sleeps on your bed, use a fragrance-free - if possible, hypoallergenic - laundry detergent and avoid fabric conditioner.

The irritation may be restricted to the part of the dog - such as the underneath of the paws or belly - which has touched the offending object. Symptoms are skin irritation - either a general problem or specific hotspots - itching (pruritus) and sometimes hair loss. Readers of our website sometimes report to us that their dog will incessantly lick one part of the body, often the paws, anus, belly or back.

Flea Bite Allergies

These are a very common canine allergy and affect dogs of all breeds. To compound the problem, many dogs with flea allergies also have inhalant allergies. Flea bite allergy is typically seasonal, worse during summer and autumn - peak time for fleas - and is worse in warmer climates where fleas are prevalent.

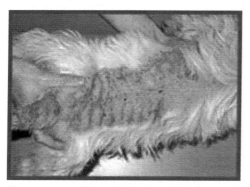

This type of allergy is not to the flea itself, but to proteins in flea saliva, which are deposited under the dog's skin when the insect feeds. Just one bite to an allergic Cavalier will cause intense and long-lasting itching. If affected, the dog will try to bite at the base of his tail and scratch a lot. Most of the damage is done by the dog's scratching, rather than the flea bite, and can result in the hair falling out or skin abrasions.

Some Cavaliers will develop hot spots. These can occur anywhere, but are often along the back and base of the tail. Flea bite allergies can only be totally prevented by keeping all fleas away from the dog. Various flea prevention treatments are available – see the section on **Parasites**. If you suspect your dog may be allergic to fleas, consult your vet for the proper diagnosis and medication.

Diet and Food Allergies

Food is the third most common cause of allergies in dogs. Cheap dog foods bulked up with grains and other ingredients can cause problems. Some owners have reported their dogs having intolerance to wheat and other grains. If you feed your dog a dry commercial dog food, make sure that it is high quality, preferably hypoallergenic, and that the first ingredient listed on the sack is *meat or poultry,* not grain. Without the correct food, a dog's whole body - not just the skin and coat - will continuously be under stress and this manifests itself in a number of ways. The symptoms of food allergies are similar to those of most allergies:

- Itchy skin affecting primarily the face, feet, ears, forelegs, armpits and anus
- Excessive scratching
- Chronic or recurring ear infections

- ❧ Hair loss
- ❧ Hot spots
- ❧ Skin infections that clear up with antibiotics, but return after the antibiotics have finished
- ❧ Possible increased bowel movements, maybe twice as many as normal

The bodily process that occurs when an animal has a reaction to a particular food agent is not very well understood, but the veterinary profession does know how to diagnose and treat food allergies. As many other problems can cause similar symptoms (and also the fact that many sufferers also have other allergies), it is important that any other conditions are identified and treated before food allergies are diagnosed.

Atopy, flea bite allergies, intestinal parasite hypersensitivities, sarcoptic mange and yeast or bacterial infections can all cause similar symptoms. This can be an anxious time for owners as vets try one thing after another to get to the bottom of the allergy.

The normal method for diagnosing a food allergy is elimination. Once all other causes have been ruled out or treated, then a food trial is the next step – and that's no picnic for owners either - see **Chapter 8. Feeding a Cavalier** for more information. As with other allergies, dogs may have short-term relief by taking fatty acids, antihistamines, and steroids, but removing the offending items from the diet is the only permanent solution.

Acute Moist Dermatitis (Hot Spots)

Acute moist dermatitis or 'hot spots' are not uncommon. A hot spot can appear suddenly and is a raw, inflamed and often bleeding area of skin. The area becomes moist and painful and begins spreading due to continual licking and chewing. They can become large, red, irritated lesions in a short pace of time. The cause is often a local reaction to an insect bite - fleas, ticks, biting flies or mosquitoes. Other causes of hot spots include:

- ❧ Allergies - inhalant allergies and food allergies
- ❧ Mites
- ❧ Ear infections
- ❧ Poor grooming
- ❧ Burs or plant awns
- ❧ Anal gland disease
- ❧ Hip dysplasia or other types of arthritis and degenerative joint disease

Once diagnosed and with the right treatment, hot spots disappear as soon as they appeared. The underlying cause should be identified and treated, if possible. Check with your vet before treating your Cavalier for fleas and ticks at the same time as other medical treatment (such as anti-inflammatory medications and/or antibiotics), as he or she will probably advise you to wait.

Treatments may come in the form of injections, tablets or creams – or your dog might need a combination of them. Your vet will probably clip and clean the affected area to help the effectiveness of any spray or ointment and your poor Cavalier might also have to wear an E-collar until the condition subsides, but usually this does not take long.

Interdigital Cysts

If your Cavalier gets a fleshy red lump between the toes that looks like an ulcerated sore or a hairless bump, then there's a good chance it is an interdigital cyst - or *interdigital furuncle* to give the condition its correct medical term. This unpleasant condition can be very difficult to get rid of, since it is often not the primary issue, but a sign of some other problem. The 'Bully breeds' (Bulldogs, French Bulldogs, Pugs, etc). are most susceptible, but some Cavaliers do suffer from them - often those that suffer from other allergies.

Actually, they are not cysts, but the result of **furunculosis**, a condition of the skin which clogs hair follicles and creates chronic infection. They can be caused by a number of factors, including allergies, obesity, poor foot conformation, mites, yeast infections, ingrown hairs or other foreign bodies, and obesity.

These nasty-looking bumps are painful for your dog, will probably cause a limp and can be a nightmare to get rid of. Vets might recommend a whole range of treatments to get to the root cause of the problem. It can be extremely expensive if your dog is having a barrage of tests or biopsies, and even then you are not guaranteed to find the underlying cause. The first thing he or she will probably do is put your dog in an E-collar to stop him licking the affected area, which will never recover properly as long as it's constantly being licked. This again is stressful for your dog.

Cavaliers are sensitive dogs and some can be resistant to E-collars - they may slump down like you've hung a 10-ton weight on their neck or just become depressed by the whole thing. You might consider putting socks on the affected foot or feet, which will work well while your dog sleeps but then you'll have to watch him or her like a hawk when awake to stop the affected areas being licked or bitten. Here are some remedies your vet may suggest:

- Antibiotics and/or steroids and/or mite killers
- Soaking the feet in Epsom salts twice daily to unclog the hair follicles
- Testing for allergies or thyroid problems
- Starting a food trial if food allergies are suspected
- Shampooing the feet
- Cleaning between the toes with medicated (benzoyl peroxide) wipes
- A referral to a veterinary dermatologist
- Surgery

If you suspect your Cavalier has an interdigital cyst, get to the vet for a correct diagnosis and then discuss the various options. A course of antibiotics may be suggested initially, along with switching to a hypoallergenic diet if a food allergy is suspected. If the condition persists, many owners get discouraged, especially when treatment may go on for many weeks.

Be wary of going on to steroid injections or repeated courses of antibiotics, as this may mean that the underlying cause of the furuncle has not been diagnosed and will persist.

 Before you resort to any drastic action, first try soaking your Cavalier's affected paw in Epsom salts for five or 10 minutes twice a day. After the soaking, clean the area with medicated wipes, which are antiseptic and control inflammation. In the US these are sold under the brand name Stridex pads in the skin care section of any grocery, or from the pharmacy. If you think the cause may be an environmental allergy, wash your dog's feet and under his belly when you return from a walk, as this will help to remove pollen and other allergens.

Surgery is a drastic option. Although it can be effective in solving the immediate problem, it will not deal with whatever is triggering the interdigital cysts in the first place. Not only is healing after this surgery a lengthy and difficult process, it also means your dog will never have the same foot as before - future orthopaedic issues and a predisposition to more interdigital cysts are a couple of problems that can occur afterwards.

All that said, your vet will understand that interdigital cysts aren't so simple to deal with, but they are always treatable. **Get the right diagnosis as soon as possible**, limit all offending factors and give medical treatment a good solid try before embarking on more drastic cures.

....

Parasites

Demodectic Mange

Demodectic Mange is also known as *red mange, follicular mange* or *puppy mange*. It is caused by the tiny mite Demodex canis — pictured - which can only be seen through a microscope. The mites actually live inside the hair follicles on the bodies of virtually every adult dog, and most humans, without causing any harm or irritation. In humans, the mites are found in the skin, eyelids and the creases of the nose...try not to think about that!

The Demodex mite spends its entire life on the host dog. Eggs hatch and mature from larvae to nymphs to adults in 20 to 35 days and the mites are transferred directly from the mother to the puppies within the first week of life by direct physical contact. Demodectic mange is not a disease of poorly-kept or dirty kennels. It is generally a disease of young dogs with inadequate or poorly developed immune systems (or older dogs suffering from a suppressed immune system).

Vets currently believe that virtually every mother carries and transfers mites to her puppies, and most are immune to the mite's effects, but a few puppies are not and they develop full-blown mange. They may have a few (less than five) isolated lesions and this is known as localised mange — often around the head. This happens in around 90% of cases.

In the other 10% of cases, it develops into generalised mange that covers the entire body or region of the body. This is most likely to develop in puppies with parents that have suffered from mange. Most lesions in either form develop after four months of age. It can also develop around the time when females have their first season and may be due to a slight dip in the bitch's immune system.

Symptoms — Bald patches are usually the first sign, usually accompanied by crusty, red skin that sometimes appears greasy or wet. Usually hair loss begins around the muzzle, eyes and other areas on the head. The lesions may or may not itch. In localised mange, a few circular crusty areas appear, most frequently on the head and front legs of three to six-month-old puppies. Most will self-heal as the puppies become older and develop their own immunity, but a persistent problem needs treatment.

With generalised mange there are bald patches over the entire coat, including the head, neck, body, legs, and feet. The skin on the head, side and back is crusty, often inflamed and oozes a clear fluid. The skin itself will often be oily to touch and there is usually a secondary bacterial infection. Some puppies can become quite ill and can develop a fever, lose their appetites and become lethargic. If you suspect your puppy has generalised demodectic mange, get him to a vet straight away.

There is also a condition called pododermatitis, when the mange affects a puppy's paws. It can cause bacterial infections and be very uncomfortable, even painful. The symptoms of this mange include hair loss on the paws, swelling of the paws (especially around the nail beds) and red/hot/inflamed areas which are often infected. Treatment is always recommended, and it can take several rounds to clear it up.

Diagnosis and Treatment – The vet will normally diagnose demodectic mange after he or she has taken a skin scraping. As these mites are present on every dog, they do not necessarily mean the dog has mange. Only when the mite is coupled with lesions will the vet diagnose mange. Treatment usually involves topical (on the skin) medication and sometimes tablets. In 90% of cases localised demodectic mange resolves itself as the puppy grows.

If the dog has just one or two lesions, these can usually be successfully treated using specific creams and spot treatments. There are also non-chemical treatments, such as the one pictured, to relieve symptoms. With the more serious generalised demodectic mange, treatment can be lengthy and expensive. The vet might prescribe an anti-parasitic dip every two weeks. Owners should always wear rubber gloves when treating their dog, and it should be applied in an area with adequate ventilation.

Note that **some dogs – especially Toy breeds like Cavaliers - can have a bad reaction to these dips,** so check with your vet as to whether it will be suitable for your dog. Most dogs with a severe issue need six to 14 dips every two weeks. After the first three or four dips, your vet will probably take another skin scraping to check the mites have gone. Dips continue for one month after the mites have disappeared, but dogs shouldn't be considered cured until a year after their last treatment.

Other options include the heartworm treatment Ivermectin. This isn't approved by the FDA for treating mange, but is often used to do so. It is usually given orally every one to two days, or by injection, and can be very effective. **Again, some dogs react badly to it.** Another drug is Interceptor (Milbemycin oxime), which can be expensive as it has to be given daily. However, it is effective on up to 80% of the dogs who did not respond to dips – but should be given with caution to pups under 21 weeks of age.

Dogs that have the generalised condition may have underlying skin infections, so antibiotics are often given for the first several weeks of treatment. Because the mite flourishes on dogs with suppressed immune systems, you should try to get to the root cause of immune system disease, especially if your Cavalier is older when he or she develops demodectic mange.

Harvest Mite

Specialist Contributors Dennis and Tina Homes have pointed out another parasitic mite that can affect Cavaliers and other animals in late summer and autumn – particularly if you walk your dog through long, grassy fields: "The orange, six-legged harvest mite is so small, it is barely visible to the human eye. It's at the larval stage when it attacks warm blooded animals – and humans; in other stages of its life it is not parasitic. The larvae feed on tissue fluid and can cause considerable discomfort to dogs.

"The larvae congregate on small clods of earth or vegetation. They are active during the day and particularly in dry, sunny weather. When a warm-blooded animal comes into contact with them, they swarm on to it and attach to the skin - particularly in sparsely-haired, thin-skinned areas. Individual larva inject a fluid with digestive enzymes which break down skin cells. The mite then sucks on the same place for two or three days until it is full, before dropping off the host, leaving a red swelling that can itch severely.

"The itching usually develops within three to six hours, but can continue for several weeks. The fluid injected by the mite is very irritating, causing the dog to scratch, bite and lick, which can result in extensive self-inflicted injury. If the skin is damaged due to scratching, these areas can also become infected."

Harvest mite larvae are only active during the day - the worst infestations occur when sitting in the sun in middle of the day. If your regular walk is through long, grassy fields, in warm weather consider going very early in the morning, before they become too active, And if you have a problem, wash all clothes you were wearing when you think the mites first attacked.

Dennis added: "There are insecticidal sprays available from your vet that can be of help, but it is more important to thoroughly wash your dog with a good insecticidal shampoo. *Thornit* is also said to be effective against mites. It is a remedy that we generally use for ear mites, but it also seems to be very effective for a variety of mites. Thornit is a powder that is based on Iodoform. The powder can be lightly dusted on to the itchy areas, or in to itchy ears. Relief usually comes within two to five days. *Yumega Plus* for dogs can help to relieve the itch as it has a combination of Omega 3 EPA from fresh salmon oil and Omega 6 GLA."

Cheyletiella (Rabbit Fur Mite)

"My dog appears to have dandruff, there's lots of white scurf in his coat," is a commonly-heard claim. Occasionally, scurf can be caused by a very dry skin or even by shampoo not being thoroughly rinsed out of the coat after a bath, but in the vast majority of cases, the parasitic Cheyletiella mite is to blame.

There are few symptoms, but a heavy infestation can cause itching, skin scaling and hair loss. The mites, their eggs and the scurf they produce have been called '*walking dandruff*', which is most frequently seen on the back and sides of the dog. Skin scales are carried through the hair coat by the mites, so the dandruff appears to be moving along the back of the animal, hence the nickname.

The mite spends its entire life cycle on the dog. Eggs are laid glued to the hair shafts and go on to form larvae, then nymph and then adult mites. They are spread by direct contact with an infected individual or infested bedding. These mites are non-burrowing and feed on the keratin layer or epidermis. They most often inhabit the dorsal coat (along the backbone or spine). The mite's life cycle lasts around 21 days on the host, which gives it plenty of time to spread to other areas and animals or humans.

Most affected dogs respond quite well to treatment, although it can sometimes take a while to completely cure the infestation. Your vet may prescribe a pyrethrin-based shampoo. Frontline spray has also been proved to be effective in killing off the mites.

After bathing with an insecticidal shampoo, it can also be quite effective if the dog is rinsed in a benzyl benzoate mixture prescribed by the vet and diluted as per the recommendations. Great care should be taken to not allow this to go anywhere near your dog's face. Always consult your vet.

Your dog's bedding area should be treated and you should also be aware that these mites can temporarily infest humans, causing a mild skin irritation and some itching. In some severe cases, open lesions may occur.

Sarcoptic Mange (Scabies)

Also known as canine scabies, this is caused by the parasite *Sarcoptes scabiei*. This microscopic mite can cause a range of skin problems, the most common of which is hair loss and severe itching. The mites can infect other animals such as foxes, cats and even humans, but prefer to live their short lives on dogs. Fortunately, there are several good treatments for this type of mange and the disease can be easily controlled.

In cool, moist environments, the mites live for up to 22 days. At normal room temperature they live from two to six days, preferring to live on parts of the dog with less hair. These are the areas you may see him scratching, although it can spread throughout the body in severe cases.

Diagnosing canine scabies can be somewhat difficult, and it is often mistaken for inhalant allergies. Once diagnosed, there are a number of effective treatments, including selamectin (Revolution – again, some dogs can have a bad reaction to this), an on-the-skin solution applied once a month which also provides heartworm prevention, flea control and some tick protection. Various Frontline products are also effective – check with your vet for the correct ones. There are also holistic remedies for many skin conditions.

Because your dog does not have to come into direct contact with an infected dog to catch scabies, it is difficult to completely protect him. Foxes and their environment can also transmit the mite so, if possible, keep your Cavalier away from areas where you know foxes are present.

Fleas

When you see your dog scratching and biting, your first thought is probably: "He's got fleas!" and you may well be right. Fleas don't fly, but they do have very strong back legs and they will take any opportunity to jump from the ground or another animal into your Cavalier's lovely warm coat. You can sometimes see the fleas if you part your dog's hair.

And for every flea that you see on your dog, there is the awful prospect of hundreds of eggs and larvae in your house or apartment. So, if your dog is unlucky enough to catch fleas, you'll have to treat your environment as well as your dog in order to completely get rid of them.

The best form of cure is prevention. Vets recommend giving dogs a preventative flea treatment every four to eight weeks. This may vary depending on your climate, the season - fleas do not breed as quickly in the cold - and how much time your dog spends outdoors. Once-a-month topical (applied to the skin) insecticides - like Frontline and Advantix - are the most commonly used flea prevention products on the market. You part the skin and apply drops of the liquid on to a small area on your dog's back, usually near the neck. Some kill fleas and ticks, and others just kill fleas - check the details.

It is worth spending the money on a quality treatment, as cheaper brands may not rid your Cavalier completely of fleas, ticks and other parasites. Sprays, dips, shampoos and collars are other options, as are tablets and injections in certain cases, such as before your dog goes into boarding kennels or has surgery. Incidentally, a flea bite is different from a flea bite allergy.

One UK breeder said that many breeders are opposed to chemical flea treatments, such as Spot On or ones from the vet, as so many dogs have been reported as reacting to the area it's applied to on the skin - and in extreme cases some have been known to have seizures. She added that when she found a flea, she simply washed all of her dogs, one after the other, and then washed every last piece of bedding and hadn't seen them since.

NOTE: There is also anecdotal evidence from owners of various breeds that the US flea and worm tablet *Trifexis* may cause severe side effects in some dogs. You may wish to read some owners' comments at: www.max-the-schnauzer.com/trifexis-side-effects-in-schnauzers.html

Ticks

A tick is not an insect, but a member of the arachnid family, like the spider. There are over 850 types of them, divided into two types: hard shelled and soft shelled. Ticks don't have wings - they can't fly, they crawl. They have a sensor called Haller's organ that detects smell, heat and humidity to help them locate food, which in some cases is a Cavalier. A tick's diet consists of one thing and one thing only – blood! They climb up onto tall grass and when they sense an animal is close, crawl on.

Ticks can pass on a number of diseases to animals and humans, the most well-known of which is **Lyme Disease**, a serious condition that causes lameness and other problems. Dogs that spend a lot of time outdoors in high risk areas, such as woods, can have a vaccination against Lime Disease.

One breeder added:" We get ticks from sand dunes sometimes and, if removed quickly, they're not harmful. We use a tick tool which has instructions in the packet. You put the forked end either side of the tick and twist it till it comes out."

If you do find a tick on your Cavalier's coat and are not sure how to get it out, have it removed by a vet or other expert. Inexpertly pulling it out yourself and leaving a bit of the tick behind can be detrimental to your dog's health. Prevention treatment is similar to that for fleas. If your Cavalier has sensitive skin, he or she might do better with a natural flea or tick remedy.

Heartworm

Heartworm is a serious and potentially fatal disease affecting pets in North America and many other parts of the world. It is caused by foot-long worms (heartworms) that live in the heart, lungs and associated blood vessels of affected pets, causing severe lung disease, heart failure and damage to other organs in the body.

The dog is a natural host for heartworms, which means that heartworms living inside the dog mature into adults, mate and produce offspring. If untreated, their numbers can increase; dogs have been known to harbour several hundred worms in their bodies. Heartworm disease causes lasting damage to the heart, lungs and arteries, and can affect the dog's health and quality of life long after the parasites are gone. For this reason, prevention is by far the best option and treatment - when needed - should be administered as early as possible.

The mosquito (pictured) plays an essential role in the heartworm life cycle. When a mosquito bites and takes a blood meal from an infected animal, it picks up baby worms that develop and mature into 'infective stage' larvae over a period of 10 to 14 days.

Then, when the infected mosquito bites another dog, cat or susceptible wild animal, the infective larvae are deposited onto the surface of the animal's skin and enter the new host through the mosquito's bite wound. Once inside a new host, it takes approximately six months for the larvae to develop into adult heartworms. Once mature, heartworms can live for five to seven years in a dog. In the early stages of the disease, many dogs show few or no symptoms. The longer the infection persists, the more likely symptoms will develop. These include:

- ❧ A mild persistent cough
- ❧ Reluctance to exercise
- ❧ Tiredness after moderate activity
- ❧ Decreased appetite
- ❧ Weight loss

As the disease progresses, dogs may develop heart failure and a swollen belly due to excess fluid in the abdomen. Dogs with large numbers of heartworms can develop sudden blockages of blood flow within the heart leading to the life-threatening caval syndrome. This is marked by a sudden onset of laboured breathing, pale gums and dark, bloody or coffee-coloured urine. Without prompt surgical removal of the heartworm blockage, few dogs survive.

Although more common in the south eastern US, heartworm disease has been diagnosed in all 50 states. And because infected mosquitoes can fly indoors, even dogs that spend much time inside the home are at risk. For that reason, the American Heartworm Society recommends that you get your dog tested every year and give your dog heartworm preventive treatment for 12 months of the year. If you live in a risk area, check that your tick and flea medication also prevents heartworm. In the UK, heartworm has only been found in imported dogs.

Thanks to the American Heartworm Society for assistance with the section.

Ringworm

This is not actually a worm, but a fungus and is most commonly seen in puppies and young dogs. It is highly infectious and often found on the face, ears, paws or tail. The ringworm fungus is most prevalent in hot, humid climates but, surprisingly, most cases occur in autumn and winter. Ringworm infections in dogs are not that common; in one study of dogs with active skin problems, less than 3% had ringworm.

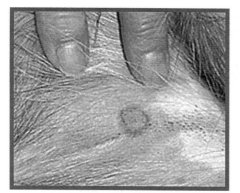

Ringworm is transmitted by spores in the soil and by contact with the infected hair of dogs and cats, which can be typically found on carpets, brushes, combs, toys and furniture. Spores from infected animals can be shed into the environment and live for over 18 months, but fortunately most healthy adult dogs have some resistance and never develop symptoms. The fungi live in dead skin, hairs and nails - and the head and legs are the most common areas affected.

Tell-tale signs are bald patches with a roughly circular shape (pictured). Ringworm is relatively easy to treat with fungicidal shampoos or antibiotics from a vet. Humans can catch ringworm from pets, and vice versa. Children are especially susceptible, as are adults with suppressed immune systems and those undergoing chemotherapy. Hygiene is extremely important.

If your dog has ringworm, wear gloves when handling him and wash your hands well afterwards. And if a member of your family catches ringworm, make sure they use separate towels from everyone else or the fungus may spread. (As a teenager I caught ringworm from horses at the stables where I worked at weekends - much to my mother's horror - and was treated like a leper by the rest of the family until it had cleared up!)

Bacterial infection (Pyoderma)

Pyoderma literally means 'pus in the skin' (yuk!) and fortunately this condition is not contagious. Early signs of this bacterial infection are itchy red spots filled with yellow pus, similar to pimples or spots in humans. They can sometimes develop into red, ulcerated skin with dry and crusty patches.

Pyoderma is caused by several things: a broken skin surface, a skin wound due to chronic exposure to moisture, altered skin bacteria, or impaired blood flow to the skin. Dogs have a higher risk of developing an infection when they have a fungal infection or an endocrine (hormone gland) disease such as hyperthyroidism, or have allergies to fleas, food or parasites.

Pyoderma is often secondary to allergic dermatitis and develops in the sores on the skin that occur as a result of scratching. Puppies often develop 'puppy pyoderma' in thinly-haired areas such as the groin and underarms. Fleas, ticks, yeast or fungal skin infections, thyroid disease, hormonal imbalances, heredity and some medications can increase the risk. If you notice symptoms, get your dog to the vet quickly before the condition develops from **superficial pyoderma** into **severe pyoderma**, which is very unpleasant and takes a lot longer to treat.

Bacterial infection, no matter how bad it may look, usually responds well to medical treatment, which is generally done on an outpatient basis. Superficial pyoderma will usually be treated with a two to six-week course of antibiotic tablets or ointment. Severe or recurring pyoderma looks awful, causes your dog some distress and can take months of treatment to completely cure. Medicated shampoos and regular bathing, as instructed by your vet, are also part of the treatment. It's also important to ensure your dog has clean, dry, padded bedding.

Canine Acne

This is not that common and - just as with humans - generally affects teenagers, often between five and eight months of age with dogs. Acne occurs when oil glands become blocked causing bacterial infection and these glands are most active in teenagers. Acne is not a major health problem as most of it will clear up once the dog becomes an adult, but it can reoccur. Typical signs are pimples, blackheads or whiteheads around the muzzle, chest or groin. If the area is irritated, then there may be some bleeding or pus that can be expressed from these blemishes.

Hormonal Imbalances

These occur in dogs of all breeds. They are often difficult to diagnose and occur when a dog is producing either too much (hyper) or too little (hypo) of a particular hormone. One visual sign is often hair loss on both sides of the dog's body. The condition is not usually itchy. Hormone imbalances can be serious as they are often indicators that glands that affect the dog internally are not working properly. However, some types can be diagnosed by special blood tests and treated effectively.

Ear Infections

Cavaliers have long, floppy, hairy ears, which makes them susceptible to ear infections.

Infection of the external ear canal (outer ear infection) is called *otitis externa* and is one of the most common types seen. The fact that your dog has recurring ear infections does not necessarily mean that his ears are the source of the problem – although they might be. One common reason for them in Cavaliers is moisture in the ear canal, which in turn allows bacteria to flourish there.

However, some dogs with chronic or recurring ear infections have inhalant or food allergies or low thyroid function (hypothyroidism). Sometimes the ears are the first sign of allergy. The underlying problem must be treated or the dog will continue to have long term ear problems. Tell-tale signs include your dog shaking his head, scratching or rubbing his ears a lot, or an unpleasant smell coming from the ears.

If you look inside the ears, you may notice a reddy brown or yellow discharge, it may also be red and inflamed with a lot of wax. Sometimes a dog may appear depressed or irritable; ear infections are painful. In chronic cases, the inside of his ears may become crusty or thickened. Dogs can have ear problems for many different reasons, including:

- Allergies, such as environmental or food allergies

- Ear mites or other parasites

- Bacteria or yeast infections

- Injury, often due to excessive scratching

- Hormonal abnormalities, e.g. hypothyroidism

- The ear anatomy and environment, e.g. excess moisture

- Hereditary or immune conditions and tumours

In reality, many Cavaliers have ear infections due to the structure of the ear. The long, hairy ears often prevent sufficient air flow inside the ear. This can lead to bacterial or yeast infections - particularly if there is moisture inside. These warm, damp and dark areas under the ear flaps provide an ideal breeding ground for bacteria.

Treatment depends on the cause and what – if any - other conditions your dog may have. Antibiotics are used for bacterial infections and antifungals for yeast infections. Glucocorticoids, such as dexamethasone, are often included in these medications to reduce the inflammation in the ear. Your vet may also flush out and clean the ear with special drops, something you may have to do daily at home until the infection clears.

A dog's ear canal is L-shaped, which means it can be difficult to get medication into the lower (horizontal) part of the ear. The best method is to hold the dog's ear flap with one hand and put the ointment or drops in with the other, if possible tilting the dog's head away from you so the liquid

flows downwards **with gravity**. Make sure you then hold the ear flap down and massage the medication into the horizontal canal before letting go of your dog, as the first thing he will do is shake his head – and if the ointment or drops aren't massaged in, they will fly out.

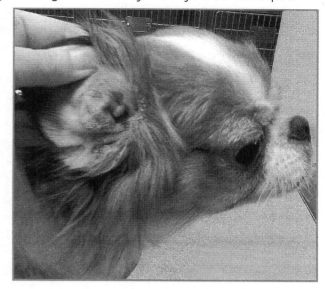

Nearly all ear infections can be successfully managed if properly diagnosed and treated. But if an underlying problem remains undiscovered, the outcome will be less favourable.

Deep ear infections can damage or rupture the eardrum, causing an internal ear infection and even permanent hearing loss. Closing of the ear canal (*hyperplasia* or *stenosis)* is another sign of severe infection. Most extreme cases of hyperplasia will eventually require surgery as a last resort; the most common procedure is called a 'lateral ear resection'. Our dog with allergies had a lateral ear resection following years of recurring ear infections and the growth of scar tissue. It was surgery or deafness, the vet said. We opted for surgery and the dog was free of ear infections ever since. However, it is an **extremely** painful procedure for the animal and should only be considered as a very last resort.

To avoid or alleviate recurring ear infections, check your dog's ears and clean them regularly. Hair should be regularly plucked from inside your Cavalier's ears – either by you or a groomer, or both. Breeder Jina Ezell, of Kalama Cavaliers, Washington State, USA, goes even further: "I completely SHAVE the underside of the ear and go into the ear canal to keep the hair clean and clear. As such, I have yet to have an ear infection."

When cleaning or plucking your dog's ears, be very careful not to put anything too far down inside. Visit YouTube to see videos of how to correctly clean without damaging them. DO NOT use cotton buds inside the ear, they are too small and can cause injury. Some owners recommend regularly cleaning the inside of ears with cotton wool and a mixture of water and white vinegar once or twice a week. If your Cavalier is one of the many that enjoys swimming, great care should be taken to ensure the inside of the ear is thoroughly dry afterwards - and after bathing at home. There is more information in **Chapter 14. Grooming.**

Consider buying elevated food and water bowls (pictured). They have higher, narrower tops than normal dog dishes and help to keep your dog's ears out of his or her food and water.

If your dog appears to be in pain, has smelly ears, or if his ear canals look inflamed, contact your vet straight away. If you can nip the first infection in the bud, there is a chance it will not return. If your dog has a ruptured or weakened eardrum, ear cleansers and medications could do more harm than good. Early treatment is the best way of preventing a recurrence.

Some Allergy Treatments

Treatments and success rates vary tremendously from dog to dog and from one allergy to another, which is why it is so important to consult a vet at the outset. Earlier diagnosis is more likely to lead to a successful treatment. Some owners whose dogs have recurring skin issues find that a course of antibiotics or steroids works wonders for their dog's sore skin and itching. However, the scratching starts all over again shortly after the treatment stops.

Food allergies require patience, a change of diet and maybe even a food trial, and the specific trigger is notoriously difficult to isolate – unless you are lucky and hit on the culprit straight away. With inhalant and contact allergies, blood and skin tests are available, followed by hypersensitisation treatment. However, these are expensive and often the specific trigger for many dogs remains unknown. So, the reality for many owners of Cavaliers with allergies is that they manage the ailment with various medications and practices, rather than curing it completely.

Our Personal Experience

After corresponding with numerous other dog owners and consulting our vet, Graham, it seems that our experiences with allergies are not uncommon. This is borne out by the dozens of dog owners who have contacted our website about their pet's allergy or sensitivities. According to Graham, more and more dogs appearing in his waiting room every spring with various types of allergies. Whether this is connected to how we breed our dogs remains to be seen.

Our dog was perfectly fine until he was about two years old when he began to scratch a lot. He

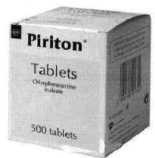

scratched more in spring and summer, which meant that his allergies were almost certainly inhalant or contact-based and related to pollens, grasses or other outdoor triggers. One option was a barrage of tests to discover exactly what he was allergic to. We decided not to do this, not because of the cost, but because our vet said it was highly likely that he was allergic to pollens. If we had confirmed an allergy to pollens, we were not going to stop taking him outside for walks, so the vet treated him on the basis of seasonal inhalant or contact allergies, probably related to pollen.

As mentioned, it's beneficial to have a shallow bath or hose outside and to rinse the dog's paws and underbelly after a walk in the countryside. This is something our vet does with his own dogs and has found that the scratching reduces as a result. Regarding medications, our dog was at first put on to a tiny dose of Piriton, an antihistamine for hay fever sufferers (human and canine) and for the first few springs and summers, this worked well.

Allergies can often change and the dog can also build up a tolerance to a treatment, which is why they can be so difficult to treat. This has been the case with us over the years. The symptoms changed from season to season, although the main ones remained and were: general scratching, paw biting and ear infections.

One year he bit the skin under his tail a lot (near the anus) and this was treated very effectively with a single steroid injection followed by spraying the area with cortisone once a day at home for a period. This type of spray can be very effective if the itchy area is small, but no good for spraying all over a dog's body. Not every owner wants to treat his or her dog with chemicals, nor feed a diet which includes preservatives, which is why this book includes alternatives.

A couple of years ago he started nibbling his paws for the first time - a habit he persisted with - although not to the extent that they become red and raw. Over the years we tried a number of treatments, all of which worked for a while, before he came off the medication in autumn for six months when plants and grasses stop growing outdoors. He managed perfectly fine the rest of the year without any treatment at all.

We fed a high quality hypoallergenic dry food. If we were starting again from scratch, knowing what we know now, I would probably investigate a raw diet or raw with biscuits, if necessary in combination with holistic remedies. Max's allergies were manageable; he loved his food, was full of energy and otherwise healthy, and lived a happy life to the age of 13 years.

One season the vet put him on a short course of steroids. These worked very well for five months, but steroids are not a long-term solution, as prolonged use can cause organ damage. Another spring, we were prescribed Atopica, a non-steroid daily tablet sold in the UK only through vets. The active ingredient is **cyclosporine**, which suppresses the immune system. Some dogs can get side

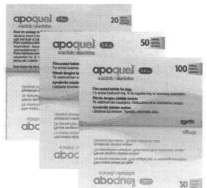

effects, although ours didn't, and holistic practitioners believe that it is harmful to the dog. This treatment was expensive, but initially extremely effective – so much so that we thought we had cured the problem completely. However, after a couple of seasons on cyclosporine he developed a tolerance to the drug and started scratching again.

A few years ago he went back on the antihistamine Piriton, a higher dose than when he was two years old, and this worked very well again. One advantage of this drug is that is it manufactured by the million for dogs and is therefore very inexpensive.

In 2013 the FDA approved **Apoquel** (oclacitinib) to control itching and inflammation in allergic dogs. In some quarters it has been hailed a wonder drug for canine allergies. In fact it proved so popular in the UK and North America that in the following two years there was a shortage of supply, with the manufacturers not being able to produce it fast enough.

We tried it with excellent results. There was some tweaking at the beginning to get the daily dose right, but it really proved effective for us. The tablets are administered according to body weight and cost around £1 or $1.50 each. It's not cheap, but Apoquel can be a miracle worker for some dogs.

NOTE: This article from Dogs Naturally magazine recommends NOT giving Apoquel to your dog: www.dogsnaturallymagazine.com/wouldnt-give-dog-new-allergy-drug - make up your own mind. Allergies are often complex and difficult to treat; you should weigh up the pros and cons in the best interests of your individual dog.

Vets often recommend adding fish oils (which contain Omega-3 fatty acids) to a daily feed to keep your dog's skin and coat healthy all year round – whether or not he has problems. We added a liquid supplement called Yumega Plus, which contains Omegas 3 and 6, to one of the two daily feeds all year round and this definitely seemed to help the skin.

When the scratching got particularly bad, we bathed our dog in an antiseborrheic shampoo (called Malaseb) twice a week for a limited time. This also helped, although was not necessary once he started on Apoquel.

The main point is that most allergies are manageable, although they may change throughout the life of the dog and you may have to alter the treatment. We've compiled some anecdotal evidence from our website from owners of dogs with various allergies; here are some of their suggestions for alleviating the problems:

Bathing - bathing your dog using shampoos that break down the oils that plug the hair follicles. These shampoos contain antiseborrheic ingredients such as benzoyl peroxide, salicylic acid, sulphur or tar. One example is Sulfoxydex shampoo, which can be followed by a cream rinse such as Episoothe Rinse afterwards to prevent the skin from drying out.

Dabbing – Using an astringent such as witch hazel or alcohop on affected areas. We have heard of zinc oxide cream being used to some effect. In the human world, this is rubbed on to mild skin abrasions and acts as a protective coating. It can help the healing of chapped skin and nappy rash in babies. Zinc oxide works as a mild astringent and has some antiseptic properties and is safe to use on dogs, *as long as you do not allow the dog to lick it off*.

Daily supplements - Vitamin E, vitamin A, zinc and omega oils all help to make a dog's skin healthy. Feed a daily supplement that contains some of these, such as fish oil, which provides omega.

Here are some specific remedies from owners. We are not endorsing them; we're just passing on the information. Check with your vet before trying any new remedies.

A medicated shampoo with natural tea tree oil has been suggested by one owner. Some have reported that switching to a fish-based diet has helped lessen scratching, while others have suggested home-cooked food is best, if you have the time to prepare the food.

Another reader said: "I have been putting a teaspoon of canola (rapeseed) oil in my dog's food every other day and it has helped with the itching. I have shampooed the new carpet in hopes of removing any of the chemicals that could be irritating her. And I have changed laundry detergent. After several loads of laundry everything has been washed."

And from another reader: "My eight-month-old dog also had a contact dermatitis around his neck and chest. I was surprised how extensive it was. The vet recommended twice-a-week baths with an oatmeal shampoo. I also applied organic coconut oil daily for a few weeks and this completely cured the dermatitis. I also put a capsule of fish oil with his food once a day and continue to give him twice-weekly baths. His skin is great now."

Many owners have tried coconut oil with some success. Here is a link to an article on the benefits of coconut oils and fish oils, check with your vet first: www.dogsnaturallymagazine.com/the-health-benefits-of-coconut-oil

 If you suspect your dog has a skin problem, ear infection or allergy, bite the bullet and get her or him to the vet straight away. You can hopefully nip it in the bud before secondary infections develop – and save a lot of heartache and money in the long run.

The Holistic Approach

As canine allergies become increasingly common, more and more owners of dogs with allergies and sensitivities are looking towards natural foods and remedies to help deal with the issues. Others are finding that their dog does well for a time with injections or medication, but then the symptoms slowly start to reappear. A holistic practitioner looks at finding the root cause of the problem and treating that, rather than just treating the symptoms.

Dr Sara Skiwski is a holistic vet working in California. She writes here about canine environmental allergies: "Here in California, with our mild weather and no hard freeze in Winter, environmental allergens can build up and cause nearly year-round issues for our beloved pets. Also seasonal allergies, when left unaddressed, can lead to year-round allergies.

"Unlike humans, whose allergy symptoms seem to affect mostly the respiratory tract, seasonal allergies in dogs often take the form of skin irritation/inflammation.

"Allergic reactions are produced by the immune system. The way the immune system functions is a result of both genetics and the environment: Nature versus Nurture. Let's look at a typical case. A puppy starts showing mild seasonal allergy symptoms, for instance a red tummy and mild itching in Spring. Off to the vet!

"The treatment prescribed is symptomatic to provide relief, such as a topical spray. The next year when the weather warms up, the patient is back again - same symptoms but more severe this time. This time the dog has very itchy skin. Again, the treatment is symptomatic - antibiotics, topical spray (hopefully no steroids), until the symptoms resolve with the season change. Fast forward to another Spring...on the third year, the patient is back again but this time the symptoms last longer, (not just Spring but also through most of Summer and into Fall).

"By Year Five, all the symptoms are significantly worse and are occurring year round. This is what happens with seasonal environmental allergies. The more your pet is exposed to the allergens they are sensitive to, the more the immune system over-reacts and the more intense and long-lasting the allergic response becomes. What to do?

"In my practice, I like to address the potential root cause at the very first sign of an allergic response, which is normally seen between the ages of six to nine months old. I do this to circumvent the escalating response year after year. Since the allergen load your environmentally-sensitive dog is most susceptible to is much heavier outdoors, I recommend two essential steps in managing the condition. They are vigilance in foot care as well as hair care.

"What does this mean? A wipe down of feet and hair, especially the tummy, to remove any pollens or allergens is key. This can be done with a damp cloth, but my favorite method is to get a spray bottle filled with Witch Hazel and spray these areas. First, spray the feet then wipe them off with a cloth, and then spray and wipe down the tummy and sides. This is best done right after the pup has been outside playing or walking. This will help keep your pet from tracking the environmental allergens into the home and into their beds. If the feet end up still being itchy, I suggest adding foot soaks in Epsom salts."

Dr Sara also stresses the importance of keeping the immune system healthy by avoiding unnecessary vaccinations or drugs: "The vaccine stimulates the immune system, which is the last thing your pet with seasonal environmental allergies needs.

"I also will move the pet to an anti-inflammatory diet. Foods that create or worsen inflammation are high in carbohydrates. An allergic pet's diet should be very low in carbohydrates, especially grains.

Research has shown that 'leaky gut,' or dysbiosis, is a root cause of immune system overreactions in both dog and cats (and some humans). Feed a diet that is not processed, or minimally processed; one that doesn't have grain and takes a little longer to get absorbed and assimilated through the gut. Slowing the assimilation assures that there are not large spikes of nutrients and proteins that come into the body all at once and overtax the pancreas and liver, creating inflammation.

"A lot of commercial diets are too high in grains and carbohydrates. These foods create inflammation which overtaxes the body and leads not just to skin inflammation, but also to other inflammatory conditions, such as colitis, pancreatitis, arthritis, inflammatory bowel disease and ear infections. Also, these diets are too low in protein, which is needed to make blood. This causes a decreased blood reserve in the body and in some of these animals this can lead to the skin not being properly nourished, starting a cycle of chronic skin infections which produce more itching."

After looking at diet, check that your dog is free from fleas and then these are some of Dr Sara's suggested supplements:

✓ **Raw (Unpasteurised) Local Honey** - an alkaline-forming food containing natural vitamins, enzymes, powerful antioxidants and other important natural nutrients, which are destroyed during the heating and pasteurisation processes. Raw honey has anti-viral, anti-bacterial and anti-fungal properties. It promotes body and digestive health, is a powerful antioxidant, strengthens the immune system, eliminates allergies, and is an excellent remedy for skin wounds and all types of infections. Bees collect pollen from local plants and their honey often acts as an immune booster for dogs living in the locality.

Dr Sara says: "It may seem odd that straight exposure to pollen often triggers allergies, but that exposure to pollen in the honey usually has the opposite effect. But this is typically what we see. In honey, the allergens are delivered in small, manageable doses and the effect over time is very much like that from undergoing a whole series of allergy immunology injections."

✓ **Mushrooms** - make sure you choose the non-poisonous ones! Dogs don't like the taste, you so may have to mask it with another food. Medicinal mushrooms are used to treat and prevent a wide array of illnesses through their use as immune stimulants and modulators, and antioxidants. The most well-known and researched are reishi, maitake, cordyceps, blazei, split-gill, turkey tail and shiitake. The mushrooms stabilise mast cells in the body, which have the histamines attached to them. Histamine is what causes much of the inflammation, redness and irritation in allergies. By helping to control histamine production, the mushrooms can moderate the effects of inflammation and even help prevent allergies in the first place.

WARNING! Mushrooms can interact with some over-the-counter and prescription drugs, so do your research as well as checking with your vet first.

✓ **Stinging Nettles** - contain biologically active compounds that reduce inflammation. Nettles have the ability to reduce the amount of histamine the body produces in response to an allergen. Nettle tea or extract can help with itching. Nettles not only help directly to decrease the itch, but also work overtime to desensitise the body to allergens, helping to reprogramme the immune system.

✓ **Quercetin** – is an over-the-counter supplement with anti-inflammatory properties. It is a strong antioxidant and reduces the body's production of histamines.

✔ **Omega-3 Fatty Acids** - these help decrease inflammation throughout the body. Adding them into the diet of all pets - particularly those struggling with seasonal environmental allergies – is very beneficial. If your dog has more itching along the top of their back and on their sides, add in a fish oil supplement. Fish oil helps to decrease the itch and heal skin lesions. The best sources of Omega 3s are krill oil, salmon oil, tuna oil, anchovy oil and other fish body oils, as well as raw organic egg yolks. If using an oil alone, it is important to give a vitamin B complex supplement.

✔ **Coconut Oil** - contains lauric acid, which helps decrease the production of yeast, a common opportunistic infection. Using a fish body oil combined with coconut oil before inflammation flares up can help moderate or even suppress your dog's inflammatory response.

Dr Sara adds: "Above are but a few of the over-the-counter remedies I like. In non-responsive cases, Chinese herbs can be used to work with the body to help to decrease the allergy threshold even more than with diet and supplements alone. Most of the animals I work with are on a program of Chinese herbs, diet change and acupuncture.

"So, the next time Fido is showing symptoms of seasonal allergies, consider rethinking your strategy to treat the root cause instead of the symptom."

With thanks to Dr Sara Skiwski, of the Western Dragon Integrated Veterinary Services, San Jose, California, for her kind permission to use her writings as the basis for this section.

....

This chapter has only just touched on the complex subject of skin disorders. As you can see, the causes and treatments are many and varied. One thing is true whatever the condition: if your Cavalier has a skin issue, seek a professional diagnosis as soon as possible before attempting to treat it yourself and before the condition becomes entrenched.

Early diagnosis and treatment give the best chance of a full recovery.

Some skin conditions cannot be completely cured, but they can be successfully managed, allowing your dog to live a happy, pain-free life. If you haven't got your puppy yet, ask the breeder if there is a history of skin issues in his or her bloodlines. Once you have your pup or adult dog, remember that regular grooming, a good quality diet and attention to cleanliness and ears go a long way in preventing or managing skin problems and ear infections in Cavaliers.

14. Grooming the Cavalier

One of the Cavalier's prize assets is its beautiful silky coat, which is quite unique. The breed is the only Spaniel to have the distinctive feathering on the feet - sometimes called *bedroom slippers!* This is usually left natural, although the hair between the pads and nails should be trimmed.

The coat is double layered with a dense undercoat and silky, straight or slightly wavy top coat; it shouldn't be curly. As well as the feet, there is also feathering on the tail, chest, legs and ears. Don't worry if your puppy has a tail which looks more like it belongs on a Pointer than a Cavalier, the feathering doesn't fully show until adulthood!

In the show world, there is a certain understated elegance and beauty to the sight of a superbly-groomed Cavalier in full flow... but this has a price, Cavaliers are pretty high maintenance when it comes to grooming – and not just show dogs. To keep a pet Cavalier's coat healthy and clean requires time and effort on the part of the owner.

And another downside of Cavaliers is that they shed - A LOT. They shed more in spring and autumn (fall), but tend to lose hair all year round. Females will shed more after each heat cycle or litter. All of this means that **Cavaliers are generally not a suitable choice for people with allergies** - or the very house-proud.

Although clean dogs by nature, if Cavs are running free, mud, grass, burrs and other organic matter can get caught up in the long coat (as is the case with all Spaniels), and then transferred to the home.

The trademark long, hairy ears also require your attention. They drag along the ground when your Cavalier does what comes natural to Spaniels, i.e. runs around with his or her nose to the ground on the trail of a scent – and they quite easily get wet and/or dirty. Regular ear cleaning should be a part of your grooming routine to prevent ear infections - the bugbear of any breed with long, floppy ears. Similarly, lack of attention to the luxuriant coat can lead to it becoming matted and smelly. Cavaliers are clean dogs by nature and if yours smells "doggie", you are not paying enough attention to grooming!

The Cavalier Coat

All Cavaliers are born with a puppy coat, which varies in texture and maintenance from an adult coat; it is generally short and wavy, whereas an adult coat is longer and straighter. The adult coat should be apparent by around the age of one year. While a puppy's coat requires very little maintenance, it is important to start handling and grooming your pup right from the beginning.

Except for exceptional circumstances, a Cavalier's coat should never be fully trimmed or shaved off - even in hot conditions, as it can ruin it. Owners Laura and Mustafa Rakla live in Dubai and have two Cavaliers, Alfred, aged two, and Bertie, who is six months younger. Laura says: "They have coped a little better with the heat than we thought for a short-nosed breed. Because of the temperature in Dubai, we did trim Alfred short in the summer and it made his coat very curly. People should not do this! It has taken over a year for it to grow back straight and glossy. We now thin the coat a lot with scissors in the summer months, but never tail or ears. Similar to other breeds, in the very hot summer their foot pads can become burned or dry from walking on the hot pavement or stone. We try to keep them mainly on the grass at these times; it wouldn't be practical if you didn't have a garden."

We advise against it, but if you do decide to have your Cavalier clippered in hot weather, leave at least an inch of coat on - and even then, it might grow back curly. If you intent to show your dog, trimming the coat with clippers is not permitted, except for the hair between the pads of the feet to make it more comfortable for walking.

If your dog has a particularly thick coat or shows signs of struggling for breath in hot weather, a better option to clipping is to buy a tool like a Coat King (pictured) which thins out the denser undercoat but leaves the outer coat the normal length. Not only is this far better for your dog's coat, but it is something you can easily do yourself at home (preferably outdoors), so saving the expense of a trip to the groomer's.

The coat comes in four colours, listed here in order of popularity: Blenheim (chestnut and white), tricolour, black and tan, and ruby. Studies show that there is no great difference in temperament or anything else between the colours; it is simply a matter of personal preference.

Tip If you haven't got your dog yet and have set your heart on a specific colour, make sure you see the parents' health certificates as well as the puppies.

Like any breed, the Cavalier can have health issues related to the coat. These are covered in detail in **Chapter 12. Cavalier Health** and **Chapter 13. Skin and Allergies.**

....

Regular Maintenance

Grooming doesn't just mean giving your Cavalier a quick tickle with a brush once a week. There are other facets that play a part in keeping your dog clean and skin-related issues at bay. Time spent grooming is also time spent bonding with your dog; this physical and emotional inter-reliance brings us closer to our pets. Cavaliers, especially, like to be close to their owners, and once they have got used to it, most LOVE being groomed, just watch their eyes glaze over when you brush them.

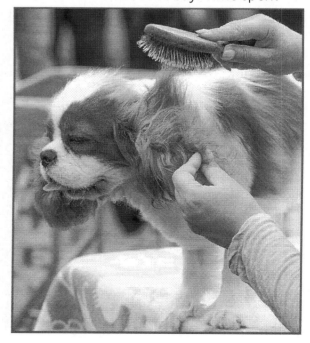

Routine grooming sessions also allow you to examine your Cavalier's coat, skin, ears, teeth, eyes, paws and nails for signs of problems. Other benefits of regular brushing are that it removes dead hair and skin, stimulates blood circulation and spreads natural oils throughout the coat, helping to keep it in good condition. Even if your dog has regular trips to the groomer's for a bath and a trim around the paws, etc., you still need to groom at home in between visits.

Cavaliers require regular grooming throughout their lives, so it's important to get a puppy used to being handled from an early age; a wilful adult will not take kindly to being groomed if he is not used to it. You can start gently brushing your puppy with a soft brush or grooming glove a week or two after you bring him or her home. If your Cavalier is resisting your grooming efforts, take him out of his comfort zone by placing him on a table or bench - make sure he can't jump off. You'd be surprised what a difference this can make once he is out of his normal environment, i.e. floor level - and at your level, where you can more easily control him (this is not recommended for puppies).

You can use a variety of tools and brushes to groom a Cavalier: a medium bristle brush, metal comb, slicker brush (pictured) and a coat thinner/de-shedder such as a Furminator or Coat King - make sure you buy the right model for a Cavalier. A few things to look out for when grooming are:

Feet - Cavaliers have fluffy, feathered hair on and under their feet (paws), which needs trimming to prevent it becoming matted. Use scissors or clippers to remove the hair between the pads on the underside of the feet and to trim any excess hair on top of the feet. Check after walks for any debris or tangles stuck in the fur around the feet - brush these out with a slicker brush – and also make sure the pads are not dry and cracked.

Eyes - These should be clean and clear. Cloudy eyes, particularly in an older dog, could be early signs of cataracts. Red or swollen tissue in the corner of the eye could be a symptom of cherry eye, which can affect dogs of all breeds. Ingrowing eyelashes are another issue which causes red, watery eyes. If your dog has an issue, you can start by gently bathing the eye(s) with warm water and cotton wool - but never use anything sharp; your dog can suddenly jump forwards or backwards, causing injury. If the eye is red or watering for a few days or more, get it checked out by a vet. If your Cav has reddish tear stains, it could be too much yeast, so check the diet. Tear stain removal products are widely available.

Dry skin - A dog's skin can dry out, especially with artificial heat in the winter months. If you spot any dry patches, for example on the pads, inner thighs or armpits, or a cracked nose, massage a little petroleum jelly or baby oil on to the dry patch.

Acne - Little red pimples on a dog's face and chin mean he has got acne. A dog can get acne at any age, not just as an adolescent. Plastic bowls can also trigger the condition, which is why stainless steel ones are often better. Daily washing followed by an application of an antibiotic cream is usually enough to get rid of the problem; if it persists, it will mean a visit to your vet.

Ear Cleaning

It is not uncommon for Cavaliers to suffer from ear infections. Breeds with pricked-up ears, like the

German Shepherd Dog, suffer far fewer ear infections than those with long, floppy ears. This is because an upright ear allows air to circulate inside, whereas covered inner ears are generally warm, dark and moist, making them a haven for bacteria and yeast. Add to that the luxuriant feathering inside and outside a Cavalier's ears and you have a prime target for recurring ear infections.

Swimming can also cause ear infections if the area under the ear flap remains wet for long periods. The wetness, combined with the warmth of an enclosed space, is an ideal breeding ground for bacteria. A good habit to get into is to towel dry under the ear flaps every time your dog goes swimming. If you bathe your dog try to keep the water away from the inside of the ears, and consider putting cotton wool balls under the ear flaps - but don't forget to remove them or your Cavalier will be even deafer than usual to your commands!

Keep an eye out for redness or inflammation of the ear flap or inner ear, or a build-up of dark wax. If your dog goes to the groomer's, ask her to pluck any excess hair from under the ear flap - this is also something you can do at home.

Also, wash or hose your dog down after swimming in the sea to keep the coat free from salt – don't forget to dry the ears afterwards.

Some owners of susceptible dogs bathe the inner ear with cotton wool and warm water or a veterinary ear cleaner as part of their regular grooming routine. Whether or not your Cavalier has issues, it is good practice to check his or her ears and eyes regularly.

Tip *Never put anything sharp or narrow, like a cotton bud (Q-tip), inside your dog's ears, as you can cause injury.*

Typical signs of an ear infection are: your dog shaking his head a lot, scratching his ears, rubbing his ears on the carpet or ground, and/or an unpleasant smell coming from the ears, which is a sign of a yeast infection. If your dog exhibits any of these signs, consult your vet A.S.A.P. as simple routine cleaning won't solve the problem, and *ear infections are notoriously difficult to get rid of* once your dog's had one.

The secret is to keep your dog's ears clean, dry and free from too much hair right from puppyhood and hope that he or she never gets one.

One breeder had this advice: "Try to never get water or liquid in the ears, including when bathing. Check weekly for any brown gunk in the ears and use a tissue to wipe it out, being careful to avoid the ear canal. At the same time, use your finger and thumb to remove whatever hair you're able to reach from the inside of the ear; this is better than using a tool, which can take too much. If you struggle to get a grip on the hair, sprinkle a little ear plucking powder in then try again."

One method of cleaning ears is to get a good quality ear cleaning solution from your vet's or local pet/grooming supply shop. Then squeeze the cleaner into one ear canal and rub the ear at the base next to the skull. Allow your dog to shake his or her head and use a cotton ball to gently wipe out any dirt and waxy build up inside the ear canal.

Method Two is to use a baby wipe and gently wipe away any dirt and waxy build up. In both cases it is important to only clean as far down the ear canal as you can see to avoid damaging the eardrum. The first method is preferred if you are also bathing your dog, as it will remove any unwanted water that may have got down into the ears during the bath. See **Chapter 13. Skin and Allergies** for more information on ear infections.

Nail Trimming

If your Cavalier is regularly exercised on grass or other soft surfaces, her nails may not be getting worn down sufficiently, so they may have to be clipped or filed. Nails should be kept short for the paws to remain healthy. Long nails interfere with the dog's gait, making walking awkward or painful and they can also break easily, usually at the base of the nail where blood vessels and nerves are located.

Get your dog used to having her paws inspected from puppyhood; it's also a good opportunity to check for other problems, such as cracked pads or interdigital cysts (swellings between the toes, often due to a bacterial infection). Be prepared; many dogs dislike having their nails trimmed, so it requires patience and persistence on your part.

To trim your dog's nails, use a specially designed clipper. Most have safety guards to prevent you cutting the nails too short. Do it before they get too long; if you can hear the nails clicking on the floor, they're too long. You want to trim only the ends, before 'the quick', (hence the expression "cut to the quick"), which is a blood vessel inside the nail. You can see where the quick ends on a white nail, but not on a dark nail.

Clip only the hook-like part of the nail that turns down. Start trimming gently, a nail or two at a time, and your dog will learn that you're not going to hurt her. If you accidentally cut the quick, stop the bleeding with some styptic powder.

Another option is to file your dog's nails with a nail grinder tool. Some dogs may have tough nails that are hard to trim and this may be less stressful for your dog, with less chance of pain or bleeding. The grinder is like an electric nail file and only removes a small amount of nail at a time. Some owners prefer to use one as it is harder to cut the quick, and many dogs prefer them to a clipper. However, you have to introduce your Cavalier gradually to the grinder – Cavs can be wimps and often don't like the noise or vibration at first. If you find it impossible to clip your dog's nails, or you are at all worried about doing it, take her to the vet or groomer - and ask him or her to squeeze your dog's anal sacs while she's there!

And while we're discussing the less appealing end of your Cavalier, let's dive straight in and talk about anal sacs. Sometimes called scent glands, these are a pair of glands located inside your dog's anus that give off a scent when she has a bowel movement.

You won't want to hear this, but problems with impacted anal glands are not uncommon in Cavaliers! When a dog passes firm stools, the glands normally empty themselves, but soft poo(p) or diarrhoea can mean that not enough pressure is exerted to empty the glands, causing discomfort. If they become infected, this results in swelling and pain. In extreme cases one or both anal glands can be removed. (A dog can manage perfectly well with one anal gland – ours did).

If your dog drags herself along on her rear end - 'scoots' - or tries to lick or scratch her anus, she could well have impacted anal glands that need squeezing, also called expressing, either by you if you know how to do it, your vet or a groomer. She might also have worms- the dog, not the groomer! Either way, it pays to keep an eye on both ends of your dog.

Keeping Teeth Healthy

Veterinary studies show that by the age of three, 80% of dogs show signs of gum or dental disease. Like other Toy breeds, the Cavalier is regarded as susceptible to dental problems because they have just as many teeth as a large dog crammed into a small mouth.

Because the Cavalier has a short muzzle, under and overbites can also be an issue. The perfect bite is a scissor bite where the top incisors are in contact with the lower incisors, but are positioned slightly in front, like two blades of a scissor if viewed from the side. In the vast majority of cases, underbites and overbites do not affect the dog's ability to chew – although they are penalised in the show ring. If an overbite is very severe, a procedure may be necessary if a tooth is growing into the opposite gum, such as tooth extraction, but this is fairly rare.

Symptoms of tooth decay include yellow and brown build-up of tartar along the gum line, red inflamed gums and persistent bad breath (halitosis). *It is important to make the time to take care of your Cavalier's teeth* – regular dental care greatly reduces the onset of gum/tooth decay and infection. If left, problems can escalate very quickly.

Without brushing, plaque coats the teeth and within three to five days this starts to harden into tartar, often turning into gingivitis (inflammation of the gums). Gingivitis is regularly accompanied by periodontal disease (infections around the teeth). This can be serious as it can in some cases lead to the infection spreading through the bloodstream to vital organs, such as heart, liver and kidneys.

Even if the infection doesn't spread beyond the mouth, bad teeth are very unpleasant for a dog, just as with a human, causing painful toothache and difficulty chewing. You can give your dog a daily dental treat, such as Dentastix or Nylabone, or regularly give her a large raw to help with dental hygiene, but you should also check and brush your Cavalier's teeth every week.

Prevention is better than cure.

Start getting your pup used to having teeth cleaned as soon as they arrive home at eight weeks or so. Take things slowly in the beginning and give your dog lots of praise. Cavaliers love your attention (and food) and many will start looking forward to tooth brushing sessions - especially if they like the flavour of the toothpaste. Use a pet toothpaste; dogs don't rinse and spit and the human variety can upset a canine's stomach.

In the beginning, get your dog used to the toothpaste by letting her lick some off your finger. If she doesn't like the flavour, try a different one. Continue until she looks forward to licking the paste - it might be instant or take days. Put a small amount on your finger and gently rub it on one of the big canine teeth at the front of her mouth. Over the next one to two weeks, rub your finger with the toothpaste all over her teeth.

Then get the right size of three-sided brush for your Cavalier's mouth and put the toothpaste in between the bristles (rather than on top) so more of it actually gets on to the teeth and gums. Allow her to get used to the toothbrush being in her mouth for several days - praise her when she licks it – before you start proper brushing. Lift her upper lip gently and place the brush at a 45° angle to the gum line. Gently move the brush backwards and forwards. Start just with her front teeth and then gradually do a few more. Do the top ones first.

You don't need to brush the inside of her teeth as the tongue keeps them relatively free of plaque. Regular brushing shouldn't take more than five minutes - well worth the time and effort when it spares your Cavalier the pain and misery of serious periodontal disease.

Some owners book their dog in for a professional clean at the local veterinary clinic every few months. However, if your Cavalier needs a deep clean, remedial work or teeth removing, he or she will have to be anaesthetised, a procedure which is to be avoided unless absolutely necessary.

Bathing Your Cavalier

If you are showing your Cavalier, he or she will probably have a bath every week. You don't need to bathe a pet Cavalier regularly, but the odd bath - perhaps once every month or two - wouldn't go amiss. Bathing helps to keep your dog's coat clean and tangle-free, and your dog looking and smelling sweet.

If your Cavalier is sporty and enjoys running through fields and swimming in muddy ponds, he or she will need more frequent baths. If your dog does regularly return from her daily walks covered in mud, hose her down before allowing her back into the house.

This is perfectly acceptable; a Cavalier's coat is designed to cope with water. A bath will also be necessary if your dog has rolled in something smelly and unmentionable, like fox or cow poo – both of which were like a magnet for our dog, Max.

Never use human shampoos on your Cavalier as these will only irritate the skin. A dog's skin has a different pH to that of a human. If you do occasionally use a shampoo on your dog, use one specially medicated for dogs - such as Malaseb or similar. They may be expensive, but last a long time. There is also a wide range of shampoos for dogs containing natural organic ingredients.

If a Cavalier is left in a dirty condition, this can cause irritation, leading to skin issues, scratching and/or excessive shedding.

Breeders on Grooming

Philippa Biddle, of Hearthfriend Cavaliers, Norfolk: "On average I spend about 10 minutes every two

days giving a thorough brush to the coat and ears and cleaning the eyes if runny. Once a week I check nails and ears. I bath non-show dogs approximately every three to four weeks. I tidy the feet underneath with scissors and trim the fluffy feet when they get excessively long."

Pictured is Hearthfriend Hocus Pocus, known as Rogue to his friends. Photo by Laura Davis.

"On older dogs I shave inside the ears to keep them clean and do a hygiene trim (around their rear end). On dogs with longer, thicker coat, I use a Coat King about once a month, depending on the season, to reduce dead undercoat. This is more important when they are moulting."

Julie Durham, Donrobby Cavaliers, Berkshire: "I DO NOT TRIM! I say if you want a short-coated dog, don't buy a Cavalier. I comb my dogs most evenings when they sit on my lap and bath them when they smell or they have rolled in something unmentionable. Once a week they have nails, teeth and ears cleaned and a jolly good comb." *Pictured is Julie's Teddy.*

Kathy Hargest, of Kathysgirls Cavaliers, Gloucestershire: "Check ears every day; knots frequently occur behind them. Give your dog a quick all-over brush every day - start this as a puppy, even though they do not need it. Check teeth, ears and claws so they become accustomed to being handled, and do not cut the hair at all."

Sandra Coles, of Twyforde Cavalier King Charles Spaniels, Devon: "Grooming is carried out weekly and more frequently with the show dogs. I don't trim unless I feel the feet need doing on some of them. Cavaliers should be free from trimming - why have a long coated breed and shave them? I am horrified when owners do this!"

Philip Lunt, of Oaktreepark Cavaliers, Staffordshire: "I spend a maximum of five minutes per day on each dog to check for any knots or tangles. Trimming is not permitted, as I show my dogs; the only allowance is the underneath of the paws/pads."

Dennis and Tina Homes, Leogem Cavaliers, Herefordshire: "We have a daily regime of grooming and teeth cleaning which on average takes 10 minutes per dog. Regular grooming keeps knots and tangles at bay and also keeps the coat clean. By grooming daily, you are made aware of any health issues, including ear infections, anal gland infections, sore and inflamed gums, fleas, ticks and hidden grass seeds in the coat. Bathing is generally undertaken when we are preparing for a dog show, otherwise every few weeks or so."

Jina Ezell, Kalama Cavaliers, Washington State, USA: "I might brush mine once a week. My Cavaliers don't have the tangled-hair issues that tend to happen within this breed. They might have a bath twice a month, but it's not on the calendar. I have a grooming basket that I bring out every weekend and, while relaxing in front of the television, I use the nail dremel, wipe out the ears and put ear powder in if they seem moist (I live in a high humidity area), brush their teeth and give a nice brushing."

Photo of Ezell's Sir William and Ezell's Princess Gracie by Andrea Bernard.

"Due to the wet, wet climate (and mud, mud, mud), I DO trim up my dogs. I trim all around the feet at least once a year in the fall and sometimes take up those lovely feathered ears and tail, again, just because it's a nuisance to keep them and the house clean in the wet months. I completely SHAVE the underside of the ear and go into the ear canal to keep the hair clean and clear. As such, I have yet to have an ear infection."

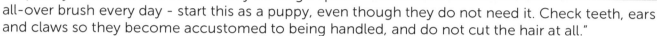

As you can see, grooming isn't just about brushing your Cavalier a couple of times a week. Cavaliers do require extra care when it comes to grooming; it's all part of the bargain when you decide that this striking breed is the dog for you.

15. The Birds and the Bees

Judging by the number of questions our website receives from owners who ask about the canine reproductive cycle and breeding their dogs, there is a lot of confusion about the doggy facts of life out there. Some owners want to know whether they should breed their dog, while others ask if and at what age they should have their dog neutered – this term can refer to both the spaying of females and the castration of males.

Owners of females often ask when she will come on heat, how long this will last and how often it will occur. Sometimes they want to know how you can tell if a female is pregnant or how long a pregnancy lasts. So here, in a nutshell, is a chapter on The Facts of Life as far as Cavalier King Charles Spaniels are concerned.

Females and Heat

Just like all other mammal females, including humans, a female Cavalier King Charles Spaniel has a menstrual cycle - or to be more accurate, an oestrus cycle (*estrus* in the US). This is the period of time when she is ready (and willing!) for mating and is more commonly called **heat** or being **on heat**, **in heat** or **in season**.

A Cavalier bitch has her first cycle from about six to 10 months old, although some may not have their first heat until 10 months to one year old. Females may follow the pattern of their mother, so if you are getting a female puppy, it may be worth asking your breeder at what age the dam (mother) first came on heat. She will then come on heat roughly every six months. There is no season of the year which corresponds to a breeding season, so it could be winter and summer or spring and autumn (fall), etc.

When a young bitch comes on heat, it is normal for her cycles to be somewhat irregular, and can take up to two years for regular cycles to develop. The timescale also becomes more erratic with old, unspayed females. Unlike women, female dogs do not stop menstruating when they reach middle age, although the heat becomes shorter and lighter. A litter for an elderly female (older than seven years) is not advisable as it can result in complications – for both mother and pups.

On average, the heat cycle will last around 21 days, but can be anything from seven to 10 days up to four weeks. Within this period there will be several days in the middle of the cycle that will be the optimum time for her to get pregnant. This is the phase called the *oestrus*. The third phase, called *dioestrus*, begins immediately afterwards. During this time, her body will produce hormones whether or not she is pregnant. Her body thinks and acts like she is pregnant. All the hormones are present; only the puppies are missing. This can sometimes lead to what is known as a 'false pregnancy'.

The first visual sign of heat that you may notice is that your dog's vulva (external sex organ, or pink bit under her tail) becomes swollen, which she will lick to keep herself clean. If you're not sure, hold a tissue against her vulva – does it turn pink or red? She will then bleed; this is sometimes called spotting. It will be a light red or brown at the beginning of the heat cycle, turning more watery after a week or so. Some females can bleed quite heavily; this is normal. But if you have any concerns, contact your vet to be on the safe side.

Females on heat often urinate more frequently than normal, or may 'mark' various objects on a walk or even in the home by doing a small pee on them! She may also start to 'mate' with your leg, other dogs or objects. These are all normal signs.

Many females naturally want to keep themselves clean by licking; others don't. If your girl leaves an unwanted trail around the house, cover anything you don't want stained. You might also consider using disposable doggy diapers/nappies (pictured) or reusable sanitary pants.

Owners have reported a variety of behavioural changes when their Cavalier has her first heat cycle. Some Cavs go off their food, or start shedding hair. Others may become more clingy - or ignore you and sulk in their beds.

While a female is on heat, she produces hormones that attract male dogs. Because dogs have a sense of smell thousands of times stronger than ours, your girl on heat is a magnet for all the males in the neighbourhood. It is believed that they can detect the scent of a female on heat up to two miles away! They may congregate around your house or follow you around the park (if you are brave or foolish enough to venture out there while she is in season), waiting for their chance to prove their manhood – or mutthood in their case.

Don't expect your precious little Cavvie princess to be fussy. Her hormones are raging when she is on heat and, during her most fertile days (Day 9-10 of heat for five or more days) she is ready, able and ... VERY willing! As she approaches the optimum time for mating you may notice her tail bending slightly to one side. She will also start to urinate more frequently. This is her signal to all those virile male dogs out there that she is ready for mating.

Although breeding requires specialised knowledge on the part of the owner, it does not stop a female on heat from being extremely interested in attention from any old mutt! To avoid an unwanted pregnancy you must keep a close eye on your female and not allow her to freely wander where she may come into contact with other dogs when she is on heat - and that includes the garden, unless it is 100% dog proof.

It is amazing the lengths some entire (uncastrated) males will go to impregnate a female on heat. Travelling great distances to follow her scent, jumping over barriers, digging under fences, chewing through doors or walls and sneaking through hedges are just some of the tactics employed by canine Casanovas on the loose. Some dogs living in the same house as a bitch in season have even been known to mate with her through the bars of a crate! If you do have an entire male, you need to physically keep him in a separate place, perhaps with an understanding friend, outdoor kennel or even boarding kennels. The desire to mate is all-consuming and can be accompanied by howling or 'marking' (urinating) indoors from a frustrated male.

Avoid taking your female out in public places while she is in season, and certainly don't let her run free if you are away from home and may encounter other dogs. During this time you can compensate for these restrictions by playing more indoor or garden games to keep her mentally and physically active. You can buy a spray which masks the natural oestrus scent of your female. Marketed under such attractive names as *"Bitch Spray"*, these will lessen the scent, but not eliminate it. They might be useful for reducing the amount of unwanted attention, but are not a complete deterrent. There is, however, no canine contraceptive and the only sure-fire way of preventing your female from becoming pregnant is spaying.

There is a "morning after pill" – actually a series of oestrogen tablets or an injection - which some vets may administer, but reported side effects are severe, including Pyometra (a potentially life-threatening infection of the womb which can affect up to one in four middle-aged females), bone marrow suppression and infertility. Unlike women, female dogs do not go through the menopause and can have puppies even when they are quite old. A litter for an elderly female (older than seven years) is not advisable as it can result in complications – for both mother and pups.

Good Breeding

Normally, responsible breeders wait until a female is fully health tested, has had one or two heat cycles and is at least 18 months to two years old before mating. Females should not be used for breeding too early; pregnancy draws on the calcium reserves needed for their own growing bones. If bred too early, they may break down structurally and have health issues in later life.

However, with Cavaliers, there is a further consideration, and it's called the **MVD Breeding Protocol.** Many Cavaliers suffer from a heart condition called *early-onset Mitral Valve Disease* (MVD) and the MVD Protocol is a set of guidelines introduced with the aim of eliminating, or greatly reducing, this hereditary disease. One of the recommendations is that Cavaliers less than two-and-a-half years' old are not used for breeding, and this is endorsed by America's Cavalier King Charles Club, USA See **Chapter 12. Health** for more details.

Good breeders also limit the number of litters from each female, as breeding can take a lot out of them. To protect females from overbreeding, the UK's Kennel Club introduced Breeding Restrictions in 2012. Now it will not register a litter from any bitch:

1. That has already had four litters.

2. If she is less than one year old at the time of mating.

3. If she is eight years or older when she whelps (gives birth).

4. If the litter is the result of any mating between father and daughter, mother and son or brother and sister.

5. If she has already had two C-Sections (Caesarean Sections).

6. In the UK, the dam has to be resident at a UK address at the date of whelping – this is to try and discourage people buying from foreign puppy farms.

Breeders then spend considerable time researching a suitable mate. The Kennel Club's **Mate Select** programme at www.thekennelclub.org.uk/services/public/mateselect is an excellent tool for UK breeders. It enables them to check the health screening results of a potential mate, and also gives a figure for the Coefficient of Inbreeding (COI), to ensure that the potential mate is not too closely related to the female, as this can lead to unhealthy puppies. The US equivalent of Mate Select is the **K9** programme at www.k9data.com

All national Cavalier King Charles Spaniel Clubs have a Code of Ethics for their breeders. Here are some of the major points from the CKCSC, USA:

- I believe that the welfare of the Cavalier King Charles Spaniel breed is of paramount importance. It supersedes any other commitment to Cavaliers, whether that be personal, competitive, or financial

- I will maintain complete and accurate records of each litter I breed and register each puppy individually

I realize that the purpose of breeding Cavalier King Charles Spaniels is to attempt to bring their natural qualities to perfection in accordance with the Breed Standard. There exists a constant danger that ignorant or disreputable breeders may, by improper practices, produce physically, mentally or temperamentally unsound specimens to the detriment of the breed. I will consult with the breeder of the dog I own and/or with some other experienced breeder before undertaking any breeding. If I decide to breed a litter, I will:

- To the best of my ability be selective with respect to the conformation, physical wellbeing, and temperament of the pair to be mated

- Breed only after a careful study and understanding of the Breed Standard, as it applies to the pedigrees of the two dogs involved, and to the dogs themselves

- To the best of my ability be selective with respect to the conformation, physical wellbeing, and temperament of the pair to be mated

- Breed only after a careful study and understanding of the Breed Standard, as it applies to the pedigrees of the two dogs involved, and to the dogs themselves

- Breed only Cavaliers registered with the CKCSC, USA, or a registry recognized by the CKCSC, USA

- I will provide all my Cavaliers with proper veterinary and home care, which includes:
  - Checking into the removal of dewclaws, including hind dewclaws if present
  - The elimination of parasites, internal or external
  - The necessary inoculations as determined by a veterinarian
  - A properly balanced nutritional diet

- I will do my best to evaluate my Cavaliers objectively and to use for breeding only those conforming closely to the Breed Standard. All others I will either have neutered before transferring them, or will transfer with a CKCSC, USA "Restricted Transfer of Dog" form, duly signed by buyer and seller, restricting the Cavalier from being used for breeding purposes

- I will to the very best of my ability screen all prospective new owners to determine their suitability and their motives for acquiring a Cavalier. Special attention will be given to the necessary commitment to financial responsibility for proper care and adequate physical facilities

- I will not allow any puppy to leave for its new home before the age of eight weeks. The CKCSC recommends ten to twelve weeks as the appropriate age for transfer

Neutering - Pros and Cons

Once a straightforward subject, this is currently a hot potato in the dog world. Dogs which are kept purely as pets – i.e. not for showing or working – have often been spayed or neutered. There is also the very real life-threatening risk of Pyometra in unspayed middle-aged females.

However, there is mounting scientific evidence that dogs should not be spayed or neutered at least until they are through puberty - regardless of what some vets currently advise. Armed with the facts, it is for each individual owner to decide what is best for their dog. (The procedure of removing ovaries or testicles is also known as a gonadectomy).

A major argument for neutering of both sexes is that there is already too much indiscriminate breeding of dogs in the world. As you will read in **Chapter 16. Cavalier Rescue**, it is estimated that 1,000 dogs are put to sleep **every hour** in the USA alone. It is for this reason that rescue organisations in North America, the UK and Australia neuter all dogs that they rehome. Some areas in the United States, e.g. LA, have even adopted a compulsory sterilisation policy: www.avma.org/Advocacy/StateAndLocal/Pages/sr-spay-neuter-laws.aspx aimed at "reducing and eventually eliminating the thousands of euthanizations conducted in Los Angeles' animal shelters every year."

The RSPCA, along with most UK vets, also promotes the benefits of neutering: www.rspca.org.uk/adviceandwelfare/pets/general/neutering. It is estimated that more than half of all dogs in the UK are spayed or castrated. Another point is that you may not have a choice. Some Puppy Contracts from KC and AKC breeders may stipulate that, except in special circumstances, you agree to neuter your Cavalier King Charles Spaniel as a Condition of Sale. Others may state that you need the breeder's permission to breed your dog.

The other side of the coin is that there is recent scientific evidence that neutering – and especially early neutering - can have a detrimental effect on the health of some dogs. In 2013, the University of California, Davis School of Veterinary Medicine published a study revealing that neutered Golden Retrievers and Labradors appear to be at a higher risk of joint disorders and cancers compared with sexually intact dogs of the same breed. Read the news report online here: http://www.aaha.org/blog/NewStat/post/2014/07/17/785809/UC-Davis-study-neutering-Golden-retrievers-Labradors.aspx A follow-up study involving both males and females (with around a 5% incidence of joint disorders in intact dogs) found that Golden Retrievers that had been neutered before six months of age were four or five times more likely to have joint problems. The same study looked at cancer. Intact females had a 3% rate of cancer, while females spayed up to eight years old were three to four times more likely to get cancer. Neutering males had "relatively minor effects." Read the full report at: http://journals.plos.org/plosone/article?id=10.1371/journal.pone.0102241

Many vets and rescue organisations currently advise spaying or castrating puppies and kittens at just a few months old. However, although there are, as yet, no studies on neutering Cavalier King Charles Spaniels, you may want to consider whether you spay a female Cavalier, or at least wait until she is three or four years of age. If you have a male and decide to neuter him, you might want to wait until he is fully grown, i.e. at least 18 months or two years of age.

There is another article, published autumn 2018 in The IAABC Journal (International Association of Animal Behavior Consultants), which highlights the pros and cons of neutering. It is written by a vet and is slightly technical, but worth a read for anyone considering spaying or neutering their dog: https://fall2018.iaabcjournal.org/2018/10/31/spay-and-neuter-surgery-effects-on-dogs The table at the end of the article summarises the pros and cons.

....

Spaying

Spaying is the term traditionally used to describe the sterilisation of a female dog so that she cannot become pregnant. This is normally done by a procedure called an *ovariohysterectomy* and involves the removal of the ovaries and uterus (womb). Although this is a routine operation, it is major abdominal surgery and she has to be anaesthetised.

One less invasive option offered by some vets is an *ovariectomy*, which removes the ovaries, but leaves the womb intact. It requires only a small incision and can even be carried out by laparoscopy (keyhole surgery). The dog is anaesthetised for a shorter time and there is less risk of infection or excess bleeding during surgery. NOTE: One breeder said that her vet had advised against getting very small dogs spayed by keyhole surgery, as it is very "fiddly." Check with your vet.

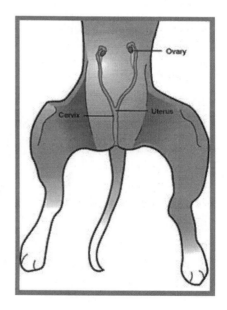

One major reason often given for not opting for an ovariectomy is that the female still runs the risk of Pyometra later in life. However, there is currently little or no scientific evidence of females that have undergone an ovariectomy contracting Pyometra at a later date.

If a female is spayed before her first heat cycle, she will have an almost zero risk of mammary cancer (the equivalent of breast cancer in women). Even after the first heat, spaying reduces the risk of this cancer by 92%. Some vets claim that the risk of mammary cancer in unspayed female dogs can be as high as one in four.

If you do wish to have your dog spayed, our advice is to wait until she is 18 months or older; and there is emerging evidence (with Retrievers) that is it better to wait until a female is four years old. Personally, I **would** consider spaying a fully grown female Cavalier King Charles Spaniel.

Spaying is a much more serious operation for females than neutering is for males. It involves an internal abdominal operation, whereas the neutering procedure is carried out on the male's testicles, which are outside his abdomen. As with any major procedure, there are pros and cons.

For:

❧ Spaying prevents infections, cancer and other diseases of the uterus and ovaries. A spayed bitch will have a greatly reduced risk of mammary cancer

- Spaying eliminates the risk of Pyometra, which results from hormonal changes in the female's reproductive tract. It also reduces hormonal changes that can interfere with the treatment of diseases like diabetes or epilepsy

- You no longer have to cope with any potential mess caused by bleeding inside the house during heat cycles

- You don't have to guard your female against unwanted attention from males as she will no longer have heat cycles

- Spaying can reduce behaviour problems, such as roaming, aggression towards other dogs, anxiety or fear (not all canine experts agree with this)

- A University of Georgia study involving 40,000 death records from the Veterinary Medical Database from 1984-2004, found that sterilised dogs lived on average 1.5 years longer: http://journals.plos.org/plosone/article?id=10.1371/journal.pone.0061082

- A spayed dog does not contribute to the pet overpopulation problem

Against:

- Complications can occur, including an abnormal reaction to the anaesthetic, bleeding, stitches breaking and infections; **these are not common**

- Occasionally there can be long-term effects connected to hormonal changes. These include weight gain or less stamina, which can occur years after spaying

- Older females may suffer some urinary incontinence, but it only affects a few spayed females. NOTE: Some younger dogs can also suffer from urinary incontinence after spaying - discuss with your vet.

- Cost. This can range from £100 to £300 in the UK (approximately $150-$500 at a vet's clinic in the USA, or around $50 at a low cost clinic, for those that qualify)

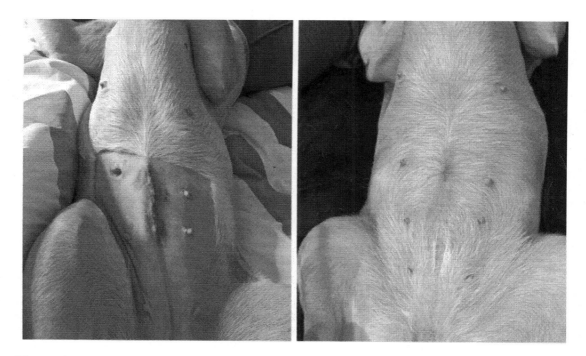

These photographs are reproduced courtesy of Guy Bunce and Chloe Spencer, of Dizzywaltz Labrador Retrievers, Berkshire, England. The one on the left shows four-year-old Disney shortly after spaying (ovariohysterectomy). The one on the right shows Disney a few weeks later

🐾 There is early evidence that spaying some Retrievers before six months of age can greatly increase the chance of joint problems developing. A further study by the same scientists indicated that the risk of cancer after spaying increased by 300% to 400%.

Neutering

Neutering male dogs involves castration (the removal of the testicles). This can be a difficult decision for some owners, as it causes a drop in the pet's testosterone levels, which some humans – men in particular! - feel affects the quality of their dog's life. Fortunately, dogs do not think like people and male dogs do not miss their testicles or the loss of sex.

Unless you specifically want to breed, work or show your dog, or he has a special job, neutering is recommended by animal rescue organisations and vets. Even then, dogs working in service or for charities are routinely neutered and this does not impair their ability to perform their duties. There are countless unwanted puppies, many of which are destroyed. There is also the problem of a lack of knowledge from the owners of some dogs, resulting in the production of poor puppies with congenital health or temperament problems.

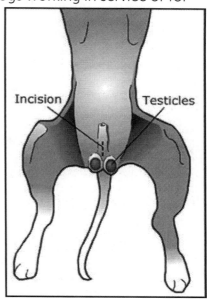

Technically, neutering can be carried out at any age over eight weeks, provided both testicles have descended. However, recent research is definitely coming down on the side of waiting until the dog is at least one year old. Surgery is relatively straightforward, and much less of a major operation for a male than spaying is for a female. Complications are less common and less severe than with spaying. Although he will feel tender afterwards, your dog should return to his normal self within a couple of days.

Dogs neutered before puberty tend to grow a little larger than dogs done later. This is because testosterone is involved in the process that stops growth, so the bones grow for longer without testosterone.

When he comes out of surgery, his scrotum (the sacs that held the testicles) will be swollen and it may look like nothing has been done. But it is normal for these to shrink slowly in the days following surgery. Here are the main pros and cons:

For:

🐾 Castration is a simple procedure, and dogs usually make a swift recovery afterwards

🐾 Behaviour problems such as aggression and wandering off are reduced (some experts disagree with this)

🐾 Unwanted sexual behaviour, such as mounting people or objects, is usually reduced or eliminated

🐾 Testicular problems such as infections, cancer and torsion (painful rotation of the testicle) are eradicated

🐾 Prostate disease, common in older male dogs, is less likely to occur

🐾 A submissive entire (un-neutered) male dog may be targeted by other dogs. After he has been neutered, he will no longer produce testosterone and so will not be regarded as much of a threat by the other males, so he is less likely to be bullied

🐾 A neutered dog is not fathering unwanted puppies

Against:

- ❧ A major scientific study focussed on Retrievers seems to show that some dogs neutered before six months of age are four to five times more likely to have joint problems

- ❧ As with any surgery, there can be bleeding afterwards; you should keep an eye on him for any blood loss after the operation. Infections can also occur, generally caused by the dog licking the wound, so try and prevent him doing this. If he persists, use an Elizabethan collar (E-collar). In the **vast majority** of cases, these problems do not occur

- ❧ Some dogs' coats may be affected (this also applies to spaying); supplementing the diet with fish oil can compensate for this

- ❧ Cost - this starts at around £80 in the UK. In the USA this might cost upwards from $100 at a private veterinary clinic, or from $50 at a low cost or Humane Society clinic

Two other phrases you may hear when discussing neutering of males and females are '*tubal ligation*' or '*vasectomy*'. Many veterinary papers have been written on these topics, but as yet, not many vets offer them as options, possibly because they have not been trained to carry out these procedures at vet school.

The first is the tying of a female's Fallopian tubes and the second is the clamping shut of the sperm ducts from the male's testicles. In both procedures, the dog continues to produce hormones (unlike with spaying and neutering), but is unable to get pregnant or father puppies. With further data on the positive effects of hormones, these operations could become more common in the future – although more vets will first have to learn these new techniques.

A new non-surgical procedure to sterilise male dogs called *Zeutering* has been developed. It involved injecting zinc gluconate into the dog's testicles. Dogs are lightly sedated but not anaesthetised. It's inexpensive, there's little recovery time and no stitches.

However, studies show that Zeutering is only 99% effective, and its long-term effects are still being researched. A downside is that, while it makes dogs sterile, they still retain some of their testosterone. Therefore habits which usually disappear with traditional castration, such as marking, roaming, following females on heat and aggression towards other males, remain.

Zeutering isn't for every dog, but worth discussing with your vet.

Here are some common myths about neutering and spaying:

Neutering or spaying will spoil the dog's character - There is no evidence that any of the positive characteristics of your dog will be altered. He or she will be just as loving, playful and loyal. Neutering may reduce aggression or roaming, especially in male dogs, because they are no longer competing to mate with a female.

A female needs to have at least one litter - There is no proven physical or mental benefit to a female having a litter.

Mating is natural and necessary - We tend to ascribe human emotions to our dogs, but they do not think emotionally about sex or having and raising a family. Unlike humans, their desire to mate or breed is entirely physical, triggered by the chemicals called hormones within their body. Without these hormones – i.e. after neutering or spaying – the desire disappears or is greatly reduced.

Male dogs will behave better if they can mate - This is simply not true; sex does not make a dog behave better. In fact, it can have the opposite effect. Having mated once, a male may show an increased interest in females. He may also consider his status elevated, which may make him harder to control or call back.

Breeders on Neutering

Philippa Biddle: "I do not sell with a spay/neuter clause, but I strongly encourage owners not to neuter or spay too early. That is before two to three seasons for a bitch and not before 20 months for a dog. I give detailed information about the disadvantages of spaying/neutering too early.

"I strongly believe they need those sex hormones to develop their body and joints and adult brain. I think they are calmer and more sensible as adults if the brain is allowed to develop naturally with the sex hormones as it should do. In my opinion, Cavaliers tend to become too sedate, lacklustre in nature and overweight if neutered early. It also affects the coat, which becomes thick, dull and unruly."

Julie Durham agrees with the timing: "I ask that males are neutered after 18 months of age and girls not before their second season."

Kathy Hargest: "I recommend that owners wait until after at least two seasons for bitches and one year for dogs at least."

Philip Lunt: "I do not place any spay/neuter clause when selling puppies, I do advise new owners that spaying/neutering should be done at least three months after a girl's first season and at nine months for a boy - but to speak with their vet for clarification on this."

Dennis and Tina Homes: "We never recommend spaying or neutering unless there is a medical problem, such as persistent phantom pregnancies in bitches or a retained testicle in a dog. In all cases not earlier than 18 to 24 months."

Sandra Coles: "I have no spay/neuter clauses, I prefer that owners keep them entire. If they do, then I advise not to spay before first season; there can be urinary tract problems and incontinence. Owners need to research and make an informed decision. I only neuter if I have to."

US breeder Jina Ezell: "I do not put spay/neuter in my contract, but speak with each owner in length about my thoughts, I put it in e-mails during the whelping phase and typically follow up with each person within a few months of placement."

Pregnancy

Regardless of how big or small the dam is, a Cavalier King Charles Spaniel pregnancy lasts for 58 to 65 days; 63 days is average. This is true of all breeds of dog. Sometimes pregnancy is referred to as the *'gestation period.'* It is recommended to take a female for a pre-natal check-up after mating. The vet should answer any questions about type of food, supplements and extra care needed, as well as informing the owner about any physical changes likely to occur in your female.

There is a blood test available that measures levels of **relaxin**. This is a hormone produced by the ovary and the developing placenta, and pregnancy can be detected by monitoring relaxin levels as early as 22 to 27 days after mating. The levels are high throughout pregnancy and then decline rapidly after the female has given birth.

A vet can usually see the puppies (but not how many) using Ultrasound from around the same time. X-rays carried out 45 days into the pregnancy show the puppies' skeletons and give the breeder a good idea of the number of puppies. They can also help to give the vet more information, which is particularly useful if the bitch has had previous whelping problems.

Here are some of the signs of pregnancy:

🐾 After mating, many females become more affectionate. (However, others may become uncharacteristically irritable and maybe even a little aggressive)

🐾 The female may produce a slight clear discharge from her vagina about one month after mating

🐾 Three or four weeks after mating, a few females experience morning sickness – if this is the case, feed little and often. She may seem more tired than usual

🐾 She may seem slightly depressed and/or show a drop in appetite. These signs can also mean there are other problems, so you should consult your vet

🐾 Her teats (nipples) will become more prominent, pink and erect 25 to 30 days into the pregnancy. Later on, you may notice a fluid coming from them

🐾 After about 35 days, or seven weeks, her body weight will noticeably increase

🐾 Many pregnant females' appetite will increase in the second half of pregnancy

🐾 Her abdomen will become noticeably larger from around day 40, although first-time mums and females carrying few puppies may not show as much

🐾 Her nesting instincts will kick in as the delivery date approaches. She may seem restless or scratch her bed or the floor

🐾 During the last week of pregnancy, females often start to look for a safe place for whelping. Some seem to become confused, wanting to be with their owners and at the same time wanting to prepare their nest. Even if the female is having a C-section, she should still be allowed to nest in a whelping box with layers of newspaper, which she will scratch and dig as the time approaches

If your female becomes pregnant – either by design or accident - your first step should be to consult a vet.

Litter Size

Generally, the larger the dog, the bigger the litter; Cavalier King Charles Spaniels are not known for having large litters. Typical litter sizes are two to six pups. However, the number of pups can vary, affected by such factors as the age of the dam and sire (mother and father), size of the gene pool and even the dam's diet. Younger and older females tend to have smaller litters.

False Pregnancies

As many as 50% or more of intact (unspayed) females may display signs of a false pregnancy. In the wild it was common for female dogs to have false pregnancies and to lactate (produce milk). This female would then nourish puppies if their own mother died.

False pregnancies occur 60 to 80 days after the female was in heat - about the time she would have given birth – and are generally nothing to worry about for an owner. The exact cause is unknown; however, hormonal imbalances are thought to play an important role. Some dogs have shown symptoms within three to four days of spaying; these include:

- Making a nest
- Mothering or adopting toys and other objects
- Producing milk (lactating)
- Appetite fluctuations
- Barking or whining a lot
- Restlessness, depression or anxiety
- Swollen abdomen
- She might even appear to go into labour

Try not to touch your dog's nipples, as touch will stimulate further milk production. If she is licking herself repeatedly, she may need an E-collar to minimise stimulation. To help reduce and eliminate milk production, you can apply cool compresses to the nipples

Under no circumstances should you restrict your Cavalier's water supply to try and prevent her from producing milk. This is dangerous as she can become dehydrated.

Some unspayed bitches may have a false pregnancy with each heat cycle. Spaying during a false pregnancy may actually prolong the condition, so better to wait until it is over to have her spayed. False pregnancy is not a disease, but an exaggerated response to normal hormonal changes. Owners should be reassured that, even if left untreated, the condition almost always resolves itself.

However, if your Cavvie appears physically ill or the behavioural changes are severe enough to worry you, visit your vet. He or she may prescribe Galastop, which very effectively stops milk production and quickly returns the hormones to normal. In rare cases, hormone treatment may be necessary. Generally, dogs experiencing false pregnancies do not have serious long-term problems, as the behaviour disappears when the hormones return to their normal levels in two to three weeks.

One exception is **Pyometra**, a serious and potentially deadly infection of the womb, caused by a hormonal abnormality. Pyometra follows a heat cycle in which fertilisation did not occur and the dog typically starts showing symptoms within two to four months. Commonly referred to as 'pyo', there are 'open' and 'closed' forms of the disease. Open pyo is usually easy to identify with a smelly discharge, so prompt treatment is easy. Closed pyo is often harder to identify and you may not even notice anything until your girl becomes feverish and lethargic. When this happens, it is very serious and time is of the essence. Typically, vets will recommend immediate spaying in an effort to save the bitch's life.

Signs of Pyometra are excessive drinking and urination, with the female trying to lick a white discharge from her vagina. She may also have a slight temperature. If the condition becomes severe, her back legs will become weak, possibly to the point where she

can no longer get up without help. Pyometra is serious if bacteria take a hold, and in extreme cases it can be fatal. It is also relatively common and needs to be dealt with promptly by a vet, who will give the dog intravenous fluids and antibiotics for several days. In most cases this is followed by spaying.

Should I Breed From My Cavalier?

The short and simple answer is: **NO, leave it to the experts** - unless you know exactly what you are doing or intend to seek expert advice. The rising cost of puppies and increasing number of dog owners are tempting more people to consider breeding their dogs. However, breeding **healthy** Cavalier King Charles Spaniels with good temperaments that conform to the Breed Standard is a skill best left to the experts.

Due to several genetic diseases which can and do affect the breed, any responsible person who is considering breeding Cavaliers needs an extensive knowledge of potential issues and health screening. You need to fully research a suitable mate with regards to health and temperament. The Kennel Club's Mate Select feature at www.thekennelclub.org.uk/services/public/mateselect/ provides details of individual dog's health screening and how closely related a potential mate is to your dog.

You also have to be prepared to part with a four-figure sum before a single pup is born. Good care, health screening and stud fees come at a cost, and Cavaliers tend to have small litters, so don't enter into this thinking you will make a lot of money. If you do it properly, you won't.

You can't just put any two dogs together and expect perfect, healthy puppies; ethical and successful breeding is much more scientific and time-consuming than that. Inexperience can result in tragic health consequences, poor specimens of the breed, the loss of pups - or even the mother. Sometimes a C-section (Caesarean section) may be necessary. In the UK, all C-sections have to be registered with the Kennel Club. These are carried out when the mother is unable to birth the pups naturally – and timing is critical. Too early and the pups may be underdeveloped or the mother can bleed to death; too late and the pups can die.

A major study published in 2010, carried out jointly by the BSAVA (British Small Animal Veterinary Association) and the UK's Kennel Club, looked at 13,141 bitches from 151 breeds and the incidence of C-Sections over a 10-year period. The resulting report at http://bit.ly/2cV6MF3 involved 1,207 litters from 670 Cavaliers and revealed that some 13% had to have C-Sections.

And since 2012, the UK's Kennel Club will no longer register puppies from a female who has had more than two C-Sections, "except for scientifically proven welfare reasons and in such cases normally provided that the application is made prior to mating."

Breeding healthy Cavalier King Charles Spaniels to type is a complex, expensive and time-consuming business when all the fees, DNA and health tests, care, nutrition and medical expenses have been taken into account.

Breeding Costs

Here's an idea of what to consider if you are seriously thinking about breeding - and doing it properly:

- Annual heart tests on the sire and dam
- Eye tests
- MRI scan for Chiari Malformation/Syringomyelia (CM/SM) – recommended in UK
- Episodic Falling (EF) – UK
- Curly Coat Dry Eye (CC/DE) – UK
- Patella Luxation - USA
- Hip Dysplasia - USA
- Pre-mate tests
- Stud fees
- Pregnancy – ultrasound scan, worming, extra food and supplements for the mother
- Equipment – whelping box, vet bed, thermometer, feeding bottles, heat mat, hibiscrub, etc.
- Birth – vet's fees, and maybe even the costs of a C-Section
- Puppies – vaccinations and worming, puppy food, coloured collars
- Kennel Club or AKC registration

And these are just the basics! Even without a C-Section, these four-figure costs are considerable and swallow up a large chunk of any profit you thought you might make. And if there is a problem with the mother, birth or puppies and you rack up vet's bills, you can actually make a loss on a litter.

Breeder Philippa Biddle added: "One extra cost and consideration in being a breeder who health tests is what happens if your potential breeding dog or bitch fails one of the tests? It costs around £2,500 to £3,000 ($3,250 to $3,900) to get a bitch puppy to breeding age, more for a stud dog, who has to be campaigned around shows to prove his quality is high enough for breeding. A male dog needs to be consistently winning at Champion show level before anyone will consider using him at stud.

"So if they fail a heart or eye test, or the MRI scan for CM/SM aged two to three years they are useless for breeding. Unethical breeders would breed anyway to at least get their money back, and say they don't bother with health testing (for a variety of lame excuses). A good breeder has to either keep the young dog for life or rehome for free, to a suitable and understanding home, i.e. family and friends. And take the loss.

"As these 'fail' dogs have come from your own well-health-tested-through-the-generation lines, the risk of them actually suffering poor health and short lives is much less than dogs that have been bred from non-tested lines, of course. But anomalies do crop up - even in well-health-tested lines. So there's a risk factor, as well as a cost factor, in running on a dog to breeding age."

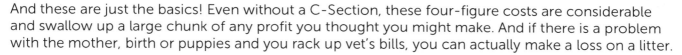

Ask Yourself This...

1. Did I get my Cavalier King Charles Spaniel from a good, ethical breeder? Dogs sold in pet stores and on general sales websites are seldom good specimens and can be unhealthy.

2. Are my dog and his or her close relatives free from health issues? Heart, eye and joint issues are just some of the illnesses Cavalier King Charles Spaniel pups can inherit. Are you 100% sure your breeding dog is free from them all? Also, an unhealthy female is also more likely to have trouble with pregnancy and whelping.

3. Does my dog conform to the Breed Standard as laid down by the Kennel Club or AKC? Do not breed from a Cavalier King Charles Spaniel that is not an excellent specimen, hoping that somehow the puppies will turn out better. They won't. Talk with experienced breeders and ask them for an honest assessment of your dog.

4. Is my female at least in her second heat cycle? The MVD Breeding Protocol goes further than that and recommends Cavalier breeders wait until the breeding pair is at least two-and-a-half years old. A female should be physically mature, able to carry a litter to term and robust enough to whelp and care for a litter. Even then, not all female Cavaliers are suitable. Some are simply poor mothers who don't care for their puppies; others don't produce enough milk - which means you have to do it.

5. Do I understand COI and its implications? Coefficient of Inbreeding measures the common ancestors of a dam and sire and indicates the probability of how genetically similar they are. Breeding from too closely-related dogs can result in health issues for the puppies.

6. Does my dog have a good temperament? Does he or she socialise well with people and other animals? Dogs with poor temperaments should not be bred, regardless of how good they look.

7. Am I financially able to provide good veterinary care for the mother and puppies, particularly if complications occur? If you are not prepared to make a significant financial commitment to a litter, then don't breed your dog. A single litter can cost thousands of pounds or dollars - and what if you only get a couple of puppies?

8. Have I got the indoor space? Mother and pups will need their own space in your home which will become messy, as new-born pups do not come into this world housetrained (potty trained). It should also be warm and draught-free.

9. Can I cope with several puppies at once?

10. Can I devote the time to breeding? Caring for mother and young pups is a 24/7 job in the beginning and involves many sleepless nights. During the day, you cannot simply go off to work or leave the house with the mother and young pups unattended. Also, it is not uncommon for a dam to be unable or unwilling to provide milk for her puppies, particularly when a C-section is involved, as it may take up to 72 hours for the anaesthesia to completely wear off. In which case, you have to tube feed the puppies every couple of hours throughout the day and night. Breeding is a huge tie.

11. Am I confident enough in my breeding programme to offer a puppy health warranty?

12. Will I be able to find good homes for all the pups and be prepared to take them back if necessary? Good breeders do not let their precious puppies go to any old home. They often have a waiting list before the litter is born.

You may have the most wonderful Cavalier King Charles Spaniel in the world, but only enter the world of canine breeding if you have the right knowledge and motivation. Don't do it just for the money or the cute factor – or to show the kids 'The Miracle of Birth!' Breeding poor examples only brings heartache in the long run when health or temperament issues develop.

Having said all of that, good Cavalier King Charles Spaniel breeders are made, not born. Like any expert, they learn over time. If you're serious, spend time researching the breed and its genetics and make sure you are going into it for the right reasons and not just for the money - ask yourself how you intend to improve the breed.

A great way of learning about breeding Cavaliers is to find a mentor, someone who is already successfully breeding Cavaliers. By 'successful' we mean somebody who is producing healthy, handsome puppies with good temperaments, not someone who is making lots of money from churning out puppies. Talk to the breeder you got your pup from, visit dog shows and make contact with established breeders or look at the Kennel Club or AKC website for details of breeders near you. Contact one of the Cavalier King Charles Spaniel Clubs and ask them to help find a suitable person who is willing to help you get started: in the UK look for: www.thecavalierclub.co.uk and http://www.ckcsc.org in the USA.

One book which a couple of breeders have recommended is **Book of the Bitch** by J. M. Evans and Kay White, which is useful for reference.

Committed Cavalier King Charles Spaniel breeders aren't in it for the cash. They use their skills and knowledge to produce healthy pups with good temperaments that conform to the Breed Standard and ultimately improve the breed.

Our strong advice is: when it comes to breeding Cavaliers, leave it to the experts or seek expert advice.

16. Cavalier Rescue

Not everybody who is thinking of getting a Cavalier gets one as a puppy from a breeder. Some people prefer to adopt a dog from a rescue organisation. What could be kinder and more rewarding than giving a poor, abandoned dog a happy and loving home for the rest of his or her life?

Not much really; adoption saves lives and gives unfortunate dogs a second chance of happiness. The problem of homeless dogs is truly depressing. It's a big issue in Britain, but even worse in the US, where the sheer numbers in kill shelters are hard to comprehend. Randy Grim states in "Don't Dump The Dog" that 1,000 dogs are being put to sleep every hour in the States.

According to Jo-Anne Cousins, former Executive Director at IDOG, who has spent many years involved in US canine rescue, the situations leading to a dog ending up in rescue can often be summed up in one phrase: 'Unrealistic expectations.'

She said: "In many situations, dog ownership was something that the family went into without fully understanding the time, money and commitment to exercise and training that it takes to raise a dog. While they may have spent hours on the internet pouring over cute puppy photos, they probably didn't read any puppy training books or look into actual costs of regular vet care, training and boarding."

That lack of thought was highlighted in a story that appeared in the Press in my Yorkshire home town. A woman went shopping on Christmas Eve in a local retail centre. She returned home £700 (more than $900) poorer with a puppy she had bought on impulse. The pup was in a rescue centre two days later. Common reasons for a dog being put into rescue include:

* A change in family circumstance, such as divorce or a new baby
* A change in work patterns
* Moving home
* An elderly owner has died or moved to a care home
* The dog develops health issues

Often, the 'unrealistic expectations' come home to roost and the dog is given up for rescue because:

* He has too much energy, needs too much exercise, knocks the kids over and/or jumps on people - young dogs are often boisterous and sometimes lack co-ordination
* He is growling and/or nipping. All puppies bite, it is their way of exploring the world; they have to be trained not to bite the things (such as humans) that they are not supposed to bite
* He chews or eats things he shouldn't
* He makes a mess in the house - housetraining requires time and patience from the owner

- He needs a lot more exercise/grooming/attention than the owner is able or prepared to give. Cavaliers are "Velcro" dogs and require a lot of attention from the owner

- He costs too much to keep - the cost of feeding, vets' bills, grooming (unless you do it yourself), etc. are not insignificant

There is, however, a ray of sunshine for some of these dogs. Every year many thousands of people in the UK, North America and countries all around the world adopt a rescue dog and the story often has a happy ending.

The Dog's Point of View...

If you are serious about adoption, then you should do so with the right motives and with your eyes wide open. If you're expecting a perfect dog, you could be in for a shock. Rescue dogs can and do become wonderful companions, but a lot of it depends on you.

Cavaliers are sensitive, loyal dogs. Sometimes those that have ended up in rescue centres are traumatised. Some may have heart, eye or other health problems. They don't understand why they have been abandoned, neglected or badly treated by their beloved owners and may arrive at your home with 'baggage' of their own until they adjust to being part of a loving family again. This may take time. Time and patience are the keys to help the dog to adjust to his or her new surroundings and family and to learn to love and trust again. Ask yourself a few questions before you take the plunge and fill in the adoption forms:

- Are you prepared to accept and deal with any problems - such as bad behaviour, chewing, timidity, aggression, jumping up or peeing/pooing in the house - which a rescue dog may initially display when arriving in your home?

- How much time are you willing to spend with your new dog to help him or her integrate back into normal family life?

- Can you take time off work to be at home and help the dog settle in at the beginning?

- Are you prepared to take on a new addition to your family that may live for another decade?

- Are you prepared to stick with the dog even if he or she develops health issues later?

Think about the implications before rescuing a dog - try and look at it from the dog's point of view...What could be worse for the unlucky dog than to be abandoned again if things don't work out between you?

Other Considerations

Adopting a rescue dog is a big commitment for all involved. It is not a cheap way of getting a Cavalier and shouldn't be viewed as such. It could cost you several hundred pounds - or dollars. You'll have adoption fees to pay and often vaccination and veterinary bills as well as worm and flea medication and spaying or neutering. Make sure you're aware of the full cost before committing.

Cavaliers that have been badly treated or have had difficult lives need plenty of time to rehabilitate. Some may have initial problems with housetraining, others may need socialisation with people and/or other dogs. And if you are serious about adoption, you may have to wait a while until a suitable dog comes up. One way of finding out if you, your family and home are suitable is to volunteer to become a foster home for one of the rescue centres. Fosters offer temporary homes until a forever home becomes available. It's a shorter-term arrangement, but still requires commitment and patience. The Cavalier King Charles Spaniel Club in the US says: "We are committed to the health and wellbeing of the breed, and therefore, we do not pay any fee for any dog that results in a profit for the puppy mill industry. The number of Cavaliers in rescue has grown dramatically, and we very much need your help."

Despite the fact that so many dogs need rehoming, it's not just the dogs that are screened - you'll also have to be vetted too. Rescue groups and shelters have to make sure that prospective adopters are suitable and they have thought through everything very carefully before making such a big decision. They also want to match you with the right dog - putting a young Cavalier with an elderly couple might not be the perfect match, for example. Or putting any Cavalier with somebody who is out at work all day would also be unsuitable, as Cavaliers are very dependent on their humans for happiness. It would be further tragedy for the dog if things did not work out in the new home.

Most rescue groups will ask a raft of personal questions - some of which may seem intrusive. If you are serious about adopting, you will have to answer them. Here are some of the details required on a typical adoption form:

- Name, address and details, including ages, of all people living in your home
- Extensive details of any other pets
- Your work hours and amount of time you spend away from the home each day
- Type of property you live in
- Size of your garden (if you have one) and height of the fence around it
- Whether you have any previous experience with Cavaliers
- Your reasons for wanting to adopt a Cavalier
- If you have ever previously given up a dog for adoption
- Whether you have any experience dealing with canine behaviour or health issues
- Details of your vet
- If you are prepared for destructive behaviour/chewing/fear/aggression/timidity/soiling inside the house/medical issues
- Whether you agree to insure your dog
- Whether you are prepared for the financial costs of dog ownership
- Whether you are willing to housetrain and obedience train the dog
- Your views on dog training methods classes
- Where your dog will sleep at night
- Whether you are prepared to accept a Cavalier cross
- Details of two personal referees

The Application form for Cavalier Rescue USA can be found on the Cavalier King Charles Spaniel Club website at: https://www.ckcsc.org/ckcsc/forms.nsf/rescueform?OpenForm

If you work away from the home, it is useful to know that as a general rule of thumb, UK rescue organisations will not place dogs in homes where they will be left alone for more than four or five hours at a stretch. After you've filled in the adoption form, a chat with a representative from the charity usually follows. There will also be an inspection visit to your home - and your vet may even be vetted!

If all goes well, you will be approved to adopt and it's then just a question of waiting for the right match to come along. When he or she does, a meeting will be arranged with the dog for all family members, you pay the adoption fee and become the proud new owner of a Cavalier.

It might seem like a lot of red tape, but the rescue groups have to be as sure as they can that you will provide a loving, forever home for the unfortunate dog. It would be terrible if the dog had to be placed back in rescue again.

All rescue organisations will neuter the dog or, if he or she is too young, specify in the adoption contract that the dog must be neutered and may not be used for breeding. Many rescue organisations have a lifetime rescue back-up policy, which means that if things don't work out, the dog must be returned to them.

Rescue Organisations

Rescue organisations are often run by volunteers who give up their time to help dogs in distress. They often have a network of foster homes, where a dog is placed until a permanent new home can be found. Foster homes are better than shelters, as Cavaliers thrive on human contact. Fostering helps to keep the dog socialised, and the people who foster are able to give sufficient attention to the individual dog in their care.

There are also online Cavalier forums where people sometimes post information about a dog that needs a new home. Even if you can't or don't want to offer a permanent home, there are other ways that you can help these worthy organisations, such as by short-term fostering or helping to raise money.

UK

There is a range of regional Cavalier rescue organisations in the UK. Visit this Kennel club page for details: https://www.thekennelclub.org.uk/services/public/findarescue/Default.aspx?breed=6149 as it gives details of regional rescue groups.

The Cavalier Club has details of the national rescue group at: http://www.cavalierrescue.co.uk and regional clubs here: http://www.thecavalierclub.co.uk/rescue/map/regmap.htm

There is also a Facebook page with details of available dogs from various organisations: https://www.facebook.com/CavalierRescueUk

If you'd be prepared to take an older dog, i.e. aged over seven years, visit the Oldies website at: https://www.oldies.org.uk/?s=cavalier

USA

The website for Cavalier Rescue USA is at: https://www.cavalierrescueusa.org

The Cavalier King Charles Spaniel Club has details of Cavalier Rescue USA, which is "an organized national team of networked volunteers who find loving homes for any Cavalier who has been released to rescue by his or her owner or caretaker." Details of regional contacts are here: http://www.ckcsc.org/ckcsc/ckcsc_inc.nsf/Founded-1954/rescontact.html

There are also general websites, such as www.petfinder.com, www.aspca.org/adopt-pet and www.adoptapet.com

This is by no means an exhaustive list, but it does cover some of the main organisations involved. If you do visit these websites, you cannot presume that the descriptions are 100% accurate. They are given in good faith, but ideas of what constitutes a 'lively' dog may vary. Some Cavaliers advertised may have other breeds in their genetic make-up. It does not mean that these are necessarily worse dogs, but if you are attracted to the Cavalier for its temperament and other assets, make sure you are looking at a Cavalier.

DON'T get a dog from eBay, Craig's List, Gumtree or any of the other general advertising websites that sell golf clubs, jewellery, old cars, washing machines, etc. You might think you are getting a bargain dog, but in the long run you may well pay the price. If the dog had been well bred and properly cared for, he or she would not be advertised on such websites - or sold in pet shops. You may be storing up a whole load of trouble for yourselves in terms of health, vets' bills and/or behaviour issues, due to poor breeding and environment.

If you haven't been put off with all of the above... Congratulations, you may be just the family or person that poor homeless Cavalier is looking for!

If you can't spare the time to adopt - and adoption means forever - you might want to consider fostering. Or you could help by becoming a home inspector or fundraiser to help keep these very worthy rescue groups providing such a wonderful service. However you decide to get involved, **Good Luck!**

Saving one dog will not change the world,
But it will change the world for one dog.

17. Caring for Senior Cavaliers

If your Cavalier has been well looked after and has suffered no serious diseases, he or she could live for 12 to 15 years. Lifespan is influenced by genetics and also by owners - how you feed, exercise and generally look after your dog will all have an impact on his or her life. At some point before the end, he or she will start to feel the effects of ageing.

Approaching Old Age

After having got up at the crack of dawn when your dog was a puppy, you may find that she now likes to sleep in longer in the morning. Physically, joints will probably become stiffer and organs - such as heart, liver and kidneys - may not function as effectively. Studies show that the heart disease MVD (Mitral Valve Disease) affects nearly all Cavaliers that reach the age of 10 years, to a greater or lesser extent.

And on the mental side - just as with humans - your dog's memory, ability to learn and awareness will start to dim.

Your faithful companion might become a bit stubborn, grumpier or a little less tolerant of lively dogs and children. She may start waking up or wandering about the house in the middle of the night, taking forever to sniff a blade of grass, or seeking out your company more often. She might even have the odd "accident" inside the house.

You may also notice that she doesn't see or hear as well as she used to. On the other hand, your old friend might not be hard of hearing at all. She might have developed that affliction common to many older dogs - ours included - of 'selective hearing.' Our 13-year-old Max had bionic hearing when it came to the word "Dinnertime" whispered from 20 yards, yet was strangely unable to hear the commands "Stay" or "Here" when we were right in front of him!

You can help ease your mature dog gracefully into old age by keeping an eye on him or her, noticing the changes and taking action to help as much as possible. This might involve a visit to the vet for supplements and/or medications, modifying your dog's environment, changing his or her diet and slowly reducing the amount of daily exercise.

Much depends on the individual dog. Just as with humans, a Cavalier of ideal weight that has been physically and mentally active all of her life is likely to age slower than an overweight, under-stimulated couch potato.

Keeping older Cavaliers at that optimum weight can be challenging as they age. Some become more food-orientated, even though they are getting less exercise. Also, their metabolisms slow down, making it easier to put on the pounds unless their daily calories are reduced. At the same time, extra weight places additional, unwanted stress on joints and organs, making them have to work harder than they should.

We normally talk about dogs being old when they reach the last third of their lives. This varies greatly from dog to dog and bloodline to bloodline. Some Cavaliers may keep remain active with little signs of ageing until the day they die, others may start to show signs of ageing at seven or eight years old. Competitively, a Cavalier is classed as a 'Veteran' at seven years old in the show ring (although nobody told the Cavalier that!)

Physical and Mental Signs of Ageing

If your Cavalier is in or approaching the last third of his life, here are some signs that his body is feeling its age:

- ❧ He has generally slowed down and no longer seems as keen to go out on his walks – or if he does want to go, he doesn't want to go as far. He is happy pottering and sniffing - and often takes forever to inspect a single clump of grass! Some are less keen to go outside in bad weather

- ❧ He gets up from lying down more slowly and he goes up and down stairs more slowly. He can no longer jump on to the couch or bed. These are all signs that his joints are stiffening, often due to arthritis

- ❧ He is getting grey hairs, particularly around the muzzle (harder to tell on a Blenheim or tricolour with their white muzzles!)

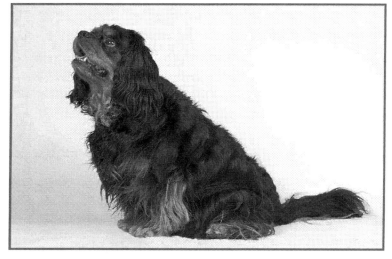

- ❧ He has put on a bit of weight

- ❧ He may have the occasional 'accident' (incontinence) inside the house

- ❧ He urinates more frequently

- ❧ He drinks more water

- ❧ He has bouts of constipation or diarrhoea

- ❧ The foot pads thicken and nails may become more brittle

- ❧ One or more lumps or fatty deposits (lipomas) develop on his body. Our Max developed two small bumps on top of his head aged 10 and we took him straight to the vet, who performed minor surgery to remove them. They were benign (harmless), but you should always get them checked out ASAP in case they are an early form of cancer - they can also grow quite rapidly, even if benign. They often appear on the chest, flanks or armpit

- ❧ He can't regulate his body temperature as he used to and so feels the cold and heat more

- ❧ He doesn't hear as well as he used to

- ❧ His eyesight may deteriorate – if his eyes appear cloudy he may be developing cataracts and you should see your vet as soon as you notice the signs. Just as with humans, most older dogs live quite well with failing eyesight

- ❧ He has bad breath (halitosis), which could be a sign of dental or gum disease. Brush your dog's teeth regularly and if the bad breath persists, get him checked out by a vet

- ❧ If he's inactive he may develop callouses on the elbows, especially if he lies down on hard surfaces – this is more common with large dogs than small ones

It's not just your dog's body that deteriorates; his mind does too. It's often part of the normal ageing process. Your dog may display some, all or none of these signs of *Canine Cognitive Dysfunction:*

- His sleep patterns change; an older dog may be more restless at night and sleepy during the day. He may start wandering around the house at odd times, causing you sleepless nights

- He barks more, sometimes at nothing or open spaces

- He stares at objects, such as walls, or wanders aimlessly around the house or garden

- He displays increased anxiety, separation anxiety or aggression; although aggression is more common with other breeds and most ageing Cavaliers remain gentle souls

- He forgets or ignores commands or habits he once knew well, such as coming when called and sometimes toilet training

- Some dogs may become more clingy and dependent, often resulting in separation anxiety. He may seek reassurance that you are near him as his faculties fade and he becomes a bit less confident and independent. Others may become a bit disengaged and less interested in human contact

Understanding the changes happening to your dog and acting on them compassionately and effectively will help ease your dog's passage through his or her senior years. Your dog has given you so much pleasure over the years, now he or she needs you to give that bit of extra care for a happy, healthy old age. You can also help your Cavalier to stay mentally active by playing gentle games and getting new toys to stimulate interest.

Helping Your Dog Age Gracefully

There are many things you can do to ease your passage into his declining years.

As dogs age they need fewer calories and less protein, so many owners switch to a food specially formulated for older dogs. These are labelled *Senior, Ageing* or *Mature.* Check the labelling; some are specifically for dogs aged over eight, others may be for 10 or 12-year-olds.

If you are not sure if a senior diet is necessary for your Cavalier, talk to your vet the next time you are there. Remember, if you do change brand, switch the food gradually over a week or so. Unlike with humans, a dog's digestive system cannot cope with sudden changes of diet. See Dennis and Tina's section **Feeding the Ageing Cavalier** later in this chapter.

Consider feeding your old dog a supplement, such as Omega-3 fatty acids for the brain and coat, or one to help joints. Our dog gets a squirt of Yumega Omega 3 and half a scoop of Joint Aid in one of his daily feeds. There are also medications and homeopathic remedies, such as melatonin which has natural sedative properties, to help relieve anxiety. Check with your vet before introducing anything new.

One of the most important things you can do for your Cavalier is regular tooth brushing throughout his or her life. Cavaliers are prone to tooth and gum decay. Not only is toothache painful and unpleasant for your dog, it can be traumatic when they have to have teeth removed under anaesthetic or when they start to lose weight due to being unable to eat properly.

Pictured enjoying looking out over their Gloucestershire garden are mother and daughter Tansy, aged 13, (left) and Hazel, 11. Photo courtesy of Kathy Hargest.

Our old dog used to be very sensitive to loud noises and the lead up to Bonfire Night was a nightmare. (This is November 5th in the UK, a cause for celebration, but a worry if you have animals as there are countless firework displays and loud bangs). However, after his hearing deteriorated, he was actually far more relaxed, as loud noises were muffled and no longer frightening to him.

If your old friend has started to ignore your verbal commands when out on a walk – either through 'switching off' or deafness - you can try a whistle to attract his or her attention and then use an exaggerated hand signal for the recall. Once your dog is looking at you, hold your arm out, palm down, at 90 degrees to your body and bring it down, keeping your arm straight, until your fingers point to your toes.

This worked very effectively with our Max. He looked, understood and then decided if he was going to come or not - but at least he knew what he should be doing! More often than not he did come back, especially if the arm signal was repeated while he was making up his mind.

Weight - no matter how old your Cavalier is, he still needs a waist! Maintaining a healthy weight with a balanced diet and regular, gentler exercise are two of the most important things you can do for your dog.

Environment - Make sure your dog has a nice soft place to rest his old bones, which may mean adding an extra blanket to his bed. This should be in a place that is not too hot or cold, as he may not be able to regulate his body temperature as well as when he was younger. He needs plenty of undisturbed sleep and should not be pestered and/or bullied by younger dogs, other animals or young children. If his eyesight is failing, move obstacles out of his way, and/or use pet barriers to reduce the chance of injuries.

Jumping on and off furniture or in or out of the car is high impact for his old joints and bones. He will need a helping hand on to and off the couch or your bed, if he's allowed up there, or even a little ramp to get in and out of the car. We bought a plastic ramp for Max as he became hesitant to jump in or out of the car. However, this proved to be a complete waste of money, as he didn't like the feel of the non-slip surface on his paws and after the first couple of tentative attempts, he steadfastly refused to set a paw on it!

Exercise - Take the lead from your dog, if he doesn't want to walk as far, then don't. But if your dog doesn't want to go out at all, you will have to coax him out. ALL old dogs need exercise, not only to keep their joints moving, but also to keep their heart, lungs and joints exercised and to help keep their minds engaged with different places, smells, etc.

Feeding the Ageing Cavalier

Longstanding breeders, owners of many senior Cavaliers over the years and breeders of the UK's Top Cavalier 2017, Dennis and Tina Homes, have written this section of the importance of the right fuel, i.e. food, as your Cavalier ages. They say: "As your dog reaches middle age, he is starting to slow down and consequently, so are all of his organs. And just because you have fed him a certain food since a puppy doesn't mean that he should continue with this diet.

"There are many commercial foods available for the senior and ageing dog. Manufactured foods for the ageing dog are different from those for puppies. Whilst puppies need plenty of protein for optimum growth, the older dog needs less protein, but it must be of a higher quality. What's needed are increased fatty acids, less sodium and higher concentrations of vitamins A, B and E. Getting the balance right for the older dog's diet is very important. If you decide that you don't want to feed a commercial diet and would much prefer a home-prepared menu, then it would be wise to start giving a good multivitamin.

"A word of warning: certain foods should not be fed to our dogs because they are toxic, or at least can cause stomach upsets or even severe diarrhoea. Onions and very large amounts of garlic can cause blood problems, mushrooms are not tolerated at all, grapes, raisins, sultanas and chocolate should not be fed. Most vegetables can be fed, but never raw tomatoes.

"Chicken and turkey are excellent because they are easily digested. So too is lamb, rabbit and game of any sort. Fish is an excellent storehouse of protein and should be fed. This could include any white, boneless, cooked fish: pilchards, sardines, mackerel, herring and salmon, which are all rich in fats, vitamin B and omega 3 oils. You can also feed tinned fish too, but do stick with the ones that are prepared and stored in oil."

Pictured are Tina and Dennis with their Leogem Cavaliers of varying ages.

"A special treat could be a couple of boiled eggs once a week. You can also make an omelette and include a little grated cheese or even some cooked vegetables. Never feed eggs raw because there is always the risk of your dog falling victim to salmonella, which eggs can carry. And if fed raw the avidin, which is the ingredient within the white of the egg, destroys the natural biotin in the egg yolk. However, if the eggs are cooked, the avidin is destroyed.

"A couple of tablespoons daily of natural yoghurt is a wonderful source of protein; it also contains vitamins and calcium. It can help to maintain a healthy flora in the gut, which in turn will help with absorption of all the vital nutrients through his food and digestion. Should your pet ever succumb to a long and protracted case of diarrhoea, the probiotics in natural yogurt will help to re-establish the healthy flora so needed within the walls of the intestine. Cottage cheese is also a good addition to a meal every now and then.

"To add fibre to any meal, boiled or sweet potatoes are good; but never feed these raw. Diced and cooked carrots, swede, parsnip, leeks, courgettes, sprouts can all be mixed with cooked meats. Other good sources of carbohydrates are pasta, wholemeal bread and brown rice. If you feel unable to feed home-produced and would rather feed a commercially-prepared food, then do read the labels. Make sure that good quality ingredients are used and avoid anything that has soya or vegetable protein, as these are cheap fillers which most dogs cannot tolerate. Some of the ills that veteran or older dogs suffer are likely to be food-induced. Kidney and liver problems are such common ailments today, and these are often caused by too much protein - above 20% - together with all the additional additive, preservatives and flavourings in some commercial foods. These toxins are stored in the kidneys and liver which will cause a breakdown and lessen the efficiency of these organs."

Tina adds a general comment: "As a groomer I see so many dogs with bad skin and poor hair growth. When I have suggested to their owners to change the diet to avoid beef, wheat and dairy products, within a couple of months the transformation from lethargic, itchy, scurfy dogs to happy and glowing little canines has to be seen to be believed. Half the time they have been in the care of their vets for years with all sorts of pills and potions, but a change in diet is often all that is needed."

When to Consult a Professional

If your dog is showing any of these signs, get him checked out by a vet:

- Excessive increased urination or drinking can be a sign of something amiss, such as reduced liver or kidney function, Cushing's disease or diabetes
- Constipation or not urinating regularly could be a sign of something not functioning properly with the digestive system or organs
- Incontinence, which could be a sign of a mental or physical problem
- Cloudy eyes, which could be cataracts
- Decreased appetite – often one of the first signs of an underlying problem
- Lumps or bumps on the body - often benign, but can occasionally be malignant (cancerous)
- Excessive sleeping or a lack of interest in you and his or her surroundings
- Diarrhoea or vomiting
- A darkening and dryness of skin that never seems to get any better - this can be a sign of hypothyroidism
- Any other out-of-the-ordinary behaviour for your dog. A change in patterns or behaviour is often your dog's way of telling you that all is not well

What the Breeders Say

Sandra Coles, of Twyforde Cavalier King Charles Spaniels, Devon, has bred and shown Cavaliers since 1974. Unlike some breeders, Sandra has always kept all of her breeding stock and eased them into old age - she currently has 15 veterans (over seven years old). What Sandra doesn't know about caring for older dogs can fit on the back of a postage stamp!

This is what she has to say: "We have 10 dogs over 10 years of age and lost our oldest one this year, Twyforde Alula Borealis (Lula), she was 15 years and one month old. I do know, however, that people have had them live until they are 16 plus. If the hearts are good there is no reason for them not to live until they are well over 10 years.

"At present none are on any heart medication. I don't frequently bath them but their coats are shiny and no scurf. Energy levels are good, even with the Oldies. I don't trim unless I feel the feet need doing on some of them.

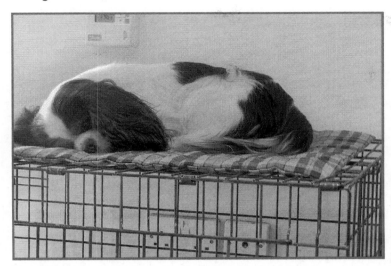

"Some of my veterans are still like puppies with a lot of character and energy. I think the reason for this is that they have a lot of exercise and are not overweight. Mimosa is 10 now and can still jump up to her favourite spot on top of the crate using the cages as steps to get there." *(Pictured)*

"Percy, who is 14, can still jump our four-foot fence! He has a little roam around our land and then comes to the front door to be let in, hoping for a biscuit.

"They do start to slow down at about 10 and do more sleeping, but they are still game for exercise and fun. Remember, like old people, they are all different. I do change to a senior diet and what they have depends on the individual dog. Some have smaller biscuits, some have two meals a day and they have added glucosamine for their joints - but they still love their raw tripe.

"Signs of old age are slowing down, stiffness in joints, being slower to get up, not wanting to go so far or as fast. They also lose more teeth or, as in the case of my 14-year-olds, have few teeth. Make sure that teeth and gums remain healthy so that they can eat properly.

"The Blenheims go greyer around the muzzle, while the tricolours seem to maintain colour better. Eyes can be a problem with cataracts developing (the same as with old people) and Dry Eye, so eyes may need more attention and some lubrication. Some dogs develop hearing loss; ears need to be checked and kept clean.

"I have not noticed any behavioural changes in mine, so I'm not sure if they suffer from dementia like old people; it's mainly their faculties like eyes, hearing and joints that suffer. Diabetes could be a problem if they become obese and hearts would definitely be affected, so it is very important to maintain a healthy weight and get them checked at regular intervals. Vets will do this for free and sometimes have free health clinics.

"Another issue can be Pyometra in bitches that have not been neutered. This usually happens when she reaches middle age or veteran and is a life-threatening condition. It is usually an emergency spay operation. Some bitches that have been spayed can become incontinent. They may need to go out more frequently and may not be able to last through the night.

"This can also happen to older dogs as well. I have one little girl called Susy, she is 10 now, and she asks to go out at about 4am. Because she is housetrained, I always get up for her.

"Some older bitches can develop mammary cancer. There is some research that says that spaying prevents this, and bitches that have had a litter are less likely to develop it. Anal glands will also need checking. Grooming and bathing is good for them as long as they are kept warm after the bath. Dry them well after being out and getting wet. My older dogs have a coat for walks and I keep them generally warmer.

"I keep a careful eye on my Oldies and, because they all live indoors, I can pick up immediately when anything is wrong."

Our photo shows a pile of Sandra's senior tricolours, ranging in age from seven to 11, enjoying a group snooze on the sofa.

Kathy Hargest, of Kathysgirls Cavaliers, Gloucestershire: "I'd say a Cavalier starts to become a senior at seven to eight years. At this time, I change to James Wellbeloved Senior Grain-Free food. I continue to give lots of raw vegetables to aid digestion. I also give Yumove joint supplement and cranberry tablets to help the waterworks.

"Signs of old age are joint stiffness and more time spent sleeping. Watch out for early morning coughing, which could be fluid retention due to a heart issue. Have the heart checked regularly - an annual Well Dog Clinic is a good idea. Teeth need to be checked regularly; a dental vet check is a good idea before they get too old for anaesthetic - again seven to eight years old. Check paws and pads for drying and cracking.

"Keep exercise the same as usual for as long as possible. They will let you know when they want to do less. Keep up with grooming, it will help to find lumps and bumps early, and they will feel better with a clean coat. Ears especially should be checked and cleaned if necessary - older dogs are more prone to yeast and urinary infections.

"My final piece of advice is to be with them when they have to leave you on that final journey."

Philippa Biddle, of Hearthfriend Cavaliers, Norfolk: "My first Cavalier lived to 15.5 years, her daughter 14.7 years and her granddaughter is a still healthy, lively 13¾ years old. The age at which Cavaliers move towards old age depends on the dog, but with mine it's around 11 to 12 years."

Pictured is Philippa's Solo (Hearthfriend Home Alone), aged nearly 14. She's called Solo as she was a singleton pup (the only puppy in the litter).

"I stick with the adult diet, but have not had a Cavalier with any particular problem like pancreatitis, diabetes or obesity. I cut down the food ration once they are spayed and always keep them slim and exercised. In terms of supplements, mine have had Fortekor tablets to support the heart and Rimidyl for arthritic pain, from the vet. I give green-lipped mussel supplement as necessary. I rely on a good quality raw diet to supply all the vitamins and nutrient they need.

"As Cavaliers age they sleep more and prefer a more relaxing environment (seeking a quiet spot in a busy household) and are less keen on walking far. Oldies need to be respected. They are less tolerant of being mangled and bounced on by puppies or children. I find they get more opinionated about their likes and dislikes! We call it *"Princess Syndrome"* in our house.

"My advice is to keep them slim, let them dictate how much exercise they can tolerate, but don't let them become couch potatoes. Keep them cool with a Cool Mat or coat on hot summer days. Don't exercise in heat or midday in summer, and Oldies are more likely to need a coat on cold days. Be sure to dry them well and keep them warm after a winter walk."

Philip Lunt, of Oaktreepark Cavaliers, Staffordshire, added: "Veteran age is over seven years; vintage is over 10 years. I mix the food between Adult and Senior/Light and all my dogs have Yumega joint tablets as a supplement. I advise owners to watch the weight, as neutered dogs can become prone to gaining the pounds. The oldest Cavalier I have had lived to 15; I have known them to live to 18 years."

The Last Lap

Huge advances in veterinary science have meant that there are countless procedures and medications that can prolong the life of your dog, and this is a good thing. But there comes a time when you do have to let go.

If your dog is showing all the signs of ageing, has an ongoing medical condition from which he or she cannot recover, is showing signs of pain, mental anxiety or distress and there is no hope of improvement, then the dreaded time has come to say goodbye. You owe it to him or her.

There is no point keeping an old dog alive if all he or she has to look forward to is pain and death. I'm getting upset as I write this, thinking of our recently-departed Max, aged 13, as well as all the wonderful dogs we have had in the past. But we have their lives in our hands and we can give them the gift of passing away peacefully and humanely at the end when the time is right.

Losing our beloved companion, our best friend, a member of the family, is truly heart-breaking for most owners. But one of the things we realise at the back of our minds when we get that lively little puppy that bounded up to meet us like we were the best person in the whole wide world is the pain that comes with it. We know that we will live longer than them and that we'll probably have to make this most painful of decisions at some point.

It's the worst thing about being a dog owner.

If your Cavalier has had a long and happy life, then you could not have done any more. You were a

great owner and your dog was lucky to have you. Remember all the good times you had together. And try not to rush out and buy another dog straight away; wait a while to grieve for your Cavalier.

Assess your current life and lifestyle and, if your situation is right, only then consider getting another dog and all that that entails in terms of time, commitment and expense.

A Cavalier coming into a happy, stable household will get off to a better start in life than a dog entering a home full of grief.

Whatever you decide to do, put the dog first.

18. A Life in Show Business

Conformation showing is highly competitive, and here Dennis and Tina Homes tell the wonderful story of their path to success - and pass on some great tips to anyone starting out. Their first Cavalier puppy, Kelly, led to a 40-year love affair with the breed, culminating in the supreme honour of breeding and owning the UK's Top Cavalier 2017, as well as two AKC Champions. Along the way they established the Leogem bloodline and became Championship judges on three continents.

Some time after Tina and I married, Tina's Labrador died and we were dogless for a couple of years. We considered a number of different breeds, but as our London house and garden were small, we decided to opt for a smaller breed.

In 1979 we visited a local town show that included a dog show. We spoke to exhibitors of various breeds and came across what we considered to be the prettiest and most affable dog at the show. We were immediately hooked on the Cavalier - this was the breed for us!

Unfortunately, we went about it in totally the wrong way and bought from a commercial breeder. We named our little Blenheim bitch Kelly and later found out that she had slipping patellas which required surgery. Kelly was never bred from, but lived to the ripe old age of 15 and still had a clear heart.

We were totally smitten with her character and temperament, so when she was six months old we decided to get her a playmate. This time we went about it in the correct way and visited a Cavalier club show and bought from a reputable breeder. Tasha was a tricolour and the daughter of Ch Jia Laertes of Tonnew, who went on to win the Toy Group at Crufts.

....

Bitten by the Show Bug

When Tasha was six months old we decided to enter her in a couple of small local summer shows, just for fun. At the time we had no intention of taking up dog showing as a regular hobby. But after winning a couple of ribbons - albeit just a third and a fourth - we quickly found ourselves on the slippery slope of dog showing!

As well as getting involved in competitive showing, we also found dog shows to be quite the social event, meeting up with other Cavalier owners, many of whom have gone on to become great friends.

A couple of years down the line we decided to breed Tasha, and from this first litter we kept a tricolour bitch that we named Leogem Tamarisk. She became the foundation bitch from which all our dogs are descended. We chose *Leogem* as our kennel name because Dennis is a Leo and Tina a Gemini - despite the fact that neither of us are interested in astrology!

Dennis and Tina are pictured here with Ch Leogem Rhapsody on the day she gained her title.

We've never been big breeders as far as breeding lots of litters goes; we just breed whenever we want another dog in our household, hopefully for showing.

We feel that the Cavalier is not just a beautiful dog to look at, but these gentle, loving little dogs have a purity of mind and spirit, and their endearing inquisitiveness and eagerness to please makes them like no other canine. These characteristics are what we fell in love with. We know that these attributes are the magic spells for Cavalier enthusiasts the world over.

Although we were showing on a regular basis, it was not until 17 years after we started that we made up our first champion. He was a Blenheim dog called Ch Leogem Lothario. Since then we have bred five more UK champions and two American AKC champions. To date our biggest success has been with Ch Leogem Renaissance JW (pictured).

As well as winning multiple challenge certificates he won **Cavalier Puppy of the Year** in both 2016 and 2017. He was able to win two years running as he did a lot of winning as a young puppy at the end of the qualifying period in 2016 and had many wins as an older puppy at the early part of 2017. He went on to become the UK's overall **Top Cavalier 2017**.

If anyone is thinking of breeding Cavaliers, obviously, breeding for good health is paramount and regular health testing of breeding stock in essential. However, we feel that the most important factor when breeding for the show ring is not to be 'kennel blind'. This is when a show exhibitor or breeder only focuses on the good points of their dog(s). No dog is perfect, they all have imperfections, but the aim of a breeder should always be to strive to breed as close to the Breed Standard as possible - and the only way to do that is to be totally aware of any faults or weaknesses that your dog(s) may have.

The late Susan Burgess of the Crisdig Cavaliers was one of the top post-war breeders and she once made a very valid statement when she said, "Judges should look for attributes, but breeders should always look for faults." All dogs have faults and you should be completely aware of both the weak points and the strengths of your breeding bitches. Study the Breed Standard very carefully and when deciding on what stud dog to mate your bitch to, it is important that you do not double up on weak points.

....

The Show Structure

Quite often owners of pet Cavaliers are attracted to entering dog shows as it combines both the excitement of competition with meeting other Cavalier owners and seeing many other Cavaliers. There are a number of different types of show:

Fun Shows are often run in conjunction with village or church fetes and any dog can enter, be it a pedigree or a crossbreed and the dog need not be registered with the Kennel Club. Most of the classes are novelty types, such as 'Dog with the Waggiest Tail', 'Prettiest Bitch' and 'Most Handsome Dog'. They often include a few pedigree classes such as Any Variety Puppy, which is for any puppy up to the age of 12 months and Any Variety Open, which is for any dog of any age.

Companion Dog Shows are similar to Fun Shows, but are licensed by the Kennel Club and have to abide by Kennel Club regulations. Like Fun Shows, they are open to both pedigree and crossbreed dogs, which do not have to be registered with the Kennel Club. The only dogs not allowed to enter are those who have already won a Challenge Certificate, a Reserve Certificate or a Junior Warrant. As well as novelty classes, they usually have a few pedigree classes. Companion Dog Shows are usually a great way for beginners to start dog show competitions.

Open Shows are licensed by the Kennel Club and only pedigree dogs registered with the Kennel Club are allowed to enter. There are three main types of Open Shows: General Open Shows, which are usually run by a regional dog club and have many different breeds. If a particular breed is not classified at one of these shows it can still be entered in an Any Variety class, such as *Any Variety Toy* or *Any Variety Terrier*. Group Open Shows are confined to breeds within a certain group such as Toy, Terrier, Hound, Gundog, Working, Pastoral and Utility. Breed Open Shows are run by clubs specializing in a particular breed and only dogs of that breed are eligible to enter.

Championship Dog Shows are the highest level of dog shows where Challenge Certificates are on offer. Again, they can be general all-breed shows, group shows or individual breed shows. They attract several thousand dogs and are usually held over three or four days. Although Challenge Certificates are on offer for most breeds, rare breeds and some breeds with very few numbers do not have Challenge Certificates awarded.

Pictured is the beautiful Ch Leogem Rhapsody.

With Fun Shows and Companion Dog Shows, you can simply turn up and enter on the day. However, entries must be made in advance either by post or online for Open and Championship Shows, usually a few weeks before the show.

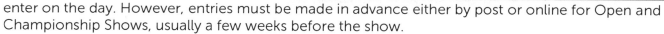

Local Ringcraft Clubs often have schedules available for local shows, and you can generally find details on the websites of the two main companies that handle show entries in the UK. They are: Fosse Data and Higham Press (Dog Biz).

If after entering a Fun Show or a Companion Dog Show you feel that you'd like to compete at a higher level, then it is advisable to join a local Ringcraft Club. A quick search online will usually find details of a local club. Here you will be shown the best way to handle and present your dog at a show. Trainers at these clubs act as judges and run their hands over the dog to check how it is put together, just like a judge at a show. This way your dog will soon get familiar with being handled. The trainers will also advise you on how to walk your dog in the show ring and how to get him or her to stand correctly.

Classes

There are quite a number of classes allowed by the Kennel Club, but most shows only have some of them. The age- restricted classes are:

Minor Puppy - Over six months but under nine months

Puppy - Six months to 12 months

Junior - Between 12 to 18 months

Yearling - Between 18 months to two years

Veteran - Dogs over seven years

Then you have the classes restricted by the number of first prizes previously won.

Open Shows

Maiden - None

Novice - Not more than three

Tyro - Not more than five

Open - For any dog, regardless of how many previous wins.

Championship Shows

Maiden – None

Novice - Not more than three

Undergraduate – None

Graduate – None; *Post Graduate* – None

Mid Limit - For dogs that have not become show Champions nor won five or more First Prizes at Championship Shows in Mid Limit, Limit or Open Classes

Limit - For dogs which have not become show Champions nor won seven or more First Prizes at Championship Shows in Limit or Open Classes

Open - For any dog regardless of how many previous wins

....

Grooming for Shows

We are often asked about grooming regimes for show dogs. We groom all our dogs daily, not just the ones that we show. This way they are kept in good condition and, by grooming on a daily basis, you can check for any problems that could arise, such as impacted anal glands, sore gums, ear infections, or things like grass seeds stuck in their coats, feet and ears.

When entering a dog show it is important to bath the dog beforehand. If the show is not too far away, you may have time to do this before leaving home, or if not, then the night before. For some dogs with rather wavy coats, it is probably best to bath the day before to allow the coat to settle.

(Library photo)

There are a multitude of different shampoos on the market and it is purely by experimenting that you'll hopefully find one that best suits your dog. Some dogs have rather greasy coats, while others may have a rather dry coat.

There are shampoos for greasy coats and also milder shampoos for dry coats. For the drier coat you may also need a conditioner after shampooing. Dogs with long coats, particularly if they are slightly wavy, do well with a *drying coat* put on afterwards - these are close-fitting netted coats.

Dogs should be thoroughly rinsed after shampooing then towel dried. They should then be dried with a hair dryer until very slightly damp. After that they should be thoroughly combed through and have the coat put on before being dried off under a hair dryer.

The drying coat should be left on for at least an hour and when removed the dog's own coat should be nice and flat. There are several makes of drying coats on the market but one of the most popular can be found at www.drydogcoats.co.uk

Pictured here is Ch Leogem Ginestra JW in a drying coat.

Judging Around the World

After we had been showing for around six years, different canine societies invited us to judge at their Open Shows. Slowly but surely, we both began to get more and more judging appointments at Open Shows in various parts of the country. After several years we were approached by different regional Cavalier Clubs to judge at their breed Open Shows.

Some 18 years after judging her first Open Show, Tina was approved by the Kennel Club to judge at Championship level and Dennis followed in her footsteps a few years later. Since then we have judged at Championship level in Germany, Denmark, the Czech Republic, Sweden, Belgium, France, Australia and the United States.

When we first started judging we both were a little nervous. We now regard it as a great honour to be asked to judge and give our opinion on all the dogs entered under us. Obviously, some exhibitors will be disappointed if we have not placed their dogs, but we endeavour to be honest in our judging and place each dog in order of merit. Judging should be conducted without fear or favour. Although we place the winning dogs in the order of 1st, 2nd, 3rd, Reserve and Very Highly Commended, we are not actually judging the dogs against each other. What we are doing is judging the dogs against the Breed Standard and placing each dog in the order of how close they are to the Breed Standard.

Judging procedure in the UK, the USA, Canada, Australia and New Zealand is very similar. In many other countries, notably in Europe, judging is done under FCI rules (Fédération Cynologique Internationale). This is an organisation which is made up of kennel clubs from a great many countries. Under these rules the main classes are:

- *Puppy* (6-9 months)
- *Junior* (9-18 months)
- *Intermediate* (15-24 months)
- *Open* (15 months and over)
- *Champion* (15 months and over)
- *Veteran* (over eight years)

In the Puppy Class, each dog is graded as Very Promising, Promising, Quite Promising or Insufficient. In the remaining classes, dogs are judged as Excellent, Very Good, Good, Quite Good or Insufficient.

When judging, we look for overall shape and breed type. No dog is perfect and we do not dwell on just one fault if all their other attributes are good. For instance, a dog may have a slightly high tail carriage when on the move, or the nose pigment maybe slightly light. But if its movement is good and the dog is of good breed type, we would not necessarily penalise on minor points, providing they are not too extreme. However, we would penalise bad temperament.

The Breed Standard says that a Cavalier should be gay and fearless, and a friendly and outgoing temperament is what a Cavalier is all about. If a dog shows aggression or is very timid and backs off, then this is not good temperament. We feel that it is important that healthy, unexaggerated dogs with sound construction and good temperament are the ones to win top honours. This is especially paramount in the case of would-be stud dogs to ensure that healthy, sound attributes are hopefully passed on to the next generation.

We would suggest to anyone who wants to show that they should join one of the Cavalier Clubs; preferably the main Cavalier Club in your country, and also one of the regional clubs – details can be found on national Cavalier club websites. By joining a club you can gain lots of information and make contact with experienced exhibitors and breeders who will be pleased to offer advice and answer any queries. Many clubs also hold health-testing days with specialist cardiologist vets and ophthalmic vets.

The Cavalier King Charles Spaniel is, in our opinion, the most wonderful of dog breeds. We feel honoured and privileged to have been so involved with Cavaliers over the last 40 years and, hopefully, to have made a positive contribution to the breed. Our main criterion has always been to try to breed quality over quantity and to breed each litter better than the last.

Pictured here are four generations of Leogem Cavaliers. Left to right: Ch Leogem Minuet aged 12 and a half; her son Ch Leogem Marcello; granddaughter Ch Leogem Rhapsody and great grandson Ch Leogem Renaissance.

Contacts
UK national Cavalier club www.thecavalierclub.co.uk USA national Cavalier club www.ckcsc.org Details of your nearest regional club can be found on these websites.

Show Dates and Results: Fosse Data - www.fossedata.co.uk/show_schedules and Higham Press (Dog Biz) - http://www.highampress.co.uk/info.asp

Useful Contacts

Cavalier King Charles Spaniel Club (USA) https://www.ckcsc.org

Cavalier Rescue USA - http://www.ckcsc.org/ckcsc/ckcsc_inc.nsf/Founded-1954/rescontact.html

American Kennel Club (AKC) - http://www.akc.org

Puppies via AKC marketplace - https://marketplace.akc.org/puppies/cavalier-king-charles-spaniel

NOTE: Only Breeders of Merit and Bred With H.E.A.R.T. breeders have been vetted by the AKC

Help finding **lost or stolen dogs**, register your dog's microchip - www.akcreunite.org

Checking the health of a puppy's parents or a mate - www.k9data.com

The Cavalier King Charles spaniel Club (UK) - http://www.thecavalierclub.co.uk

Cavalier Rescue UK - www.thecavalierclub.co.uk/start.html

Kennel Club (UK) - www.thekennelclub.org.uk

Kennel Club Assured Breeders:
www.thekennelclub.org.uk/services/public/acbr/Default.aspx?breed=Cavalier+King+Charles+Spaniel

Kennel Club Mate Select - www.thekennelclub.org.uk/services/public/mateselect

Champdogs (UK) - breeders advertising *"health tested"* dogs must show Champdogs the relevant certificates: www.champdogs.co.uk/breeds/cavalier-king-charles-spaniel

Detailed information on Cavalier health - http://www.cavalierhealth.org

http://cavaliermatters.org is another useful website

Association of Pet Dog Trainers USA www.apdt.com

Association of Pet Dog Trainers UK www.apdt.co.uk

Canadian Association of Professional Pet Dog Trainers www.cappdt.ca

Dog foods - Useful information on grain-free and hypoallergenic food: www.dogfoodadvisor.com
UK dog food advice: www.allaboutdogfood.co.uk

There are also **internet forums** are a good source of information from other owners, including:
http://www.cavaliers.co.uk and www.forum.breedia.com/dogs/cavalier-king-charles-spaniel

....

List of Contributors

Dennis and Tina Homes, Leogem Cavaliers, Herefordshire, UK

Jina Ezell, Kalama Cavaliers, Washington State, USA kalamacavaliers@gmail.com
www.facebook.com/KalamaCavaliers

Sandra Coles, Twyforde Cavalier King Charles Spaniels, Devon, UK www.twyfordecavaliers.com

Philippa Biddle, Hearthfriend Cavaliers, Norfolk, UK
www.facebook.com/hearthfriend

Kathy Hargest, Kathysgirls Cavaliers, Gloucestershire, UK

Julie Durham, Donrobby Cavaliers, Berkshire, UK
http://donrobby.co.uk

Philip Lunt, Oaktreepark Cavaliers, Staffordshire, UK

Owners Nicola Byam-Cook, Hampshire, and Laura and Mustafa Rakla, Dubai

Dr Sara Skiwski, holistic vet and proprietor, The Western Dragon Integrated Veterinary Solutions, California, USA www.thewesterndragon.com

Disclaimer

This book has been written to provide helpful information on Cavalier King Charles Spaniels. It is not meant to be used, nor should it be used, to diagnose or treat any medical condition. For diagnosis or treatment of any animal medical problem, consult a qualified veterinarian.

The author is not responsible for any specific health or allergy conditions that may require medical supervision and is not liable for any damages or negative consequences from any treatment, action, application or preparation, to any animal or to any person reading or following the information in this book.

The views expressed by contributors to this book are solely personal and do not necessarily represent those of the author. References are provided for informational purposes only and do not constitute endorsement of any websites or other sources.

Author's Notes:

Half the people reading this book will have a female dog and the other half will have a male dog. I have alternated between the masculine pronoun 'he' and feminine pronoun 'she' in an effort to make this book as relevant as possible for all new and prospective owners.

The Cavalier King Charles Handbook uses UK English, except where Americans have been quoted, when the original US English has been preserved.

The term "Cavalier" has been widely used throughout the book to refer to The Cavalier King Charles Spaniel.